American Childhoods

AN ANTHOLOGY

David Willis McCullough, Editor

LITTLE, BROWN AND COMPANY

BOSTON   TORONTO

Acknowledgments of permission
to reprint copyrighted material
appear on pages 403–405.

Library of Congress Cataloging-in-Publication Data

American childhoods.

    1. United States—Biography. 2. Children—
United States—Biography. I. McCullough, David W.
CT215.A665 1987   920'.073   86-27472
ISBN 0-316-55544-4

RRD VA

*Published simultaneously in Canada
by Little, Brown & Company (Canada) Limited*

PRINTED IN THE UNITED STATES OF AMERICA

For two D. D. McC's: my mother and my sister

Contents

American
Childhoods

Introduction

by David Willis McCullough

CHILDHOOD is a concept made up by adults looking back over their shoulders. To a child, childhood is simply life. Definitions and analysis come later.

Most adults in the business of writing about childhood like to point out that they are involved in a relatively new line of work. It has been nearly two thousand years since Saint Paul observed that when he was a child he spoke and acted as a child and that when he became a man he put aside childish things, but enjoying those childish things is a recent luxury. Until a century or so ago childhood was a very serious affair. The typical child, as one properly sardonic scholar has pointed out, was buried in the local graveyard. Infant mortality was the leading cause of death, and the average life span of the survivors, who were usually working as adults by the time they were ten years old, was all too brief. Childhood, clearly, was too important to waste on idleness. For optimists, there were trades and professions to be passed on. For pessimists, who would consider themselves realists, young souls had to be made morally ready for the terrible Last Judgment.

In spite of the adults' grim notions of how they should be spending their time, children have always found ways of playing. Ancient tombs of all cultures are littered with far too many toys to assume otherwise. But over the last two hundred years, beginning at about the time the United States was born, a new notion of childhood began to evolve. Childhood became recognized as a unique period. Children were no longer seen simply as under-ripe adults who had not reached full growth. Credit Jean-Jacques Rousseau or Sigmund Freud or Dr. Lister and the discovery of germs, but childhood became at once safer and more respected. Adults began to take childhood seriously not because of the dangers children faced or because of their potential as future adults but because childhood itself began to be seen as something special. And although young people living through it may have found it hard to believe, childhood became a period that was remembered, usually none too accurately, with nostalgia and romance.

The way children are portrayed in popular American paintings made between the eighteenth and early twentieth centuries reveals how notions of childhood have changed. In the early colonial portraits children are little adults, gussied up in miniature adult clothing; and although they might be toying with pet birds or squirrels, or holding, in the case of girls, flowers or pieces of fruit, they are a pretty sullen lot. As the years went by and the country moved into its own Victorian age, infants began to look like Baby Jesus (especially when teamed up with saintly-looking mothers), and older children started having fun. At least the boys did. Girls were always well behaved, playing house or dressing up their dolls (already in the roles of little mothers and housekeepers), but boys were allowed to raise hell. Girls may play with kittens, but boys are shown tormenting them in a jolly boys-will-be-boys way. Happy boys steal apples or sneak under circus tents or take off their clothes and jump into the old swimming hole. There was even a popular genre of child-labor pictures — bootblacks, newspaper sellers, field hands — with everyone smiling and, in the case of black children, singing. It would take the camera to discover the harsh side of putting children to work.

In 1913, when Theodore Roosevelt was invited to visit Brazil and explore some little-known backwater of the Amazon, he replied: "I had to go. It was my last chance to be a boy." That was a remarkable admission. Here was a man, fifty-five years old, who earlier had been president of the United States for nearly eight years, daydreaming of returning to some mythical golden age of boyhood. As usual, Roosevelt, who flourished during what was probably the high-water mark of childhood romanticism, was simply proclaiming the spirit of his time. A decade or so later, Americans began to realize — or perhaps simply to admit — that childhood was more than sunshine and pranks, that just possibly what was going on in the mind of a child was as important and as secret as those old-timers who worried about infant damnation feared. The American cult of childhood continued, but now the stakes would be higher, the focus on youth more intense and, with luck, more clear-eyed.

The forty Americans who recall their childhoods in this anthology are a varied lot. Spanning a period of more than two hundred years, from Ben Franklin in British Boston to two nearly anonymous young bystanders in the riot-torn Alabama of the 1960s, they represent a mixture of whites, blacks, Indians, and Asians. Some are American-born; some are not. Some are concerned about being American, either because their families are newcomers or because they have been Americans for generations. Others do not give a thought to their nationality. Some write of surviving in a hostile world, some of enjoying the comforts of affluence. Some are proud of setting off on their own, others of having the support of a family. Most recall days in which something unusual happened — the day they were kidnapped by Indians, or went to work in a factory, or traded their first horse, or won a championship basketball game. Others remember ordinary days spent hunting or going to school or daydreaming about somewhere more exotic than home. Many write about the realization that the life they had accepted as being perfectly ordinary was, in the eyes of outsiders and strangers, quite extraordinary.

Joseph Heller once wrote: "Most people I've met who have a penchant for reminiscing about their childhoods are looking back on unhappy ones." But that does not quite tell the whole story. There are many unhappy situations remembered here — a childhood spent in slavery, or in an internment camp during World War II, or dealing with a mentally confused parent, or coming to terms with rape — but it is important to remember that the author of an autobiography is by definition a survivor and survivors tend to have about themselves a certain inescapable joy in having pulled through. The childhoods may have been unhappy, but the surviving child rarely is.

Style in autobiography, as in painting, has changed over the years. In the earliest autobiographies distinguished ancestors may be cataloged, but childhoods are skipped over. Even those two great godfathers of modern autobiography Giacomo Casanova and Benvenuto Cellini do not begin the stories of their lives until they are sexually mature — which was, after all, when the best anecdotes were supposed to begin. The early years simply did not matter. (And women, it might be added, rarely wrote about their lives at all.) Later, mentioning childhood incidents became acceptable if some moral lesson could be drawn from them, although annotated lists of books dutifully read were usually given more space.

But from the days of Davy Crockett on, American autobiographers began to devote more attention to their early years. And, as with popular painting, boys were allowed their pranks while girls, in reflection, remained more solemn. As time went on, writers became franker, less superficially respectful of adults (although skepticism of authority is a hallmark of American childhood reminiscences from the very beginning), more cutting in their humor, more willing — even eager — to admit living secret lives that would have horrified their parents.

There are several qualities that seem to unite the reminiscences in this collection. One is the authors' obvious belief in the importance of place. Almost everyone heard from tries hard to make us see the scenes of childhood. Indeed first memories are usually of places — Henry Adams's was of a kitchen with a yellow-colored floor, for instance, and Davy Crockett's of a waterfall his brothers were nearly washed over (Davy, of course, saved the day by running for help) — and in many cases places are recalled far more vividly than people.

Another common quality seems to be an almost boundless sense of optimism, a sense — and I suspect this is a very American quality — that anything is possible, that all experience can be seized upon and used to some advantage. Lucy Larcom, sent at thirteen to work in the textile mills of Lowell, Massachusetts, turns her situation into an opportunity to learn about literature. Charlotte Forten, a free black forced in the decade before the Civil War to leave Philadelphia because of its segregated schools, goes to Salem, Massachusetts, where she becomes active in the abolitionist movement. On a far different level, young Lincoln Steffens discovers and absorbs a whole new world on the dusty streets of Sacramento when he is given a horse at the age of eight; and a half a century later, in the same city, Richard Rodriguez discovers an even wider world by learning to read English.

Another common bond is an awareness of race. It is a theme that runs through this book because it is a theme that runs through American history: the Indians who got here first, the whites who came to conquer a new world they believed it was their manifest destiny to rule, the blacks who came in chains, and the Asians who arrived — or were imported — to serve the whites. From the very beginning there was racial tension and bloodshed, and the children of all races grew up reflecting the tension, and sometimes learning from it.

A final common bond, and an even more curious one, is the way the writers regard their parents. From beginning to end, with few exceptions (Gloria Steinem is one), parents are treated with incredible caution. They are rarely attacked or criticized (one thinks of the wariness with which abused children protect their parents), but it is amazing how often mothers and fathers are simply not included in these memories of growing up. Absent parents may be missed, as in the cases of Pierrepont Noyes or William Humphrey, but living, breathing parents tend to be pushed to one side (while lavish attention is sometimes paid to grandparents) as though one of the first acts of independence for an autobiographer is to free himself from those who so dominated his childhood. Why, after all, write an autobiography if you are not going to be the star?

Which brings up the subject of lies — or "stretchers," as Huck Finn called them in his autobiography. It is very possible that there are more stretchers — and more varieties of stretchers — in this book than in any other book published this season. Policemen like to say that there is no one more untrustworthy than an eye witness. Espionage experts say the same thing about refugees fleeing the battlefields. But they are only talking about facts. On a factual level there is little doubt that this anthology is a minefield. Except for entries from three diaries, all the selections were written long after childhood had ended. Think of your own favorite childhood story. Think of it again. How much of it do you really remember? How much do you simply remember from having told it before? How much of it was told to you in the first place by someone else? One of the favorite pastimes of many children is asking to be told about those days they were too young to remember. But since childhood is largely a state of mind, facts as such are not all that important. What someone thinks happened in his childhood, did happen. What someone wishes to pass off as having happened is also worth hearing for the wish rather than the fact.

A large part of the pleasure of reading autobiography is purely narcissistic. I suspect it is almost impossible to read someone else's memoirs without making up your own as comparison. The reader finds himself comparing his memories of high school with Joe Brainard's or Jim Carroll's, or comparing the stories he has heard of his grandfather the coal miner with the stories Henry Adams heard of his grandfather the president. Most memoirs of famous people are fascinating up to the point that they become famous — Charlie Chaplin's autobiography is a fine example — and then they tend to become ragbags of gossip and catch-as-catch-can philosophizing. Once fame comes along most of us have to give up the comparative autobiographies we were composing in our minds. But we have all had a childhood. We have something to compare.

It is probably worth ending these comments with some definitions. Childhood, for the purposes of this collection, ends at sixteen. By that time the boy or girl has had enough contact with the world outside the family to temper dreams with reality and to know that there are possibilities to dream about that were never before expected.

And what is an American childhood? What besides geography defines a boy growing up in an upstate New York utopian community, a girl in Seattle dutifully observing the niceties of the Japanese New Year, a boy prowling the streets of Brooklyn, a girl spending her first winter in a sod hut on the Colorado prairie, a boy witnessing a bloody battle between members of his tribe and the invading white men, a girl supporting her family by selling drawings to a local newspaper? One girl's father came from China to practice medicine in Hawaii; another's was a slave. Rich man, poor man, beggar man, thief. Yet they all grow up believing in the freedom to move on and discover new worlds. Young Davy Crockett runs away from home. Young H. L. Mencken explores Baltimore while staying safely with his family. Young Jim Carroll wins a scholarship to play basketball with a whole new crowd. Parents can pull up stakes and move their families to another part of town, to another city, to the country. In search of a new life, they can go west or head north. They can choose to come to America in the first place. There is always room — or so it seems — for a new adventure. Or the hope of one. And that is the common thread of all these memoirs.

Gouverneur Morris is one of the American forefathers who never became a household word, but still he was there at the beginning, a friend of the more famous men, a delegate at the constitutional convention in Philadelphia. Looking around at his contemporaries — Washington, Hamilton, Adams, Jefferson, and the rest — he said, "This generation will die away and give place to a race of Americans." His generation, he was saying, were not the Americans. They were yet to come. It is their voices, the voices of Americans yet to come, that fill this book.

———•◦∞◦•———

Benjamin Franklin

Benjamin Franklin (1706–1790) seems to get credit, whether he deserves it or not, for inventing everything from bifocals to the American post office system. He is also one of the authentic inventors of American autobiography. Although not published until after his death, Franklin's unfinished Autobiography *was written in bits and pieces between 1771 and 1778, largely while he was living abroad.*

In it Franklin observes the unwritten rules of eighteenth-century memoirists. He writes at length about his ancestors (omitted here), stresses the importance of his education (although in his case it was hardly orthodox), and even when telling of a boyhood prank is careful to draw a moral lesson from it. But if Franklin's method was traditional, his observations were American.

For Franklin and most of his contemporaries, childhood was too serious a time to waste. It was, literally, an apprenticeship. Ben was at work in his brother's Boston printing shop when he was twelve. By the time he was sixteen, he was regularly publishing essays in the New England Courant *under the name of Silence Dogood.*

The excerpt reprinted here begins just after his father left England for the New World. Notice the elaborate epitaph Franklin copies with obvious pride from his parents' gravestone, composed — and paid for, he lets us know — by himself. When it came time for an epitaph of his own, it read, simply, "Benjamin Franklin, Printer."

From *The Autobiography of Benjamin Franklin*

JOSIAH, MY FATHER, married young, and carried his wife with three children into New England, about 1682. The conventicles having been forbidden by law, and frequently disturbed, induced some considerable men of his acquaintance to remove to that country, and he was prevailed with to accompany them thither, where they expected to enjoy their mode of religion with freedom. By the same wife he had four children more; born there, and by a second wife ten more, in all seventeen;

of which I remember thirteen sitting at one time at his table, who all grew up to be men and women, and married; I was the youngest son, and the youngest child but two, and was born in Boston, New England. My mother, the second wife, was Abiah Folger, daughter of Peter Folger, one of the first settlers of New England, of whom honorable mention is made by Cotton Mather, in his church history of that country entitled *Magnalia Christi Americana*, as *"a godly, learned Englishman,"* if I remember the words rightly. I have heard that he wrote sundry small occasional pieces, but only one of them was printed, which I saw now many years since. It was written in 1675, in the home-spun verse of that time and people, and addressed to those then concerned in the government there. It was in favor of liberty of conscience, and in behalf of the Baptists, Quakers, and other sectaries that had been under persecution, ascribing the Indian wars, and other distresses that had befallen the country, to that persecution, as so many judgments of God to punish so heinous an offense, and exhorting a repeal of those uncharitable laws. The whole appeared to me as written with a good deal of decent plainness and manly freedom. The six concluding lines I remember, though I have forgotten the two first of the stanza; but the purport of them was, that his censures proceeded from good will, and therefore he would be known to be the author.

> *"Because to be a libeller (says he)*
> *I hate it with my heart;*
> *From Sherburne town, where now I dwell*
> *My name I do put here;*
> *Without offense your real friend,*
> *It is Peter Folgier."*

My elder brothers were all put apprentices to different trades. I was put to the grammar-school at eight years of age, my father intending to devote me, as the tithe of his sons, to the service of the Church. My early readiness in learning to read (which must have been very early, as I do not remember when I could not read), and the opinion of all his friends, that I should certainly make a good scholar, encouraged him in this purpose of his. My uncle Benjamin, too, approved of it, and proposed to give me all his short-hand volumes of sermons, I suppose as a stock to set up with, if I would learn his character. I continued, however, at the grammar-school not quite one year, though in that time I had risen gradually from the middle of the class of that year to be the head of it, and farther was removed into the next class above it, in order to go with that into the third at the end of the year. But my father, in the meantime, from a view of the expense of a college education, which having so large a family he could not well afford, and the mean living many so educated were afterwards able to obtain, — reasons that he gave to his friends in my hearing, — altered his first intention, took me from the grammar-school, and sent me to a school for writing and arithmetic, kept by a then famous man, Mr. George Brownell, very successful in his profession generally, and that by mild, encouraging methods. Under him I acquired fair writing pretty soon, but I failed in the arithmetic, and made no progress in it. At ten years old I was taken home to assist my father in his business, which was that of a tallow-chandler and sope-boiler; a business he was not bred to, but had assumed on his arrival in New England, and on finding his dying trade would not maintain his family, being in little request. Accordingly, I was employed in cutting wick for the candles, filling the dipping mold and the molds for cast candles, attending the shop, going of errands, etc.

I disliked the trade, and had a strong inclination for the sea, but my father declared against it; however, living near the water, I was much in and about it, learnt early to swim well, and to manage boats; and when in a boat or canoe with other boys, I was commonly allowed to govern, especially in any case of difficulty; and upon other occasions I was generally a leader among the boys, and sometimes led them into scrapes, of which I will mention one instance, as it shows an early projecting public spirit, tho' not then justly conducted.

There was a salt-marsh that bounded part of the mill-pond, on the edge of which, at high water, we used to stand to fish for minnows. By much trampling, we had made it a mere quagmire. My proposal was to build a wharf there fit for us to stand upon, and I showed my comrades a large heap of stones, which were intended for a new house near the marsh, and which would very well suit our purpose. Accordingly, in the evening, when the workmen were gone, I assembled a number of my play-fellows, and working with them diligently like so many emmets, sometimes two or three to a stone, we brought them all away and built our little wharf. The next morning the workmen were surprised at missing the stones, which were found in our wharf. Inquiry was made after the removers; we were discovered and complained of; several of us were corrected by our fathers; and, though I pleaded the usefulness of the work, mine convinced me that nothing was useful which was not honest.

I think you may like to know something of his person and
character. He had an excellent constitution of body, was of middle
stature, but well set, and very strong; he was ingenious, could draw
prettily, was skilled a little in music, and had a clear, pleasing voice, so
that when he played psalm tunes on his violin and sung withal, as he
sometimes did in an evening after the business of the day was over, it
was extremely agreeable to hear. He had a mechanical genius too,
and, on occasion, was very handy in the use of other tradesmen's
tools; but his great excellence lay in a sound understanding and solid
judgment in prudential matters, both in private and publick affairs.
In the latter, indeed, he was never employed, the numerous family
he had to educate and the straitness of his circumstances keeping him
close to his trade; but I remember well his being frequently visited by
leading people, who consulted him for his opinion in affairs of the
town or of the church he belonged to, and showed a good deal of
respect for his judgment and advice: he was also much consulted by
private persons about their affairs when any difficulty occurred,
and frequently chosen an arbitrator between contending parties. At
his table he liked to have, as often as he could, some sensible friend
or neighbor to converse with, and always took care to start some
ingenious or useful topic for discourse, which might tend to improve the minds of his children. By this means he turned our
attention to what was good, just, and prudent in the conduct of life;
and little or no notice was ever taken of what related to the victuals
on the table, whether it was well or ill dressed, in or out of season,
of good or bad flavor, preferable or inferior to this or that other
thing of the kind, so that I was bro't up in such a perfect inattention to those matters as to be quite indifferent what kind of food was
set before me, and so unobservant of it that to this day if I am asked
I can scarcely tell a few hours after dinner what I dined upon. This
has been a convenience to me in travelling, where my companions
have been sometimes very unhappy for want of a suitable
gratification of their more delicate, because better instructed, tastes
and appetites.

My mother had likewise an excellent constitution: she suckled all
her ten children. I never knew either my father or mother to have
any sickness but that of which they dy'd, he at eighty-nine, and she
at eighty-five years of age. They lie buried together at Boston, where
I some years since placed a marble over their grave, with this inscription:

JOSIAH FRANKLIN
And
ABIAH his wife,
Lie here interred.
They lived lovingly together in wedlock
Fifty-five years
Without an estate, or any gainful employment,
By constant labor and industry
With God's blessing,
They maintained a large family
Comfortably,
And brought up thirteen children
And seven grandchildren
Reputably.
From this instance, reader
Be encouraged to diligence in thy calling,
And distrust not Providence.
He was a pious and prudent man;
She, a discreet and virtuous woman.
Their youngest son,
In filial regard to their memory,
Places this stone.
J. F. born 1655, died 1744, Ætat 89.
A. F. born 1667, died 1752,——85.

By my rambling digressions I perceive myself to be grown old. I us'd to write more methodically. But one does not dress for private company as for a publick ball. 'Tis perhaps only negligence.

To return: I continued thus employed in my father's business for two years, that is, till I was twelve years old; and my brother John, who was bred to that business, having left my father, married, and set up for himself at Rhode Island, there was all appearance that I was destined to supply his place, and become a tallow-chandler. But my dislike to the trade continuing, my father was under apprehensions that if he did not find one for me more agreeable, I should break away and get to sea, as his son Josiah had done, to his great vexation. He therefore sometimes took me to walk with him, and see joiners, bricklayers, turners, braziers, etc., at their work, that he might observe my inclination and endeavour to fix it on some trade or other on land. It has ever since been a pleasure to me to see good workmen handle their tools; and it has been useful to me, having learnt so much by it as to be able to do little jobs myself in my house when a workman could not readily be got, and to construct little machines for my experiments, while the intention of making the experiment was fresh and warm in my mind. My father at last fixed upon the cutler's trade, and my uncle Benjamin's son Samuel, who was bred to that business in London, being about that time established in Boston, I was sent to be with him some time on liking. But his expectations of a fee with me displeasing my father, I was taken home again.

From a child I was fond of reading, and all the little money that came into my hands was ever laid out in books. Pleased with the *Pilgrim's Progress,* my first collection was of John Bunyan's works in separate little volumes. I afterward sold them to enable me to buy R. Burton's *Historical Collections;* they were small chapmen's books, and cheap, forty or fifty in all. My father's little library consisted chiefly of books in polemic divinity, most of which I read, and have since often regretted that, at a time when I had such a thirst for knowledge, more proper books had not fallen in my way, since it was now resolved I should not be a clergyman. Plutarch's *Lives* there was in which I read abundantly, and I still think that time spent to great advantage. There was also a book of De Foe's, called an *Essay on Projects,* and another of Dr. Mather's called *Essays to do Good,* which perhaps gave me a turn of thinking that had an influence on some of the principal future events of my life.

This bookish inclination at length determined my father to make me a printer, though he had already one son (James) of that profession. In 1717 my brother James returned from England with a press and letters to set up his business in Boston. I liked it much better than that of my father, but still had a hankering for the sea. To prevent the apprehended effect of such an inclination, my father was impatient to have me bound to my brother. I stood out some time, but at last was persuaded, and signed the indentures when I was yet but twelve years old. I was to serve as an apprentice till I was twenty-one years of age, only I was to be allowed journeyman's wages during the last year. In a little time I made great proficiency in the business, and became a useful hand to my brother. I now had access to better books. An acquaintance with the apprentices of booksellers enabled me sometimes to borrow a small one, which I was careful to return soon and clean. Often I sat up in my room reading the greatest part of the night, when the book was borrowed in the evening and to be returned early in the morning, lest it should be missed or wanted.

And after some time an ingenious tradesman, Mr. Matthew Adams, who had a pretty collection of books, and who frequented our printing-house, took notice of me, invited me to his library, and very kindly lent me such books as I chose to read. I now took a fancy to poetry, and made some little pieces; my brother, thinking it might turn to account, encouraged me, and put me on composing occasional ballads. One was called *The Lighthouse Tragedy,* and contained an account of the drowning of Captain Worthilake, with his two daughters; the other was a sailor's song, on the taking of *Teach* (or Blackbeard) the pirate. They were wretched stuff, in the Grub-street-ballad style; and when they were printed he sent me about the town to sell them. The first sold wonderfully; the event, being recent, having made a great noise. This flattered my vanity; but my father discouraged me by ridiculing my performances, and telling me verse-makers were generally beggars. So I escaped being a poet, most probably a very bad one; but as prose writing has been of great use to me in the course of my life, and was a principal means of my advancement, I shall tell you how, in such a situation, I acquired what little ability I have in that way.

There was another bookish lad in the town, John Collins by name, with whom I was intimately acquainted. We sometimes disputed, and very fond we were of argument, and very desirous of confuting one another, which disputatious turn, by the way, is apt to become a very bad habit, making people often extremely disagreeable in company by the contradiction that is necessary to bring it into practice; and thence, besides souring and spoiling the conversation, is productive of disgusts and, perhaps, enmities where you may have occasion for friendship. I had caught it by reading my father's books of dispute about religion. Persons of good sense, I have since observed, seldom fall into it, except lawyers, university men, and men of all sorts that have been bred at Edinborough.

A question was once, somehow or other, started between Collins and me, of the propriety of educating the female sex in learning, and their abilities for study. He was of opinion that it was improper, and that they were naturally unequal to it. I took the contrary side, perhaps a little for dispute's sake. He was naturally more eloquent, had a ready plenty of words, and sometimes, as I thought, bore me down more by his fluency than by the strength of his reasons. As we parted without settling the point, and were not to see one another again for some time, I sat down to put my arguments in writing which I copied fair and sent to him. He answered, and I replied. Three or four letters of a side had passed, when my father happened to find my papers and read them. Without entering into the discussion, he took occasion to talk to me about the manner of my writing; observed that, though I had the advantage of my antagonist in correct spelling and pointing (which I ow'd to the printing-house), I fell far short in elegance of expression, in method and in perspicuity, of which he convinced me by several instances. I saw the justice of his remarks, and thence grew more attentive to the manner in writing, and determined to endeavor at improvement.

About this time I met with an odd volume of the *Spectator*. It was the third. I had never before seen any of them. I bought it, read it over and over, and was much delighted with it. I thought the writing excellent, and wished, if possible, to imitate it. With this view I took some of the papers, and, making short hints of the sentiment in each sentence, laid them by a few days, and then, without looking at the book, try'd to compleat the papers again, by expressing each hinted sentiment at length, and as fully as it had been expressed before, in any suitable words that should come to hand. Then I compared my *Spectator* with the original, discovered some of my faults and corrected them. But I found I wanted a stock of words, or a readiness in recollecting and using them, which I thought I should have acquired before that time if I had gone on making verses; since the continual occasion for words of the same import, but of different length, to suit the measure, or of different sound for the rhyme, would have laid me under a constant necessity of searching for variety, and also have tended to fix that variety in my mind, and make me master of it. Therefore I took some of the tales and turned them into verse; and, after a time, when I had pretty well forgotten the prose, turned them back again. I also sometimes jumbled my collections of hints into confusion, and after some weeks endeavoured to reduce them into the best order, before I began to form the full sentences and compleat the paper. This was to teach me method in the arrangement of thoughts. By comparing my work afterwards with the original, I discovered my faults and amended them; but I sometimes had the pleasure of fancying that, in certain particulars of small import, I had been lucky enough to improve the method or the language, and this encouraged me to think I might possibly in time come to be a tolerable

English writer, of which I was extremely ambitious. My time for these exercises and for reading was at night, after work or before it began in the morning, or on Sundays, when I contrived to be in the printing-house alone, evading as much as I could the common attendance on public worship which my father used to exact of me when I was under his care, and which indeed I still thought a duty, though I could not, as it seemed to me, afford time to practise it.

When about 16 years of age I happened to meet with a book, written by one Tryon, recommending a vegetable diet. I determined to go into it. My brother, being yet unmarried, did not keep house, but boarded himself and his apprentices in another family. My refusing to eat flesh occasioned an inconveniency, and I was frequently chid for my singularity. I made myself acquainted with Tryon's manner of preparing some of his dishes, such as boiling potatoes or rice, making hasty pudding, and a few others, and then proposed to my brother, that if he would give me, weekly, half the money he paid for my board, I would board myself. He instantly agreed to it, and I presently found that I could save half what he paid me. This was an additional fund for buying books. But I had another advantage in it. My brother and the rest going from the printing-house to their meals, I remained there alone, and, despatching presently my light repast, which often was no more than a bisket or a slice of bread, a handful of raisins, or a tart from the pastry-cook's and a glass of water, had the rest of the time, till their return, for study, in which I made the greater progress, from that greater cleverness of head and quicker apprehension which usually attend temperance in eating and drinking.

John Adams

John Adams (1735–1826) was George Washington's vice-president, the second president of the United States, and founder of a line of Adamses that was to be heard from in American political and intellectual life until the early years of the twentieth century. He began his autobiography in 1802, two years after he was defeated for reelection by Thomas Jefferson.

The memoir is as sketchy an account of a New England boyhood as Benjamin Franklin's, but franker in its domestic details. Life in rural Braintree (now Quincy), Massachusetts, with the middle-class Adams family was clearly more comfortable than it had been at Josiah Franklin's candle shop in Boston. But amid some practical lessons on the difficulty of farming and a fourteen-year-old's realistic worries about the entrance exams at Harvard, John Adams introduces two basically American subjects that surface repeatedly throughout this collection: guns and sex.

From *The Autobiography of John Adams*

MY FATHER married Susanna Boylston in October 1734, and on the 19th of October 1735 I was born. As my Parents were both fond of reading, and my father had destined his first born, long before his birth to a public Education I was very early taught to read at home and at a School of Mrs. Belcher the Mother of Deacon Moses Belcher, who lived in the next house on the opposite side of the Road. I shall not consume much paper in relating the Anecdotes of my Youth. I was sent to the public School close by the Stone Church, then kept by Mr. Joseph Cleverly, who died this Year 1802 at the Age of Ninety. Mr. Cleverly was through his whole Life the most indolent Man I ever knew (*excepting Mr. Wibirt*) though a tolerable Schollar and a Gentleman. His inattention to his Schollars was such as gave me a disgust to Schools, to books and to study and I spent my time as idle Children do in making and sailing boats and Ships upon the Ponds and Brooks, in making and flying Kites, in driving hoops, playing marbles, playing

Quoits, Wrestling, Swimming, Skaiting and above all in shooting, to which Diversion I was addicted to a degree of Ardor which I know not that I ever felt for any other Business, Study or Amusement.

My Enthusiasm for Sports and Inattention to Books, allarmed my Father, and he frequently entered into conversation with me upon the Subject. I told him [I did not] love Books and wished he would lay aside the thoughts of sending me to Colledge. What would you do Child? Be a Farmer. A Farmer? Well I will shew you what it is to be a Farmer. You shall go with me to Penny ferry tomorrow Morning and help me get Thatch. I shall be very glad to go Sir. — Accordingly next morning he took me with him, and with great good humour kept me all day with him at Work. At night at home he said Well John are you satisfied with being a Farmer. Though the Labour had been very hard and very muddy I answered I like it very well Sir. Ay but I dont like it so well: so you shall go to School to day. I went but was not so happy as among the Creek Thatch. My School master neglected to put me into Arithmetick longer than I thought was right, and I re-sented it. I procured me Cockers I believe and applyd myself to it at home alone and went through the whole Course, overtook and passed by all the Schollars at School, without any master. I dared not ask my fathers Assistance because he would have disliked my Inattention to my Latin. In this idle Way I passed on till fourteen and upwards, when I said to my Father very seriously I wished he would take me from School and let me go to work upon the Farm. You know said my father I have set my heart upon your Education at Colledge and why will you not comply with my desire. Sir I dont like my Schoolmaster. He is so negligent and so cross that I never can learn any thing under him. If you will be so good as to perswade Mr. Marsh to take me, I will apply myself to my Studies as closely as my nature will admit, and go to Colledge as soon as I can be prepared. Next Morning the first I heard was John I have perswaded Mr. Marsh to take you, and you must go to school there to day. This Mr. Marsh was a Son of our former Minister of that name, who kept a private Boarding School but two doors from my Fathers. To this School I went, where I was kindly treated, and I began to study in Earnest.* My Father soon

---

* Some fragmentary notes taken down by Harriet Welsh from John Adams's conver-sations in 1823 slightly amplify his recollections of his school days:

... "I was about nine or ten years old at that time and soon learn'd the use of the gun and became strong enough to lift it. I used to take it to school and leave it in the entry and the moment it was over went into the field to kill crows and squirrels and I tried to

observed the relaxation of my Zeal for my Fowling Piece, and my daily encreasing Attention to my Books. In a little more than a Year Mr. Marsh pronounced me fitted for Colledge. On the day appointed at Cambridge for the Examination of Candidates for Admission I mounted my horse and called upon Mr. Marsh, who was to go with me. The Weather was dull and threatened rain. Mr. Marsh said he was unwell and afraid to go out. I must therefore go alone. Thunder struck at this unforeseen disappointment, And terrified at the Thought of introducing myself to such great Men as the President and fellows of a Colledge, I at first resolved to return home: but foreseeing the Grief of my father and apprehending he would not only be offended with me, but my Master too whom I sincerely loved, I arroused my self, and collected Resolution enough to proceed. Although Mr. Marsh had assured me that he had seen one of the Tutors the last Week and had said to him, all that was proper for him to say if he should go to Cambridge; that he was not afraid to trust me to an Examination and was confident I should acquit my self well and be honourably admitted; yet I had not the same confidence in my self, and suffered a very melancholly Journey. Arrived at Cambridge I presented myself according to my directions and underwent the usual Examination by the President Mr. Holyoke and the Tutors Flint, Hancock, Mayhew and Marsh. Mr. Mayhew into whose Class We were to be admitted, presented me a Passage of English to translate into Latin. It was long and casting my Eye over it I found several Words the latin for which did not occur to my memory. Thinking that I must

---

see how many I could kill: at last Mr. Cleverly found this out and gave me a most dreadful scolding and after that I left the gun at an old woman's in the neighborhood. I soon became large enough to go on the marshes to kill wild fowl and to swim and used to beg so hard of my father and mother to let me go that they at last consented and many a cold boisterous day have I pass'd on the beach without food waiting for wild fowl to go over — often *lying* in wait for them on the cold ground — to hide myself from them. I cared not what I did if I could but get away from school, and confess to my shame that I sometimes play'd truant. At last I got to be thirteen years of age and my life had been wasted. I told my father if I must go to College I must have some other master for I detested the one I had and should not be fitted ever if I staid with him but if he would put me to Mr. Marsh's school I would endeavor to get my lessons and make every exertion to go. He said I knew it was an invariable rule with Mr. M. not to take any boys belonging to the town — he only took eight or ten to live with him. However I said so much to him that he said he would try, and after a great deal of persuasion Master Marsh consented. The next day after he did so I took my books and went to him. I fulfill'd my promise and work'd diligently and in eighteen months was fitted for college. He lived where Hardwicke now keeps a shop opposite to where the Cleverlys live. . . . Mr. Marsh was a good instructor and a man of learning. The house I learn'd my letters in was opposite my father's nearly and I have pulled it down within this twenty years."

translate it without a dictionary, I was in a great fright and expected to be turned by, an Event that I dreaded above all things. Mr. Mayhew went into his Study and bid me follow him. There Child, said he is a dictionary, there a Gramar, and there Paper, Pen and Ink, and you may take your own time. This was joyfull news to me and I then thought my Admission safe. The Latin was soon made, I was declared Admitted and a Theme given me, to write on in the Vacation. I was as light when I came home as I had been heavy when I went: my Master was well pleased and my Parents very happy. I spent the Vacation not very profitably chiefly in reading Magazines and a British Apollo. I went to Colledge at the End of it and took the Chamber assigned me and my place in the Class under Mr. Mayhew. I found some better Schollars than myself, particularly Lock, Hemmenway and Tisdale. The last left Colledge before the End of the first Year, and what became of him I know not. Hemmenway still lives a great divine, and Lock has been President of Harvard Colledge a Station for which no Man was better qualified. With these I ever lived in friendship, without Jealousy or Envy. I soon became intimate with them, and began to feel a desire to equal them in Science and Literature. In the Sciences especially Mathematicks, I soon surpassed them, mainly because, intending to go into the Pulpit, they thought Divinity and the Classicks of more Importance to them. In Litterature I never overtook them.

Here it may be proper to recollect something which makes an Article of great importance in the Life of every Man. I was of an amorous disposition and very early from ten or eleven Years of Age, was very fond of the Society of females. I had my favorites among the young Women and spent many of my Evenings in their Company and this disposition although controlled for seven Years after my Entrance into College returned and engaged me too much till I was married. I shall draw no Characters nor give any enumeration of my youthfull flames. It would be considered as no compliment to the dead or the living: This I will say — they were all modest and virtuous Girls and always maintained this Character through Life. No Virgin or Matron ever had cause to blush at the sight of me, or to regret her Acquaintance with me. No Father, Brother, Son or Friend ever had cause of Grief or Resentment for any Intercourse between me and any Daughter, Sister, Mother, or any other Relation of the female Sex. My Children may be assured that no illegitimate Brother or Sister exists or ever existed. These Reflections, to me consolatory beyond all expression, I am able to make with truth and sincerity and I presume I am indebted for this blessing to my Education. My Parents held every Species of Libertinage in such Contempt and horror, and held up constantly to view such pictures of disgrace, of baseness and of Ruin, that my natural temperament was always overawed by my Principles and Sense of decorum. This Blessing has been rendered the more prescious to me, as I have seen enough of the Effects of a different practice. Corroding Reflections through Life are the never failing consequence of illict amours, in old as well as in new Countries. The Happiness of Life depends more upon Innocence in this respect, than upon all the Philosophy of Epicurus, or of Zeno without it. I could write Romances, or Histories as wonderfull as Romances of what I have known or heard in France, Holland and England, and all would serve to confirm what I learned in my Youth in America, that Happiness is lost forever if Innocence is lost, at least untill a Repentance is undergone so severe as to be an overballance to all the gratifications of Licentiousness. Repentance itself cannot restore the Happiness of Innocence, at least in this Life.

John McCullough

John McCullough (1748–1823) had no doubt told the story of his boyhood captivity by Indians many times before he got around to writing it down. By that time there was a popular genre of horrifying kidnap tales. But the odd thing about John's story is how matter-of-fact it is, how unhorrifying. Even with the surprising twist his adventure takes toward the end, McCullough's deadpan prose style seems to proclaim his honesty. If he were making it up, the reader suspects, he would have told a taller tale. In fact, no one bothered publishing his Life with the Aborigines, *from which this excerpt is taken, until 1912, when his great-grandson had it privately published.*

McCullough was the son of a northern-Irish immigrant who settled near Mercersburg, Pennsylvania. There John, about eight years old, and his younger brother were grabbed by Indians (accompanied by a Frenchman) and taken west. He was sixteen when he returned home. Later, he would marry twice, have six children, and become a local justice of the peace — "a position that in those olden days was always filled by the very best men of the community," his great-grandson assures us in his preface to the autobiography.

From *Life with the Aborigines*

ON THE 26TH OF JULY, 1756, my parents and my oldest sister went home to pull flax, accompanied by one John Allen, a neighbor, who had business at Fort Loudon, and promised to come that way in the evening to accompany them back. Allen had proceeded but about two miles toward Loudon until he heard the Indians had killed a man that morning, about a mile and a half from where my parents were at work; he then, instead of going back to accompany them home agreeably to his promise, took a circuitous route of about six or seven miles, for fear of the Indians. When he came home, my brother and I were playing on the great road, a short distance from the house; he told us to go immediately to the house, or the Indians would catch us, adding,

at the same time, that he supposed they had killed our father and
mother by that time.

We were small, I was about eight years old, my brother was but five;
we went to the house, the people were all in a bustle, making ready to
go to a fort about a mile off. I recollect of hearing them say, that
somebody should go and give my parents notice; none would venture
to go; my brother and I concluded that we would go ourselves, accordingly we laid off our trowsers and went off in our shirts unno-
ticed by any person, leaving a little sister about two years old, sleeping
in bed; when we got in sight of the house we began to halloo and sing,
rejoicing that we had got home; when we came within about fifty or
sixty yards of the house, all of a sudden the Indians came rushing out
of a thicket upon us; they were six in number, to wit, five Indians and
one Frenchman; they divided into two parties; three rushed across
the path before, and three behind us. This part of the scene appears
to me yet, more like a dream than anything real: my brother screamed
aloud the instant we saw them; for my part, it appeared to me that the
one party were Indians, and the other white people; they stopped
before us, I was making my way betwixt two of them, when one of the
hind part pulled me back by my shirt; they instantly ran up a little hill
to where they had left their baggage; there they tied a pair of moccasins on my feet; my brother at that instant broke off from them,
running towards the house, screaming as he went; they brought him
back, and started off as fast as I was able to run along with them, one
of them carrying my brother on his back. We ran along side of the
field where my parents were at work, they were only intercepted from
our view by a small ridge in the field, that lay parallel to the course we
were running; when we had got about seventy or eighty perches from
the field, we sat down in a thicket of bushes, where we heard our
father calling us; two of the Indians ran off towards the house, but
happily missed him, as he had returned back to the field, supposing
we had gone back again.

The other four started off with us as fast as I was able to travel
along with them, jumping across every road we came to, one catching
me by each arm and slinging me over the road to prevent our tracks
from being discovered.

We travelled all that day, observing still when we came to an eminence, one of them would climb a tree, and point out the course they
should take, in order, I suppose, to avoid being discovered. It came on
rain towards evening, we travelled on till a good while after night; at

last we took up our lodging under a large tree, they spread down a blanket for us to lie on, and laid another over us, an Indian laid down at our head and feet. At break of day we started again; about sun-rise we heard a number of axes at a short distance from us, we also discovered where logs had been dragged on the ground the day before; they immediately took the alarm and made off as quick as possible. Towards evening we stopped on the side of a mountain; two of the Indians and the Frenchman, went down into the valley, leaving one to take care of us; they were not long gone till we heard them shooting, in a short time they came back, carrying a parcel of hogs on their backs, and a fowl they had killed; also a parcel of green apples in their bosoms; they gave us some of the apples, which was the first nourishment we got from the time we were taken. We then went down the mountain into an obscure place, where they kindled a fire and singed the hair off the hogs and roasted them, the fowl they roasted for us; we had not been long there till we heard the war halloo up the run from where we had our fire, the two Indians came to us, whom I mentioned had ran towards the house when they heard our father calling us; they had a scalp with them, by the color of the hair I concluded it had been my father's, but I was mistaken, it was the scalp of the man they killed the morning before they took us; the scalp they made two of, and dried them at the fire. After roasting the meat and drying the scalps, we took the mountain again, when we had got about half way up, we stopped and sat down on an old log — after a few minutes rest they rose up one after another and went to the sides of rocks and old logs and began to scrape away the leaves, where they drew out blankets, bells, a small kettle and several other articles which they had hidden when they were coming down. We got over the mountain that evening, about sunset we crossed a large road in sight of a waste house, we went about a quarter of a mile further and encamped by the side of a large run; one of them went about two or three hundred yards from the camp and shot a deer and brought it to the camp on his back. I had been meditating my escape from the time we crossed the road.

Shortly after dark we laid down, I was placed next to the fire, my brother next, and an Indian laid down on the edge of the blanket behind us; I awoke sometime in the night and aroused my brother, whispering to him to rise, and we would go off, he told me that he could not go, I told him that I would go myself, he replied that he did not care. I got up as softly as I could, but had not gone more than three or four yards from the fire till the Indian who lay at our backs raised his head and said, "Where you go?" I told him I was going to p—s, he said, "make haste, come sleep." I went and laid down again.

Next morning four of the Indians and the Frenchman went off on a scout, leaving one to take care of us. About the middle of the day, they came running the way we came the evening before — they hallooed as soon as they came in sight [and] by the time they got to the camp, the one who took care of us had all their things thrown upon their blankets; the one who took care of us took me on his back and ran as fast as he could, for about a quarter of a mile, then threw me down, broke a twig and switched me along until we got on the mountain again; about an hour after, we began to gather whortleberries, as they were very plenty on the mountains; lucky indeed for us, for I verily believe we would have starved, had it not been for the berries, for we could not eat the meat without bread or salt. We got off the mountain that evening, and encamped in a thicket; it rained that night and the next morning; they had made a shade of some of their spare blankets; we were long in starting the next morning. Whilst we were sitting about the fire, we heard the report of two guns at a little distance directly the way we came the evening before; they started up in an instant, and picked up their blankets and other articles; the one who carried me before took me on his back and ran as fast as he could, for about a mile, then threw me down and whipped me along as he had done the day before. It must be observed that they always carried my brother time about; for my part it was the only two rides I got from the day I was taken, till we got to Fort Duquesne (now Pittsburg). I must pass over many occurrences that happened on our way to Pittsburg, excepting one or two.

The morning before we came to Kee-ak-kshee-man-nit-toos, which signifies Cut Spirit, an old town at the junction of La-el-han-neck, or Middle Creek, and Quin-nim-mough-koong, or Can-na-maugh, or Otter Creek, as the word signifies.

The morning before we got there, they pulled all the hair out of our heads, except a small spot on the crown, which they left. We got to the town about the middle of the day, where we got some squashes to eat; the next morning we set out for Fort Duquesne — the morning after that we came to several Indian camps — they gave us some bread, which was the first we tasted from the time we were taken.

About a mile or two before we came to the fort, we met an old Indian, whose dress made him appear very terrifying to us; he had a brown coat on him, no shirt, his breast bare, a breech-clout, a pair of leggins and moccasins, his face and breast painted rudely with vermillion and verdigris, a large bunch of artificial hair, dyed of a crimson color, fixed on the top or crown of his head, a large triangle piece of silver hanging below his nose, that covered almost the whole of his upper lip; his ears (which had been cut according to their peculiar custom) were stretched out with fine brass wire, made in the form (but much larger) of what is commonly fixed in suspenders, so that, perhaps, he appeared something like what you might apprehend to be a likeness of the devil. As he approached toward us, the rest said something to him, — he took hold of me by the arm, and lashed me about from side to side, at last he threw me from him as far as he was able, then took hold of my brother, and served him the same way. Shortly after that, they stopped and painted us, tying or fixing a large bunch of hawk's feathers on the top of each of our heads, then raised the war halloo, viz. one halloo for each scalp, and one for each prisoner, still repeating at certain intervals; we met several Indians who came running out to meet us — we were taken to the middle of their encampment into one of their chief's huts; after they had given a narrative of their adventure, the old chief drew out a small bag from behind his bed and took out a large belt of wampum and fixed it round my neck; we then started down to the fort, a great number of Indians of both sexes were paraded on each side of the path to see us as we went along; some of them were shoving in little fellows to strike us, and others advising me to strike them, but we seemed to be both afraid of each other; we were taken into a French house, where a number of Indians were sitting on the floor; one of the chiefs took my brother by the hand and handed him to a Frenchman who was standing at a room door, which was the last sight I had of him; after that he took me by the hand, and made a speech for about half an hour, then handed me to an Indian who was sitting on the hearth smoking his pipe; he took me between his legs, (he could talk very good English) and asked me several questions, telling me that I was his brother, that the people had killed a brother of his about a year before, and that these good men (meaning the warriors who took us) had gone and brought me to replace his deceased brother; he also told me that he had been raised amongst the white people, and that he had been taught to read when he was young, but that he had almost forgot it. I believe that he was telling me the truth, for he knew all the letters and figures. He then took me by the hand and led me to the Al-leege-eon-ing, or Allegheny River, which signifies an impression made by the foot of a human being, for said they, the land is so rich about it that a person cannot travel through the lands adjoining it without leaving the mark of their feet. We got in a canoe and went across the river, where a great number of Indians were encamped.

He led me through their encampment; towards evening we came back. Shortly after our return two young fellows took me by the hand and led me to the river, we got into a canoe and paddled about thirty or forty yards from the shore, when they laid down their paddles and laid hold of me by the wrists, and plunged me over head and ears under the water, holding me down until I was almost smothered, then drew me up to get breath. They repeated several times. I had no other thought, but they were going to drown me.

I was at every interval pleading with them not to drown me; at last one of them said, "me no killim, me washim." I plead with them to let me into shallow water, and I would wash myself, accordingly they did — I then began to rub myself; they signified me to dive; I dipped my face into the water and raised it up as quick as I could; one of them stepped out of the canoe and laid hold me on back of my neck, and held me down to the bottom, till I was almost smothered, before he let me go. I then waded out; they put a new ruffled shirt on me, telling me that I was then an Indian, and that they would send me away to the rest of their friends. Accordingly I was sent off the next day with a female friend, to an uncle of my adopted brother's, who lived at a town called She-nang-go, on Beaver Creek.

Nothing remarkable happened on our journey, excepting several falls that I got off a young horse I was set on to ride. On the third or fourth night we arrived in She-nang-go, about an hour after dark; after the female friend whom I was sent with had informed the family who I was, they set up a lamentable cry, for some time; when their lamentation was over, they came to me one after another and shook me by the hand, in token that they considered me to stand in the same relationship to them as the one in whose stead I was placed. The next morning I was presented to my uncle, with whom I lived about a year. He was blind of one eye — a very good natured man.

In the beginning of winter he used to raise me up by daylight every morning, and make me sit down in the creek up to my chin in the cold water, in order to make me hardy as he said, whilst he would sit on the bank smoking his pipe, until he thought I had been long enough in the water, he would then bid me to dive. After I came out of the water he would order me not to go near the fire until I would be dry. I was kept at that until the water was frozen over, he would then break the ice for me and send me in as before. Some time in the winter, perhaps not long before Christmas, I took very sick; I lay all winter at the fire side, and an old squaw attended me, (what little attendance I got); she used to go out in the snow and hunt up herbs by the old tops; the roots of which she would boil and make a kind of drink for me. She would never suffer me to taste cold water or any kind of flesh, or anything that was sweet or salt. The only nourishment that I was suffered to take, was hominy, or dumplings, made of coarse Indian meal boiled in water. As I said before, I lay all winter at the fire side; I had nothing but a small blanket to cover me, part of which I drew under me for my bed, my legs drew up so that I was obliged to crawl when I had occasion to go out of doors. I remained in that situation until corn planting time, when I began to get better. They anointed my knees and hams with bear's oil, and made me keep my knees stretched out as tight as I could bear them, by which means I got the use of my joints in about a month's time. Shortly after I got able to run about, a dreadful accident happened at my hands, in the following manner: the most of the Indians of the town were either at their corn-fields or out a fishing — my uncle had been unwell for some time — he was below the town at the creek side, where he had an Indian doctor sweating him and conjuring out his disorder. He had a large pistol, which he had hung up by the guard at the head of his bed, — there were two brothers, relations of ours, the oldest was per- haps about my age, the other about two years younger. The oldest boy took down the pistol and cocked it, threatening for diversion to shoot his brother; the little fellow ran off from us — I assisted him to let down the cock of the pistol, which he held in his left hand with the muzzle towards his body, and his right hand against the cock; I would then (after cautioning him to turn the muzzle past his body) draw the trigger and he would let down the cock slowly. I advised him several times to lay by the pistol, which he would do; but as soon as his brother would come back to us, he would get it again. At last his brother got afraid and would not come near us any more. He then threatened to shoot me; I fled out of the house from him. The town lay in a semi-circular form, round a bend of the creek; there hap- pened to be a woman at the upper end of the town, (as we lived at the lower end), that had observed me when I fled out of the house from him — he immediately called me back to assist him to let down the cock; I refused to go, unless he would turn the butt end of the pistol to me, which he did, I went in, in haste (and forgot to caution him to hold the muzzle to one side) and drew the trigger; the consequence was, the pistol went off and shot him in the stomach, the pistol flew out of our hands; he laid his hands across his breast and ran out of the house, screaming aloud as he ran; I ran out of the house and looked after him, he went towards their own door, (about forty or fifty yards off), and quit screaming before he fell; — it was late in the evening; his mother and grandmother were coming from their corn-field at that instant; his grandmother just cast her eye towards him, as she came past him, and came to me where I was standing; before they got near me, I told her that Watook, (for that was his name), had shot himself; she turned away from me without saying anything. In a short time all the Indians in the town collected about me, examining me, and getting me to show them what way he took to shoot himself; I told them that he took the pistol in his left hand and held the muzzle to his thumb; I held to the one story. At last the woman (whom I mentioned had seen me when I fled out of the house from him) came and told them that she was standing out of doors looking at me across the bend of the creek, at the time she heard the report of the pistol, and that I was standing a considerable distance from the house at the time — at which they all dispersed. . . .

It happened to be the first funeral that I had seen amongst them, and not being acquainted with their customs, I was put to a terrible fright; shortly after dark they began to fire their guns, which they always do when any one dies. As all the family had gone to the wake, I was left by myself in the house; when the firing began I concluded that they were about to take my life; I therefore crept under a bed that was set upon forks drove into the ground, a considerable height off the floor, where I lay as close to the wall as I could get, till about break of day, when I was roused by the report of their guns again. I did not go near the corpse — however I heard them say, that he bled none, as the colfing and the blaze of the powder had followed the ball into his body. There were several young squaws who had seen us running about with the pistol; they frequently charged me with being the cause of the boy's death, which I always denied, but Queek-queek-co-mooch-que, a little white girl, (a prisoner) who lived with the family that the deceased belonged to, was like to be the worst evidence against me, — she told them that she saw me have the pistol in my hands several times — but the woman's evidence overruled the whole of them; however their minds were not entirely divested of the thoughts that I had taken his life, as they often cast it up to me afterwards, that I had shot Watook; especially when I would happen to get into a quarrel with any of the little fellows, they would tell me that I had killed one of them already, and that I wanted to kill another; however I declared the thing was merely accidental. When I reflect upon the above accident, and the circumstances attending it, my mind flows with gratitude to that Almighty Being whose wise providence directs the affairs of the world; I do not say that a lie is justifiable in the sight of God, yet I am led to believe that the woman was guided by providence in telling a manifest falsehood which, perhaps, was the means of prolonging my days. . . .

Sometime while we resided at Kseek-he-oong, or Salt Licks, Mossooh-whese, or Ben Dickson, invented a kind of punishment to inflict on boys who would do mischief, such as quarreling, plundering watermelon, or cucumber patches, etc., in the following manner: — there is a kind of fish that abounds in western waters, called a gar, that has a very long bill, and long sharp teeth; he took the bill of one of those fish, and wrapped a thin rag around it, projecting the teeth through the rag. He took any one who would do any kind of mischief, and after wetting their thighs and legs, he would score them from the hip down to the heel, three or four times on each thigh and leg, and some times, if they were found guilty, a second or third time, he would score them from the top of the shoulder down to the wrists, and from the top of the shoulder, on the back, to the contrary hip, crossways. It happened once, that a nephew of his, a very mischievous boy, threw the entrails of a turtle in my face, then ran off as quick as he could from me around the house; I picked up a stone and pursued him, and threw it after him; it happened to light on the top of his head, and knocked him down, and cut his head badly, or, it is probable, he would have concealed it, as he well knew what the consequences would be; for his back, arms, thighs and legs were almost constantly raw, by the frequent punishments he got for his mischief.

However, Mos-sooh-whese happened to be out a fishing at the time; he was informed when he came home of what had taken place; I was apprehensive of would be my doom, and was advised by my friends to hide myself; accordingly I got into a small addition to the house, where a number of bails of deer skin and fur were piled up; I had not been long there until I heard him inquiring for me; they told him that I had gone down to the creek and was not returned yet: he therefore ordered one of my brothers, (who had been with him a fishing the day before), to stand up until he would score him: as my brother was partly man grown, he refused; a struggle ensued — however, my brother was obliged to give up. The reason he gave for punishing others who were not present at the time the mischief was done, was, that if they should be present at the time that any one was prompting mischief, he should do his best endeavor to prevent it, or inform against those who had done it — as the informer was always exempted from the punishment aforesaid. I then heard him say, that, if I was to stay away a year he would score me; he then went to the creek on the hunt of me; after he was gone, they told me that I might as well come out as conceal myself; accordingly I did. In a short time he came back, grinning and showing his teeth as if he had got a prize; he ordered me to stand up at the side of a post; I obeyed his orders — he then took and wet my thighs and legs, to prevent the skin from tearing: he took the gar's bill, and gave me four scores, or scrapes, with it, from the point of the hip down to the heel — the mark of which I will carry to my grave.

My oldest brother was from home at the time the above punishment was inflicted on us; he came home that same night; I scarcely ever saw him more out of humour, than when he found the way we had been treated. He said, (whether he was in earnest or not, I cannot tell), that if he had been at home, he would have applied his tim-ma-heek-can, to Mos-sooh-whese's head, rather than suffer such an ignominious punishment, as he conceived it, to be inflicted on any of his family. However, he told Mos-sooh-whese never to do the like again without his consent. . . .

Whilst we were living at Kseek-he-oong, one Andrew Wilkins, a trader came to the town and was taken ill while there — he sent me to the other end of the town with some beads, to purchase a fowl for him, to work off a physic with; when I came back he was sitting alone in the house: as he could talk the Indian tongue tolerably well, he began to question me about where I was taken from; I told him from Conococheague — he asked my name; I told him.

As soon as he returned to Shippensburg, (which was his place of residence), he informed my father that he had seen me, which was the first account they received of me, from the time I was taken. The next spring we moved to a town about fifteen miles off, called Mo-hon-ing, which signifies a lick.

Some time in the summer following, my father came to Mo-hon-ing and found me out. I was shy in speaking to him, even by an interpreter, as I had at the time forgotten my mother tongue. My Indian brother not being at home, my father returned to Pittsburg and left me.

The fall following, my father went out to Fort Venenggo, or French Creek, along with Wilkins. Wilkins sent a special messenger to Mo-hon-ing, for my brother to take me to Venenggo, telling him that my father would purchase me from him; accordingly he took me off without letting me know his intention, or, it is probable, I would not have gone with him. When we got to Venenggo, we encamped about a mile from the garrison; my brother went to the garrison to bargain with my father for me, but told me nothing of it. The next morning my father and two others came to our camp, and told me that my brother wanted to see me at the fort; I went along with them; when we got there he told me that I must go home with my father, to see my mother and the rest of my friends; I wept bitterly, — all to no purpose; my father was ready to start; they laid hold of me and set me on a horse — I threw myself off; they set me on again and tied my legs under the horse's belly and started away for Pittsburg: we encamped about ten or fifteen miles from Venenggo; before we lay down, my father took his garters and tied my arms behind my back; however, I had them loose before my father laid down; I took care to keep it concealed from them by keeping my arms back as if they were tied. About midnight I arose from between my father and John Simeons, who was to accompany us to Pittsburg; I stepped out from the fire and sat down as if I had a real necessity for doing so; my father and Simeons arose and mended the fire; whilst they were laying the chunks together I ran off as fast as I could; I had got near a hundred yards from the camp when I heard them hunting a large dog which they had along with them, after me; I thought the dog would certainly overtake me; I therefore climbed up a tall tree as fast as I could; the dog stopped at the root of the tree, but as they continued to hunt him on, he ran off again — they came past the tree: after they passed by me, I climbed further up, until I got to some limbs where I could rest myself; the dog came back and stood a considerable time at the foot of the tree — then returned to the fire; I could see them distinctly from where I was; I remained on the tree about an hour; I then went down and steered through the woods till I found the road; I went about two or three miles along it, and the wolves were making a hideous noise all around me; I went off the road a short distance and climbed up a dogwood sapling and fixed myself on the branches of it, where I remained till break of day; I then got on the road again; I ran along as fast as I was able for about five miles, where I came to an Indian camp; they told me that I had better not keep the road, alleging that I would certainly be pursued; I took their advice and went off the road immediately, and steered through the woods till I got to where my friends were encamped; they advised me to take along the road that we came, when we came there; telling me that they were going to return home that day; I made no delay but went on about ten miles, and there waited till they came up with me. Not long after I left them my father came to the camp; they denied that they had seen me — supposing that I had gone on to Mo-hon-ing by myself, telling him that if I had, that they would take me to Pittsburg that fall.

Soon after we got home to Mo-hon-ing, instead of taking me to Pittsburg, agreeable to their promise, they set out on their fall hunt, taking me along with them; we staid out till some time in the winter before we returned. . . .

Sometime in the summer, whilst we were living at Kta-ho-ling, a great number of Indians collected at the forks of Moosh-king-oong, perhaps there were about three hundred or upwards; their intention was to come to the settlement and make a general massacre of the whole people, without any regard to age or sex; they were out about ten days when the most of them returned; having held a council, they concluded that it was not safe for them to leave their towns destitute of defence. However, several parties went on to different parts of the settlements; it happened that three of them, whom I was well acquainted with, came to the neighborhood of where I was taken from — they were young fellows — perhaps none of them more than twenty-years of age, — they came to a school house, where they murdered and scalped the master and all the scholars, except one, who survived after he was scalped, a boy of about ten years old, and a full cousin of mine. I saw the Indians when they returned home with the scalps; some of the old Indians were very much displeased at them for killing so many children, especially Neep-paugh-whese, or Night Walker, an old chief or half king, — he ascribed it to cowardice, which was the greatest affront he could offer them.

In the fall we were alarmed by a report that the white people were marching out against them, which, in a short time proved to be true; Col. Parquett, with an army, was then actually marching out against them. As the Delaware nation was always on the frontier, (which was the nation I was amongst), they had the first notice of it, and immediately gave the alarm to the other nations adjoining them. A council was called; the result was, that they were scarce of ammunition, and were not able to fight him; that they were then destitute of clothing; and that, upon the whole, it was best to come on terms of peace with the white people. Accordingly they sent off special messengers to meet the army on their march, in order to let them know that they were disposed to come on terms of peace with them. The messengers met the army at Tuscalaways.

They crept up to the camp after dark, and informed the guard that they were sent by their nation to sue for peace. The commander of the army sent for them to come into camp; they went and delivered their mission. The Colonel took care to take hostages for their fidelity; the remainder were suffered to return; but he told them he would march his army on to Moosh-king-oong, where he expected to meet their chiefs and warriors, to come on terms of peace with him, assuring them at the same time, that he would not treat with them, but upon condition, that they would deliver up all the prisoners they had in their possession. The messengers returned and gave a narrative of their mission. The Sha-a-noo-wack, or Shawanese, were not satisfied with the terms; however, as the Delaware had left hostages with the commander of the army, the Shawanese acquiesced to come on terms of peace, jointly with the other tribes. Accordingly the army marched on to Moosh-king-oong. The day they arrived there, an express was sent off to one of their nearest towns, to inform them that they were ready to treat with them. We then lived about ten miles from Moosh-king-oong; accordingly they took all the prisoners to the camp, myself amongst the rest, and delivered us up to the army. We were immediately put under a guard, — a few days after, we were sent under a strong guard to Pittsburg. On our way two of the prisoners made their escape, to wit, one Rhoda Boyd and Elizabeth Studibaker, and went back to the Indians.

I never heard whether they were brought back or not. There were about two hundred of us — we were kept a few days in Pittsburg. There was one, John Martin, from the Big Cove, came to Pittsburg after his family who had been taken by the Indians the fall before I was taken: he got leave from the Colonel to bring me down along with his family. I got home about the middle of December, 1764, being absent (as I heard my parents say) eight years, four months, and sixteen days. Previous to my return, my father had sold his plantation, where I was taken from, and bought another four miles from the former, where I have resided ever since.

Davy Crockett

At the end of this excerpt from his autobiography, David Crockett (1786–1836) complains that when he was fifteen years old, he still could not read a word. It is more than likely that when A Narrative of the Life of David Crockett, of the State of Tennessee *was published in 1834, Congressman Crockett could not read any better than he did at fifteen. The book was dictated, rushed into print because more than one bogus Crockett autobiography had already come onto the market. Whatever its other qualities, the sound of the book is the authentic sound of American frontier speech.*

Crockett's youthful adventures on the loose should probably not be accepted at face value, but they are a lively — and early — statement of the freewheeling "on the road" spirit of boyhood adventure that would become part of American childhood folklore.

Davy Crockett was elected to Congress thanks largely to his tall tales of killing bears and other wilderness adventures. He also won a reputation for his sly political humor, some of which manages to slip into these pages.

Two years after the Narrative *was published, Crockett was killed at the Alamo, fighting with the Texans in their war against Mexico. A Mexican officer who saw him die described him as "the naturalist David Crockett, well-known in North America for his unusual adventures." Young Davy was twelve when these particular adventures begin.*

From *A Narrative of the Life of David Crockett, of the State of Tennessee*

MY . . . FATHER . . . took it into his head to send me to a little country school, which was kept in the neighbourhood by a man whose name was Benjamin Kitchen; though I believe he was no way connected with the cabinet. I went four days, and had just began to learn my letters a little, when I had an unfortunate falling out with one of the scholars, — a boy much larger and older than myself. I knew well enough that though the school-house might do for a still hunt, it wouldn't do for a *drive,* and so I concluded to wait until I could get him out, and then I was determined to give him salt and vinegar. I waited till in the evening, and when the larger scholars were spelling, I slip'd out, and going some distance along his road, I lay by the way-side in the bushes, waiting for him to come along. After a while he and his company came on sure enough, and I pitched out from the bushes and set on him like a wild cat. I scratched his face all to a flitter jig, and soon made him cry out for quarters in good earnest. The fight being over, I went on home, and the next morning was started again to school; but do you think I went? No, indeed. I was very clear of it; for I expected the master would lick me up, as bad as I had the boy. So, instead of going to the school-house, I laid out in the woods all day until in the evening the scholars were dismissed, and my brothers, who were also going to school, came along, returning home. I wanted to conceal this whole business from my father, and I therefore persuaded them not to tell on me, which they agreed to.

Things went on in this way for several days; I starting with them to school in the morning, and returning with them in the evening, but lying out in the woods all day. At last, however, the master wrote a note to my father, inquiring why I was not sent to school. When he read this note, he called me up, and I knew very well that I was in a devil of a hobble, for my father had been taking a few *horns,* and was in a good condition to make the fur fly. He called on me to know why I had not been at school? I told him I was afraid to go, and that the master would whip me, for I knew quite well if I was turned over to this old Kitchen, I should be cooked up to a cracklin, in little or no time. But I soon found that I was not to expect a much better fate at home; for my father told me, in a very angry manner, that he would whip me an eternal sight worse than the master, if I didn't start immediately to the school. I tried again to beg off; but nothing would do, but to go to the school. Finding me rather too slow about starting, he gathered about a two year old hickory, and broke after me. I put out with all my might, and soon we were both up to the top of our speed. We had a tolerable tough race for about a mile; but mind me, not on the school-house road, for I was trying to get as far the t'other way as possible. And I yet believed, if my father and the schoolmaster could both have levied on me about that time, I should never have been called on to sit in the councils of the nation, for I think they would have used me up. But fortunately for me, about this time, I saw just before me a hill, over which I made headway, like a young steam-boat. As soon as I had passed over it, I turned to one side, and hid myself in the bushes. Here I waited until the old gentleman passed by, puffing and blowing, as tho' his steam was high enough to burst his boilers. I waited until he gave up the hunt, and passed back again: I then cut out, and went to the house of an acquaintance a few miles off, who was just about to start with a drove. His name was Jesse Cheek, and I hired myself to go with him, determining not to return home, as home and the school-house had both become too hot for me. I had an elder brother, who also hired to go with the same drove. We set out and went on through Abbingdon, and the county seat of Withe county, in the state of Virginia; and then through Lynchburgh, by Orange court-house, and Charlottesville, passing through what was called Chester Gap, on to a town called Front Royal, where my em-ployer sold out his drove to a man by the name of Vanmetre; and I was started homeward again, in company with a brother of the first owner of the drove, with one horse between us; having left my brother to come on with the balance of the company.

I travelled on with my new comrade about three days' journey; but much to his discredit, as I then thought, and still think, he took care all the time to ride, but never to tie; at last I told him to go ahead, and I would come when I got ready. He gave me four dollars to bear my expenses upwards of four hundred miles, and then cut out and left me.

I purchased some provisions, and went on slowly, until at length I fell in with a waggoner, with whom I was disposed to scrape up a hasty acquaintance. I inquired where he lived, and where he was going, and all about his affairs. He informed me that he lived in Greenville, Tennessee, and was on his way to a place called Gerardstown, fifteen miles below Winchester. He also said, that after he should make his journey to that place, he would immediately return to Tennessee. His name was Adam Myers, and a jolly good fellow he seemed to be. On a little reflection, I determined to turn back and go with him, which I did; and we journeyed on slowly as waggons commonly do, but merrily enough. I often thought of home, and, indeed, wished bad enough to be there; but, when I thought of the school-house, and Kitchen, my master, and the race with my father, and the big hickory he carried, and of the fierceness of the storm of wrath that I had left him in, I was afraid to venture back; for I knew my father's nature so well, that I was certain his anger would hang on to him like a turkle does to a fisherman's toe, and that, if I went back in a hurry, he would give me the devil in three or four ways. But I and the waggoner had travelled two days, when we met my brother, who, I before stated, I had left behind when the drove was sold out. He persuaded me to go home, but I refused. He pressed me hard, and brought up a great many mighty strong arguments to induce me to turn back again. He pictured the pleasure of meeting my mother, and my sisters, who all loved me dearly, and told me what uneasiness they had already suffered about me. I could not help shedding tears, which I did not often do, and my affections all pointed back to those dearest friends, and as I thought, nearly the only ones I had in the world; but then the promised whipping — that was the thing. It came right slap down on every thought of home; and I finally determined that make or break, hit or miss, I would just hang on to my journey, and go ahead with the waggoner. My brother was much grieved at our parting, but he went his way, and so did I. We went on until at last we got to Gerardstown, where the waggoner tried to get a back load, but he could not without going to Alexandria. He engaged to go there, and I concluded that I would wait until he returned. I set in to work for a man by the name of John Gray, at twenty-five cents per day. My labour, however, was light, such as ploughing in some small grain, in which I succeeded in pleasing the old man very well. I continued working for him until the waggoner got back, and for a good long time afterwards, as he continued to run his team back and forward, hauling to and from Baltimore. In the next spring, from the proceeds of my daily labour, small as it was, I was able to get me some decent clothes, and concluded I would make a trip with the waggoner to Baltimore, and see what sort of a place that was, and what sort of folks lived there. I gave him the balance of what money I had for safe keeping, which, as well as I recollect, was about seven dollars. We got on well enough until we came near Ellicott's Mills. Our load consisted of flour, in barrels. Here I got into the waggon for the purpose of changing my clothing, not thinking that I was in any danger; but while I was in there we were met by some wheelbarrow men, who were working on the road, and the horses took a scare and away they went, like they had seen a ghost. They made a sudden wheel around, and broke the waggon tongue slap, short off, as a pipe-stem; and snap went both of the axletrees at the same time, and of all devilish flouncing about of flour barrels that ever was seen, I reckon this took the beat. Even *a rat* would have stood a bad chance in a *straight* race among them, and not much better in a crooked one; for he would have been in a good way to be ground up as fine as ginger by their rolling over him. But this proved to me, that if a fellow is born to be hung, he will never be drowned; and, further, that if he is born for a seat in Congress, even flour barrels can't make a mash of him. All these dangers I escaped unhurt, though, like most of the officeholders of these times, for a while I was afraid to say my soul was my own; for I didn't know how soon I should be knocked into a cocked hat, and get my walking papers for another country.

We put our load into another waggon, and hauled ours to a workman's shop in Baltimore, having delivered the flour, and there we intended to remain two or three days, which time was necessary to repair the runaway waggon. While I was there, I went, one day, down to the wharf, and was much delighted to see the big ships, and their sails all flying; for I had never seen any such things before, and indeed, I didn't believe there were any such things in all nature. After a short time my curiosity induced me to step aboard of one, where I was met by the captain, who asked me if I didn't wish to take a voyage to London? I told him I did, for by this time I had become pretty well weaned from home, and I cared but little where I was, or where I went, or what become of me. He said he wanted just such a boy as I was, which I was glad to hear. I told him I would go and get my clothes, and go with him. He enquired about my parents, where they lived, and all about them. I let him know that they lived in Tennessee, many hundred miles off. We soon agreed about my intended voyage, and I went back to my friend, the waggoner, and informed him that I was going to London, and wanted my money and clothes. He refused to let me have either, and swore that he would confine me, and take me back to Tennessee. I took it to heart very much, but he kept so close and constant a watch over me, that I found it impossible to escape from him, until he had started homeward, and made several days' journey on the road. He was, during this time, very ill to me, and threatened me with his waggon whip on several occasions. At length I resolved to leave him at all hazards; and so, before day, one morning, I got my clothes out of his waggon, and cut out, on foot, without a farthing of money to bear my expenses. For all other friends having failed, I determined then to throw myself on Providence, and see how that would use me. I had gone, however, only a few miles when I came up with another waggoner, and such was my situation, that I felt more than ever the necessity of endeavouring to find a friend. I therefore concluded I would seek for one in him. He was going westwardly, and

very kindly enquired of me where I was travelling? My youthful resolution, which had brooked almost every thing else, rather gave way
at this enquiry; for it brought the loneliness of my situation, and every
thing else that was calculated to oppress me, directly to view. My first
answer to his question was in a sprinkle of tears, for if the world had
been given to me, I could not, at that moment, have helped crying. As
soon as the storm of feeling was over, I told him how I had been
treated by the waggoner but a little before, who kept what little money
I had, and left me without a copper to buy even a morsel of food.

He became exceedingly angry, and swore that he would make the
other waggoner give up my money, pronouncing him a scoundrel,
and many other hard names. I told him I was afraid to see him, for he
had threatened me with his waggon whip, and I believed he would
injure me. But my new friend was a very large, stout-looking man,
and as resolute as a tiger. He bid me not to be afraid, still swearing he
would have my money, or whip it out of the wretch who had it.

We turned and went back about two miles, when we reached the
place where he was. I went reluctantly; but I depended on my friend
for protection. When we got there, I had but little to say; but approaching the waggoner, my friend said to him, "You damn'd rascal,
you have treated this boy badly." To which he replied, it was my fault.
He was then asked, if he did not get seven dollars of my money, which
he confessed. It was then demanded of him; but he declared most
solemnly, that he had not that amount in the world; that he had spent
my money, and intended paying it back to me when we got to Tennessee. I then felt reconciled, and persuaded my friend to let him
alone, and we returned to his waggon, geared up, and started. His
name I shall never forget while my memory lasts; it was Henry Myers.
He lived in Pennsylvania, and I found him what he professed to be,
a faithful friend and a clever fellow.

We traveled together for several days, but at length I concluded to
endeavour to make my way homeward; and for that purpose set out
again on foot, and alone. But one thing I must not omit. The last
night I staid with Mr. Myers, was at a place where several other
waggoners also staid. He told them, before we parted, that I was a
poor little straggling boy, and how I had been treated; and that I was
without money, though I had a long journey before me, through a
land of strangers, where it was not even a wilderness.

They were good enough to contribute a sort of money-purse, and
presented me with three dollars. On this amount I travelled as far as

Montgomery court-house, in the state of Virginia, where it gave out. I set to work for a man by the name of James Caldwell, a month, for five dollars, which was about a shilling a day. When this time was out, I bound myself to a man by the name of Elijah Griffith, by trade a hatter, agreeing to work for him four years. I remained with him about eighteen months, when he found himself so involved in debt, that he broke up, and left the country. For this time I had received nothing, and was, of course, left without money, and with but very few clothes, and them very indifferent ones. I, however, set in again, and worked about as I could catch employment, until I got a little money, and some clothing; and once more cut out for home. When I reached New River, at the mouth of a small stream, called Little River, the white caps were flying so, that I couldn't get any body to attempt to put me across. I argued the case as well as I could, but they told me there was great danger of being capsized, and drowned, if I attempted to cross. I told them if I could get a canoe I would venture, caps or no caps. They tried to persuade me out of it; but finding they could not, they agreed I might take a canoe, and so I did, and put off. I tied my clothes to the rope of the canoe, to have them safe, whatever might happen. But I found it a mighty ticklish business, I tell you. When I got out fairly on the river, I would have given the world, if it had belonged to me, to have been on shore. But there was no time to lose now, so I just determined to do the best I could, and the devil take the hindmost. I turned the canoe across the waves, to do which, I had to turn it nearly up the river, as the wind came from that way; and I went about two miles before I could land. When I struck land, my canoe was about half full of water, and I was as wet as a drowned rat. But I was so much rejoiced, that I scarcely felt the cold, though my clothes were frozen on me; and in this situation, I had to go about three miles, before I could find any house, or fire to warm at. I, however, made out to get to one at last, and then I thought I would warm the inside a little, as well as the outside, that there might be no grumbling.

So I took "a leetle of the creater," — that warmer of the cold, and cooler of the hot, — and it made me feel so good that I concluded it was like the negro's rabbit, "good any way." I passed on until I arrived in Sullivan county, in the state of Tennessee, and there I met my brother, who had gone with me when I started from home with the cattle drove.

I staid with him a few weeks, and then went on to my father's, which place I reached late in the evening. Several waggons were there for the night, and considerable company about the house. I enquired if I could stay all night, for I did not intend to make myself known, until I saw whether any of the family would find me out. I was told that I could stay, and went in, but had mighty little to say to any body. I had been gone so long, and had grown so much, that the family did not at first know me. And another, and perhaps a stronger reason was, they had no thought or expectation of me, for they all had long given me up for finally lost.

After a while, we were all called to supper. I went with the rest. We had all sat down to the table and begun to eat, when my eldest sister recollected me: she sprung up, ran and seized me around the neck, and exclaimed, "Here is my lost brother."

My feelings at this time it would be vain and foolish for me to attempt to describe. I had often thought I felt before, and I suppose I had, but sure I am, I never had felt as I then did. The joy of my sisters and my mother, and, indeed, of all the family, was such that it humbled me, and made me sorry that I hadn't submitted to a hundred whippings, sooner than cause so much affliction as they had suffered on my account. I found the family had never heard a word of me from the time my brother left me. I was now almost *fifteen* years old; and my increased age and size together with the joy of my father, occasioned by my unexpected return, I was sure would secure me against my long dreaded whipping; and so they did. But it will be a source of astonishment to many, who reflect that I am now a member of the American Congress, — the most enlightened body of men in the world, — that at so advanced an age, the age of fifteen, I did not know the first letter in the book.

Lucy Larcom

Lucy Larcom (1824–1893) is the sort of poet we do not seem to have anymore. Her role was that of a kindly Sunday-school teacher pointing out the beauty of nature, the goodness of God, and the frailty of man to a large circle of readers she assumed — quite properly — to be female. A verse from a poem in her popular Childhood Songs *reads:*

> If I were a sunbeam,
> I know where I'd go:
> Into lowliest hovels
> Dark with want and woe;
> Till sad hearts looked upward,
> I would shine and shine;
> Then they'd think of heaven,
> Their sweet home and mine.

As her autobiography A New England Girlhood, Outlined from Memory *makes clear, Lucy Larcom was familiar with the "lowliest hovels." She was born in Beverly, Massachusetts, the daughter of a retired shipmaster turned shopkeeper. After her father's death, her mother gave up running the store and moved the family to Lowell, where the widow became a housekeeper in a boardinghouse and her daughters went to work in the mills.*

Lucy's seemingly naive portrait of the difficult financial times as seafaring Massachusetts entered the industrial age — with all her crotchets, prejudices, and boundless optimism — probably tells us more about everyday life in pre–Civil War New England than do most academic studies of the period. Later, Lucy would move to Illinois, where she attended school and became a teacher, a poet, and an active abolitionist. Among her books is An Idyl of Work, *a long narrative poem based on her experiences in the Lowell mills. A* New England Girlhood *was published in 1889, four years before her death.*

From "Schoolroom and Meeting-house," "Beginning to Work," and "By the River,"
A New England Girlhood, Outlined from Memory

THERE WERE only two or three houses between ours and the main street, and then our lane came out directly opposite the finest house in town, a three-story edifice of brick, painted white, the "Colonel's" residence. There was a spacious garden behind it, from which we caught glimpses and perfumes of unknown flowers. Over its high walls hung boughs of splendid great yellow sweet apples, which, when they fell on the outside, we children considered as our perquisites. When I first read about the apples of the Hesperides, my idea of them was that they were like the Colonel's "pumpkin-sweetings."

Beyond the garden were wide green fields which reached eastward down to the beach. It was one of those large old estates which used to give to the very heart of our New England coast-towns a delightful breeziness and roominess.

A coach-and-pair was one of the appurtenances of this estate, with a coachman on the box; and when he took the family out for an airing we small children though it was a sort of Cinderella-spectacle, prepared expressly for us.

It was not, however, quite so interesting as the Boston stage-coach, that rolled regularly every day past the head of our lane into and out of its head-quarters, a big, unpainted stable close at hand. This stage-coach, in our minds, meant the city, — twenty miles off; an immeasurable distance to us then. Even our elders did not go there very often.

In those early days, towns used to give each other nicknames, like school-boys. Ours was called "Bean-town"; not because it was especially devoted to the cultivation of this leguminous edible, but probably because it adhered a long time to the Puritanic custom of saving Sunday-work by baking beans on Saturday evening, leaving them in the oven over-night. After a while, as families left off heating their ovens, the bean-pots were taken by the village baker on Saturday afternoon, who returned them to each house early on Sunday morning, with the pan of brown bread that went with them. The jingling of the baker's bells made the matter a public one.

The towns through which our stage-coach passed sometimes called it the "bean-pot." The Jehu who drove it was something of a wag. Once, coming through Charlestown, while waiting in the street for a

resident passenger, he was hailed by another resident who thought
him obstructing the passage, with the shout, —

"Halloo there! Get your old bean-pot out of the way!"

"I will, when I have got my pork in," was the ready reply. What the
sobriquet of Charlestown was, need not be explained.

We had a good opportunity to watch both coaches, as my father's
shop was just at the head of the lane, and we went to school up-stairs
in the same building. After he left off going to sea, — before my
birth, — my father took a store for the sale of what used to be called
"West India goods," and various other domestic commodities.

The school was kept by a neighbor whom everybody called "Aunt
Hannah." It took in all the little ones about us, no matter how young
they were, provided they could walk and talk, and were considered
capable of learning their letters.

A ladder-like flight of stairs on the outside of the house led up to
the schoolroom, and another flight, also outside, took us down into a
bit of a garden, where grew tansy and spearmint and southernwood
and wormwood, and, among other old-fashioned flowers, an abun-
dance of many-tinted four o'clocks, whose regular afternoon-opening
just at the close of school, was a daily wonder to us babies. From the
schoolroom window we could watch the slow hands of the town clock,
and get a peep at what was going on in the street, although there was
seldom anybody in sight except the Colonel's gardener or coachman,
going into or out of the driveway directly opposite. It was a very still
street; the front windows of the houses were generally closed, and a
few military-looking Lombardy poplars stood like sentinels on guard
before them.

Another shop — a very small one — joined my father's, where three
shoemakers, all of the same name — the name our lane went by — sat
at their benches and plied their "waxed ends." One of them, an elderly man, tall and erect, used to come out regularly every day, and
stand for a long time at the corner, motionless as a post, with his nose
and chin pointing skyward, usually to the north-east. I watched his
face with wonder, for it was said that "Uncle John" was "weatherwise,"
and knew all the secrets of the heavens.

Aunt Hannah's schoolroom and "our shop" are a blended memory
to me. As I was only a baby when I began to go to school, I was often
sent down-stairs for a half hour's recreation not permitted to the
older ones. I think I looked upon both school and shop entirely as
places of entertainment for little children.

The front shop-window was especially interesting to us children, for there were in it a few glass jars containing sticks of striped barley-candy, and red and white peppermint-drops, and that delectable achievement of the ancient confectioner's art, the "Salem gibraltar." One of my first recollections of my father is connected with that window. He had taken me into the shop with him after dinner, — I was perhaps two years old, — and I was playing beside him on the counter when one of his old sea-comrades came in, whom we knew as "Captain Cross." The Captain tried to make friends with me, and, to seal the bond, asked my father to take down from its place of exhibition a strip of red peppermints dropped on white paper, in a style I particularly admired, which he twisted around my neck, saying, —

"Now I've bought you! Now you are my girl. Come, go home with me!"

His words sounded as if he meant them. I took it all in earnest, and ran, scared and screaming, to my father, dashing down the sugar-plums I wanted so much, and refusing even to bestow a glance upon my amused purchaser. My father pacified me by taking me on his shoulders and carrying me "pickaback" up and down the shop, and I clung to him in the happy consciousness that I belonged to him, and that he would not let anybody else have me; though I did not feel quite easy until Captain Cross disappeared. I suppose that this little incident has always remained in my memory because it then for the first time became a fact in my consciousness that my father really loved me as I loved him. He was not at all a demonstrative man, and any petting that he gave us children could not fail to make a permanent impression.

I think that must have been also the last special attention I received from him, for a little sister appeared soon after, whose coming was announced to me with the accompaniment of certain mysterious hints about my nose being out of joint. I examined that feature carefully in the looking-glass, but could not discover anything unusual about it. It was quite beyond me to imagine that our innocent little baby could have anything to do with the possible disfigurement of my face, but she did absorb the fondness of the whole family, myself included, and she became my father's playmate and darling, the very apple of his eye. I used sometimes to wish I were a baby too, so that he would notice me, but gradually I accepted the situation.

Aunt Hannah used her kitchen or her sitting-room for a school-room, as best suited her convenience. We were delighted observers of her culinary operations and other employments. If a baby's head nodded, a little bed was made for it on a soft "comforter" in the corner, where it had its nap out undisturbed. But this did not often happen; there were so many interesting things going on that we seldom became sleepy.

Aunt Hannah was very kind and motherly, but she kept us in fear of her ferule, which indicated to us a possibility of smarting palms. This ferule was shaped much like the stick with which she stirred her hasty pudding for dinner, — I thought it was the same, — and I found myself caught in a whirlwind of family laughter by reporting at home that "Aunt Hannah punished the scholars with the pudding-stick."

There was one colored boy in school, who did not sit on a bench, like the rest, but on a block of wood that looked like a backlog turned endwise. Aunt Hannah often called him a "blockhead," and I supposed it was because he sat on that block. Sometimes, in his absence, a boy was made to sit in his place for punishment, for being a "blockhead" too, as I imagined. I hoped I should never be put there. Stupid little girls received a different treatment, — an occasional rap on the head with the teacher's thimble; accompanied with a half-whispered, impatient ejaculation, which sounded very much like "Numskull!" I think this was a rare occurrence, however, for she was a good-natured, much-enduring woman. . . .

I began to go to school when I was about two years old, as other children about us did. The mothers of those large families had to resort to some means of keeping their little ones out of mischief, while they attended to their domestic duties. Not much more than that sort of temporary guardianship was expected of the good dame who had us in charge.

But I learned my letters in a few days, standing at Aunt Hannah's knee while she pointed them out in the spelling-book with a pin, skipping over the "a b abs" into words of one and two syllables, thence taking a flying leap into the New Testament, in which there is concurrent family testimony that I was reading at the age of two years and a half. Certain it is that a few passages in the Bible, whenever I read them now, do not fail to bring before me a vision of Aunt Hannah's somewhat sternly smiling lips, with her spectacles just above them, far down on her nose, encouraging me to pronounce the hard words. I think she tried to choose for me the least difficult verses, or perhaps those of which she was herself especially fond. Those which

I distinctly recall are the Beatitudes, the Twenty-third Psalm, parts of the first and fourteenth chapters of the Gospel of St. John, and the thirteenth chapter of the First Epistle to the Corinthians.

I liked to say over the "Blessèds," — the shortest ones best, — about the meek and the pure in heart; and the two "In the beginnings," both in Genesis and John. Every child's earliest and proudest Scriptural conquest in school was, almost as a matter of course, the first verse in the Bible. . . .

The Sabbath mornings in those old times had a peculiar charm. They seemed so much cleaner than other mornings! The roads and the grassy footpaths seemed fresher, and the air itself purer and more wholesome than on week-days. Saturday afternoon and evening were regarded as part of the Sabbath (we were taught that it was heathenish to call the day Sunday); work and playthings were laid aside, and every body, as well as every thing, was subject to rigid renovation. Sabbath morning would not have seemed like itself without a clean house, a clean skin, and tidy and spotless clothing.

The Saturday's baking was a great event, the brick oven being heated to receive the flour bread, the flour-and-Indian, and the rye-and-Indian bread, the traditional pot of beans, the Indian pudding, and the pies; for no further cooking was to be done until Monday. We smaller girls thought it a great privilege to be allowed to watch the oven till the roof of it should be "white-hot," so that the coals could be shoveled out.

Then it was so still, both out of doors and within! We were not allowed to walk anywhere except in the yard or garden. I remember wondering whether it was never Sabbath-day over the fence, in the next field; whether the field was not a kind of heathen field, since we could only go into it on week-days. The wild flowers over there were perhaps Gentile blossoms. Only the flowers in the garden were well-behaved Christians. It was Sabbath in the house, and possibly even on the doorstep; but not much farther. The town itself was so quiet that it scarcely seemed to breathe. The sound of wheels was seldom heard in the streets on that day; if we heard it, we expected some unusual explanation.

I liked to go to meeting, — not wholly oblivious to the fact that going there sometimes implied wearing a new bonnet and my best white dress and muslin "vandyke," of which adornments, if *very* new, I vainly supposed the whole congregation to be as admiringly aware as I was myself.

But my Sabbath-day enjoyment was not wholly without drawbacks. It was so hard, sometimes, to stand up through the "long prayer," and to sit still through the "ninthlies," and "tenthlies," and "finallys" of the sermon! It was impressed upon me that good children were never restless in meeting, and never laughed or smiled, however their big brothers tempted them with winks or grimaces. And I did want to be good.

I was not tall enough to see very far over the top of the pew. I think there were only three persons that came within range of my eyes. One was a dark man with black curly hair brushed down in "bangs" over his eyebrows, who sat behind a green baize curtain near the outside door, peeping out at me, as I thought. I had an impression that he was the "tidy-man," though that personage had become mythical long before my day. He had a dragonish look, to me; and I tried never to meet his glance.

But I did sometimes gaze more earnestly than was polite at a dear, demure little lady who sat in the corner of the pew next ours, her downcast eyes shaded by a green calash, and her hidden right hand gently swaying a long-handled Chinese fan. She was the deacon's wife, and I felt greatly interested in her movements and in the expression of her face, because I thought she represented the people they called "saints," who were, as I supposed, about the same as first cousins to the angels.

The third figure in sight was the minister. I did not think he ever saw me; he was talking to the older people, — usually telling them how wicked they were. He often said to them that there was not one good person among them; but I supposed he excepted himself. He seemed to me so very good that I was very much afraid of him. I was a little afraid of my father, but then he sometimes played with us children: and besides, my father was only a man. I thought the minister belonged to some different order of beings. Up there in the pulpit he seemed to me so far off — oh! a great deal farther off than God did. His distance made my reverence for him take the form of idolatry. The pulpit was his pedestal. If any one had told me that the minister ever did or thought anything that was wrong, I should have felt as if the foundations of the earth under me were shaken. I wondered if he ever did laugh. Perhaps it was wicked for a minister even to smile.

One day, when I was very little, I met the minister in the street; and he, probably recognizing me as the child of one of his parishioners, actually bowed to me! His bows were always ministerially profound, and I was so overwhelmed with surprise and awe that I forgot to make the proper response of a "curtsey," but ran home as fast as I could go, to proclaim the wonder. It would not have astonished me any more, if one of the tall Lombardy poplars that stood along the sidewalk had laid itself down at my feet. . . .

During my father's life, a few years before my birth, his thoughts had been turned towards the new manufacturing town growing up on the banks of the Merrimack. He had once taken a journey there, with the possibility in his mind of making the place his home, his limited income furnishing no adequate promise of a maintenance for his large family of daughters. From the beginning, Lowell had a high reputation for good order, morality, piety, and all that was dear to the old-fashioned New Englander's heart.

After his death, my mother's thoughts naturally followed the direction his had taken; and seeing no other opening for herself, she sold her small estate, and moved to Lowell, with the intention of taking a corporation-house for mill-girl boarders. Some of the family objected, for the Old World traditions about factory life were anything but attractive; and they were current in New England until the experiment at Lowell had shown that independent and intelligent workers invariably give their own character to their occupation. My mother had visited Lowell, and she was willing and glad, knowing all about the place, to make it our home.

The change involved a great deal of work. "Boarders" signified a large house, many beds, and an indefinite number of people. Such piles of sewing accumulated before us! A sewing-bee, volunteered by the neighbors, reduced the quantity a little, and our child-fingers had to take their part. But the seams of those sheets did look to me as if they were miles long!

My sister Lida and I had our "stint," — so much to do every day. It was warm weather, and that made it the more tedious, for we wanted to be running about the fields we were so soon to leave. One day, in sheer desperation, we dragged a sheet up with us into an apple-tree in the yard, and sat and sewed there through the summer afternoon, beguiling the irksomeness of our task by telling stories and guessing riddles.

It was hardest for me to leave the garret and the garden. In the old houses the garret was the children's castle. The rough rafters, — it was always an unfinished room, otherwise not a true garret, — the music of the rain on the roof, the worn sea-chests with their miscellaneous treasures, the blue-roofed cradle that had sheltered ten blue-eyed babies, the tape-looms and reels and spinning-wheels, the herby smells, and the delightful dream corners, — these could not be taken with us to the new home. Wonderful people had looked out upon us from under those garret-eaves. Sindbad the Sailor and Baron Munchausen had sometimes strayed in and told us their unbelievable stories; and we had there made acquaintance with the great Caliph Haroun Alraschid.

To go away from the little garden was almost as bad. Its lilacs and peonies were beautiful to me, and in a corner of it was one tiny square of earth that I called my own, where I was at liberty to pull up my pinks and lady's delights every day, to see whether they had taken root, and where I could give my lazy morning-glory seeds a poke, morning after morning, to help them get up and begin their climb. Oh, I should miss the garden very much indeed!

It did not take long to turn over the new leaf of our home experience. One sunny day three of us children, my youngest sister, my brother John, and I, took with my mother the first stage-coach journey of our lives, across Lynnfield plains and over Andover hills to the banks of the Merrimack. We were set down before an empty house in a yet unfinished brick block, where we watched for the big wagon that was to bring our household goods.

It came at last; and the novelty of seeing our old furniture settled in new rooms kept us from being homesick. One after another they appeared, — bedsteads, chairs, tables, and, to me most welcome of all, the old mahogany secretary with brass-handled drawers, that had always stood in the "front room" at home. With it came the barrel full of books that had filled its shelves, and they took their places as naturally as if they had always lived in this strange town. . . .

For the first time in our lives, my little sister and I became pupils in a grammar school for both girls and boys, taught by a man. I was put with her into the sixth class, but was sent the very next day into the first. I did not belong in either, but somewhere between. And I was very uncomfortable in my promotion, for though the reading and spelling and grammar and geography were perfectly easy, I had never studied anything but mental arithmetic, and did not know how to "do a sum." We had to show, when called up to recite, a slateful of sums, "done" and "proved." No explanations were ever asked of us.

The girl who sat next to me saw my distress, and offered to do my sums for me. I accepted her proposal, feeling, however, that I was a miserable cheat. But I was afraid of the master, who was tall and gaunt, and used to stalk across the school-room, right over the desk-tops, to find out if there was any mischief going on. Once, having caught a boy annoying a seat-mate with a pin, he punished the offender by pursuing him around the school-room, sticking a pin into his shoulder whenever he could overtake him. And he had a fearful leather strap, which was sometimes used even upon the shrinking palm of a little girl. If he should find out that I was a pretender and deceiver, as I knew that I was, I could not guess what might happen to me. He never did, however. I was left unmolested in the ignorance which I deserved. But I never liked the girl who did my sums, and I fancied she had a decided contempt for me.

There was a friendly looking boy always sitting at the master's desk; they called him "the monitor." It was his place to assist scholars who were in trouble about their lessons, but I was too bashful to speak to him, or to ask assistance of anybody. I think that nobody learned much under that régime, and the whole school system was soon after entirely reorganized.

Our house was quickly filled with a large feminine family. As a child, the gulf between little girlhood and young womanhood had always looked to me very wide. I supposed we should get across it by some sudden jump, by and by. But among these new companions of all ages, from fifteen to thirty years, we slipped into womanhood without knowing when or how.

Most of my mother's boarders were from New Hampshire and Vermont, and there was a fresh, breezy sociability about them which made them seem almost like a different race of beings from any we children had hitherto known.

We helped a little about the housework, before and after school, making beds, trimming lamps, and washing dishes. The heaviest work was done by a strong Irish girl, my mother always attending to the cooking herself. She was, however, a better caterer than the circumstances required or permitted. She liked to make nice things for the table, and, having been accustomed to an abundant supply, could never learn to economize. At a dollar and a quarter a week for board, (the price allowed for mill-girls by the corporations) great care in expenditure was necessary. It was not in my mother's nature closely to calculate costs, and in this way there came to be a continually increasing leak in the family purse. The older members of the family did everything they could, but it was not enough. I heard it said one day, in a distressed tone, "The children will have to leave school and go into the mill."

There were many pros and cons between my mother and sisters before this was positively decided. The mill-agent did not want to take us two little girls, but consented on condition we should be sure to attend school the full number of months prescribed each year. I, the younger one, was then between eleven and twelve years old.

I listened to all that was said about it, very much fearing that I should not be permitted to do the coveted work. For the feeling had already frequently come to me, that I was the one too many in the overcrowded family nest. Once, before we left our old home, I had heard a neighbor condoling with my mother because there were so many of us, and her emphatic reply had been a great relief to my mind: —

"There isn't one more than I want. I could not spare a single one of my children."

But her difficulties were increasing, and I thought it would be a pleasure to feel that I was not a trouble or burden or expense to anybody. So I went to my first day's work in the mill with a light heart. The novelty of it made it seem easy, and it really was not hard, just to change the bobbins on the spinning-frames every three quarters of an hour or so, with half a dozen other little girls who were doing the same thing. When I came back at night, the family began to pity me for my long, tiresome day's work, but I laughed and said, —

"Why, it is nothing but fun. It is just like play."

And for a little while it was only a new amusement; I liked it better than going to school and "making believe" I was learning when I was not. And there was a great deal of play mixed with it. We were not occupied more than half the time. The intervals were spent frolicking around among the spinning-frames, teasing and talking to the older girls, or entertaining ourselves with games and stories in a corner, or exploring, with the overseer's permission, the mysteries of the carding-room, the dressing-room, and the weaving-room.

I never cared much for machinery. The buzzing and hissing and whizzing of pulleys and rollers and spindles and flyers around me often grew tiresome. I could not see into their complications, or feel interested in them. But in a room below us we were sometimes allowed to peer in through a sort of blind door at the great water-wheel that carried the works of the whole mill. It was so huge that we could only watch a few of its spokes at a time, and part of its dripping rim, moving with a slow, measured strength through the darkness that shut it in. It impressed me with something of the awe which comes to us in thinking of the great Power which keeps the mechanism of the universe in motion. Even now, the remembrance of its large, mysterious movement, in which every little motion of every noisy little wheel was involved, brings back to me a verse from one of my favorite hymns: —

> "Our lives through various scenes are drawn,
>   And vexed by trifling cares,
>   While Thine eternal thought moves on
>   Thy undisturbed affairs."

There were compensations for being shut in to daily toil so early. The mill itself had its lessons for us. But it was not, and could not be, the right sort of life for a child, and we were happy in the knowledge that, at the longest, our employment was only to be temporary.

When I took my next three months at the grammar school, everything there was changed, and I too was changed. The teachers were kind, and thorough in their instruction; and my mind seemed to have been ploughed up during that year of work, so that knowledge took root in it easily. It was a great delight to me to study, and at the end of the three months the master told me that I was prepared for the high school.

But alas! I could not go. The little money I could earn — one dollar a week, besides the price of my board — was needed in the family, and I must return to the mill. It was a severe disappointment to me, though I did not say so at home. I did not at all accept the conclusion of a neighbor whom I heard talking about it with my mother. His daughter was going to the high school, and my mother was telling him how sorry she was that I could not.

"Oh," he said, in a soothing tone, "my girl hasn't got any such head-piece as yours has. Your girl doesn't need to go."

Of course I knew that whatever sort of a "head-piece" I had, I did need and want just that very opportunity to study. I think the resolution was then formed, inwardly, that I *would* go to school again, some time, whatever happened. I went back to my work, but now without enthusiasm. I had looked through an open door that I was not willing to see shut upon me.

I began to reflect upon life rather seriously for a girl of twelve or thirteen. What was I here for? What could I make of myself? Must I submit to be carried along with the current, and do just what everybody else did? No: I knew I should not do that, for there was a certain Myself who was always starting up with her own original plan or aspiration before me, and who was quite indifferent as to what people generally thought.

Well, I would find out what this Myself was good for, and that she should be! . . .

There was but one summer holiday for us who worked in the mills — the Fourth of July. We made a point of spending it out of doors, making excursions down the river to watch the meeting of the slow Concord and the swift Merrimack; or around by the old canal-path, to explore the mysteries of the Guard Locks; or across the bridge, clambering up Dracut Heights, to look away to the dim blue mountains.

On that morning it was our custom to wake one another at four o'clock, and start off on a tramp together over some retired road whose chief charm was its unfamiliarity, returning to a very late breakfast, with draggled gowns and aprons full of dewy wild roses. No matter if we must get up at five the next morning and go back to our humdrum toil, we should have the roses to take with us for company, and the sweet air of the woodland which lingered about them would scent our thoughts all day, and make us forget the oily smell of the machinery.

We were children still, whether at school or at work, and Nature still held us close to her motherly heart. Nature came very close to the mill-gates, too, in those days. There was green grass all around them; violets and wild geraniums grew by the canals; and long stretches of open land between the corporation buildings and the street made the town seem country-like.

The slope behind our mills (the "Lawrence" Mills) was a green lawn; and in front of some of them the overseers had gay flower-gardens; we passed in to our work through a splendor of dahlias and hollyhocks. . . .

The transition from childhood to girlhood, when a little girl has had an almost unlimited freedom of out-of-door life, is practically the toning down of a mild sort of barbarianism, and is often attended by a painfully awkward self-consciousness. I had an innate dislike of conventionalities. I clung to the child's inalienable privilege of running half wild; and when I found that I really was growing up, I felt quite rebellious.

I was as tall as a woman at thirteen, and my older sisters insisted upon lengthening my dresses, and putting up my mop of hair with a comb. I felt injured and almost outraged because my protestations against this treatment were unheeded; and when the transformation in my visible appearance was effected, I went away by myself and had a good cry, which I would not for the world have had them know about, as that would have added humiliation to my distress. And the greatest pity about it was that I too soon became accustomed to the situation. I felt like a child, but considered it my duty to think and behave like a woman. I began to look upon it as a very serious thing to live. The untried burden seemed already to have touched my shoulders. For a time I was morbidly self-critical, and at the same time extremely reserved. The associates I chose were usually grave young women, ten or fifteen years older than myself; but I think I felt older and appeared older than they did.

Childhood, however, is not easily defrauded of its birthright, and mine soon reasserted itself. At home I was among children of my own age, for some cousins and other acquaintances had come to live and work with us. We had our evening frolics and entertainments together, and we always made the most of our brief holiday hours. We had also with us now the sister Emilie of my fairy-tale memories, who had grown into a strong, earnest-hearted woman. We all looked up to her as our model, and the ideal of our heroine-worship; for our deference to her in every way did amount to that.

She watched over us, gave us needed reproof and commendation, rarely cosseted us, but rather made us laugh at what many would have considered the hardships of our lot. She taught us not only to accept the circumstances in which we found ourselves, but to win from them courage and strength. When we came in shivering from our work, through a snow-storm, complaining of numb hands and feet, she would say cheerily, "But it doesn't make you any warmer to *say* you are cold;" and this was typical of the way she took life generally, and tried to have us take it. She was constantly denying herself for our sakes, without making us feel that she was doing so. But she did not let us get into the bad habit of pitying ourselves because we were not as "well off" as many other children. And indeed we considered ourselves pleasantly situated; but the best of it all was that we had *her*.

Her theories for herself, and her practice, too, were rather severe;

but we tried to follow them, according to our weaker abilities. Her custom was, for instance, to take a full cold bath every morning before she went to her work, even though the water was chiefly broken ice; and we did the same whenever we could be resolute enough. It required both nerve and will to do this at five o'clock on a zero morning, in a room without a fire; but it helped us to harden ourselves, while we formed a good habit. The working-day in winter began at the very earliest daylight, and ended at half-past seven in the evening.

Another habit of hers was to keep always beside her at her daily work something to study or to think about. At first it was "Watts on the Improvement of the Mind," arranged as a textbook, with questions and answers, by the minister of Beverly who had made the thought of the millennium such a reality to his people. She quite wore this book out, carrying it about with her in her working-dress pocket. After that, "Locke on the Understanding" was used in the same way. She must have known both books through and through by heart. Then she read Combe and Abercrombie, and discussed their physics and metaphysics with our girl boarders, some of whom had remarkably acute and well-balanced minds. Her own seemed to have turned from its early bent toward the romantic, her taste being now for serious and practical, though sometimes abstruse, themes. I remember that Young and Pollok were her favorite poets.

I could not keep up with her in her studies and readings, for many of the books she liked seemed to me very dry. I did not easily take to the argumentative or moralizing method, which I came to regard as a proof of the weakness of my own intellect in comparison with hers. I would gladly have kept pace with her if I could. Anything under the heading of "Didactick," like some of the pieces in the old "English Reader," used by school-children in the generation just before ours, always repelled me. But I thought it necessary to discipline myself by reading such pieces, and my first attempt at prose composition, "On Friendship," was stiffly modeled after a certain "Didactick Essay" in that same English Reader.

My sister, however, cared more to watch the natural development of our minds than to make us follow the direction of hers. She was really our teacher, although she never assumed that position. Certainly I learned more from her about my own capabilities, and how I might put them to use, than I could have done at any school we knew of, had it been possible for me to attend one.

I think she was determined that we should not be mentally

defrauded by the circumstances which had made it necessary for us to begin so early to win our daily bread. This remark applies especially to me, as my older sisters (only two or three of them had come to Lowell) soon drifted away from us into their own new homes or occupations, and she and I were left together amid the whir of spindles and wheels.

One thing she planned for us, her younger housemates, — a dozen or so of cousins, friends, and sisters, some attending school, and some at work in the mill, — was a little fortnightly paper, to be filled with our original contributions, she herself acting as editor.

. . . Our little sheet was called "The Diving Bell," probably from the sea-associations of the name. We kept our secrets of authorship very close from everybody except the editor, who had to decipher the handwriting and copy the pieces. It was, indeed, an important part of the fun to guess who wrote particular pieces. After a little while, however, our mannerisms betrayed us. One of my cousins was known to be the chief story-teller, and I was recognized as the leading rhymer among the younger contributors; the editor-sister excelling in her versifying, as she did in almost everything.

It was a cluster of very conscious-looking little girls that assembled one evening in the attic room, chosen on account of its remoteness from intruders (for we did not admit even the family as a public; the writers themselves were the only audience); to listen to the reading of our first paper. We took Saturday evening, because that was longer than the other work-day evenings, the mills being closed earlier. Such guessing and wondering and admiring as we had! But nobody would acknowledge her own work, for that would have spoiled the pleasure. Only there were certain wise hints and maxims that we knew never came from any juvenile head among us, and those we set down as "editorials." . . .

Our small venture set some of us imagining what larger possibilities might be before us in the far future. We talked over the things we should like to do when we should be women out in the active world; and the author of [one] story horrified us by declaring that she meant to be distinguished when she grew up for something, even if it was for something bad! She did go so far in a bad way as to plagiarize a long poem in a subsequent number of the "Diving Bell"; but the editor found her out, and we all thought that a reproof from Emilie was sufficient punishment.

I do not know whether it was fortunate or unfortunate for me that

I had not, by nature, what is called literary ambition. I knew that I had a knack at rhyming, and I knew that I enjoyed nothing better than to try to put thoughts and words together, in any way. But I did it for the pleasure of rhyming and writing, indifferent as to what might come of it. For any one who could take hold of every-day, practical work, and carry it on successfully, I had a profound respect. To be what is called "capable" seemed to me better worth while than merely to have a taste or talent for writing, perhaps because I was conscious of my deficiencies in the former respect. But certainly the world needs deeds more than it needs words. I should never have been willing to be *only* a writer, without using my hands to some good purpose besides.

My sister, however, told me that here was a talent which I had no right to neglect, and which I ought to make the most of. I believed in her; I thought she understood me better than I understood myself; and it was a comfort to be assured that my scribbling was not wholly a waste of time. So I used pencil and paper in every spare minute I could find.

Our little home-journal went bravely on through twelve numbers. Its yellow manuscript pages occasionally meet my eyes when I am rummaging among my old papers, with the half-conscious look of a waif that knows it has no right to its escape from the waters of oblivion.

While it was in progress my sister Emilie became acquainted with a family of bright girls, near neighbors of ours, who proposed that we should join them, and form a little society for writing and discussion, to meet fortnightly at their house. We met, — I think I was the youngest of the group, — prepared a Constitution and By-Laws, and named ourselves "The Improvement Circle." If I remember rightly, my sister was our first president. The older ones talked and wrote on many subjects quite above me. I was shrinkingly bashful, as half-grown girls usually are, but I wrote my little essays and read them, and listened to the rest, and enjoyed it all exceedingly. Out of this little "Improvement Circle" grew the larger one whence issued the "Lowell Offering," a year or two later.

At this time I had learned to do a spinner's work, and I obtained permission to tend some frames that stood directly in front of the river-windows, with only them and the wall behind me, extending half the length of the mill, — and one young woman beside me, at the farther end of the row. She was a sober, mature person, who scarcely thought it worth her while to speak often to a child like me; and I was, when with strangers, rather a reserved girl; so I kept myself occupied with the river, my work, and my thoughts. And the river and my thoughts flowed on together, the happiest of companions. Like a loitering pilgrim, it sparkled up to me in recognition as it glided along, and bore away my little frets and fatigues on its bosom. When the work "went well," I sat in the window-seat, and let my fancies fly whither they would, — downward to the sea, or upward to the hills that hid the mountain-cradle of the Merrimack.

The printed regulations forbade us to bring books into the mill, so I made my window-seat into a small library of poetry, pasting its side all over with newspaper clippings. In those days we had only weekly papers, and they had always a "poet's corner," where standard writers were well represented, with anonymous ones, also. I was not, of course, much of a critic. I chose my verses for their sentiment, and because I wanted to commit them to memory; sometimes it was a long poem, sometimes a hymn, sometimes only a stray verse. . . .

The last window in the row behind me was filled with flourishing house plants — fragrant-leaved geraniums, the overseer's pets. They gave that corner a bowery look; the perfume and freshness tempted me there often. Standing before that window, I could look across the room and see girls moving backwards and forwards among the spinning-frames, sometimes stooping, sometimes reaching up their arms, as their work required, with easy and not ungraceful movements. On the whole, it was far from being a disagreeable place to stay in. The girls were bright-looking and neat, and everything was kept clean and shining. The effect of the whole was rather attractive to strangers.

My grandfather came to see my mother once at about this time and visited the mills. When he had entered our room, and looked around for a moment, he took off his hat and made a low bow to the girls, first toward the right, and then toward the left. We were familiar with his courteous habits, partly due to his French descent; but we had never seen anybody bow to a room full of mill girls in that polite way, and some one of the family afterwards asked him why he did so. He looked a little surprised at the question, but answered promptly and with dignity, "I always take off my hat to ladies."

His courtesy was genuine. Still, we did not call ourselves ladies. We did not forget that we were working-girls, wearing coarse aprons suitable to our work, and that there was some danger of our becoming drudges. I know that sometimes the confinement of the mill became very wearisome to me. In the sweet June weather I would lean far out of the window, and try not to hear the unceasing clash of sound inside. Looking away to the hills, my whole stifled being would cry out

> *"Oh, that I had wings!"*

Still I was there from choice, and

> *"The prison unto which we doom ourselves,*
> *No prison is."*

And I was every day making discoveries about life, and about myself. I had naturally some elements of the recluse, and would never, of my own choice, have lived in a crowd. I loved quietness. The noise of machinery was particularly distasteful to me. But I found that the crowd was made up of single human lives, not one of them wholly uninteresting, when separately known. I learned also that there are many things which belong to the whole world of us together, that no one of us, nor any few of us, can claim or enjoy for ourselves alone. I discovered, too, that I could so accustom myself to the noise that it became like a silence to me. And I defied the machinery to make me its slave. Its incessant discords could not drown the music of my thoughts if I would let them fly high enough. Even the long hours, the early rising, and the regularity enforced by the clangor of the bell were good discipline for one who was naturally inclined to dally and to dream, and who loved her own personal liberty with a willful rebellion against control. Perhaps I could have brought myself into the limitations of order and method in no other way.

Like a plant that starts up in showers and sunshine and does not know which has best helped it to grow, it is difficult to say whether the hard things or the pleasant things did me most good. But when I was sincerest with myself, as also when I thought least about it, I know that I was glad to be alive, and to be just where I was.

Andrew Taylor Still

Born in Virginia and raised in frontier communities in Tennessee and Missouri, Andrew Taylor Still (1828–1917) was the son of a Methodist minister who went west with his family to, as the son put it, "educate the heathen, and tell them all about steam." This mixture of orthodoxy and modernity is something of a theme in Still's boyhood recollections, but a stronger one is the joy of hunting: "I was like all boys," he wrote, "a little lazy and fond of a gun." Although he remained with his family, Still's memoirs are solidly in the Davy Crockett tradition.

Largely educated by his father, Still would later dabble in traditional medicine, fight for a time with John Brown in the more violent wing of the antislavery movement, serve as an officer in the Kansas militia in the Civil War, and after the war become the founder of osteopathic medicine, a healing method that uses body manipulation in addition to other techniques. His autobiography was first published in 1897.

From "Early Life — Schoolboy Days, and the Unsparing Rod,"
The Autobiography of Andrew Taylor Still

IN THE SPRING OF 1836, as I now remember, while father was a member of the Holston conference of the M. E. Church of Tennessee, he was transferred by that body to Missouri as a missionary.

We left Tennessee, starting from New Market, Jefferson County, with two wagons, seven horses, and eight in family, and began an overland journey for seven weeks to Macon County, Mo. We had a pleasant time, good roads, and nice traveling until we reached the low land on the Ohio River bottoms opposite Cairo, Ill. Here we began to find some deep mud for a few miles until we reached the river. But long before we reached it, we heard the whistle of a steamboat. We all wanted to see the mouth that could pucker and whistle so squealingly loud. "Oh, my! we could hear it roar just as plain as you could hear a rooster crow if he were on top your head." Just think of that! Meeting a man in the road, father asked how far it was to the river, and he said it was six or seven miles. We whipped up all the teams and pushed on, for we were determined to see that boat, — see it pucker its mouth and whistle. Our ideas of steam were very crude, and we had much company then of the kind who knew but little of steam engines of any other kind of machinery. We drove up to the banks of the river, and there it was, big as life, full of people, cattle, horses, sheep, merchandise, and movers, but they cut no figure with us. The boat was the sight; we saw it, and knew all that could be known. We had seen a real steamboat, and it was a whopper, too. It soon steamed up the river and went out of sight, but we supposed we knew all about steamboats, and this one afforded food for conversation for many days after.

We were now ready to go to North Missouri as missionaries, and educate the heathen, and tell them all about steam. . . .

I was like all boys, a little lazy and fond of a gun. I had three dogs, — a spaniel for the water, a hound for the fox, and a bulldog for bear and panthers. My gun for many years was the old flint-lock, which went chuck, fizz, bang; so you see, to hit where you wanted to, you had to hold still a long time, — and, if the powder was damp in the pan, much longer, for there could be no bang until the fizzing was exhausted, and fire could reach the touch-hole leading to the powder-charge behind the hall. All this required skill and a steady nerve, to hit the spot.

I was called a good judge of dogs, and quoted as authority on the subject. A hound, to be a great dog, must have a flat, broad, and thin tongue, deep-set eyes, thin, long ears, very broad, raised some at the head, and hanging three inches below the under-jaw. The roof of his mouth had to be black, the tail long and very slim, for good coon-dog. Such kind of pups I was supposed to sell for a dollar each, though I usually gave them away. When I went to the woods, armed with my flint-lock and accompanied by my three dogs, they remained with me until I said, "Seize him, Drummer!" which command sent Drummer out on a prospecting trip. When I wanted squirrels I threw a stick up a tree and cried: "Hunt him up, Drummer!" In a short time the faithful beast had treed a squirrel. When I wanted deer I hunted toward the wind, keeping Drummer behind me. When he scented a deer he walked under my gun, which I carried point front. I was always warned by his tail falling that I was about as close as I could get to my game without starting it up from the grass.

This old-fashioned flint-lock hunting was under the Van Buren and Polk's administration; but when Harrison — "old Tip" — came in, I possessed a cap-lock gun. Now I was a "man." "Big Injun me." To pull the trigger was "bang" at once, and I was able to shoot deer "on the run." Shot-guns were not in use at that time, but the frontiersman became very expert with the rifle. I could hit a hawk, wild goose, or any bird that did not fly too high or too fast for my aim. I killed a great number of deer, turkeys, eagles, wildcats, and foxes. My frontier life made me very fleet of foot. Brother Jim and I ran down and caught sixteen foxes in the month of September, 1839. Fearing some one will regard this as a fish story, I will explain that during the summer and fall some kind of disease got among the foxes, and we found them lying in the hot road in the dust, feeble and shaking, as though they had the fever and ague, and were incapable of running away from us. I have never since tried to outrun a fox.

As furs were not worth a cent in September, our sixteen foxes were useless, but during the following winter we caught a mink, and concluded to go to market with its fur as we must have a five-cent bar of lead before we could shoot other game. So I saddled my horse Selim, and went to Bloomington (nine miles) to exchange my mink-skin for lead. The barter was made with my good friend Thomas Sharp (an uncle of Rev. George Sharp, of Kirksville, Mo.), and soon the hide was with his other furs, from coons' and opossums'. Then I mounted Selim and started for home to tell Jim that I had found a permanent market for mink-skins at five cents apiece. In a short time I shot a deer, and had a buck-skin to add to the fur trade, and took my "big" fifty cents in powder, lead, and caps. . . .

My frontier experience varied. I enjoyed advantages which few others had. My father, who was a man educated to do all kinds of work, was a minister, doctor, farmer, and a practical millwright. My mother was a natural mechanic, and made cloth, clothing, and pies to perfection. She believed "to spare the rod would spoil the child," and she did use the rod in a homeopathic way. My father said if you wish to get meal in a bag, hold the mouth open. If you wish to get sense in your head, hold it open. If you wish to ride a horse, get on his back; and if one wished to be a skillful rider, hold on to him. My mother said if you wish to drink milk, put it in your mouth, and not on your clothes; for there was but one way to drink milk. My father, being a farmer, concluded that a little cornfield education would be good with my millwright knowledge, and at an early age I was taught to hold the teams, and do the duties of farm life, until I could manage teams, harrows, plows, and scrapers. When I came from the cornfield for dinner, father told me I could rest myself by carrying slop to the hogs. I did not mind the work; it was the exercise that bothered my mind. When I passed old Dan, the colored man, he would say: "De crown is for de faifful," and many other words of encouragement, such as "Go and brung de eggs," "Start a little smoke under de meat," and then he would sing the "Sweet Bye and Bye" for my edification. In due course of time I entered my gawk age, for a long journey. I was awkward, ignorant, and slovenly until I got into my mother's real training-school, in which she used soap and switches freely. After which it seemed I had more spring in my heels and head than ever before. She gave me two buckets and a cup, and told me to go and milk the cows, and be in a hurry about it, so as to help her and Dan'l shear the sheep. By seven o'clock we were in the sheep-pen. Old Dan'l says, "Ketch dat sheep," mother reiterated, "Catch that sheep," and Aunt Becky echoed, "Catch me one." By this time "old black Rachel" came in with her shears, and said: "I wants one too." And right here is where the gawk was knocked out. When I caught a sheep for her, the old ram said, "It is time for music," and sprawled me with his head, causing me to howl, and the others to laugh. This incident taught me to look backward and forward, upward and downward, right and left, and never sleep in the enemy's country, but always be on guard.

My instructors, thinking I was well enough trained to be admitted into better society, I was permitted to go with Dan'l to the timber, to be instructed in chopping wood, splitting rails, burning brush, and clearing up the ground for the plow. All went off well except once or twice, when old Dan'l revived my see-ability by playing ram until I could see a limb as big as your finger. He then closed with the proverb, " 'Cleanliness is next to godliness.' I wants all dis trash cleaned up, every moufful of it." At noon he gave the welcome information, "Come on, we's gwine to dinner." When we came near the house, we met Aunt Becky, and she told us the preacher had come to take dinner, and for me to water his horse, take the saddle off, curry him down, then come into the smokehouse and she would give me a piece of pie, but it was not large as my hunger. She said she had something to tell me.

"What is it?" I asked.

"Maybe that man will be your uncle some day. If you will stay in the smokehouse and wait till the second table, I will bring you out the chicken gizzard." I took her at her word and got the gizzard, and she got the preacher, and became the wife of a circuit-rider. Not long after I took a great notion that I would be a circuit-rider, too. I mounted horses, mules, and calves, and tried to look like a preacher. My favorite clerical steed was a calf which had a very stately step. I took him out to the meadow with a halter, mounted him, and began to play preacher. All went well; and I was wondering where my appointment would be, when a snake ran under my calf's nose, and I spread all my preach-ability on the ground before the calf as I sprawled on my back, and it has been there ever since. . . .

My father owned a farm and raised a large amount of corn, and had a great many horses, mules, cattle, sheep, and hogs to feed on it, so our crops were consumed at home. We had so much corn to husk and crib that we were compelled to commence very early, in order to get it stored away before cold weather. When we were all in our teens, my eldest brother nineteen, the next seventeen, and myself about fifteen, we gathered corn from early morn till late in the evening, fed the stock, ate our suppers, and prepared for a good hunt for coons, foxes, opossums, and skunks. We always took a gun, an ax, a big butcher-knife, and flint and steel to make fire. We had a polished cow's horn which we could blow as loud as the horns that overthrew the walls of Jericho. As brother Jim was a great talker, we made him chief horn-blower. He went into the yard, and bracing himself, tooted and tooted and split the air for miles, while the dogs collected around him and roared and howled. You never heard such sweet music as brother Jim and the dogs made. Shortly after his melodies began, we were in line of march, front, middle and rear rank, and soon journeyed to the woods to hunt opossums, polecats, coons, wildcats, foxes, and turkeys. Our dogs had a classic education, hunting and killing all classes of "varmints." When on a coon hunt we kept back all the dogs with us but two, Drum and Rouser. The roofs of their mouths were black, their ears long and thin, and their tails very slim. If we wanted coons first, we told Jim to toot for coons, which he could do very nicely. At his sound of music, Drum and Rouser moved off in the darkness, and after some minutes Drum was sure to break the silence by yelping and roaring on the track. The bark of the dog indicated to our trained ear the kind of game he was after. If he barked slow and loud we were pretty sure he had treed a coon; if he barked quick and sharp, we booked him for a fox. If he barked fast and loud we could count on a polecat. In case it was a skunk we ran to the dogs as fast as possible, and ordered Jim at the same time to blow the horn to call them off, for if they ever got the skunk's perfume on them it was so stinking strong that the scent of the animals was destroyed for other game. Sometimes a young untrained dog had the temerity to take hold of a skunk and spoil the hunt, so that all that was left for us was to let the bugle sound the retreat, and go home. The skunk possesses two wonderful powers: he can stink louder and faster than any other known animals; and if you do not kill him, within a few hours he will re-absorb all of his disgusting odors and go away; such is the power and quality placed in him by nature. I would advise you to never kill a skunk, unless you leave his body just where he falls. By so doing the stench will disappear in a very short time. In him you have one of the finest lessons of nature: he gives forth only what he absorbs from his surroundings. . . .

About the year 1852 I killed a great number of deer. I skinned, salted, and dried the meat, supplying not only myself, but my neighbors with all they wanted. One afternoon I killed a very fine young deer, brought him home, and put him in the smokehouse. My clothes, saddle, and horse were badly stained with the blood of the animal. It being late after changing clothes, I took a bucket and went to a lot adjoining my stable to milk my cow. In the lot I had about twenty large hogs. I sat down, and was milking the cow, when all at once the hogs jumped up and ran to the further side of the lot, sniffing the air in great terror. I looked to see the cause of their flight, and there in plain view, within thirty feet of me, stood a monster panther not less than nine or ten feet long from the point of his nose to the end of his tail, and fully three feet high. I was milking in a tin bucket, which made a great deal of noise, so he did not molest either myself or the hogs, but jumped out of the pen and ran to the timber. Then he began to roar and scream like a woman in distress. I was very fond of his music, but the farther it was away the sweeter it sounded. I am glad he didn't think enough of me to spend any more time in my company than he did. No doubt it was the blood on the horse and saddle that brought him there. I did not ask him, and only guessed that he came for a haunch of venison.

One day while driving home in my ox-wagon I came upon three

panthers in the road, — two old beasts and one young one. I had neither rifle nor knife to defend myself, and had they attacked me they would have killed my oxen and myself. My dogs saw the dangerous brutes, and made a bold charge upon them, and they ran up a tree. No doubt they had seated themselves to feast upon my oxen. Even when they had reached safety in the tree-top, they cast fierce, hungry glances at us. I cracked my whip, which sounded very much like a pistol, and they sprang out of the tree-top and ran off into the thick woods. I drove my oxen home in a hurry, every hair on my head feeling as stiff as a knitting-needle, and I never had any more desire to encounter panthers. . . .

. . . My adventures were not confined alone to panthers, deers, skunks, and coons. We had an enemy far more subtle and dangerous than either. His fang was poisonous and his bite often meant death. I refer to the snakes of Missouri of an early day. I have killed thousands of them, big and little, long and short, from ten feet in length to six inches, and all colors, red, black, blue, green, copper, spotted, — dangerous and harmless. They were so abundant in the timber and prairie country in the early days that it was necessary to carry a club about the size of a common walking-stick, three or four feet long, as protection. All persons carried something in their hands to kill snakes during the warm weather. Many kinds were very poisonous. I remember a man named Smith Montgomery who was bitten on the foot in the harvest-field, while he was at work barefooted. The snake's tooth penetrated a vein which carries the blood to the heart, and he cried: "I am bitten by a rattlesnake!" walked toward the other men, but after taking about six steps sank to the ground and was instantly dead. The poison of the rattlesnake produces a numb feeling, which runs all through the body, and the lungs and heart cease to move as soon as the blood is conveyed to the heart and the poison gets into the large blood-vessels. . . .

As I was traveling through some timber-land with my friend Jim Jessee, we saw in front of us a very large rattlesnake, six feet in length. I proposed to Jim to have some fun out of the gentleman. I drew my knife from my belt, cut down and trimmed up a bush, left the upper limb, so as to make a fork, with which I straddled his neck, while with other sticks I opened his mouth and filled it with hartshorn (aqua ammonia); then we let him loose and stepped back to see the fun. To our great surprise he never cut a caper. The ammonia had done its work instantaneously. I tied his tail to a bush, thinking he might be only temporarily inactive. At the end of six hours I returned to find him dead and in the possession of the green flies. By the experiment I learned that ammonia would destroy the snake's deadly virus. In all cases of snake-bite, after that, I always used ammonia as an antidote, and if it was not handy I would use soda or some other alkali with equal success, but not equal in activity. I would advise you to always have a little ammonia or soda in your pocket when going among snakes.

U. S. Grant

Ulysses S. Grant (1822–1885), Civil War hero and eighteenth president of the United States, usually lands near the bottom of the list whenever anyone tries to rank the presidents. His White House years may have been dreadful, but when it comes to rating presidential autobiographies, Grant's is usually called the best of that fairly sad lot. When his Personal Memoirs *were published in two volumes in 1885 and 1886, the prose style was so admired that a rumor went around saying they had actually been ghostwritten by Mark Twain — who was, in fact, their publisher. But Grant wrote them himself, completing them just two days before his death, a race against cancer that was probably the general's most heroic victory since the battle of Vicksburg.*

He was born Hiram Ulysses Grant in Point Pleasant, Ohio. His friends would later call him Sam, and, as he makes clear in these early pages from his memoirs, he did not care all that much for school. (It would be hard to find any male in this entire collection willing to admit to liking school.) What he did like, even at an early age, was buying and selling horses. Which brings to mind something a later president once wrote on the subject: "You know," a young Harry S. Truman wrote to his future wife, "horse trading is the cause of the death of truth in America."

From "Ancestors — Birth — Boyhood," *Personal Memoirs of U. S. Grant*

THE SCHOOLS, at the time of which I write, were very indifferent. There were no free schools, and none in which the scholars were classified. They were all supported by subscription, and a single teacher — who was often a man or a woman incapable of teaching much, even if they imparted all they knew — would have thirty or forty scholars, male and female, from the infant learning the a-b-c's up to the young lady of eighteen and the boy of twenty, studying the highest branches taught — the three R's, "Reading, 'Riting,

'Rithmetic." I never saw an algebra, or other mathematical work higher than the arithmetic, in Georgetown, until after I was appointed to West Point. I then bought a work on algebra in Cincinnati; but having no teacher, it was Greek to me.

My life in Georgetown was uneventful. From the age of five or six until seventeen I attended the subscription schools of the village, except during the winters of 1836–37 and 1838–39. The former period was spent in Maysville, Kentucky, attending the school of Richeson and Rand; the latter in Ripley, Ohio, at a private school. I was not studious in habit, and probably did not make progress enough to compensate for the outlay for board and tuition. At all events, both winters were spent in going over the same old arithmetic which I knew every word of before, and repeating, "A noun is the name of a thing," which I had also heard my Georgetown teachers repeat until I had come to believe it — but I cast no reflections upon my old teacher, Richeson. He turned out bright scholars from his school, many of whom have filled conspicuous places in the service of their States. Two of my contemporaries there — who, I believe, never attended any other institution of learning — have held seats in Congress, and one, if not both, other high offices; these are Wadsworth and Phister.

My father was, from my earliest recollection, in comfortable circumstances, considering the times, his place of residence, and the community in which he lived. Mindful of his own lack of facilities for acquiring an education, his greatest desire in maturer years was for the education of his children. Consequently, as stated before, I never missed a quarter from school from the time I was old enough to attend till the time of leaving home. This did not exempt me from labor. In my early days every one labored, more or less, in the region where my youth was spent, and more in proportion to their private means. It was only the very poor who were exempt. While my father carried on the manufacture of leather, and worked at the trade himself, he owned and tilled considerable land. I detested the trade, preferring almost any other labor; but I was fond of agriculture, and of all employment in which horses were used. We had, among other lands, fifty acres of forest within a mile of the village. In the fall of the year choppers were employed to cut enough wood to last a twelvemonth. When I was seven or eight years of age I began hauling all the wood used in the house and shops. I could not load it on the wagons, of course, at that time, but I could drive, and the choppers would load, and some one at the house unload. When about eleven years old I was strong enough to hold a plow. From that age until seventeen I did all the work done with horses, such as breaking up the land, furrowing, plowing corn and potatoes, bringing in the crops when harvested, hauling all the wood, besides tending two or three horses, a cow or two, and sawing wood for stoves, etc., while still attending school. For this I was compensated by the fact that there was never any scolding or punishing by my parents; no objection to rational enjoyments, such as fishing, going to the creek a mile away to swim in summer, taking a horse and visiting my grandparents in the adjoining county, fifteen miles off, skating on the ice in winter, or taking a horse and sleigh when there was snow on the ground.

While still quite young I had visited Cincinnati, forty-five miles away, several times, alone; also Maysville, Kentucky, often, and once Louisville. The journey to Louisville was a big one for a boy of that day. I had also gone once with a two-horse carriage to Chillicothe, about seventy miles, with a neighbor's family, who were removing to Toledo, Ohio, and returned alone; and had gone once, in like manner, to Flat Rock, Kentucky, about seventy miles away. On this latter occasion I was fifteen years of age. While at Flat Rock, at the house of a Mr. Payne, whom I was visiting with his brother, a neighbor of ours in Georgetown, I saw a very fine saddle-horse, which I rather coveted, and proposed to Mr. Payne, the owner, to trade him for one of the two I was driving. Payne hesitated to trade with a boy, but asking his brother about it, the latter told him that it would be all right, that I was allowed to do as I pleased with the horses. I was seventy miles from home, with a carriage to take back, and Mr. Payne said, he did not know that his horse had ever had a collar on. I asked to have him hitched to a farm-wagon, and we would soon see whether he would work. It was soon evident that the horse had never worn harness before; but he showed no viciousness, and I expressed a confidence that I could manage him. A trade was at once struck, I receiving ten dollars difference.

The next day Mr. Payne of Georgetown and I started on our return. We got alone very well for a few miles, when we encountered a ferocious dog that frightened the horses and made them run. The new animal kicked at every jump he made. I got the horses stopped, however, before any damage was done, and without running into anything. After giving them a little rest to quiet their fears, we started again. That instant the new horse kicked, and started to run once more. The road we were on struck the turnpike within half a mile of the point where the second runaway commenced, and there was an embankment twenty or more feet deep on the opposite side of the pike. I got the horses stopped on the very brink of the precipice. My new horse was terribly frightened, and trembled like an aspen; but he was not half so badly frightened as my companion. Mr. Payne, who deserted me after this last experience, and took passage on a freight-wagon for Maysville. Every time I attempted to start my new horse would commence to kick. I was in quite a dilemma for a time. Once in Maysville, I could borrow a horse from an uncle who lived there; but I was more than a day's travel from that point. Finally I took out my bandanna — the style of handkerchief in universal use then — and with this blindfolded my horse. In this way I reached Maysville safely the next day, no doubt much to the surprise of my friend. Here I borrowed a horse from my uncle, and the following day we proceeded on our journey.

About half my school-days in Georgetown were spent at the school of John D. White, a North Carolinian, and the father of Chilton White, who represented the district in Congress for two terms during the rebellion. Mr. White was always a Democrat in politics, and Chilton followed his father. He had two elder brothers — all three being schoolmates of mine at their father's school — who did not go the same way. The second brother died before the rebellion began; he was a Whig and afterward a Republican. His eldest brother was a Republican, and a brave soldier during the rebellion. Chilton is reported as having told of an earlier horse-trade of mine. As he told the story, there was a Mr. Ralston living within a few miles of the village, who owned a colt which I very much wanted. My father had offered twenty dollars for it, but Ralston wanted twenty-five. I was so anxious to have the colt that after the owner left I begged to be allowed to take him at the price demanded. My father yielded, but said twenty dollars was all the horse was worth, and told me to offer that price; if it was not accepted I was to offer twenty-two and a half, and if that would not get him, to give the twenty-five. I at once mounted a horse and went for the colt. When I got to Mr. Ralston's house I said to him: "Papa says I may offer you twenty dollars for the colt, but if you won't take that, I am to offer twenty-two and a half, and if you won't take that to give you twenty-five." It would not take a Connecticut man to guess the price finally agreed upon. White's story is nearly true. I certainly showed very plainly that I had come for the colt, and meant to have him. I could not have been over eight years old at the time. This transaction caused me great heartburning. The story got out among the boys of the village, and it was a long time before I heard the last of it. Boys enjoy the misery of their companions, at least village boys in that day did, and in later life I have found that all adults are not free from the peculiarity. I kept the horse until he was four years old, when he went blind, and I sold him for twenty dollars. When I went to Maysville to school, in 1836, at the age of fourteen, I recognized my colt as one of the blind horses working on the treadwheel of the ferry-boat.

I have described enough of my early life to give an impression of the whole. I did not like to work; but I did as much of it, while young, as grown men can be hired to do in these days, and attended school at the same time. I had as many privileges as any boy in the village, and probably more than most of them. I have no recollection of ever having been punished at home, either by scolding or by the rod. But at school the case was different. The rod was freely used there, and I was not exempt from its influence. I can see John D. White, the school-teacher, now, with his long beech-switch always in his hand. It was not always the same one, either. Switches were brought in bundles from a beech-wood near the school-house, by the boys of whose benefit they were intended. Often a whole bundle would be used up in a single day. I never had any hard feelings against my teacher, either while attending school, or in later years when reflecting upon my experience. Mr. White was a kind-hearted man, and was much respected by the community in which he lived. He only followed the universal custom of the period, and that under which he had received his own education.

James L. Smith

In the North at least, slave narratives were a popular form of literature in the middle years of the nineteenth century. Written — or dictated — by former slaves, they provided dramatic and shocking scenes of life on the southern plantations, and since the slaves were usually runaways, there was often a breathless chase somewhere toward the end. In one tidy package they combined spellbinding adventure with a proper morally uplifting message. Indeed, many of the incidents that Harriet Beecher Stowe used so successfully in her novel Uncle Tom's Cabin *had already been established as standard elements of the nonfiction slave narratives.*

James L. Smith's Autobiography *was published in 1881, after the narrative craze had passed its peak. Before the war, Smith , who seems to have been born in the early 1820s, had escaped from a plantation in Virginia and made his way to Connecticut on the underground railway. In Norwich he worked as a shoemaker and became an active Methodist lay-preacher. In one of the last chapters in his book he writes of his return in 1867 to the old plantation, of visiting the shop where he learned cobbling, of tracking down his brother, of drinking from the old spring. He also visits the "great house," where the widow of his former owner is so happy to see him that she invites him to dinner. He accepts "as an appreciation of her kindness" and before he leaves gives her "a nice pair of shoes, for which she is very thankful."*

From "Birth and Childhood,"
The Autobiography of James L. Smith

MY BIRTHPLACE was in Northern Neck, Northumberland Country, Virginia. My mother's name was Rachel, and my father's was Charles. Our cabin home was just across the creek. This creek formed the head of the Wycomco River. Thomas Langsdon, my master, lived on one side of the creek, and my mother's family — which was very large — on the opposite side. Every year a new comer was added to our humble cabin home, till she gave birth to the eleventh child. My mother had just so much cotton to spin every day as her stint. I lived here till I was quite a lad.

There was a man who lived near us whose name was Haney, a coach maker by trade. He always had his timber brought up to the creek. One day he ordered one of his slave women to go down and bring up some of the timber. She took with her a small lad, about my size, to assist her. She came along by our cabin, as it was near the place where the timber was, and asked me to go along with her to help her. I asked mother if I could go. She decidedly said "No!" As my mother was sick, and confined to her bed at that time, I took this opportunity to steal away, unknown to her. We endeavored, at first, to carry a large piece of timber — the woman holding one end, I the other, and the boy in the middle. Before we had gone far her foot struck something that caused her to fall, so that it jarred my end, causing it to drop on my knee. The boy being in the middle, the full weight of the timber fell on his foot, crushing and mangling it in a most shocking manner. After this accident, the woman and boy started for home, carrying some smaller pieces of timber with them.

After a few days of painful sickness, mortification took place in the little boy's foot, and death claimed him for his own. My grandmother hearing my voice of distress came after me and brought me home. At the time she did not think I was hurt very seriously. My mother called me to her bedside and punished me for disobeying her. After a day or two my knee began to contract, to shrink. This caused my mother to feel that there was something very serious about it, and as soon as she was able to get around, she went to the "great house," the home of Thos. Langsdon, and told him that I was badly hurt, and that something must be done for me. He asked her what was the matter. She told him what had happened to me, and how seriously I was hurt with the timber. After hearing this sad news, he said he had niggers enough without me; I was not worth much any how, and he did not care if I did die. He positively declared that he should not employ a physician for me. As there was no medical remedy applied to my knee, it grew worse and worse until I could not touch my foot to the ground without the most intense pain. There was a doctor in the neighborhood at this time, and mother knowing it sent me to see him, unknowingly to my master. He examined my knee and said, as it had been out of joint so long it would be a difficult matter to break it over again and then set it. He told my mother to take me home and bathe it in cold spring water to prevent it from ulcerating, for if it should it would kill me.

When I was able to walk around with my lameness, Thomas Langsdon took me across the creek to his house to do chores. I was then quite a boy. After a while my leg commenced swelling, and after that ulcerating. It broke in seven places. I was flat on my back for seven or eight weeks before I could raise myself without help. I suffered every thing but death itself, and would have died if it had not been for Miss Ayers, who was house-keeper in the "great house." She came into the kitchen every day to dress my knee, till I could get around. Not having any shoes, and being exposed to the weather, I took a heavy cold which caused my knee to ulcerate. When I was able to get around, the father of my young master was taken sick, and was confined to his bed for months. I, with another boy about my size and age — six or seven years — sat by his bedside. We took our turns alternately, the boy so many hours and I so many, to keep the flies off from him. After a while the old man died, then I was relieved from fighting or contending with flies.

After this I went across the creek to help my mother, as I was not large enough to be of any service on the plantation. In the course of time my young master died, also his wife, leaving two sons, Thomas and John Langsdon. My young master chose for us (slaves) a guardian, who hired us all out. As my mother gave birth to so many children, it made her not very profitable as a servant, and instead of being let out to the highest bidder, was let out to the lowest one that would support her for the least money. Hence my father, though a slave, agreed to take her and the children, and support them for so much money.

My father's master had a brother by the name of Thad. Guttridge, who lived in Lancaster County, who died, leaving his plantation to his brother, (my father's master). My father was then sent to take charge of this new plantation, and moved my mother and the children with him into the "great house;" my mother as mistress of the house.

This Thad. Guttridge had a woman by the name of Cecilia, or Cella, as she was called, whom he kept as house-keeper and mistress, by whom he had one child, a beautiful girl almost white. After this new arrangement was made for my father to take charge of the new plantation, this woman Cella, was turned out of her position as house-keeper to a field hand, to work on the plantation in exchange with my mother.

This was not very agreeable to Cella, so she sought or contrived some plan to avenge herself. So one Saturday night Cella went off, and did not return till Sunday night. When she did return she brought with her some whisky, in two bottles. She asked father if he would like to take a dram; and, not thinking there would be any trouble resulting from it, he replied: "Yes." Giving him the bottle, he took a drink. She then gave the other bottle to my mother, and she took a drink. Afterwards, Cella gave us children some out of the same bottle that my mother drank from. Father went to bed that night, complaining of not feeling very well. The next morning he was worse, and continued to grow worse until he was very low. His master was immediately sent for, who came in great haste. On his arrival he found father very low, not able to speak aloud. My master, seeing in what a critical condition he was, sent for a white doctor, who came, and gave father some medicine. He grew worse every time he took the medicine. There was an old colored doctor who lived some ten miles off. Some one told Bill Guttridge that he had better see him, and, perhaps he could tell what was the matter with my father. Bill Guttridge went to see this colored doctor. ·

The doctor looked at his cards, and told him that his Charles was poisoned, and even told him who did it, and her motive for doing it. Her intention was to get father and mother out of their place, so that she could get back again. Little did she think that the course she took would prove a failure. The doctor gave Guttridge a bottle of medicine, and told him to return in haste, and give father a dose of it. He did so. I saw him coming down the lane towards the house, at full speed. He jumped off his horse, took his saddle-bags and ran into the house. He called my mother to give him a cup, so he could pour out some of the medicine. He then raised my father up, and gave him some of it out of the cup. After he had laid him down, and replaced the covering over him again, he took his hickory cane and went out into the kitchen — Cella sat here with her work — with an oath told her: "You have poisoned my Charles." He had no sooner uttered these words, when he flew at her with his cane. As he was very much enraged, he commenced beating her over the head and shoulders till he had worn the cane out. After he had stopped beating her in this brutal manner her head was swollen or puffed to such size that it was impossible to recognize who she was; she did not look like the same woman. Not being satisfied with this punishment, he told her that he intended repeating it in the morning. In the morning, when he went to look for her, she was gone. He stayed with father till he was able to sit up. When he returned home — which was about ten miles — he left word with father that if Cella came home, to bind her and send her down to him.

This was in the fall of the year. Some months passed before we saw Cella again. The following spring, while the men were cleaning up the new land, Cella came to them; they took and brought her to the house. Father was then able to walk about the house, but was unable to work much. He had her tied, and put behind a man on horseback and carried down to his master, who took her and put her on board a vessel to be sent to Norfolk. He sold her to some one there. This was the last time we ever saw, or heard from her.

We lived here quite a number of years on Lancaster plantation. Finally my father's master sold it, and also his brother's daughter, Cella's child. We then returned from Lancaster plantation to Northern Neck, Va., and lived nearly in the same place, called Hog Point; we lived here quite a number of years. Mr. Dick Mitchell, my master's guardian, took me away from my mother to Lancaster County, on his plantation, where I lived about six months. I used to do chores about the house, and card rolls for the women. Being lame unfitted me for a field hand, so I had to do work about the house, to help the women.

Our dress was made of tow cloth; for the children, nothing was furnished them but a shirt; for the older ones, a pair of pantaloons or a gown, in addition, according to the sex. Besides these, in the winter season an overcoat, or a round jacket; a wool hat once in two or three years for the men, and a pair of coarse brogan shoes once a year. We dwelt in log cabins, and on the bare ground. Wooden floors were an unknown luxury to the slave. There was neither furniture nor bedsteads of any description; our beds were collections of straw and old rags, thrown down in the corners; some were boxed in with boards, while others were old ticks filled with straw. All ideas of decency and refinement were, of course, out of the question.

Our mode of living in Virginia was not unlike all other slave states. At night, each slept rolled up in a coarse blanket; one partition, which was an old quilt or blanket, or something else that answered the purpose, was extended across the hut; wood partitions were unknown to the doomed slave. A water pail, a boiling pot, and few gourds made up the furniture. When the corn had been ground in a hand-mill, and then boiled, the pot was swung from the fire and the children squatted around it, with oyster shells for spoons. Sweet potatoes, oysters and crabs varied the diet. Early in the morning the mothers went off to the fields in companies, while some women too old to do anything but wield a stick were left in charge of the strangely silent and quiet babies. The field hands having no time to prepare any thing for their morning meals, took up hastily a piece of hoe-cake and bacon, or any thing that was near at hand, and then, with rakes or hoes in the hand, hurried off to the fields at early dawn, for the loud horn called them to their labors. Heavy were their hearts as they daily traversed the long cotton rows. The overseer's whip took no note of aching hearts.

The allowance for the slave men for the week was a peck-and-a-half of corn meal, and two pounds of bacon. The women's allowance was a peck of meal, and from one pound-and-a-half to two pounds of bacon; and so much for each child, varying from one-half to a peck a week, and of bacon, from one-half to a pound a week. In order to make our allowance hold out, we went crabbing or fishing. In the winter season we used to go hunting nights, catching oysters, coons and possums. When I was home, the slaves used to bake their hoe-cakes on hoes; these hoes were larger than those used in the northern states. Another way for cooking them was to rake the ashes and then put the meal cake between the ashes and the fire — this was called ash pone; and still another way was to bake the bare cake in a Dutch oven, heated for the purpose — that was called oven pone. This latter way of baking them was much practiced, or customary at the home of the slave-holders.

The "great house," so called by the plantation hands, was the home where the master and his family lived. The kitchen was an apartment by itself in the yard, a little distance from the "great house," so as to face the front part of the house; others were built in the back yard. The kitchens had one bed-room attached to them.

One night I went crabbing, and was up most all night; a boy accompanied me. We caught a large mess of crabs, and took them home with us. The next day I had to card for one of the women to spin, and, being up all night, I could hardly keep my eyes open; every once in a while I would fall asleep. Mrs. Mitchell could look through her window into the kitchen, it being in front of the "great house." She placed herself in the portico, to see that I worked. When I fell into a quiet slumber she would halloo out and threaten to cowhide me; but, for all that, I could not keep awake. Seeing that I did not heed her threatenings, she took her rawhide and sewing and seated herself close by me, saying she would see if she could keep me awake. She asked me what was the matter; I told her I felt sick. (I was a great hand to feign sickness). She asked me what kind of sickness; I told her I had the stomach ache and could not work. Thinking that something did ail me, she sent Alfred, the slave boy, into the house after her medicine chest; she also told him to bring her the decanter of whisky. She then poured out a tumbler most full of whisky and then made me drink all of it. After drinking it I was worse than I was before, for I was so drunk I could not see what I was doing. Every once in a while when I fell asleep she would give me a cut with the rawhide. At last, night came and I was relieved from working so steady. When I was not carding I was obliged to knit; I disliked it very much; I was very slow; it used to take me two or three weeks to knit one stocking, and when I had finished it you could not tell what the color was.

I had also to drive the calves for the milk-woman to milk. One afternoon, towards night, I stopped my other work to hunt up the calves and have them at the cow-pen by the time the milk-woman came, with the cows; I went in one of the quarters, and being tired, I sat down on a bench, and before I knew it I fell asleep and slept till after dark. The milk-woman came with the cows, but there were no calves there. She hallooed for me, but I was not within hearing. As the cow-pen was not far from the "great house" the mistress heard her. At last the milk-woman came to the "great house" to see what had become of me, but no Lindsey could be found. She went to the kitchen where the milk pails were kept, took them, and then drove the calves up herself and went to milking. Before she had finished, I awoke and started for the kitchen for the pails. When I got there, Mrs. Mitchell was standing up in the middle of the kitchen floor. She asked me where I had been; I told her I fell asleep in the quarters' and forgot myself. She said she would learn me how to attend to my business, so she told Alfred to go into the "great house" and bring her the rawhide. I stood there trembling about mid-way of the floor. Taking the cow-hide, and lifting her large arms as high as she could, [she] applied it to my back. The sharp twang of the rawhide, as it struck my shoulders, raised me from the floor.

Jinny (the cook) told me afterwards, that when Mrs. Mitchell struck me I jumped about four feet, and did not touch the floor again till I was out doors. She followed me to the door and just had time to see me turn the corner of the "great house." I then ran down towards the cow-pen. The cook told me the way I was running as I turned the corner, that she did not believe that there was a dog or horse on the plantation that could have caught me. I went to the cow-pen and helped the woman to finish milking, and stayed around till I thought that Mrs. Mitchell had gone into the "great house." But to my astonishment when I went to the kitchen again, behold, there she was still waiting for me. She asked me why I ran from her; I told her that it hurt me so bad when she struck me, that I did not know that I was running. She said the next time she whipped me that she would have me tied, then she guessed I would not run. She left me off that night by promising her that I would do better, and never run from her again.

Mrs. Mitchell was a very cruel woman; I have seen her whip Jinny in a very brutal manner. There was a large shade tree that stood in the yard; she would make Jinny come out under this tree, and strip her shoulders all bare; then she would apply the rawhide to her bare back until she had exhausted her own strength, and was obliged to call some of the house servants to bring her a chair. While she was resting, she would keep Jinny still standing. After resting her weary arms, she commenced again. Thus she whipped and rested, till she had applied fifty blows upon her suffering back. There was not a spot upon her naked back to lay a finger but there would be a gash, gushing forth the blood; every cut of the rawhide forced an extraordinary groan from the suffering victim; she then sent her back to the kitchen, with her back sore and bleeding, to her work. We slaves often talked the matter over amongst ourselves, and wondered why God suffered such a cruel woman to live. One night, as we were talking the matter over, Jinny exclaimed: "De Lord bless me, chile, I do not believe dat dat devil will ever die, but live to torment us."

After a while I left there for Hog Point, to live with my mother. In the course of a year or two old Mrs. Mitchell sickened, and died.

After she died, I went down to see the folks on the plantation. After my arrival, they told me that just before she breathed her last, she sent for Jinny to come to her bedroom. As she entered, she looked up and said: "Jinny, I am going to die, and I suppose you are glad of it." Jinny replied: "No, I am not." After pretending to cry, she came back to the kitchen and exclaimed: "Dat old devil is going to die, and I am glad of it." When her mistress died her poor back had a brief respite for a while. I do not know what took place upon the plantation after this.

As my young master became of age about this time, Mr. Mitchell gave the guardianship to him. During this time my mother died; then I was bound out to his uncle, John Langsdon, to learn the shoemaker's trade. John Langsdon was a very kind man, and struck me but once the whole time I was with him in Fairfield, and then it was my own fault. One day, while I was at work in the shop, I put my work down and went out; while I was out, I stepped into the "great house." His two sons were in the house shelling corn; some words passed between his eldest son and me, which resulted in a fight. Mr. Langsdon was looking out of the shop window and saw us fighting; so he caught up a stick and struck me three or four times, and then drove me off to the shop to my work. I took hold of shoe-making very readily; I had not been there a great while when I could make a shoe, or a boot — this I acquired by untiring industry. He used to give me my stint, a pair of shoes a day. I remained with him four years.

The first cruel act of my master, as soon as he became of age, and took his slaves home, was to sell one of my mother's children, whose name was Cella, who was carried off by a trader. We never saw or heard from her again. Oh! how it rent my mother's heart; although her heart was almost broken by grief and despair, she bore this shock in silent but bitter agony. Her countenance exhibited an anxious and sorrowful expression, and her manner gave evidence of a deep settled melancholy. This, and other troubles which she was compelled to pass through, and constant toil and exposure so shattered her physical frame that disease soon preyed upon her, that hastened her to the grave. Ah! I saw not the death-angel, as with white wings he approached. When the hour came for her departure from earth there was but a slight struggle, a faint gasp, and the freed spirit went to its final home. Gone where there are neither bonds nor tortures, sorrow and weeping are unknown.

My mother was buried in a field where there was no other dead deposited; no stone marks her resting place; no fragrant flowers adorn the sod that covers her silent house.

My father soon followed my mother to the grave; then we children were left fatherless and motherless in the cold world. My father's death was very much felt as a good servant, being quick and energetic, rendered him a favorite with his master. When my father was about to die, he called his children, those who were at home around him, as no medicine could now retard the steady approach of the death-angel. When we assembled about him he bade us all farewell, saying, there was but one thing that troubled him, and that was, not one of us professed religion. When I heard that, and saw his sunken eye and hollow cheek, my heart sank within me. Oh! how those words did cut me, like a two-edged sword. From that day I commenced to seek the Lord with all my heart, and never stopped till I found Him. After my father's death, my eldest sister took charge of the younger children, until her master took her home.

One cold morning, while I lived at Hog Point, we looked out and saw three men coming towards the house. One was Mr. Haney, the other one was one of his neighbors, and the last one was his slave. Near our cabin home was a large oak tree; they took this doomed slave down to this tree, and stripped him entirely naked; then they threw a rope across a limb and tied him by his wrists, and drew him up so that his feet cleared the ground. They then applied the lash to his bare back till the blood streamed and reddened the ground underneath where he hung. After whipping him to their satisfaction, they took him down, and led him bound through our yard. I looked at him as he passed, and saw the great ridges in his back as the blood was pouring out of them, and it was as a dagger to my heart. They took him and forced him to work, with his back sore and bleeding. He came to our cabin, a night or two afterwards; my mother asked him what Mr. Haney beat him for; he said it was for nothing only because he did not work enough for him; he did all he could, but the unreasonable master demanded more. I never saw him any more, for shortly after this we moved away.

Joanna Draper

In 1937, when Joanna Draper was eighty-three years old and living in Tulsa, Oklahoma, she told an interviewer from the Federal Writers' Project about her life as a slave on a Mississippi plantation before, during, and just after the Civil War. She was eight years old when her story begins, and she remembers the coming of the war, the first appearance of the Ku Klux Klan, and the fact that no one ever bothered to tell her that slavery had been abolished. She also remembers things her master said to her mistress when they assumed no one was paying attention.

From a Federal Writers' Project interview

MOST FOLKS can't remember many things happened to 'em when they only eight years old, but one of my biggest tribulations come about that time, and I never will forget it! That was when I was took away from my own mammy and pappy and sent off and bound out to another man, 'way off two-three hundred miles away from where I live. And that's the last time I ever see either one of them, or any my own kinfolks!

Where I was born was at Hazlehurst, Mississippi. Just a little piece east of Hazlehurst, close to the Pearl River, and that place was a kind of new plantation what my master, Dr. Alexander, bought when he moved into Mississippi from up in Virginia awhile before the war.

They said my mammy brings me down to Mississippi, and I was born just right after she got there. My mammy's name was Margaret, and she was born under the Ramsons, back in Tennessee. She belonged to Dave Ramson, and his pappy had come to Tennessee to settle on war land, and he had knowed Dr. Alexander's people back in Virginia too. My pappy's name was Addison, and he always belonged to Dr. Alexander. Old Doctor bought my mammy 'cause my pappy liked her. Old Doctor live in Tennessee a little while before he go on down to Mississippi.

Old Doctor's wife named Dinah, and she sure was a good woman, but I don't remember about Old Doctor much. He was away all the time, it seem like.

When I is about six year old, they take me into the big house to learn to be a house woman, and they show me how to cook and clean up and take care of babies. That big house wasn't very fine, but it was mighty big and cool, and made out of logs with a big hall, but it didn't have no long gallery like most the houses around there had.

They was lots of big trees in the yard, and most the ground was new ground round that place, 'cause Old Doctor just started to done farming on it when I was took away, but he had some more places not so far away, over toward the river, that was old ground and made big crops for him. I went to one of the places one time, but they wasn't nobody on 'em but niggers and a white overseer. I don't know how many niggers Old Doctor had, but Master John Deeson say he had about a hundred.

At Old Doctor's house I didn't have to work very hard. Just had to help the cooks and peel the potatoes and pick the guineas and chickens and do things like that. Sometime I had to watch the baby. He was a little boy, and they would bring him into the kitchen for me to watch. I had to git up way before daylight and make the fire in the kitchen fireplace and bring in some fresh water, and go get the milk what been down in the spring all night, and do things like that until breakfast ready. Old Master and Old Mistress come in the big hall to eat in the summer, and I stand behind them and shoo off the flies.

Old Doctor didn't have no spinning and weaving niggers 'cause he say they don't do enough work, and he buy all the cloth he use for everybody's clothes. He can do that 'cause he had lots of money. He was big rich, and he keep a whole lot of hard money in the house all the time, but none of the slaves know it but me. Sometimes I would have the baby in the mistress' room and she would git three or four big wood boxes full of hard money for us to play with. I would make fences out of the money all across the floor, to keep the baby satisfied, and when he go to sleep I would put the money back in the boxes. I never did know how much they is, but a whole lot.

Even after the war start Old Doctor have that money, and he would exchange money for people. Sometimes he would go out and be gone for a long time, and come back with a lot more money he got from somewhere.

Right at the first they made him a high officer in the war, and he done doctoring somewhere at a hospital most of the time. But he could go on both sides of the war, and sometime he would come in at night and bring Old Mistress pretty little things, and I heard him tell her he got them in the North.

One day I was fanning him, and I asked him is he been to the North, and he kick out at me and tell to shut up my black mouth, and it nearly scared me to death the way he look at me! Nearly every time he been gone and come in and tell Mistress he been in the North, he have a lot more hard money to put away in them boxes, too!

One evening 'long come a man and eat supper at the house and stay all night. He was a nice-mannered man, and I like to wait on him. The next morning I hear him ask Old Doctor what is my name, and Old Doctor start in to try to sell me to that man. The man say he can't buy me 'cause Old Doctor say he want a thousand dollars, and then Old Doctor say he will bind me out to him.

I run away from the house and went out to the cabin where my mammy and pappy was, but they tell me to go back to the big house 'cause maybe I am just scared. But about that time Old Doctor and the man come, and Old Doctor make me go with the man. We go in his buggy a long ways off to the south, and after he stop two or three night at people's houses and put me out to stay with the niggers, he come to his own house. I ask him how far it is back home, and he say about a hundred miles or more, and laugh, and ask me if I knew how far that is.

I wants to know if I can go back to my mammy sometime, and he say "Sure, of course you can, some of these times. You don't belong to me, Jo, I's just your boss and not your master."

He live in a big old rottendy house, but he ain't farming none of the land. Just as soon as he git home, he go off again, and sometimes he only come in at night for a little while.

His wife's name was Kate and his name was Mr. John. I was there about a week before I found out they name was Deeson. They had two children, a girl about my size, name Joanna like me, and a little baby boy, name Johnny. One day Mistress Kate tell me I the only nigger they got. I been thinking maybe they had some somewhere on a plantation, but she say they ain't got no plantation and they ain't been at that place very long either.

That little girl Joanna and me kind of take up together, and she was a might nice-mannered little girl, too. Her mammy raised her good.

Her mammy was mighty sickly all the time, and that's the reason they bind me to do the work.

Mr. John was in some kind of business in the war too, but I never see him with no soldier clothes on but one time. One night he come in with them on, but the next morning he come to breakfast in just his plain clothes again. Then he go off again.

I sure had a hard row at that house. It was old and rackety, and I had to scrub off the staircase and the floors all the time, and git the breakfast for Mistress Kate and the two children. Then I could have my own breakfast in the kitchen. Mistress Kate always get the supper, though.

Some days she go off with the two children and leave me at the house all day by myself, and I think maybe I run off, but I didn't know where to go.

After I been at the place two years, Mr. John come home and stay. He done some kind of trading in Jackson, Mississippi, and he would be gone three or four days at a time, but I never did know what kind of trading it was.

About the time he come home to stay I seen the first Ku Klux I ever seen one night. I was going down the road in the moonlight, and I heard a hog grunting out in the bushes at the side of the road. I just walk right on and in a little ways I hear another hog in some more bushes. This time I stop and listen, and they's another hog grunts across the road, and about that time two mens dressed up in long white shirts steps out into the road in front of me! I was so scared the goose bumps jump up all over me 'cause I didn't know what they is! They didn't say a word to me, but just walked on past me and went on back the way I had come. Then I see two more mens step out of the woods, and I run from that as fast as I can go!

I ast Miss Kate what they is, and she say they Ku Klux, and I better not go walking off down the road any more. I seen them two-three times after that, though, but they was riding horses them times.

I stayed at Mr. John's place two more years, and he got so grumpy and his wife got so mean I make up my mind to run off. I bundle up my clothes in a little bundle and hide them, and then I wait until Miss Kate take the children and go off somewhere, and I light out on foot. I had me a piece of that hard money what Master Doctor Alexander had give me one time at Christmas. I had kept it all that time, and nobody knowed I had it, not even Joanna. Old Doctor told me it was fifty dollars, and I thought I could live on it for a while.

I never had been away from the place, not even to another plantation in all the four years I was with the Deesons, and I didn't know which-a-way to go, so I just started west.

I been walking about all evening, it seem like, and I come to a little town with just a few houses. I see a nigger man and ask him where I can git something to eat, and I say I got fifty dollars.

"What you doing with fifty dollars, child? Where you belong at, anyhow?" he ask me, and I tell him I belong to Master John Deeson, but I is running away. I explain that I just bound out to Mr. John, but Dr. Alexander my real master, and then that man tell me the first time I knowed it that I ain't a slave no more!

That man Deeson never did tell me, and his wife never did!

Well, that man asked me about the fifty dollars, and then I found out that it was just fifty cents!

I can't begin to tell about all the hard times I had working for something to eat and roaming around after that. I don't know why I never did try to git back up around Hazlehurst and hunt up my pappy and mammy, but I reckon I was just ignorant and didn't know how to go about it. Anyways, I never did see them no more.

Mark Twain

Mark Twain — who as Samuel Langhorne Clemens (1835–1910) grew up in the Mississippi River town of Hannibal, Missouri — claimed to remember very little of his early childhood. He recalled that he was told by members of his family that he was "a sickly and precarious and tiresome and uncertain child" who lived on medicine until he was seven. Long afterwards he asked his mother, then in her late eighties, about those years.

> *"I suppose that during all that time you were uneasy about me?"*
> *"Yes, the whole time," she answered.*
> *"Afraid I wouldn't live?"*
> *After a long pause, ostensibly to think out the facts. "No, afraid you would."*

That story appears in his posthumously published Autobiography, *which is short on childhood information other than anecdotes that relate to scenes in such novels as* Tom Sawyer, Huckleberry Finn, *and* The Gilded Age. *In fact, his father was a Virginian who had gone west hoping to strike it rich in land speculation. Samuel dropped out of school at twelve and, like Ben Franklin, went to work for a printer. In 1856, pursuing the boyhood dream he writes about in this chapter from* Life on the Mississippi, *he became an apprentice to a steamboat pilot and worked on the river until the outbreak of the Civil War, when, after a brief spell in the Confederate Army, he took off for the California goldfields. There, he turned to journalism and short fiction and began to make a reputation for himself as a frontier humorist. In 1870, he settled in Hartford, Connecticut, and over the next twenty years wrote most of the novels for which he would be remembered. In 1883, a year before the publication of* Huckleberry Finn, *the nonfictional — or, at least, only vaguely fictionalized —* Life on the Mississippi *appeared, combining autobiography with history and travel writing as Mark Twain's bittersweet love letter to the river.*

"The Boys' Ambition," *Life on the Mississippi*

WHEN I WAS A BOY, there was but one permanent ambition among my comrades in our village on the west bank of the Mississippi River. That was, to be a steamboatman. We had transient ambitions of other sorts, but they were only transient. When a circus came and went, it left us all burning to become clowns; the first negro minstrel show that ever came to our section left us all suffering to try that kind of life; now and then we had a hope that, if we lived and were good, God would permit us to be pirates. These ambitions faded out, each in its turn; but the ambition to be a steamboatman always remained.

Once a day a cheap, gaudy packet arrived upward from St. Louis, and another downward from Keokuk. Before these events, the day was glorious with expectancy; after them, the day was a dead and empty thing. Not only the boys, but the whole village, felt this. After all these years I can picture that old time to myself now, just as it was then: the white town drowsing in the sunshine of a summer's morning; the streets empty, or pretty nearly so; one or two clerks sitting in front of the Water Street stores, with their splint-bottomed chairs tilted back against the walls, chins on breasts, hats slouched over their faces, asleep — with shingle-shavings enough around to show what broke them down; a sow and a litter of pigs loafing along the sidewalk, doing a good business in watermelon rinds and seeds; two or three lonely little freight piles scattered about the "levee"; a pile of "skids" on the slope of the stone-paved wharf, and the fragrant town drunkard asleep in the shadow of them; two or three wood flats at the head of the wharf, but nobody to listen to the peaceful lapping of the wavelets against them; the great Mississippi, the majestic, the magnificent Mississippi, rolling its mile-wide tide along, shining in the sun; the dense forest away on the other side; the "point" above the town, and the "point" below, bounding the river-glimpse and turning it into a sort of sea, and withal a very still and brilliant and lonely one. Presently a film of dark smoke appears above one of those remote "points"; instantly a negro drayman, famous for his quick eye and prodigious voice, lifts up the cry, "S-t-e-a-m-boat a-comin'!" and the scene changes! The town drunkard stirs, the clerks wake up, a furious clatter of drays follows, every house and store pours out a human contribution and all in a twinkling the dead town is alive and moving. Drays, carts, men, boys, all go hurrying from many quarters to a common center, the wharf. Assembled there, the people fasten their eyes upon the coming boat as upon a wonder they are seeing for the first time. And the boat *is* rather a handsome sight, too. She is long and sharp and trim and pretty; she has two tall, fancy-topped chimneys, with a gilded device of some kind swung between them; a fanciful pilot-house, all glass and "gingerbread," perched on top of the "texas" deck behind them; the paddle-boxes are gorgeous with a picture or with gilded rays above the boat's name; the boiler-deck, the hurricane-deck, and the texas deck are fenced and ornamented with clean white railings; there is a flag gallantly flying from the jack-staff; the furnace doors are open and the fires glaring bravely; the upper decks are black with passengers; the captain stands by the big bell, calm, imposing, the envy of all; great volumes of the blackest smoke are rolling and tumbling out of the chimneys — a husbanded grandeur created with a bit of pitch-pine just before arriving at a town; the crew are grouped on the forecastle; the broad stage is run far out over the port bow, and an envied deck-hand stands picturesquely on the end of it with a coil of rope in his hand; the pent steam is screaming through the gauge-cocks; the captain lifts his hand, a bell rings, the wheels stop; then they turn back, churning the water to foam, and the steamer is at rest. Then such a scramble as there is to get aboard, and to get ashore, and to take in freight and to discharge freight, all at one and the same time; and such a yelling and cursing as the mates facilitate it all with! Ten minutes later the steamer is under way again, with no flag on the jack-staff and no black smoke issuing from the chimneys. After ten more minutes the town is dead again, and the town drunkard asleep by the skids once more.

My father was a justice of the peace, and I supposed he possessed the power of life and death over all men, and could hang anybody that offended him. This was distinction enough for me as a general thing; but the desire to be a steamboatman kept intruding, nevertheless. I first wanted to be a cabin-boy, so that I could come out with a white apron on and shake a table-cloth over the side, where all my old comrades could see me; later I thought I would rather be the deck-hand who stood on the end of the stage-plank with the coil of rope in his hand, because he was particularly conspicuous. But these were only day-dreams — they were too heavenly to be contemplated as real possibilities. By and by one of our boys went away. He was not heard of for a long time. At last he turned up as apprentice engineer or "striker" on a steamboat. This thing shook the bottom out of all my Sunday-school teachings. That boy had been notoriously worldly, and

I just the reverse; yet he was exalted to this eminence, and I left in obscurity and misery. There was nothing generous about this fellow in his greatness. He would always manage to have a rusty bolt to scrub while his boat tarried at our town, and he would sit on the inside guard and scrub it, where we all could see him and envy him and loathe him. And whenever his boat was laid up he would come home and swell around the town in his blackest and greasiest clothes, so that nobody could help remembering that he was a steamboatman; and he used all sorts of steamboat technicalities in his talk, as if he were so used to them that he forgot common people could not understand them. He would speak of the "labboard" side of a horse in an easy, natural way that would make one wish he was dead. And he was always talking about "St. Looy" like an old citizen; he would refer casually to occasions when he was "coming down Fourth Street," or when he was "passing by the Planter's House," or when there was a fire and he took a turn on the brakes of "the old Big Missouri"; and then he would go on and lie about how many towns the size of ours were burned down there that day. Two or three of the boys had long been persons of consideration among us because they had been to St. Louis once and had a vague general knowledge of its wonders, but the day of their glory was over now. They lapsed into a humble silence, and learned to disappear when the ruthless "cub"-engineer approached. This fellow had money, too, and hair-oil. Also an ignorant silver watch and a showy brass watch-chain. He wore a leather belt and used no suspenders. If ever a youth was cordially admired and hated by his comrades, this one was. No girl could withstand his charms. He "cut out" every boy in the village. When his boat blew up at last, it diffused a tranquil contentment among us such as we had not known for months. But when he came home the next week, alive, renowned, and appeared in church all battered up and bandaged, a shining hero, stared at and wondered over by everybody, it seemed to us that the partiality of Providence for an undeserving reptile had reached a point where it was open to criticism.

This creature's career could produce but one result, and it speedily followed. Boy after boy managed to get on the river. The minister's son became an engineer. The doctor's and the postmaster's sons became "mud clerks"; the wholesale liquor dealer's son became a barkeeper on a boat; four sons of the chief merchant, and two sons of the county judge, became pilots. Pilot was the grandest position of all. The pilot, even in those days of trivial wages, had a princely salary —

from a hundred and fifty to two hundred and fifty dollars a month, and no board to pay. Two months of his wages would pay a preacher's salary for a year. Now some of us were left disconsolate. We could not get on the river — at least our parents would not let us.

So, by and by, I ran away. I said I would never come home again till I was a pilot and could come in glory. But somehow I could not manage it. I went meekly aboard a few of the boats that lay packed together like sardines at the long St. Louis wharf, and humbly inquired for the pilots, but got only a cold shoulder and short words from mates and clerks. I had to make the best of this sort of treatment for the time being, but I had comforting day-dreams of a future when I should be a great and honored pilot, with plenty of money, and could kill some of these mates and clerks and pay for them.

Charlotte L. Forten

Charlotte Forten (1838–1914) was the daughter of a freeborn black, James Forten, who served as a cabin boy aboard a privateer during the American Revolution, was captured by the British, and spent some time in England — where he met his first abolitionists — before he returned to Philadelphia and amassed a fortune in the sailmaking business.

Charlotte was educated by tutors at home until she was sixteen. After being denied admission to a segregated school in Philadelphia, she was sent off to Salem, Massachusetts, a place her father believed to be free of prejudice. There she stayed at the home of a family friend, the well-known mulatto abolitionist Charles Lenox Remond, and began keeping a diary that is rich in many enthusiasms she shared with her father: a love of England ("my beloved England," she sometimes calls it) and a passionate following of the leaders of the abolitionist movement.

Charlotte was not one to pass up a good antislavery demonstration or a fiery sermon, and although she was probably more politically aware than most of her fellow students at the integrated Higginson Grammar School for Girls, she shared their typically Victorian fondness for strolling in cemeteries.

On July 4, 1855, the year following the diary entries excerpted here, Charlotte wrote: "The patriots, poor fools, were celebrating the anniversary of their vaunted independence. Strange! that they cannot feel their own degradation — the weight of the chains which they have imposed upon themselves." Later that year she was graduated and began teaching in Salem. In 1862, while the Civil War was still in progress, she went south to Port Royal, South Carolina, to teach captured slaves who had been isolated so long on an offshore island they did not speak English. In 1878, she married Francis Grimke, a Presbyterian minister whose mother was a slave. His father, a white plantation owner, was the brother of the famous Grimke sisters, the early women's rights activists.

From "Salem Schooldays,"
The Journal of Charlotte L. Forten

Wednesday, May 24, 1854. Rose at five. The sun was shining brightly through my window, and I felt vexed with myself that he should have risen before me; I shall not let him have that advantage again very soon. How bright and beautiful are these May mornings! — The air is so pure and balmy, the trees are in full blossom, and the little birds sing sweetly. I stand by the window listening to their music, but suddenly remember that I have an Arithmetic lesson which employs me until breakfast; then to school, recited my lessons, and commenced my journal. After dinner practiced a music lesson, did some sewing, and then took a pleasant walk by the water. I stood for some time, admiring the waves as they rose and fell, sparkling in the sun, and could not help envying a party of boys who were enjoying themselves in a sailing-boat. On my way home, I stopped at Mrs. Putnam's and commenced reading "Hard Times," a new story by Dickens. . . .

Thursday, May 25, 1854. Did not intend to write this evening, but have just heard of something which is worth recording; — something which must ever rouse in the mind of every true friend of liberty and humanity, feelings of the deepest indignation and sorrow. Another fugitive from bondage [Anthony Burns] has been arrested; a poor man, who for two short months has trod the soil and breathed the air of the "Old Bay State," was arrested like a criminal in the streets of her capital, and is now kept strictly guarded, — a double police force is required, the military are in readiness; and all this is done to prevent a man, whom God has created in his own image, from regaining that freedom with which he, in common with every other human being, is endowed. I can only hope and pray most earnestly that Boston will not again disgrace herself by sending him back to a bondage worse than death; or rather that she will redeem herself from the disgrace which his arrest alone has brought upon her. . . .

Friday, May 26, 1854. Had a conversation with Miss [Mary] Shepard about slavery; she is, as I thought, thoroughly opposed to it, but does not agree with me in thinking that the churches and ministers are generally supporters of the infamous system; I believe it firmly. Mr. Barnes, one of the most prominent of the Philadelphia clergy, who does not profess to be an abolitionist, has declared his belief that 'the American church is the bulwark of slavery.' Words cannot express all that I feel; all that is felt by the friends of Freedom, when thinking of this great obstacle to the removal of slavery from our land. Alas! that it should be so. — I was much disappointed in not seeing the eclipse, which, it was expected would be the most entire that has taken place for years; but the weather was rainy, and the sky obscured by clouds; so after spending half the afternoon on the roof of the house in eager expectation, I saw nothing; heard since that the sun made his appearance for a minute or two, but I was not fortunate enough to catch even that momentary glimpse of him. . . .

Saturday, May 27. . . . Returned home, read the Anti-Slavery papers, and then went down to the depot to meet father, he had arrived in Boston early in the morning, regretted very much that he had not reached there the evening before to attend the great meeting at Faneuil Hall. He says that the excitement in Boston is very great; the trial of the poor man takes place on Monday. We scarcely dare to think of what may be the result; there seems to be nothing too bad for these Northern tools of slavery to do.

Sunday, May 28. A lovely day; in the morning I read in the Bible and wrote letters; in the afternoon took a quiet walk in Harmony Grove [cemetery], and as I passed by many an 'unknown grave,' the question 'who sleeps below?' rose often to my mind, and led to a long train of thoughts, of whose those departed ones might have been, how much beloved, how deeply regretted and how worthy of such love and such regret. I love to walk on the Sabbath, for all is so peaceful; the noise and labor of everyday life has ceased; and in perfect silence we can commune with Nature and with Nature's God. . . .

Tuesday, May 30. Rose very early and was busy until nine o'clock; then, at Mrs. Putnam's urgent request, went to keep store for her while she went to Boston to attend the Anti-Slavery Convention. I was very anxious to go, and will certainly do so tomorrow; the arrest of the alleged fugitive will give additional interest to the meetings, I should think. His trial is still going on and I can scarcely think of anything else. . . .

Wednesday, May 31. . . . Sarah [Redmond] and I went to Boston in the morning. Everything was much quieter — outwardly than we expected, but still much real indignation and excitement prevail. We walked past the Court-House, which is now lawlessly converted into a prison, and filled with soldiers, some of whom were looking from the windows, with an air of insolent authority which made my blood boil, while I felt the strongest contempt for their cowardice and servility.

We went to the meeting, but the best speakers were absent, engaged in the most arduous and untiring efforts in behalf of the poor fugitive; but though we missed the glowing eloquence of [Wendell] Phillips, [William Lloyd] Garrison, and [Theodore] Parker, still there were excellent speeches made, and our hearts responded to the exalted sentiments of Truth and Liberty which were uttered. The exciting intelligence which occasionally came in relation to the trial, added fresh zeal to the speakers, of whom Stephen Foster and his wife were the principal. The latter addressed, in the most eloquent language, the women present, entreating them to urge their husbands and brothers to action, and also to give their aid on all occasions in our just and holy cause. — I did not see father the whole day; he, of course, was deeply interested in the trial. — Dined at Mr. Garrison's; his wife is one of the loveliest persons I have ever seen, worthy of such a husband. At the table, I watched earnestly the expression of that noble face, as he spoke beautifully in support of the non-resistant principles to which he has kept firm; his is indeed the very highest Christian spirit, to which I cannot hope to reach, however, for I believe in 'resistance to tyrants,' and would fight for liberty until death. We came home in the evening, and felt sick at heart as we passed through the streets of Boston on our way to the depot, seeing the military as they rode along, ready at any time to prove themselves the minions of the South.

Thursday, June 1st. . . . The trial is over at last; the commissioner's decision will be given to-morrow. We are all in the greatest suspense; what will that decision be? Alas! that any one should have the power to decide the right of a fellow being to himself! It is thought by many that he will be acquitted of the *great crime* of leaving a life of bondage, as the legal evidence is not thought sufficient to convict him. But it is only too probable that they will sacrifice him to propitiate the South, since so many at the North dared oppose the passage of the infamous Nebraska Bill. — Miss Putnam was married this evening. Mr. Frothingham performed the ceremony, and in his prayer alluded touchingly to the events of this week; he afterwards in conversation with the bridegroom, (Mr. Gilliard), spoke in the most feeling manner about this case; — his sympathies are all on the right side. The wedding was a pleasant one; the bride looked very lovely; and we enjoyed ourselves as much as is possible in these exciting times. It is impossible to be happy now.

Friday, June 2. Our worst fears are realized; the decision was against poor Burns, and he has been sent back to a bondage worse, a thousand times worse than death. Even an attempt at rescue was utterly impossible; the prisoner was completely surrounded by soldiers with bayonets fixed, a cannon loaded, ready to be fired at the slightest sign. To-day Massachusetts has again been disgraced; again has she shewed her submission to the Slave Power; and Oh! with what deep sorrow do we think of what will doubtless be the fate of that poor man, when he is again consigned to the horrors of Slavery. With what scorn must that government be regarded, which cowardly assembles thousands of soldiers to satisfy the demands of slaveholders; to deprive of his freedom a man, created in God's own image, whose sole offence is the color of his skin! And if resistance is offered to this outrage, these soldiers are to shoot down American citizens without mercy; and this by the express orders of a government which proudly boasts of being the freeest [*sic*] in the world; this on the very soil where the Revolution of 1776 began; in sight of the battle-field, where thousands of brave men fought and died in opposing British tyranny, which was nothing compared with the American oppression of to-day. In looking over my diary, I perceive that I did not mention that there was on the Friday night after the man's arrest, an attempt made to rescue him, but although it failed, on account of there not being men enough engaged in it, all honor should be given to those who bravely made the attempt. I can write no more. A cloud seems hanging over me, over all our persecuted race, which nothing can dispel.

Sunday, June 4. A beautiful day. The sky is cloudless, the sun shines warm and bright, and a delicious breeze fans my cheek as I sit by the window writing. How strange it is that in a world so beautiful, there can be so much wickedness; on this delightful day, while many are enjoying themselves in their happy homes, not poor Burns only, but millions beside are suffering in chains; and how many Christian ministers to-day will mention him, or those who suffer with him? . . . To-morrow school commences, and although the pleasure I shall feel in again seeing my beloved teacher, and in resuming my studies will be much saddened by recent events, yet they shall be a fresh incentive to more earnest study, to aid me in fitting myself for laboring in a holy cause, for enabling me to do much towards changing the condition of my oppressed and suffering people. Would that those with whom I shall recite to-morrow could sympathize with me in this; would that they could look upon all God's creatures without respect to color, feeling that it is character alone which makes the true man or woman!

I earnestly hope that the time will come when they will feel thus. . . .

Monday, June 5. Rose very early, after passing a sleepless night. Studied my lessons, and then went to school. Miss [Elizabeth] Church and I counted the merits of the first and second classes for Miss Shepard; after school, had an hour's conversation with her about slavery and prejudice. I fully appreciate her kindness, and sympathy with me; she wishes me to cultivate a Christian spirit in thinking of my enemies; I know it is right, and will endeavor to do so, but it does seem very difficult. . . .

Wednesday, June 7. After school returned home and did some ironing; then practised a music lesson. In the afternoon, read Mr. Parker's sermon on "The New Crime Against Humanity," written with his usual truthful eloquence. I wish that I could have heard him deliver it. The subject naturally possesses the greatest interest to me. . . .

Saturday, June 10. Received two letters, one from father. . . . To my great disappointment, father has decided not to remove to N[ew] England. He is, as I feared he would be, much prejudiced against it on account of the recent slave case, or, he says, he is so against Boston, and I think he extends that feeling to the whole state at least. I shall write to-morrow, and use every argument I can think of, to induce him to change his opinion. I do not wish to have my long-cherished plan of our having together a pleasant N[ew] England home, defeated. In the afternoon went to impart the unwelcome tidings to Miss [Sarah] Remond, who assured me that she had been quite certain of it before. She had a volume of Mrs. Browning's poems, from which I read "Prometheus Bound" and "Casa Guidi Windows". . . .

Monday, June 12. Did not feel very well this morning, but was much better after taking a walk. . . . I enjoyed the novelty of wandering over the hills, and ascending some of the highest of them, had a fine view of the town and harbor. It seemed like a beautiful landscape; and I wished for the artist's power or the poet's still richer gift to immortalize it. I stood and watched the last rays of the glorious sun as it slowly disappeared behind the hills, lending a beautiful tinge, to the water of a winding, romantic little stream that flowed at our feet; and felt so much delighted that it was with reluctance that I left the spot, and turned my steps homeward. . . .

Friday, June 16. Another delightful morning; the sky is cloudless, the sun is shining brightly; and, as I sit by the window, studying, a robin redbreast perched on the large apple tree in the garden, warbles his morning salutation in my ear; — music far sweeter to me than the clearer tones of the Canary birds in their cages, for they are captives, while he is free! I would not keep even a bird in bondage. . . .

Saturday, June 17. A bad headache has prevented my enjoying the fine weather to-day, or taking as much exercise as I generally do. Did some sewing on my return from school. — Read the Liberator, then practised a music lesson. . . . In the evening Miss [Sarah] Remond read aloud Mr. Frothingham's Sermon, whose stern truths shocked so many of his congregation. We, of course, were deeply interested in it, and felt grateful to this truly Christian minister for his eloquent defence of oppressed humanity. While Miss R[emond] was reading, Miss Osborne came in, and said she believed that we never talked or read anything but Anti-Slavery; she was quite tired of it. We assured her that she could never hear anything better; and said it was natural that we should speak and read much, on a subject so interesting to us. . . .

Tuesday, June 20. Rose very early and took a pleasant walk in Danvers. I noticed that nearly every house we passed, however humble in other respects, was adorned with beautiful flowers. The sun has just risen and was shedding his bright rays over hills and trees, lending an additional charm to the beauty of the scene. . . . Went to school. The weather was oppressively hot; one could scarcely study. — In the afternoon wrote a composition; subject, "A Day In June," which was very appropriate. — On my return home, commenced reading Macaulay's History of England. I know that I shall like it, as I do everything that relates to England; there is a charm for me even in its very name. . . .

Friday, June 23. Saw some engravings of castles and mountains in Wales. The scenery was wild and beautiful. How very grand those mountains appear, towering to the very clouds! I should love to see them, and those old, ruined castles, now overgrown with ivy, whose stately rooms, once filled with the gay and the beautiful, are now desolate, and mouldering to decay. — After school, read in the History of England. — Then did some sewing, while Sarah [Remond] read aloud Mr. [Charles L.] Remond's speech in the Convention, which I like very much. . . .

Sunday, June 25. Have been writing nearly all day. — This afternoon went to an Anti-Slavery meeting in Danvers, from which I have just returned. Mr. Foss spoke eloquently, and with that warmth and sincerity which evidently come from the heart. He said he was rejoiced that the people at the North were beginning to feel that slavery is no longer confined to the black man alone, but that they too must wear the yoke; and they are becoming roused on the subject at last. . . . As we walked home, Miss [Sarah] Remond and I were wishing that we could have an anti-slavery meeting in the neighborhood every Sunday, and as well attended as this was. . . .

Monday, June 26.   Went to the Essex Institute and saw many curiosities. Mr. King showed us some specimens from his botanical garden; they were highly magnified; the first we saw was a very small portion of the green slime found in impure water; when seen through the microscope, it appeared like a large piece of seaweed and looked very beautiful. — Then we saw the first growth of a pear tree; every fibre and the many little cells of which it is composed where plainly visible; it resembled another, and still smaller portion of green slime when magnified. Mr. King told us that in the beginning every vegetable substance is composed of the same kind of cells and fibres; so that the largest elm-tree in its first growth resembles this slimy substance. He showed us a very small water-flea so highly magnified that we could see the heart and every palpitation very plainly. . . .

Sunday, July 2.   A delightful day — In the morning read several chapters in the New Testament. The third verse of the last chapter of Hebrews — "Remember them that are in bonds as bound with them" suggested many thougths to my mind: *Remember the poor slave as bound with him.* How few even of those who are opposed to slavery realize this! If they felt thus so ardent, so untiring, would be their efforts that they would soon accomplish the overthrow of this iniquitous system. All honor for the noble few who do feel for the suffering bondman *as bound with him,* and act accordingly! . . .

Friday, July 7.   This afternoon heard a very interesting lecture on Ecuador, and received much useful information concerning that beautiful country; the variety of its climate, soil and productions; the grandeur of its mountain scenery; the splendor of its capital, and the character, dress and manners of its inhabitants. — On my return home, found that Mrs. [C. L.] Remond, with her usual kindness, had arranged that I should take her place in the carrige. I had a delightful ride on the sea shore. The waves looked very beautiful as they rose and fell sparkling in the sunlight. And in the distance, a steamboat which to us appeared to be standing perfectly still, though perhaps in reality it was gliding rapidly over the calm, and deep blue water of the bay, seemed like a single white cloud in the azure sky. We passed "High Rock," at the foot of which stood the residence of the far-famed "Moll Pitcher," the weird heroine of Whittier's beautiful poem. . . . I enjoyed the ride the more because Mr. Redmond allowed me to drive nearly all the way.

Saturday, July 8.   This morning took a very pleasant walk with Miss [Mary] Shepard. We walked through Harmony Grove; the air was pure and balmy, and the trees and flowers looked very beautiful as they waved over the last resting-place of many a loved and lost one. Miss Shepard read several exquisite poems written by the sister of Mrs. Hemans; they are full of deep, tender feeling, and one, a lament for the loss of her loved and highly gifted sister, was particularly touching and beautiful. . . .

Monday, July 10.   I have seen to-day a portrait of Hawthorne, one of the finest that has ever been taken of him. He has a splendid head. That noble, expansive brow bears the unmistakeable impress of genius and superior intellect. And in the depths of those dark, expressive eyes there is a strange, mysterious influence which one feels in reading his works, and which I felt most forcibly when reading that thrilling story "The Scarlet Letter." Yet there is in his countenance no trace of that gloom which pervades some of his writings; particularly that strange tale "The Unpardonable Sin," and many of the "Twice Told Tales." After reading them, I had pictured the author to myself as very dark and gloomy-looking. But I was agreeably disappointed. Grave, earnest, thoughtful, he appears, but not gloomy. His sister, who, with much kindness showed me his portrait, is very singular-looking. She has an eerie, spectral look which instantly brought to my mind the poem of "The Ancient Mariner," and for a moment gave me the strange, undefined feeling of dread and yet of fascination which I so powerfully experienced while reading that ghostly tale. But her cordial, pleasant manner quickly dispelled this feeling. And I soon realized that however peculiar she might appear, or be in reality, she was no "shadowy visitant from another world," as at first I could almost have fancied. She showed me another portrait of Hawthorne taken when he was very young. His countenance, though glowing with genius, has more of the careless, sanguine expression of youth than the profound, elevated thought which distinguishes his maturer years, and gives to his fine face and to his deeply interesting writings that mysterious charm which is felt and acknowledged by all. Miss Hawthorne showed me a piece of the English yew, the "sepulchral yew," whose dark branches are seen in every country churchyard of England and seems there the emblem of mourning as the "weeping willow" here. . . .

Saturday, July 15. Have been very busy today. — On my return from school did some sewing, and made some gingerbread. — Afterwards adopted "Bloomer" costume and ascended the highest cherry tree, which being the first feat of the kind ever performed by me, I deem worthy of note. — Obtained some fine fruit, and felt for the time "monarch of all I surveyed," and then descended from my elevated position. — In the evening spent some time very delightfully with Miss [Mary] Shepard looking over her beautiful books and many elegant little curiosities. . . .

Friday, July 28. This morning Miss Creamer, a friend of our teacher, came into the school. She is a very learned lady; a Latin teacher in Troy Seminary, and an authoress. I certainly did feel some alarm, when I saw her entering the room. But she was so very kind and pleasant that I soon felt more at ease. She asked us a few questions and told an amusing anecdote of one of her pupils. She seems to be a very nervous and excitable person, and I found myself frequently contrasting her appearance with that of our dear teacher, who looked so perfectly calm and composed, that I began to flatter myself that she was not experiencing any uneasiness about our acquitting ourselves creditably. I rather think that I was mistaken in this. But we felt very happy to hear her say afterwards that she was much pleased, and though we did very well. I do think reading one's compositions before strangers is a trying task. If I were to tell Mrs. R[emond] this, I know she would ask how I could expect to become what I often say I should like to be — an Anti-Slavery lecturer. But I think that I should then trust to the inspiration of the subject. — This evening read "Poems of Phillis Wheatly [*sic*]," an African slave, who lived in Boston at the time of the Revolution. She was a wonderfully gifted woman, and many of her poems are very beautiful. Her character and genius afford a striking proof of the falseness of the assertion made by some that hers is an inferior race. . . .

Tuesday, August 1. To-day is the twentieth anniversary of British emancipation. The joy that we feel at an event so just and so glorious is greatly saddened by thoughts of the bitter and cruel oppression which still exists in our own land, so proudly claiming to be "the land of the free." And how very distant seems the day when she will follow the example of "the mother country," and liberate her millions of suffering slaves! This morning I went with Mr. and Mrs. R[emond] to the celebration at Abington. The weather was delightful, and a very large number of persons was assembled in the beautiful grove. Mr.

Garrison, Wendell Phillips and many other distinguished friends of freedom were present, and spoke eloquently. Mr. Garrison gave an interesting account of the rise and progress of the anti-slavery movement in Great Britain. I had not seen Mr. Higginson before. He is very fine looking, and has one of the deepest, richest voices that I have ever heard. I was much pleased with Mr. M'Cluer, a genial, warm-hearted Scotchman who was arrested in Boston during the trial of Burns. He has a broad, Scotch accent which I was particularly delighted to hear as I have been reading very much about Scotland lately. The sadness that I had felt was almost entirely dissipated by the hopeful feelings expressed by the principal speakers. And when they sang the beautiful songs for the occasion, there was something very pleasant in the blending of so many voices in the open air. And still more pleasant to think that it was for a cause so holy that they had assembled then and there. Sarah [Remond] and I had a sail in one of those charming little row-boats which are my particular favorites. It was very delightful to me to feel that I was so near the water; and I could not resist the temptation to cool my hands in the sparkling waves. . . . On returning home we stopped in Boston and passed some time very pleasantly in the Common listening to the music which enlivened the stillness of the sultry night. It was quite late when we reached home. And I retired to rest feeling that this had been one of the happiest days of my life, and thinking hopefully of the happy glorious day when every fetter shall be broken, and throughout this land there shall no longer be a single slave!

Saturday, August 5. To-day vacation commenced. — How busy we have been this morning in school! Lizzie [Church] and I cleared desks and drawers, arranged books and papers, and put everything in order, rejoicing that we could be of the slightest assistance to our dear teacher [Miss Mary Shepard]. I felt very sad to part with that kind friend, even for a few weeks. She gently reproved me when we were parting, for not returning her embrace. I fear she thought me cold, but it was not so. I know not why it is that when I think and feel the most, I say the least. I suppose it is my nature, not to express by word or action how much I really feel. . . .

Tuesday, August 8. Miss [Mary] Shepard has not gone away yet, and this morning I took a delightful walk with her in Harmony Grove. Never did it look so beautiful as on this very loveliest of summer mornings, so happy, so peaceful one almost felt like resting in that quiet spot, beneath the soft, green grass. My teacher talked to me of a beloved sister who is sleeping here. As she spoke, it almost seemed to me as if I had known her; one of those noble, gentle, warm-hearted spiritual beings, too pure and heavenly for his world. . . .

Friday, August 11. I have been thinking lately very much about death, — that strange, mysterious, awful reality, that is constantly around and among us, that power which takes away from us so many of those whom we love and honor, or those who have persecuted and oppressed us, our bitter enemies whom we vainly endeavor not to hate. Oh! I long to be good, to be able to meet death calmly and fearlessly, strong in faith and holiness. . . .

Wednesday, August 16. . . . This evening I had a conversation with Mr. N about the "spiritual rappings." — He is a firm believer in their "spiritual" origin. He spoke of the different manner in which the different "spirits" manifested their presence, — some merely *touching* the mediums, others thoroughly *shaking* them, etc. I told him that I thought I required a very "thorough shaking" to make me a believer. Yet I must not presume to say that I entirely disbelieve that which the wisest cannot understand.

Thursday, August 17. My birthday — How much I feel to-day my own utter insignificance! It is true the years of my life are but few. But have I improved them as I should have done? No! I feel grieved and ashamed to think how very little I know to what I should know of what is really good and useful. May this knowledge of my *want* of knowledge be to me a fresh incentive to more earnest, thoughtful action, more persevering study! I trust, I believe it will. . . .

Friday, August 25. Our usually quiet city has been quite noisy for the last two days with the drums and other accompaniments of the military. — I shall be thankful when their "muster" is over. I never liked soldiers, and since the disgraceful capture of poor Burns, they are more hateful to me than ever.

Henry Adams

*Henry Brooks Adams (1838–1918) was the grandson of John Quincy Adams
and the great-grandson of John Adams. His father, minister to England
during the American Civil War, declined the only nongovernmental job he was
ever offered, the presidency of Harvard. All this, this matter of being an
Adams, weighed heavily on Henry.*

*His early years in Quincy, Massachusetts (called Braintree when his great-
grandfather was born there), are covered in this chapter from* The Education
of Henry Adams. *Later Henry studied law, served as his father's secretary,
and, after moving to Washington, D.C., taught history and took up writing.
His books include two novels (admirers of one of them,* Democracy, *often call
it America's best political novel) and a number of historical studies, including*
Mont-Saint-Michel and Chartres. *Like much of his work,* The Education,
*with its utter disdain for the word "I," was first published privately (in 1906);
the commercial edition became available six months after Adams's death.*

*Before settling into Henry's ironically ornate concerns over what it meant to
come toward the end of the Adamses' line, it might be instructive for the reader
to go back and take a look at Great-grandfather John's far simpler account of
what it was like at the beginning.*

"Quincy (1838–1848)," *The Education of Henry Adams*

UNDER THE SHADOW of Boston State House, turning its back on the
house of John Hancock, the little passage called Hancock Avenue
runs, or ran, from Beacon Street, skirting the State House grounds, to
Mount Vernon Street, on the summit of Beacon Hill; and there, in the
third house below Mount Vernon Place, February 16, 1838, a child
was born, and christened later by his uncle, the minister of the First
Church after the tenets of Boston Unitarianism, as Henry Brooks
Adams.

Had he been born in Jerusalem under the shadow of the Temple and circumcised in the Synagogue by his uncle the high priest, under the name of Israel Cohen, he would scarcely have been more distinctly branded, and not much more heavily handicapped in the races of the coming century, in running for such stakes as the century was to offer; but, on the other hand, the ordinary traveller, who does not enter the field of racing, finds advantage in being, so to speak, ticketed through life, with the safeguards of an old, established traffic. Safeguards are often irksome, but sometimes convenient, and if one needs them at all, one is apt to need them badly. A hundred years earlier, such safeguards as his would have secured any young man's success; and although in 1838 their value was not very great compared with what they would have had in 1738, yet the mere accident of starting a twentieth-century career from a nest of associations so colonial — so troglodytic — as the First Church, the Boston State House, Beacon Hill, John Hancock and John Adams, Mount Vernon Street and Quincy, all crowding on ten pounds of unconscious babyhood, was so queer as to offer a subject of curious speculation to the baby long after he had witnessed the solution. What could become of such a child of the seventeenth and eighteenth centuries, when he should wake up to find himself required to play the game of the twentieth? Had he been consulted, would he have cared to play the game at all, holding such cards as he held, and suspecting that the game was to be one of which neither he nor any one else back to the beginning of time knew the rules or the risks or the stakes? He was not consulted and was not responsible, but had he been taken into the confidence of his parents, he would certainly have told them to change nothing as far as concerned him. He would have been astounded by his own luck. Probably no child, born in the year, held better cards than he. Whether life was an honest game of chance, or whether the cards were marked and forced, he could not refuse to play his excellent hand. He could never make the usual plea of irresponsibility. He accepted the situation as though he had been a party to it, and under the same circumstances would do it again, the more readily for knowing the exact values. To his life as a whole he was a consenting, contracting party and partner from the moment he was born to the moment he died. Only with that understanding — as a consciously assenting member in full partnership with the society of his age — had his education an interest to himself or to others.

As it happened, he never got to the point of playing the game at all; he lost himself in the study of it, watching the errors of the players;

but this is the only interest in the story, which otherwise has no moral and little incident. A story of education — seventy years of it — the practical value remains to the end in doubt, like other values about which men have disputed since the birth of Cain and Abel; but the practical value of the universe has never been stated in dollars. Although every one cannot be a Gargantua-Napoleon-Bismarck and walk off with the great bells of Notre Dame, every one must bear his own universe, and most persons are moderately interested in learning how their neighbors have managed to carry theirs.

This problem of education, started in 1838, went on for three years, while the baby grew, like other babies, unconsciously, as a vegetable, the outside world working as it never had worked before, to get his new universe ready for him. Often in old age he puzzled over the question whether, on the doctrine of chances, he was at liberty to accept himself or his world as an accident. No such accident had ever happened before in human experience. For him, alone, the old universe was thrown into the ash-heap and a new one created. He and his eighteenth-century, troglodytic Boston were suddenly cut apart — separated forever — in act if not in sentiment, by the opening of the Boston and Albany Railroad; the appearance of the first Cunard steamers in the bay; and the telegraphic messages which carried from Baltimore to Washington the news that Henry Clay and James K. Polk were nominated for the Presidency. This was in May, 1844; he was six years old; his new world was ready for use, and only fragments of the old met his eyes.

Of all this that was being done to complicate his education, he knew only the color of yellow. He first found himself sitting on a yellow kitchen floor in strong sunlight. He was three years old when he took this earliest step in education; a lesson of color. The second followed soon; a lesson of taste. On December 3, 1841, he developed scarlet fever. For several days he was as good as dead, reviving only under the careful nursing of his family. When he began to recover strength, about January 1, 1842, his hunger must have been stronger than any other pleasure or pain, for while in after life he retained not the faintest recollection of his illness, he remembered quite clearly his aunt entering the sick-room bearing in her hand a saucer with a baked apple.

The order of impressions retained by memory might naturally be that of color and taste, although one would rather suppose that the sense of pain would be first to educate. In fact, the third recollection

of the child was that of discomfort. The moment he could be removed, he was bundled up in blankets and carried from the little
house in Hancock Avenue to a larger one which his parents were to
occupy for the rest of their lives in the neighboring Mount Vernon
Street. The season was midwinter, January 10, 1842, and he never
forgot his acute distress for want of air under his blankets, or the
noises of moving furniture.

As a means of variation from a normal type, sickness in childhood
ought to have a certain value not to be classed under any fitness or
unfitness of natural selection; and especially scarlet fever affected
boys seriously, both physically and in character, though they might
through life puzzle themselves to decide whether it had fitted or
unfitted them for success; but this fever of Henry Adams took greater
and greater importance in his eyes, from the point of view of education, the longer he lived. At first, the effect was physical. He fell
behind his brothers two or three inches in height, and proportionally
in bone and weight. His character and processes of mind seemed to
share in this fining-down process of scale. He was not good in a fight,
and his nerves were more delicate than boys' nerves ought to be. He
exaggerated these weaknesses as he grew older. The habit of doubt;
of distrusting his own judgment and of totally rejecting the judgment
of the world; the tendency to regard every question as open; the
hesitation to act except as a choice of evils; the shirking of responsibility; the love of line, form, quality; the horror of ennui; the passion
for companionship and the antipathy to society — all these are well-
known qualities of New England character in no way peculiar to individuals but in this instance they seemed to be stimulated by the
fever, and Henry Adams could never make up his mind whether, on
the whole, the change of character was morbid or healthy, good or
bad for his purpose. His brothers were the type; he was the variation.

As far as the boy knew, the sickness did not affect him at all, and he
grew up in excellent health, bodily and mental, taking life as it was
given; accepting its local standards without a difficulty, and enjoying
much of it as keenly as any other boy of his age. He seemed to himself
quite normal, and his companions seemed always to think him so.
Whatever was peculiar about him was education, not character, and
came to him, directly and indirectly, as the result of that eighteenth-
century inheritance which he took with his name.

The atmosphere of education in which he lived was colonial, revolutionary, almost Cromwellian, as though he were steeped, from his

greatest grandmother's birth, in the odor of political crime. Resistance to something was the law of New England nature; the boy looked out on the world with the instinct of resistance; for numberless generations his predecessors had viewed the world chiefly as a thing to be reformed, filled with evil forces to be abolished, and they saw no reason to suppose that they had wholly succeeded in the abolition; the duty was unchanged. That duty implied not only resistance to evil, but hatred of it. Boys naturally look on all force as an enemy, and generally find it so, but the New Englander, whether boy or man, in his long struggle with a stingy or hostile universe, had learned also to love the pleasure of hating; his joys were few.

Politics, as a practice, whatever its professions, had always been the systematic organization of hatreds, and Massachusetts politics had been as harsh as the climate. The chief charm of New England was harshness of contrasts and extremes of sensibility — a cold that froze the blood, and a heat that boiled it — so that the pleasure of hating — one's self if no better victim offered — was not its rarest amusement; but the charm was a true and natural child of the soil, not a cultivated weed of the ancients. The violence of the contrast was real and made the strongest motive of education. The double exterior nature gave life its relative values. Winter and summer, cold and heat, town and country, force and freedom, marked two modes of life and thought, balanced like lobes of the brain. Town was winter confinement, school, rule, discipline; straight, gloomy streets, piled with six feet of snow in the middle; frosts that made the snow sing under wheels or runners; thaws when the streets became dangerous to cross; society of uncles, aunts, and cousins who expected children to behave themselves, and who were not always gratified; above all else, winter represented the desire to escape and go free. Town was restraint, law, unity. Country, only seven miles away, was liberty, diversity, outlawry, the endless delight of mere sense impressions given by nature for nothing, and breathed by boys without knowing it.

Boys are wild animals, rich in the treasures of sense, but the New England boy had a wider range of emotions than boys of more equable climates. He felt his nature crudely, as it was meant. To the boy Henry Adams, summer was drunken. Among senses, smell was the strongest — smell of hot pine-woods and sweet-fern in the scorching summer noon; of new-mown hay; of ploughed earth; of box hedges; of peaches, lilacs, syringas; of stables, barns, cow-yards; of salt water and low tide on the marshes; nothing came amiss. Next to smell came taste, and the children knew the taste of everything they saw or touched, from pennyroyal and flagroot to the shell of a pignut and the letters of a spelling-book — the tasteof A-B, AB, suddenly revived on the boy's tongue sixty years afterwards. Light, line, and color as sensual pleasures, came later and were as crude as the rest. The New England light is glare, and the atmosphere harshens color. The boy was a full man before he ever knew what was meant by atmosphere; his idea of pleasure in light was the blaze of a New England sun. His idea of color was a peony, with the dew of early morning on its petals. The intense blue of the sea, as he saw it a mile or two away, from the Quincy hills; the cumuli in a June afternoon sky; the strong reds and greens and purples of colored prints and children's picture-books, as the American colors then ran; these were ideals. The opposites or antipathies, were the cold grays of November evenings, and the thick, muddy thaws of Boston winter. With such standards, the Bostonian could not but develop a double nature. Life was a double thing. After a January blizzard, the boy who could look with pleasure into the violent snow-glare of the cold white sunshine, with its intense light and shade, scarcely knew what was meant by tone. He could reach it only by education.

Winter and summer, then, were two hostile lives, and bred two separate natures. Winter was always the effort to live; summer was tropical license. Whether the children rolled in the grass, or waded in the brook, or swam in the salt ocean, or sailed in the bay, or fished for smelts in the creeks, or netted minnows in the salt-marshes, or took to the pine-woods and the granite quarries, or chased muskrats and hunted snapping-turtles in the swamps, or mushrooms or nuts on the autumn hills, summer and country were always sensual living, while winter was always compulsory learning. Summer was the multiplicity of nature; winter was school.

The bearing of the two seasons on the education of Henry Adams was no fancy; it was the most decisive force he ever knew; it ran through life, and made the division between its perplexing, warring, irreconcilable problems, irreducible opposites, with growing emphasis to the last year of study. From earliest childhood the boy was accustomed to feel that, for him, life was double. Winter and summer, town and country, law and liberty, were hostile, and the man who pretended they were not, was in his eyes a schoolmaster — that is, a man employed to tell lies to little boys. Though Quincy was but two hours' walk from Beacon Hill, it belonged in a different world. For two hundred years, every Adams, from father to son, had lived within sight of State Street, and sometimes had lived in it, yet none had ever taken kindly to the town, or been taken kindly by it. The boy inherited his double nature. He knew as yet nothing about his great-grandfather, who had died a dozen years before his own birth: he took for granted that any great-grandfather of his must have always been good, and his enemies wicked; but he divined his great-grandfather's character from his own. Never for a moment did he connect the two ideas of Boston and John Adams; they were separate and antagonistic; the idea of John Adams went with Quincy. He knew his grandfather John Quincy Adams only as an old man of seventy-five or eighty who was friendly and gentle with him, but except that he heard his grandfather always called "the President," and his grandmother "the Madam," he had no reason to suppose that his Adams grandfather differed in character from his Brooks grandfather who was equally kind and benevolent. He liked the Adams side best, but for no other reason than that it reminded him of the country, the summer, and the absence of re-straint. Yet he felt also that Quincy was in a way inferior to Boston, and that socially Boston looked down on Quincy. The reason was clear enough even to a five-year old child. Quincy had no Boston style. Little enough style had either; a simpler manner of life and thought could hardly exist, short of cave-dwelling. The flint-and-steel with which his grandfather Adams used to light his own fires in the early morning was still on the mantelpiece of his study. The idea of a livery or even a dress for servants, or of an evening toilette, was next to blasphemy. Bathrooms, water-supplies, lighting, heating, and the whole array of domestic comforts, were unknown at Quincy. Boston had already a bathroom, a water-supply, a furnace, and gas. The superiority of Boston was evident, but a child liked it no better for that.

The magnificence of his grandfather Brooks's house in Pearl Street or South Street has long ago disappeared, but perhaps his country house at Medford may still remain to show what impressed the mind of a boy in 1845 with the idea of city splendor. The President's place at Quincy was the larger and older and far the more interesting of the two; but a boy felt at once its inferiority in fashion. It showed plainly enough its want of wealth. It smacked of colonial age, but not of Boston style or plush curtains. To the end of his life he never quite overcame the prejudice thus drawn in with his childish breath. He never could compel himself to care for nineteenth-century style. He was never able to adopt it, any more than his father or grandfather or great-grandfather had done. Not that he felt it as particularly hostile, for he reconciled himself to much that was worse; but because, for some remote reason, he was born an eighteenth-century child. The old house at Quincy was eighteenth century. What style it had was in its Queen Anne mahogany panels and its Louis Seize chairs and sofas. The panels belonged to an old colonial Vassall who built the house; the furniture had been brought back from Paris in 1789 or 1801 or 1817, along with porcelain and books and much else of old diplomatic remnants; and neither of the two eighteenth-century styles — neither English Queen Anne nor French Louis Seize — was comfortable for a boy, or for any one else. The dark mahogany had been painted white to suit daily life in winter gloom. Nothing seemed to favor, for a child's objects, the older forms. On the contrary, most boys, as well as grown-up people, preferred the new, with good reason, and the child felt himself distinctly at a disadvantage for the taste.

Nor had personal preference any share in his bias. The Brooks grandfather was as amiable and as sympathetic as the Adams grandfather. Both were born in 1767, and both died in 1848. Both were kind to children, and both belonged rather to the eighteenth than to the nineteenth centuries. The child knew no difference between them except that one was associated with winter and the other with summer; one with Boston, the other with Quincy. Even with Medford, the association was hardly easier. Once as a very young boy he was taken to pass a few days with his grandfather Brooks under charge of his aunt, but became so violently homesick that within twenty-four hours he was brought back in disgrace. Yet he could not remember ever being seriously homesick again.

The attachment to Quincy was not altogether sentimental or wholly sympathetic. Quincy was not a bed of thornless roses. Even there the curse of Cain set its mark. There as elsewhere a cruel universe combined to crush a child. As though three or four vigorous brothers and sisters, with the best will, were not enough to crush any child, every one else conspired towards an education which he hated. From cradle to grave this problem of running order through chaos, direction through space, discipline through freedom, unity through multiplicity, has always been, and must always be, the task of education, as it is the moral of religion, philosophy, science, art, politics, and economy; but a boy's will is his life, and he dies when it is broken, as the colt dies in harness, taking a new nature in becoming tame. Rarely has the boy felt kindly towards his tamers. Between him and his master has always been war. Henry Adams never knew a boy of his generation to like a master, and the task of remaining on friendly terms with one's own family, in such a relation, was never easy.

All the more singular it seemed afterwards to him that his first serious contact with the President should have been a struggle of will, in which the old man almost necessarily defeated the boy, but instead of leaving, as usual in such defeats, a lifelong sting, left rather an impression of as fair treatment as could be expected from a natural enemy. The boy met seldom with such restraint. He could not have been much more than six years old at the time — seven at the utmost — and his mother had taken him to Quincy for a long stay with the President during the summer. What became of the rest of the family he quite forgot; but he distinctly remembered standing at the house door one summer morning in a passionate outburst of rebellion against going to school. Naturally his mother was the immediate victim of his rage; that is what mothers are for, and boys also; but in this case the boy had his mother at unfair disadvantage, for she was a guest, and had no means of enforcing obedience. Henry showed a certain tactical ability by refusing to start, and he met all efforts at compulsion by successful, though too vehement protest. He was in fair way to win, and was holding his own, with sufficient energy, at the bottom of the long staircase which led up to the door of the President's library, when the door opened, and the old man slowly came down. Putting on his hat, he took the boy's hand without a word, and walked with him, paralyzed by awe, up the road to the town. After the first moments of consternation at this interference in a domestic dispute, the boy reflected that an old gentleman close on eighty would never trouble himself to walk near a mile on a hot summer morning over a shadeless road to take a boy to school, and that it would be strange if a lad imbued with the passion of freedom could not find a corner to dodge around, somewhere before reaching the school door. Then and always, the boy insisted that this reasoning justified his apparent submission; but the old man did not stop, and the boy saw all his strategical points turned, one after another, until he found himself seated inside the school, and obviously the centre of curious if not malevolent criticism. Not till then did the President release his hand and depart.

The point was that this act, contrary to the inalienable rights of boys, and nullifying the social compact, ought to have made him dislike his grandfather for life. He could not recall that it had this effect even for a moment. With a certain maturity of mind, the child must have recognized that the President, though a tool of tyranny, had done his disreputable work with a certain intelligence. He had shown no temper, no irritation, no personal feeling, and had made no display of force. Above all, he had held his tongue. During their long walk he had said nothing; he had uttered no syllable of revolting cant about the duty of obedience and the wickedness of resistance to law; he had shown no concern in the matter; hardly even a consciousness of the boy's existence. Probably his mind at that moment was actually troubling itself little about his grandson's iniquities, and much about the iniquities of President Polk, but the boy could scarcely at that age feel the whole satisfaction of thinking that President Polk was to be the vicarious victim of his own sins, and he gave his grandfather credit for intelligent silence. For this forbearance he felt instinctive respect. He admitted force as a form of right; he admitted even temper, under protest; but the seeds of a moral education would at that moment have fallen on the stoniest soil in Quincy, which is, as every one knows, the stoniest glacial and tidal drift known in any Puritan land.

Neither party to this momentary disagreement can have felt rancor, for duing these three or four summers the old President's relations with the boy were friendly and almost intimate. Whether his older brothers and sisters were still more favored he failed to remember, but he was himself admitted to a sort of familiarity which, when in his turn he had reached old age, rather shocked him, for it must have sometimes tried the President's patience. He hung about the library; handled the books; deranged the papers; ransacked the drawers; searched the old purses and pocket-books for foreign coins; drew the sword-cane; snapped the travelling-pistols; upset everything in the corners, and penetrated the President's dressing-closet where a row of tumblers, inverted on the shelf, covered caterpillars which were supposed to become moths or butterflies, but never did. The Madam bore with fortitude the loss of the tumblers which her husband purloined for these hatcheries; but she made protest when he carried off her best cut-glass bowls to plant with acorns or peachstones that he might see the roots grow, but which, she said, he commonly forgot like the caterpillars.

At that time the President rode the hobby of tree-culture, and some fine old trees should still remain to witness it, unless they have been improved off the ground; but his was a restless mind, and although he took his hobbies seriously and would have been annoyed had his grandchild asked whether he was bored like an English duke, he probably cared more for the processes than for the results, so that his grandson was saddened by the sight and smell of peaches and pears, the best of their kind, which he brought up from the garden to rot on his shelves for seed. With the inherited virtues of his Puritan ancestors, the little boy Henry conscientiously brought up to him in his study the finest peaches he found in the garden, and ate only the less perfect. Naturally he ate more by way of compensation, but the act showed that he bore no grudge. As for his grandfather, it is even possible that he may have felt a certain self-reproach for his temporary rôle of schoolmaster — seeing that his own career did not offer proof of the worldly advantages of docile obedience — for there still exists somewhere a little volume of critically edited Nursery Rhymes with the boy's name in full written in the President's trembling hand on the fly-leaf. Of course there was also the Bible, given to each child at birth, with the proper inscription in the President's hand on the fly-leaf; while their grandfather Brooks supplied the silver mugs.

So many Bibles and silver mugs had to be supplied, that a new house, or cottage, was built to hold them. It was "on the hill," five minutes' walk above "the old house," with a far view eastward over Quincy Bay, and northward over Boston. Till his twelfth year, the child passed his summers there, and his pleasures of childhood mostly centered in it. Of education he had as yet little to complain. Country schools were not very serious. Nothing stuck to the mind except home impressions, and the sharpest were those of kindred children; but as influences that warped a mind, none compared with the mere effect of the back of the President's bald head, as he sat in his pew on Sundays, in line with that of President Quincy, who, though some ten years younger, seemed to children about the same age. Before railways entered the New England town, every parish church showed half-a-dozen of these leading citizens, with gray hair, who sat on the main aisle in the best pews, and had sat there, or in some equivalent dignity, since the time of St. Augustine, if not since the glacial epoch. It was unusual for boys to sit behind a President grandfather, and to read over his head the tablet in memory of a President great-grandfather, who had "pledged his life, his fortune, and his sacred honor" to secure the independence of his country and so forth; but boys naturally supposed, without much reasoning, that other boys had the equivalent of President grandfathers, and that churches would always go on, with the bald-headed leading citizens on the main aisle, and Presidents or their equivalents on the walls. The Irish gardener once said to the child: "You'll be thinkin' you'll be President too!" The casualty of the remark made so strong an impression on his mind that he never forgot it. He could not remember ever to have thought on the subject; to him, that there should be a doubt of his being President was a new idea. What had been would continue to be. He doubted neither about Presidents nor about Churches, and no one suggested at that time a doubt whether a system of society which had lasted since Adam would outlast one Adams more.

The Madam was a little more remote than the President, but more decorative. She stayed much in her own room with the Dutch tiles, looking out on her garden with the box walks, and seemed a fragile creature to a boy who sometimes brought her a note or a message, and took distinct pleasure in looking at her delicate face under what seemed to him very becoming caps. He liked her refined figure; her gentle voice and manner; her vague effect of not belonging there, but to Washington or to Europe, like her furniture, and writing-desk with little glass doors above and little eighteenth-century volumes in old binding, labelled "Peregrine Pickle" or "Tom Jones" or "Hannah More." Try as she might, the Madam could never be Bostonian, and it was her cross in life, but to the boy it was her charm. Even at that age, he felt drawn to it. The Madam's life had been in truth far from Boston. She was born in London in 1775, daughter of Joshua Johnson, an American merchant, brother of Governor Thomas Johnson of Maryland; and Catherine Nuth, of an English family in London. Driven from England by the Revolutionary War, Joshua Johnson took his family to Nantes, where they remained till the peace. The girl Louisa Catherine was nearly ten years old when brought back to London, and her sense of nationality must have been confused; but the influence of the Johnsons and the services of Joshua obtained for him from President Washington the appointment of Consul in London on the organization of the Government in 1790. In 1794 President Washington appointed John Quincy Adams Minister to The Hague. He was twenty-seven years old when he returned to London, and found the Consul's house a very agreeable haunt. Louisa was then twenty.

At that time, and long afterwards, the Consul's house, far more than the Minister's, was the centre of contact for travelling Americans, either official or other. The Legation was a shifting point, between

1785 and 1815; but the Consulate, far down in the City, near the Tower, was convenient and inviting; so inviting that it proved fatal to young Adams. Louisa was charming, like a Romney portrait, but among her many charms that of being a New England woman was not one. The defect was serious. Her future mother-in-law, Abigail, a famous New England woman whose authority over her turbulent husband, the second President, was hardly so great as that which she exercised over her son, the sixth to be, was troubled by the fear that Louisa might not be made of stuff stern enough, or brought up in conditions severe enough, to suit a New England climate, or to make an efficient wife for her paragon son, and Abigail was right on that point, as on most others where sound judgment was involved; but sound judgment is sometimes a source of weakness rather than of force, and John Quincy already had reason to think that his mother held sound judgments on the subject of daughters-in-law which human nature, since the fall of Eve, made Adams helpless to realize. Being three thousand miles away from his mother, and equally far in love, he married Louisa in London, July 26, 1797, and took her to Berlin to be the head of the United States Legation. During three or four exciting years, the young bride lived in Berlin; whether she was happy or not, whether she was content or not, whether she was socially successful or not, her descendants did not surely know; but in any case she could by no chance have become educated there for a life in Quincy or Boston. In 1801 the overthrow of the Federalist Party drove her and her husband to America, and she became at last a member of the Quincy household, but by that time her children needed all her attention, and she remained there with occasional winters in Boston and Washington, till 1809. Her husband was made Senator in 1803, and in 1809 was appointed Minister to Russia. She went with him to St. Petersburg, taking her baby, Charles Francis, born in 1807; but broken-hearted at having to leave her two older boys behind. The life at St. Petersburg was hardly gay for her; they were far too poor to shine in that extravagant society; but she survived it, though her little girl baby did not, and in the winter of 1814–15, alone with the boy of seven years old, crossed Europe from St. Petersburg to Paris, in her travelling-carriage, passing through the armies, and reaching Paris in the *Cent Jours* after Napoleon's return from Elba. Her husband next went to England as Minister, and she was for two years at the Court of the Regent. In 1817 her husband came home to be Secretary of State, and she lived for eight years in F

Street, doing her work of entertainer for President Monroe's administration. Next she lived four miserable years in the White House. When that chapter was closed in 1829, she had earned the right to be tired and delicate, but she still had fifteen years to serve as wife of a Member of the House, after her husband went back to Congress in 1833. Then it was that the little Henry, her grandson, first remembered her, from 1845 to 1848, sitting in her panelled room, at breakfast, with her heavy silver teapot and sugar-bowl and cream-jug, which still exist somewhere as an heirloom of the modern safety-vault. By that time she was seventy years old or more, and thoroughly weary of being beaten about a stormy world. To the boy she seemed singularly peaceful, a vision of silver gray, presiding over her old President and her Queen Anne mahogany; an exotic, like her Sèvres china; an object of deference to every one, and of great affection to her son Charles; but hardly more Bostonian than she had been fifty years before, on her wedding-day, in the shadow of the Tower of London.

Such a figure was even less fitted than that of her old husband, the President, to impress on a boy's mind, the standards of the coming century. She was Louis Seize, like the furniture. The boy knew nothing of her interior life, which had been, as the venerable Abigail, long since at peace, foresaw, one of severe stress and little pure satisfaction. He never dreamed that from her might come some of those doubts and self-questionings, those hesitations, those rebellions against law and discipline, which marked more than one of her descendants; but he might even then have felt some vague instinctive suspicion that he was to inherit from her the seeds of the primal sin, the fall from grace, the curse of Abel, that he was not of pure New England stock, but half exotic. As a child of Quincy he was not a true Bostonian, but even as a child of Quincy he inherited a quarter taint of Maryland blood. Charles Francis, half Marylander by birth, had hardly seen Boston till he was ten years old, when his parents left him there at school in 1817, and he never forgot the experience. He was to be nearly as old as his mother had been in 1845, before he quite accepted Boston, or Boston quite accepted him.

A boy who began his education in these surroundings, with physical strength inferior to that of his brothers, and with a certain delicacy of mind and bone, ought rightly to have felt at home in the eighteenth century and should, in proper self-respect, have rebelled against the standards of the nineteenth. The atmosphere of his first ten years must have been very like that of his grandfather at the same age, from

1767 till 1776, barring the battle of Bunker Hill, and even as late as 1846, the battle of Bunker Hill remained actual. The tone of Boston society was colonial. The true Bostonian always knelt in self-abasement before the majesty of English standards; far from concealing it as a weakness, he was proud of it as his strength. The eighteenth century ruled society long after 1850. Perhaps the boy began to shake it off rather earlier than most of his mates.

Indeed this prehistoric stage of education ended rather abruptly with his tenth year. One winter morning he was conscious of a certain confusion in the house in Mount Vernon Street, and gathered, from such words as he could catch, that the President, who happened to be then staying there, on his way to Washington, had fallen and hurt himself. Then he heard the word paralysis. After that day he came to associate the word with the figure of his grandfather, in a tall-backed, invalid armchair, on one side of the spare bedroom fireplace, and one of his old friends, Dr. Parkman or P. P. F. Degrand, on the other side, both dozing.

The end of this first, or ancestral and Revolutionary, chapter came on February 21, 1848 — and the month of February brought life and death as a family habit — when the eighteenth century, as an actual and living companion, vanished. If the scene on the floor of the House, when the old President fell, struck the still simple-minded American public with a sensation unusually dramatic, its effect on a ten-year-old boy, whose boy-life was fading away with the life of his grandfather, could not be slight. One had to pay for Revolutionary patriots; grandfathers and grandmothers; Presidents; diplomats; Queen Anne mahogany and Louis Seize chairs, as well as for Stuart portraits. Such things warp young life. Americans commonly believed that they ruined it, and perhaps the practical common-sense of the American mind judged right. Many a boy might be ruined by much less than the emotions of the funeral service in the Quincy church, with its surroundings of national respect and family pride. By another dramatic chance it happened that the clergyman of the parish, Dr. Lunt, was an unusual pulpit orator, the ideal of a somewhat austere intellectual type, such as the school of Buckminster and Channing inherited from the old Congregational clergy. His extraordinary re-fined appearance, his dignity of manner, his deeply cadenced voice, his remarkable English and his fine appreciation, gave to the funeral service a character that left an overwhelming impression on the boy's mind. He was to see many great functions — funerals and festivals —

in after-life, till his only thought was to see no more, but he never again witnessed anything nearly so impressive to him as the last services at Quincy over the body of one President and the ashes of another.

The effect of the Quincy service was deepened by the official ceremony which afterwards took place in Faneuil Hall, when the boy was taken to hear his uncle, Edward Everett, deliver a Eulogy. Like all Mr. Everett's orations, it was an admirable piece of oratory, such as only an admirable orator and scholar could create; too good for a ten-year-old boy to appreciate at its value; but already the boy knew that the dead President could not be in it, and had even learned why he would have been out of place there; for knowledge was beginning to come fast. The shadow of the War of 1812 still hung over State Street; the shadow of the Civil War to come had already begun to darken Faneuil Hall. No rhetoric could have reconciled Mr. Everett's audience to his subject. How could he say there, to an assemblage of Bostonians in the heart of mercantile Boston, that the only distinctive mark of all the Adamses, since old Sam Adams's father a hundred and fifty years before, had been their inherited quarrel with State Street, which had again and again broken out into riot, bloodshed, personal feuds, foreign and civil war, wholesale banishments and confiscations, until the history of Florence was hardly more turbulent than that of Boston? How could he whisper the word Hartford Convention before the men who had made it? What would have been said had he suggested the chance of Secession and Civil War?

Thus already, at ten years old, the boy found himself standing face to face with a dilemma that might have puzzled an early Christian. What was he? — where was he going? Even then he felt that something was wrong, but he concluded that it must be Boston. Quincy had always been right, for Quincy represented a moral principle — the principle of resistance to Boston. His Adams ancestors must have been right, since they were always hostile to State Street. If State Street was wrong, Quincy must be right! Turn the dilemma as he pleased, he still came back on the eighteenth century and the law of Resistance; of Truth; of Duty, and of Freedom. He was a ten-year-old priest and politician. He could under no circumstances have guessed what the next fifty years had in store, and no one could teach him; but sometimes, in his old age, he wondered — and could never decide — whether the most clear and certain knowledge would have helped him. Supposing he had seen a New York stock-list of 1900, and had studied the statistics of railways, telegraphs, coal, and steel — would he have quitted his eighteenth-century, his ancestral prejudices, his abstract ideals, his semi-clerical training, and the rest, in order to perform an expiatory pilgrimage to State Street, and ask for the fatted calf of his grandfather Brooks and a clerkship in the Suffolk Bank?

Sixty years afterwards he was still unable to make up his mind. Each course had its advantages, but the material advantages, looking back, seemed to lie wholly in State Street.

Charles Eastman (Ohiyesa)

In spite of his many accomplishments, Charles Alexander Eastman (1858–1939) spent much of his life playing the part of the white man's favorite redskin. When it came time — as it did at the 1933 Century of Progress Exposition in Chicago — to give someone a medal celebrating "what an Indian could achieve," Eastman, or Ohiyesa, as he liked to call himself, was often the one called upon.

Eastman's maternal grandfather was a white army officer named Seth Eastman, who won considerable fame for his paintings of western life. Seth's wife Mary, a Virginian, was well known, at least in the South, for her novel Aunt Phillis's Cabin, or Southern Life As It Is, *an answer to* Uncle Tom's Cabin. *Based on her experiences as an army wife at Fort Snelling, Minnesota, she also wrote several books on Indian legends and folklore. The introduction to Charles Eastman's autobiography of his adult years,* From the Deep Woods to Civilization, *does not mention Mary but says that Seth was married to the daughter of Chief Cloudman, a Sioux, and that their daughter married Many Lightnings and had five children. The youngest, born in Redwood Falls, Minnesota, was named The Pitiful Last (in Sioux) because his mother died in childbirth. Years later, after playing in a hard-won lacrosse game, the boy was renamed Ohiyesa, The Winner.*

Charles Eastman grew up with his Sioux grandmother and her family in Minnesota and Canada, was graduated from Dartmouth, and then went on to Boston University for a medical degree. He served as a physician on the Pine Ridge Reservation, where he treated the casualties of the Wounded Knee massacre, and also acted as an attorney in Washington on legal matters concerning the Sioux nation. But he was best known in the white world for his many books that presented a romanticized but factually detailed portrait of Plains Indian life. Indian Boyhood, *from which this excerpt is taken, deals with Ohiyesa's earliest memories. Published in 1902, it was Eastman's first book. The more fanciful collections of legends and stories prepared for reading around Boy Scout campfires came later.*

"An Indian Sugar Camp," *Indian Boyhood*

WITH THE FIRST MARCH THAW the thoughts of the Indian women of my childhood days turned promptly to the annual sugar-making. This industry was chiefly followed by the old men and women and the children. The rest of the tribe went out upon the spring fur-hunt at this season, leaving us at home to make the sugar.

The first and most important of the necessary utensils were the huge iron and brass kettles for boiling. Everything else could be made, but these must be bought, begged or borrowed. A maple tree was felled and a log canoe hollowed out, into which the sap was to be gathered. Little troughs of basswood and birchen basins were also made to receive the sweet drops as they trickled from the tree.

As soon as these labors were accomplished, we all proceeded to the bark sugar house, which stood in the midst of a fine grove of maples on the bank of the Minnesota river. We found this hut partially filled with the snows of winter and the withered leaves of the preceding autumn, and it must be cleared for our use. In the meantime a tent was pitched outside for a few days' occupancy. The snow was still deep in the woods, with a solid crust upon which we could easily walk; for we usually moved to the sugar house before the sap had actually started, the better to complete our preparations.

My grandmother worked like a beaver in these days (or rather like a muskrat, as the Indians say; for this industrious little animal sometimes collects as many as six or eight bushels of edible roots for the winter, only to be robbed of his store by some of our people). If there was prospect of a good sugaring season, she now made a second and even a third canoe to contain the sap. These canoes were afterward utilized by the hunters for their proper purpose.

During our last sugar-making in Minnesota, before the "outbreak," my grandmother was at work upon a canoe with her axe, while a young aunt of mine stood by. We boys were congregated within the large, oval sugar house, busily engaged in making arrows for the destruction of the rabbits and chipmunks which we knew would come in numbers to drink the sap. The birds also were beginning to return, and the cold storms of March would drive them to our door. I was then too young to do much except look on; but I fully entered into the spirit of the occasion, and rejoiced to see the bigger boys industriously sharpen their arrows, resting them against the ends of the long sticks which were burning in the fire, and occasionally cutting a chip from the stick. In their eagerness they paid little attention to this circumstance, although they well knew that it was strictly forbidden to touch a knife to a burning ember.

Suddenly loud screams were heard from without and we all rushed out to see what was the matter. It was a serious affair. My grandmother's axe had slipped, and by an upward stroke nearly severed three of the fingers of my aunt, who stood looking on, with her hands folded upon her waist. As we ran out the old lady, who had already noticed and reproved our carelessness in regard to the burning embers, pursued us with loud reproaches and threats of a whipping. This will seem mysterious to my readers, but is easily explained by the Indian superstition, which holds that such an offense as we had committed is invariably punished by the accidental cutting of some one of the family.

My grandmother did not confine herself to canoe-making. She also collected a good supply of fuel for the fires, for she would not have much time to gather wood when the sap began to flow. Presently the weather moderated and the snow began to melt. The month of April brought showers which carried most of it off into the Minnesota river. Now the women began to test the trees — moving leisurely among them, axe in hand, and striking a single quick blow, to see if the sap would appear. The trees, like people, have their individual characters; some were ready to yield up their life-blood, while others were more reluctant. Now one of the birchen basins was set under each tree, and a hardwood chip driven deep into the cut which the axe had made. From the corners of this chip — at first drop by drop, then more freely — the sap trickled into the little dishes.

It is usual to make sugar from maples, but several other trees were also tapped by the Indians. From the birch and ash was made a dark-colored sugar, with a somewhat bitter taste, which was used for medicinal purposes. The box-elder yielded a beautiful white sugar, whose only fault was that there was never enough of it!

A long fire was now made in the sugar house, and a row of brass kettles suspended over the blaze. The sap was collected by the women in tin or birchen buckets and poured into the canoes, from which the kettles were kept filled. The hearts of the boys beat high with pleasant anticipations when they heard the welcome hissing sound of the boiling sap! Each boy claimed one kettle for his especial charge. It was his duty to see that the fire was kept up under it, to watch lest it boil over, and finally, when the sap became sirup, to test it upon the snow, dipping it out with a wooden paddle. So frequent were these tests that for the first day or two we consumed nearly all that could be made; and it was not until the sweetness began to pall that my grandmother set herself in earnest to store up sugar for future use. She made it into cakes of various forms, in birchen molds, and sometimes in hollow canes or reeds, and the bills of ducks and geese. Some of it was pulverized and packed in rawhide cases. Being a prudent woman, she did not give it to us after the first month or so, except upon special occasions, and it was thus made to last almost the year around. The smaller candies were reserved as an occasional treat for the little fellows, and the sugar was eaten at feasts with wild rice or parched corn, and also with pounded dried meat. Coffee and tea, with their substitutes, were all unknown to us in those days.

Every pursuit has its trials and anxieties. My grandmother's special tribulations, during the sugaring season, were the upsetting and gnawing of holes in her birch-bark pans. The transgressors were the rabbit and squirrel tribes, and we little boys for once became useful, in shooting them with our bows and arrows. We hunted all over the sugar camp, until the little creatures were fairly driven out of the neighborhood. Occasionally one of my older brothers brought home a rabbit or two, and then we had a feast.

The sugaring season extended well into April, and the returning birds made the precincts of our camp joyful with their songs. I often followed my older brothers into the woods, although I was then but four or five years old. Upon one of these excursions they went so far that I ventured back alone. When within sight of our hut, I saw a chipmunk sitting upon a log, and uttering the sound he makes when he calls to his mate. How glorious it would be, I thought, if I could shoot him with my tiny bow and arrows! Stealthily and cautiously I approached, keeping my eyes upon the pretty little animal, and just as I was about to let fly my shaft, I heard a hissing noise at my feet. There lay a horrid snake, coiled and ready to spring! Forgetful that I was a warrior, I gave a loud scream and started backward; but soon recollecting myself, looked down with shame, although no one was near. However, I retreated to the inclined trunk of a fallen tree, and there, as I have often been told, was overheard soliloquizing in the following words: "I wonder if a snake can climb a tree!"

I remember on this occasion of our last sugar bush in Minnesota, that I stood one day outside of our hut and watched the approach of a visitor — a bent old man, his hair almost white, and carrying on his back a large bundle of red willow, or kinnikinick, which the Indians use for smoking. He threw down his load at the door and thus saluted us: "You have indeed perfect weather for sugar-making."

It was my great-grandfather, Cloud Man, whose original village was on the shores of Lakes Calhoun and Harriet, now in the suburbs of the city of Minneapolis. He was the first Sioux chief to welcome the Protestant missionaries among his people, and a well-known character in those pioneer days. He brought us word that some of the peaceful sugar-makers near us on the river had been attacked and murdered by roving Ojibways. This news disturbed us not a little, for we realized that we too might become the victims of an Ojibway war party. Therefore we all felt some uneasiness from this time until we returned heavy laden to our village.

Black Elk

In 1930, the Nebraska poet John G. Neihardt went to the Pine Ridge Reservation of the Oglala Sioux to do research for a long poem on the Indian Messiah movement that flourished among the Sioux in the 1880s and ended with the Wounded Knee massacre in 1890. There he met Black Elk (1863–1950), a holy man and mystic, cousin of Chief Crazy Horse and survivor of the battle of Little Big Horn. Black Elk spoke no English, but using an interpreter, usually his son, he in time told Neihardt not only his own personal story but also the history of his tribe and his mystical vision of a better world. The result, edited and possibly rewritten a bit by Neihardt, was Black Elk Speaks, *published in 1932.*

This excerpt covers Black Elk's earliest memories, his first mystical experiences, an early tribal clash with white men (recalled by a slightly older friend), and a successful bison hunt. Black Elk would later travel for three years throughout the United States and Europe with Buffalo Bill's Wild West Show. But unlike his contemporary Charles Eastman (Ohiyesa), he was never tempted to become a part of the white man's world. Like Eastman, however, he clearly wanted the white man to know his own and his people's story.

From "Early Boyhood," "The Great Vision," "The Bison Hunt," and "At the Soldiers' Town," *Black Elk Speaks*

I AM A LAKOTA of the Ogalala band. My father's name was Black Elk, and his father before him bore the name, and the father of his father, so that I am the fourth to bear it. He was a medicine man and so were several of his brothers. Also, he and the great Crazy Horse's father were cousins, having the same grandfather. My mother's name was White Cow Sees; her father was called Refuse-to-go, and her mother, Plenty Eagle Feathers. I can remember my mother's mother and her father. My father's father was killed by the Pawnees when I was too little to know, and his mother, Red Eagle Woman, died soon after.

I was born in the Moon of the Popping Trees (December) on the Little Powder River in the Winter When the Four Crows Were Killed (1863), and I was three years old when my father's right leg was broken in the Battle of the Hundred Slain.* From that wound he limped until the day he died, which was about the time when Big Foot's band was butchered on Wounded Knee (1890). He is buried here in these hills.

I can remember that Winter of the Hundred Slain as a man may remember some bad dream he dreamed when he was little, but I can not tell just how much I heard when I was bigger and how much I understood when I was little. It is like some fearful thing in a fog, for it was a time when everything seemed troubled and afraid.

I had never seen a Wasichu† then, and did not know what one looked like; but every one was saying that the Wasichus were coming and that they were going to take our country and rub us all out and that we should all have to die fighting. It was the Wasichus who got rubbed out in that battle, and all the people were talking about it for a long while; but a hundred Wasichus was not much if there were others and others without number where those came from.

I remember once that I asked my grandfather about this. I said: "When the scouts come back from seeing the prairie full of bison somewhere, the people say the Wasichus are coming; and when strange men are coming to kill us all, they say the Wasichus are coming. What does it mean?" And he said, "That they are many."

When I was older, I learned what the fighting was about that winter and the next summer. Up on the Madison Fork the Wasichus had found much of the yellow metal that they worship and that makes them crazy, and they wanted to have a road up through our country to the place where the yellow metal was; but my people did not want the road. It would scare the bison and make them go away, and also it would let the other Wasichus come in like a river. They told us that they wanted only to use a little land, as much as a wagon would take

---

* The Fetterman Fight, commonly described as a "massacre," in which Captain Fetterman and 81 men were wiped out on Peno Creek near Fort Phil Kearney, December 21, 1866.

† A term used to designate the white man, but having no reference to the color of his skin.

between the wheels; but our people knew better. And when you look about you now, you can see what it was they wanted.

Once we were happy in our own country and we were seldom hungry, for then the two-leggeds and the four-leggeds lived together like relatives, and there was plenty for them and for us. But the Wasichus came, and they have made little islands for us and other little islands for the four-leggeds, and always these islands are becoming smaller, for around them surges the gnawing flood of the Wasichu; and it is dirty with lies and greed.

A long time ago my father told me what his father told him, that there was once a Lakota holy man, called Drinks Water, who dreamed what was to be; and this was long before the coming of the Wasichus. He dreamed that the four-leggeds were going back into the earth and that a strange race had woven a spider's web all around the Lakotas. And he said: "When this happens, you shall live in square gray houses, in a barren land, and beside those square gray houses you shall starve." They say he went back to Mother Earth soon after he saw this vision, and it was sorrow that killed him. You can look about you now and see that he meant these dirt-roofed houses we are living in, and that all the rest was true. Sometimes dreams are wiser than waking.

And so when the soldiers came and built themselves a town of logs there on the Piney Fork of the Powder, my people knew they meant to have their road and take our country and maybe kill us all when they were strong enough. Crazy Horse was only about 19 years old then, and Red Cloud was still our great chief. In the Moon of the Changing Season (October) he called together all the scattered bands of the Lakota for a big council on the Powder River, and when we went on the warpath against the soldiers, a horseback could ride through our villages from sunrise until the day was above his head, so far did our camp stretch along the valley of the river; for many of our friends, the Shyela [Cheyennes] and the Blue Clouds [Arapahoes], had come to help us fight.

And it was about when the bitten moon was delayed (last quarter) in the Time of the Popping Trees when the hundred were rubbed out. My friend, Fire Thunder here, who is older than I, was in that fight and he can tell you how it was.

FIRE THUNDER SPEAKS:

I was 16 years old when this happened, and after the big council on the Powder we had moved over to the Tongue River where we were camping at the mouth of Peno Creek. There were many of us there. Red Cloud was over all of us, but the chief of our band was Big Road. We started out on horseback just about sunrise, riding up the creek toward the soldiers' town on the Piney, for we were going to attack it. The sun was about half way up when we stopped at the place where the Wasichu's road came down a steep, narrow ridge and crossed the creek. It was a good place to fight, so we sent some men ahead to coax the soldiers out. While they were gone, we divided into two parts and hid in the gullies on both sides of the ridge and waited. After a long while we heard a shot up over the hill, and we knew the soldiers were coming. So we held the noses of our ponies that they might not whinny at the soldiers' horses. Soon we saw our men coming back, and some of them were walking and leading their horses, so that the soldiers would think they were worn out. Then the men we had sent ahead came running down the road between us, and the soldiers on horseback followed, shooting. When they came to the flat at the bottom of the hill, the fighting began all at once. I had a sorrel horse, and just as I was going to get on him, the soldiers turned around and began to fight their way back up the hill. I had a six-shooter that I had traded for, and also a bow and arrows. When the soldiers started back, I held my sorrel with one hand and began killing them with the six-shooter, for they came close to me. There were many bullets, but there were more arrows — so many that it was like a cloud of grasshoppers all above and around the soldiers; and our people, shooting across, hit each other. The soldiers were falling all the while they were fighting back up the hill, and their horses got loose. Many of our people chased the horses, but I was not after horses; I was after Wasichus. When the soldiers got on top, there were not many of them left and they had no place to hide. They were fighting hard. We were told to crawl up on them, and we did. When we were close, someone yelled: "Let us go! This is a good day to die. Think of the helpless ones at home!" Then we all cried, "Hoka hey!" and rushed at them. I was young then and quick on my feet, and I was one of the first to get in among the soldiers. They got up and fought very hard until not one of them was alive. They had a dog with them, and he started back up the road for the soldiers' town, howling as he ran. He was the only one left. I did not shoot at him because he looked too sweet, but many did shoot, and he died full of arrows. So there was nobody left of the soldiers. Dead men and horses and wounded Indians were scattered all the way up the hill, and their blood was frozen, for a storm had come up and it was very cold and getting colder all the time. We left all the dead lying there, for the ground was solid, and we picked up our wounded and started back; but we lost most of them before we reached our camp at the mouth of the Peno. There was a big blizzard that night; and some of the wounded who did not die on the way, died after we got home. This was the time when Black Elk's father had his leg broken.

BLACK ELK CONTINUES:

I am quite sure that I remember the time when my father came home with a broken leg that he got from killing so many Wasichus, and it seems that I can remember all about the battle too, but I think I could not. It must be the fear that I remember most. All this time I was not allowed to play very far away from our tepee, and my mother would say, "If you are not good the Wasichus will get you."

We must have broken camp at the mouth of the Peno soon after the battle, for I can remember my father lying on a pony drag with bison robes all around him, like a baby, and my mother riding the pony. The snow was deep and it was very cold, and I remember sitting in another pony drag beside my father and mother, all wrapped up in fur. We were going away from where the soldiers were, and I do not know where we went, but it was west.

It was a hungry winter, for the deep snow made it hard to find the elk; and also many of the people went snowblind. We wandered a long time, and some of the bands got lost from each other. Then at last we were camping in the woods beside a creek somewhere, and the hunters came back with meat.

I think it was this same winter when a medicine man, by the name of Creeping, went around among the people curing snowblinds. He would put snow upon their eyes, and after he had sung a certain sacred song that he had heard in a dream, he would blow on the backs of their heads and they would see again, so I have heard. It was about the dragonfly that he sang, for that was where he got his power, they say.

When it was summer again we were camping on the Rosebud, and I did not feel so much afraid, because the Wasichus seemed farther away and there was peace there in the valley and there was plenty of meat. But all the boys from five or six years up were playing war. The little boys would gather together from the different bands of the tribe and fight each other with mud balls that they threw with willow sticks. And the big boys played the game called Throwing-Them-Off-Their-

Horses, which is a battle all but the killing; and sometimes they got hurt. The horsebacks from the different bands would line up and charge upon each other, yelling; and when the ponies came together on the run, they would rear and flounder and scream in a big dust, and the riders would seize each other, wrestling until one side had lost all its men, for those who fell upon the ground were counted dead.

When I was older, I, too, often played this game. We were always naked when we played it, just as warriors are when they go into battle if it is not too cold, because they are swifter without clothes. Once I fell off on my back right in the middle of a bed of prickly pears, and it took my mother a long while to pick all the stickers out of me. I was still too little to play war that summer, but I can remember watching the other boys, and I thought that when we all grew up and were big together, maybe we could kill all the Wasichus or drive them far away from our country.

It was in the Moon When the Cherries Turn Black (August) that all the people were talking again about a battle, and our warriors came back with many wounded. It was The Attacking of the Wagons,* and it made me afraid again, for we did not win that battle as we did the other one, and there was much mourning for the dead. Fire Thunder was in that fight too, and he can tell you how it was that day.

FIRE THUNDER SPEAKS:

It was very bad. There is a wide flat prairie with hills around it, and in the middle of this the Wasichus had put the boxes of their wagons in a circle, so that they could keep their mules there at night. There were not many Wasichus, but they were lying behind the boxes and they shot faster than they ever shot at us before. We thought it was some new medicine of great power that they had, for they shot so fast that it was like tearing a blanket. Afterwards I learned that it was because they had new guns that they loaded from behind, and this was the first time they used these guns.† We came on after sunrise. There were many, many of us, and we meant to ride right over them and rub them out. But our ponies were afraid of the ring of fire the guns of the Wasichus made, and would not go over. Our women were watching us from the hills and we could hear them singing and

---

* The Wagon Box Fight, which took place about six miles west of Fort Phil Kearney on August 2, 1867.

† Breech-loading Springfields.

mourning whenever the shooting stopped. We tried hard, but we could not do it, and there were dead warriors and horses piled all around the boxes and scattered over the plain. Then we left our horses in a gulch and charged on foot, but it was like green grass withering in a fire. So we picked up our wounded and went away. I do not know how many of our people were killed, but there were very many. It was bad.

BLACK ELK CONTINUES:

I do not remember where we camped that winter but it must have been a time of peace and of plenty to eat.

STANDING BEAR SPEAKS:

I am four years older than Black Elk, and he and I have been good friends since boyhood. I know it was on the Powder that we camped where there were many cottonwood trees. Ponies like to eat the bark of these trees and it is good for them. That was the winter when High Shirt's mother was killed by a big tree that fell on her tepee. It was a very windy night and there were noises that 'woke me, and then I heard that an old woman had been killed, and it was High Shirt's mother.

BLACK ELK CONTINUES:

I was four years old then, and I think it must have been the next summer that I first heard the voices. It was a happy summer and nothing was afraid, because in the Moon When the Ponies Shed (May) word came from the Wasichus that there would be peace and that they would not use the road any more and that all the soldiers would go away. The soldiers did go away and their towns were torn down; and in the Moon of Falling Leaves (November), they made a treaty with Red Cloud that said our country would be ours as long as grass should grow and water flow. You can see that it is not the grass and the water that have forgotten.

Maybe it was not this summer when I first heard the voices, but I think it was, because I know it was before I played with bows and arrows or rode a horse, and I was out playing alone when I heard them. It was like somebody calling me, and I thought it was my mother, but there was nobody there. This happened more than once, and always made me afraid, so that I ran home.

It was when I was five years old that my Grandfather made me a bow and some arrows. The grass was young and I was horseback. A thunder storm was coming from where the sun goes down, and just as I was riding into the woods along a creek, there was a kingbird sitting on a limb. This was not a dream, it happened. And I was going to shoot at the kingbird with the bow my Grandfather made, when the bird spoke and said: "The clouds all over are one-sided." Perhaps it meant that all the clouds were looking at me. And then it said: "Listen! A voice is calling you!" Then I looked up at the clouds, and two men were coming there, headfirst like arrows slanting down; and as they came, they sang a sacred song and the thunder was like drumming. I will sing it for you. The song and the drumming were like this:

> "Behold, a sacred voice is calling you;
> All over the sky a sacred voice is calling."

I sat there gazing at them, and they were coming from the place where the giant lives (north). But when they were very close to me, they wheeled about toward where the sun goes down, and suddenly they were geese. Then they were gone, and the rain came with a big wind and a roaring.

I did not tell this vision to any one. I liked to think about it, but I was afraid to tell it. . . .

What happened after that until the summer I was nine years old is not a story. There were winters and summers, and they were good; for the Wasichus had made their iron road* along the Platte and traveled there. This had cut the bison herd in two, but those that stayed in our country with us were more than could be counted, and we wandered without trouble in our land. . . .

One morning the crier came around the circle of the village calling out that we were going to break camp. The advisers were in the council tepee, and he cried to them: "The advisers, come forth to the center and bring your fires along." It was their duty to save fire for the people, because we had no matches then.

"Now take it down, down!" the crier shouted. And all the people began taking down their tepees, and packing them on pony drags.

Then the crier said: "Many bison, I have heard; many bison, I have heard! Your children, you must take care of them!" He meant to keep the children close while traveling, so that they would not scare the bison.

* The Union Pacific Railway.

Then we broke camp and started in formation, the four advisers first, a crier behind them, the chiefs next, and then the people with the loaded pony drags in a long line, and the herd of ponies following. I was riding near the rear with some of the smaller boys, and when the people were going up a long hill, I looked ahead and it made me feel queer again for a little while, because I remembered the nation walking in a sacred manner on the red road in my vision. But this was different, and I forgot about it soon, for something exciting was going to happen, and even the ponies seemed to know.

After we had been traveling awhile, we came to a place where there were many turnips growing, and the crier said: "Take off your loads and let your horses rest. Take your sticks and dig turnips for yourselves." And while the people were doing this, the advisers sat on a hill nearby and smoked. Then the crier shouted: "Put on your loads!" and soon the village was moving again.

When the sun was high, the advisers found a place to camp where there was wood and also water; and while the women were cooking all around the circle I heard people saying that the scouts were returning, and over the top of a hill I saw three horsebacks coming. They rode to the council tepee in the middle of the village and all the people were going there to hear. I went there too and got up close so that I could look in between the legs of the men. The crier came out of the council tepee and said, speaking to the people for the scouts: "I have protected you; in return you shall give me many gifts." The scouts then sat down before the door of the tepee and one of the advisers filled the sacred pipe with chacun sha sha, the bark of the red willow, and set it on a bison chip in front of him, because the bison was sacred and gave us both food and shelter. Then he lit the pipe, offered it to the four quarters, to the Spirit above and to Mother Earth, and passing it to the scouts he said: "The nation has depended upon you. Whatever you have seen, maybe it is for the good of the people you have seen." The scouts smoked, meaning that they would tell the truth. Then the adviser said: "At what place have you stood and seen the good? Report it to me and I will be glad."

One of the scouts answered: "You know where we started from. We went and reached the top of a hill and there we saw a small herd of bison." He pointed as he spoke.

The adviser said: "Maybe on the other side of that you have seen the good. Report it." The scout answered: "On the other side of that we saw a second and larger herd of bison."

Then the adviser said: "I shall be thankful to you. Tell me all that you have seen out there."

The scout replied: "On the other side of that there was nothing but bison all over the country."

And the adviser said: "Hetchetu aloh!"*

Then the crier shouted like singing: "Your knives shall be sharpened, your arrows shall be sharpened. Make ready, make haste; your horses make ready! We shall go forth with arrows. Plenty of meat we shall make!"

Everybody began sharpening knives and arrows and getting the best horses ready for the great making of meat.

Then we started for where the bison were. The soldier band went first, riding twenty abreast, and anybody who dared go ahead of them would get knocked off his horse. They kept order, and everybody had to obey. After them came the hunters, riding five abreast. The people came up in the rear. Then the head man of the advisers went around picking out the best hunters with the fastest horses, and to these he said: "Good young warriors, my relatives, your work I know is good. What you do is good always; so to-day you shall feed the helpless. Perhaps there are some old and feeble people without sons, or some who have little children and no man. You shall help these, and whatever you kill shall be theirs." This was a great honor for young men.

Then when we had come near to where the bison were, the hunters circled around them, and the cry went up, as in a battle, "Hoka hey!" which meant to charge. Then there was a great dust and everybody shouted and all the hunters went in to kill — every man for himself. They were all nearly naked, with their quivers full of arrows hanging on their left sides, and they would ride right up to a bison and shoot him behind the left shoulder. Some of the arrows would go in up to the feathers and sometimes those that struck no bones went right straight through. Everybody was very happy.

STANDING BEAR SPEAKS:

I remember that hunt, for before that time I had only killed a calf. I was thirteen years old and supposed to be a man, so I made up my mind I'd get a yearling. One of them went down a draw and I raced after him on my pony. My first shot did not seem to hurt him at all; but my pony kept right after him, and the second arrow went in half

* "It is so indeed."

way. I think I hit his heart, for he began to wobble as he ran and blood came out of his nose. Hunters cried "Yuhoo!" once when they killed, but this was my first big bison, and I just kept on yelling "Yuhoo!" People must have thought I was killing a whole herd, the way I yelled. When he went down, I got off my horse and began butchering him myself, and I was very happy. All over the flat, as far as I could see, there were men butchering bison now, and the women and the old men who could not hunt were coming up to help. And all the women were making the tremolo of joy for what the warriors had given them. That was in the Moon of Red Cherries (July). It was a great killing.

BLACK ELK CONTINUES:

I was well enough to go along on my pony, but I was not old enough to hunt. So we little boys scouted around and watched the hunters; and when we would see a bunch of bison coming, we would yell "Yuhoo" like the others, but nobody noticed us.

When the butchering was all over, they hung the meat across the horses' backs and fastened it with strips of fresh bison hide. On the way back to the village all the hunting horses were loaded, and we little boys who could not wait for the feast helped ourselves to all the raw liver we wanted. Nobody got cross when we did this.

During this time, women back at camp were cutting long poles and forked sticks to make drying racks for the meat. When the hunters got home they threw their meat in piles on the leaves of trees.

Then the advisers all went back into the council tepee, and from all directions the people came bringing gifts of meat to them, and the advisers all cried "Hya-a-a-a!," after which they sang for those who had brought them the good gifts. And when they had eaten all they could, the crier shouted to the people: "All come home! It is more than I can eat!" And people from all over the camp came to get a little of the meat that was left over.

The women were all busy cutting the meat into strips and hanging it on the racks to dry. You could see red meat hanging everywhere. The people feasted all night long and danced and sang. Those were happy times.

There was a war game that we little boys played after a big hunt. We went out a little way from the village and built some grass tepees, playing we were enemies and this was our village. We had an adviser, and when it got dark he would order us to go and steal some dried meat from the big people. He would hold a stick up to us and we had to bite off a piece of it. If we bit a big piece we had to get a big piece of meat, and if we bit a little piece, we did not have to get so much. Then we started for the big people's village, crawling on our bellies, and when we got back without getting caught, we would have a big feast and a dance and make kill talks, telling of our brave deeds like warriors. Once, I remember, I had no brave deed to tell. I crawled up to a leaning tree beside a tepee and there was meat hanging on the limbs. I wanted a tongue I saw up there in the moonlight, so I climbed up. But just as I was about to reach it, the man in the tepee yelled "Ye-a-a!" He was saying this to his dog, who was stealing some meat too, but I thought the man had seen me, and I was so scared I fell out of the tree and ran away crying.

Then we used to have what we called a chapped breast dance. Our adviser would look us over to see whose breast was burned most from not having it covered with the robe we wore; and the boy chosen would lead the dance while we all sang like this:

> *"I have a chapped breast.*
> *My breast is red.*
> *My breast is yellow."*

And we practiced endurance too. Our adviser would put dry sunflower seeds on our wrists. These were lit at the top, and we had to let them burn clear down to the skin. They hurt and made sores, but if we knocked them off or cried Owh!, we would be called women. . . .

After all the meat was dried, the six bands* of our nation that had come together about the time when the great vision came to me, broke camp at the mouth of Willow Creek and scattered in all directions. A small part of our band, the Ogalalas, started south for the Soldiers' Town [Fort Robinson] on Smoky Earth River (the White), for some of our relatives were there and we wanted to see them and have a feast of aguiapi and paezhuta sapa with chahumpi ska in it.† All the rest of the Ogalalas stayed in that country with Crazy Horse, who would have nothing to do with the Wasichus. This was late in the Moon When the Cherries are Ripe (July) and we boys had a good time playing. There were not many boys in our small band, and we all played together. I

---

* Ogalalas, Brules, Sans Arcs, Black Kettles, Hunkpapas, Minneconjous.

† Aguiapi, "brown all over," bread. Paezhuta sapa, "black medicine," coffee. Chahumpi ska, "white juice of the tree," sugar.

had quit thinking about my vision. The queer feeling had left me and I was not bashful any more; but whenever a thunder storm was coming I felt happy, as though somebody were coming to visit me.

We camped first on Powder River, then on the headwaters of the north fork of Good River (the Cheyenne) where there is a big butte that we called Sits-With-Young-One, because it has a little butte beside it. Then we camped on Driftwood Creek, then on the Plain of Pine Trees, and next on Plum Creek. When we got there, the plums were turning red, but they were not quite ripe yet. My grandfather went out and got some big red ones and they tasted good. When we got to War Bonnet Creek, which is not very far from the Soldiers' Town, my aunt and other relatives were there waiting for us with bread and coffee, and we had a big feast. I was sick all that night, and the next day my parents made me ride on a pony drag, because they were afraid I would surely die this time. But I think it was only too much bread and coffee, and maybe the plums. We camped again at Hips Hill, and by this time most of our people from the Soldiers' Town were among us. The next day about twenty tepees of us went on, and the rest stayed back. We camped with our relatives by White Butte near the Soldiers' Town and stayed there all winter, and we had a good time sliding down hill with sleds made out of bison jaws and ribs tied together with rawhide.

I was ten years old that winter, and that was the first time I ever saw a Wasichu. At first I thought they all looked sick, and I was afraid they might just begin to fight us any time, but I got used to them.

That winter one of our boys climbed the flagpole and chopped it off near the top. This almost made bad trouble, for the soldiers surrounded us with their guns; but Red Cloud, who was living there, stood right in the middle without a weapon and made speeches to the Wasichus and to us. He said the boy who did it must be punished, and he told the Wasichus it was foolish for men to want to shoot grown people because their little boys did foolish things in play; and he asked them if they ever did foolish things for fun when they were boys. So nothing happened after all.

Pierrepont Noyes

Pierrepont Noyes (1870–1959) once wrote:

I was born and brought up in a strange world — a world bounded on four walls of isolation; a world wherein the customs, laws, religions, and social formulas accumulated by civilization came to us only as faint cries of philistine hordes outside our walls. Wherein that protected area, a prophet and his faithful followers, having separated themselves from the rest of mankind, were trying to live as lived those members of the Primitive Christian Church of whom it was written, "No man called aught his own." That world was called Oneida Community, and that prophet was my father.

The prophet John Humphrey Noyes's Oneida Community was different from most of the utopian settlements that flourished in upstate New York in the middle of the nineteenth century. It was more middle-class, more intellectual, and — based on an industrial economy (the manufacture of animal traps and silver plate) rather than agriculture — it was financially successful. Noyes preached Perfectionism (men and women, if they lived right, could become as pure as Christ) and what he called "Bible communism." But what got him into trouble with his neighbors was the community's practice of what outsiders called "free love." In Noyes's theory of "complex marriage," every man was considered the husband of every woman, every woman the wife of every man.

But the love was far from free. Matches might have been made in heaven, but they were arranged on earth by Noyes, with, it was claimed, the participants' approval. Noyes paired his flock off according to his theories of eugenics, called stirpiculture, and couples who "enjoyed the presence" (a nicely tidy Oneida Community euphemism) without the approval of the prophet would often find the husband being packed off for a stay at the community's farm at Wallingford, Connecticut.

Pierrepont Noyes, or Pip, as he was usually called, saw the breakup of his father's dream, with John Humphrey fleeing to Canada before he died in 1886. At sixteen, Pip joined the world outside the wall by going first to Colgate

University in nearby Hamilton and then to Harvard. Later he ran the community's silver-plate business and held several appointed positions in state and federal government. He spent most of his adult years living in the Mansion House, where he grew up, married to Corinna Kinsley, whom he had met many years before as a playmate in the community's Children's House.

From "An East Room Child," "I Graduate to the South Room," "A Child's World," and "My Mother," *My Father's House*

I WAS BORN at high noon, August 18, 1870. A band was playing at the time and just outside my nursery window the usually quiet old Quadrangle, with its spreading shade trees and moss-grown, ivy-covered "reservoir," was alive with hurrying strangers. An "Excursion" had arrived, one of those Ontario & Western Railway excursions which periodically, during the seventies, brought a thousand or more visitors to eat the Community's far-famed vegetable dinner, to wander about the grounds, and, I suppose, to see what manner of people lived in this Community and how they lived. At that particular moment these excursionists were being entertained with a concert in the great hall of the Mansion House. . . .

Somewhere in the misty dawn of life I made the discovery that the world into which I had been born was called "Oneidacommunity." I learn from the report of relatives that, like other Community children, I remained in the care of my mother until I was able to walk: probably fourteen or fifteen months. Then, at the age when all Community children were brought together, I was transferred to a department called the Drawing Room. I remember nothing about my life in the Drawing Room, but assume that I was cared for meticulously, as I afterward saw the Drawing Room children cared for. I have been told that in the early 1870's the stirpicultural experiment was a general family enthusiasm and the Drawing Room was frequented by visitors.

It may be imagination, but I seem to remember a time when the Mansion House with its surrounding park was the entire world and "our folks" the population thereof. Later, but still in that twilight zone, I made another discovery. We children were watching the cows being driven along the road to their milking. Behind them I saw a man and a dog and someone told me the man was a "hired man." I remember puzzling for a long time over nice, old, bewhiskered Mr. Taylor. What was a "hired man"?

The answer to that question enlarged my horizon. We were still the center of the world just as, for the ancients, this earth was the center of the universe, but I now recognized that there were, somewhere "beyond the hedge," many strange people sometimes called "hired men" and again "outsiders."

So much for the period of infancy wherein the distinction between fact and fancy, between one's own recollections and the reports of others, is a doubtful one. My first valid memories begin at the age of four.

We were in the East Room. There were six of us sitting in high chairs about a large, round, maroon-colored table eating oatmeal and applesauce. The oatmeal half filled homemade tin porringers and the applesauce took the place of sugar and cream. I remember especially the pink color and delicious flavor of that applesauce. It must have been made from the fruit of an Early Joe tree which used to stand on the north lawn above the Dunn Cottage, for whenever I have been served with Early Joe applesauce the flavor has taken me back to the East Room.

The East Room, by the way, stood for something more than a room. It was a badge of class, a sort of sophomoric class, located between the babies of the Drawing Room and the older children of the South Room. My memories of life in the East Room are extremely vague. From the reports of older people I judge that it was much like life in the modern day nurseries to which children of three or four years are sent, excepting that the women who tended us in the East Room were also responsible for our sleeping arrangements. We had many playthings — blocks, marble rollers, rocking horses, and, I am told, were encouraged to pore over picture books, mostly homemade linen scrapbooks.

From what I have heard I am led to suspect that the desire of our elders to discover moral superiority in us "stirpicultural" children was disappointed, that those who lived closely with us acknowledged, at least to themselves, that at the age of four we were much like other children of the same age. We were selfish little animals. The women who cared for us spent much of their time settling differences of opinion as to who should have a certain toy.

I remember clearly just one feature of the East Room. It was a prancing horse with flowing mane and tail and its body all covered with hair. Shockey — that was the horse's name — pranced on delightfully elastic springs. To sit in a real saddle on its back with our feet in bright nickeled stirrups, and pitch back and forth with the motion of the pony, was the most popular amusement in the room. I think that the first time I ever encountered the word "quarrel" was in connection with that pony. Probably I had been unduly insistent on my turn at riding. The East Room impresses me as another of those remarkable anticipations of modern systems for child training which I find throughout the recollections of my earlier years.

I have a vague recollection of visiting the Drawing Room where many infants were creeping around the floor or playing on a platform, raised and railed-in so that they might safely look out the windows. More distinctly I remember our feeling of superiority to them. Were they not confined and watched and taken outdoors in carriages, while we of the East Room were allowed, within certain limitations, to play by ourselves in the sandbed and even wander over the lawns?

On the other hand, the South Room children, the older children, were granted a freedom which to us seemed infinite; even more, they had attained to such dignity of personality as to command our respect and envy. There were twenty or thirty of those privileged seniors, boys and girls between the ages of six and twelve, and they constituted the solid citizenship of the Children's House.

There again is a name which was more than the designation for a place. The Children's House was an institution. At the time it never occurred to me to question the applicability of the word "house," although the children's department occupied only a small section of the Community buildings. It was years later that I learned the origin of this colloquialism. It seems that, in the earlier days, the children's quarters were in a wooden house which stood at the edge of the south terrace and, when the great brick mansion was built in the 1860's and the children were installed in its southern wing, the earlier name persisted.

After that breakfast of oatmeal and applesauce, I find a hiatus in my memory — a period of obscurity, unillumined by any clear recollections or well-defined pictures — a hiatus extending to my Wallingford visit, in 1875. . . .

My brother, John Humphrey, one year my senior, had been living at Wallingford for some time before my visit. I am told that I accosted him with a quotation from the thirteenth chapter of First Corinthians which the children at Oneida had been learning by rote, "I am become as sounding brass or a tinkling cymbal." I cannot believe that he was greatly interested by either the brass or the cymbals. I was just a new boy to him and soon he was showing me all the wonders of the place, the pet lamb, the "mustang pony" and the yoke of huge oxen named Buck and Berry which Mr. Bristol used for his plowing.

I had not been there long before he took me back of the woodshed and proceeded to demonstrate his skill in cutting up potatoes. Whether he was cutting them for planting or for rat-bait, or merely seized on potatoes as excuse for exhibiting his dexterity with a new knife, I do not remember. What I do recall is the ugly gash inflicted on his finger when the knife cut through the potato in his hand. To this day Humphrey has a little finger made stiff by that cut.

That seemed bad enough, but worse was to follow. After his finger had been dressed, I sought to comfort him by sharing one of those little, hard "motto" candies which we children set much store by and, in trying to cut it, sliced off, or nearly off, a section of the fleshy portion of my thumb. Thereupon a "meeting" was called and we were introduced to our first "criticism."

My father summed up our moral turpitude by the statement that we were evidently "under a bad principality." "Principalities and powers" were familiar and awesome portents in my childhood and always depressed my spirits as much as normally buoyant spirits could be depressed. In some of my father's early writings I find a discussion of evil principalities and powers based on a quotation from Ephesians 6:11, but when a child I supposed that these were in some way connected with the Primitive Church.

My memory of the family sitting room at Wallingford is colored with the gloom of that criticism. It was a large room with a great fireplace and marble mantel at one end; the first fireplace I had ever seen. I remember it as a dark room. This, however, may have been a measure of my spiritual depression at the time. We two little culprits sat side by side on a great haircloth sofa with our hands bandaged and our feet sticking straight out in front of us. My father, as I recollect it, kept his eyes closed most of the time and wrinkled his forehead with a flexion of the skin which fascinated me. I remember also that Mr. Herrick and my aunt Harriet Skinner were there and that they did most of the criticizing.

Mr. Herrick was a strange combination of hearty camaraderie, quick sympathy and warm human affection, with a fanatic religiosity. In general, he was our companion, almost our playfellow, but always his affectionate smile could change on the instant to tight-lipped severity, and his voice ring with a challenge to the powers of evil. This meant anything condemned by John Humphrey Noyes or his theology. Mr. Herrick was a typical Community joiner. He left a wife and children and a high church pulpit in New York City to come to the Community, and thereafter his wife taught his children that their father was insane.

Aunt Harriet was my father's sister and his stanch supporter through all his life; she was beautifully homely, at least in my eyes, with many freckles, sandy hair and almost masculine features. Aunt Harriet possessed many of the same qualities as Mr. Herrick. She was fond of both Humphrey and me, but held the Community's war against sin and worldliness above all other considerations. Often, as a child, I sensed a struggle between her love for "John's children" and her loyalty to his spiritual severities. I can still see her strong profile as I saw it that day in the Wallingford parlor, and can hear her say with judgment-day sternness, "You boys will have to learn —"

The only other person I recall, in the circle which surrounded us during this criticism was "Miss" Fanny Leonard (we called all adult females Miss). She was a middle-aged woman with a sweet, kindly face and a large goiter which somewhat distracted my attention from the proceedings, in spite of their solemnity.

At the end, if I remember rightly, we were convicted of "pleasure seeking" and were told to "confess Christ a good spirit." That formula — "confess Christ" — with or without specific additions was an essential part of the Community liturgy. Of all the holidays and feast days and fast days celebrated at Oneida, the 20th of February had first place. It was on that date in 1834 that John Humphrey Noyes "confessed Christ his Savior from all sin."

The group of believers who gathered around him at Oneida in 1848 adopted his "confession" as a ritual. The words, which meant little to me when a child save as the formula for getting into good relations with a dimly sensed heavenly hierarchy, were to them an acknowledgment that Christ had the power to free their lives from sin. We children said, " 'fess Christ" or " 'fess Christ a good spirit," without clear understanding but with firm confidence that we were in some way acquiring merit, just as orthodox Protestant children probably feel when they kneel down to pray, or Catholic children when they say their beads. . . .

It was some time before my sixth birthday that I was graduated into the South Room. Sixteen others, nine boys and seven girls, were graduated at the same time and our common emergence laid the foundation for a class spirit which has remained strong upon us all to this day. I have a vivid recollection of the excitement attending our "moving up": the discovery of our names over hooks assigned for outdoor wraps in the South Room closet; the locating, each child, his locker in the sinkroom cupboard where, thenceforward, he was to keep rubbers and leather boots; more than all, our freedom to wander over the home domain with less oversight.

One incident that comes back to me suggests a megalomania to be accounted for — and perhaps excused — by our sudden elevation in the social scale. Several of the younger boys, left behind in the East Room, were playing in the sand-bed near the South Tower: Ethelbert, Karl, Grosvenor, I remember. [My cousin] Dick and I, self-hypnotized by our new dignity or being just ordinary liars — I am not sure which — proceeded to establish a temporary dictatorship over them. We insisted that we had the authority to admit them to the South Room or keep them out as we pleased. If I remember rightly, Karl revolted, and refused to obey our orders, whereupon Dick pronounced an edict of excommunication against the rebel and assured the others that they alone would be graduated.

As the reader will have inferred, the children of the Community were brought up, not by their parents, but by a "department." Mr. William Kelly — we called him Papa Kelly — was the head of that department. Miss Chloe and Miss Libby, the "mothers of the Children's House," put on our mittens and rubbers and made sure that when we came indoors our clothes were dry. They fed us wormwood tea and sulphur-and-molasses every spring, administered "drops" when an epidemic of sore eyes threatened, and saw to it that at least three times a day we were clean and properly fed.

Papa Kelly was an earnest man, lean and spiritually athletic. He had a thin, sandy beard, and an equally thin voice which rasped and clicked whenever he approached serious matters. He presided at five-o'clock Children's Meeting. Sometimes he quoted from one of John Humphrey Noyes's "home talks." Always he read passages from the

Bible and expounded texts, mostly dealing with "love your neighbor," "disobedience," or "God's punishment of the wicked."

In the *Oneida Circular,* 1874, I read that at the age of three I asked my mother:

"Is God really good?"

"Of course, child."

"Is He ever funny?"

"Yes, He does funny things sometimes."

"Well, does He ever laugh?"

This story brings back to me the naïve mentality of an age when I was incapable of conceiving any but an anthropomorphic God. Even at the age of five, He was still a man, a good man, an all-powerful man; in addition, God seemed stricter than Papa Kelly. I recall how intimately that word "strict" was associated in my mind with Papa Kelly.

At times he meted out punishment for the spiritual good of some erring youngster and as a warning to others. I respected him highly. Dick maintains that he resents his whippings to this day, but, personally, I cannot remember any unjust punishments. As a rule, when whipped, I knew my guilt and felt it a fair and just comeuppance. Further, I believed Papa Kelly to be a custodian of that "salvation" which was the special and wonderful asset of the Community. At an early age we were impressed with the primal necessity of being "saved" and I recognized in him a plenary representative of my father who, I knew, dealt directly with the heavenly agencies of salvation.

When Children's Meeting was over, we filed into the sinkroom where we washed our hands and faces under the rigid inspection of one of the mothers of the Children's House. In the next room Miss Jane Abbot brushed our hair. She had a habit of grasping our chins and tapping our heads smartly with the brush as she asked, "Right or left?" Then she parted our hair on the side where we had announced a "cowlick." I have a vivid recollection of a wart on Miss Jane's nose which her viselike grip always brought into the direct line of my vision. After her ministrations we marched, two and two, across the Quadrangle to the dining room.

There were two dining rooms, airy and well lighted and large enough to accommodate a dozen oblong tables each seating six people, and two or three "round tables." The round tables had stationary rims wide enough to hold a plate, cup and saucer, while the circular center with the service of food and condiments revolved. This central portion could be easily turned to bring anything desired opposite a diner's plate. The round table was hailed as a valuable invention, but I have heard members admit that its mechanics offered temptation to bad manners. There was a story that old Mr. Newhouse would let others turn the table until a desirable dish was opposite his plate; then with his thumb he would stop it and help himself to the food he wanted. We children were grouped together at the long tables and it was a proud day for me when a friend or parent invited me to sit with them at one of the round tables. Perhaps when I grew older I could sit there every day.

In the early days of the Community, the menus were simple — meager, in fact, according to the stories told us. But when I was a child the food was both abundant and excellent, although still simple. We had a wide range of vegetables, nicely cooked, delicious homemade wheat and graham bread, plenty of milk, and, in place of meat which was rarely allowed, eggs, fish, cheese or creamy meat gravies. Although living in the pie belt, pie was regarded as a menace to children; so our dessert covered a wide range of puddings — rice, tapioca, sago, custards. Our diet, and our manners as well, were carefully watched by mothers of the Children's House.

At what age we were allowed to carry our used dishes out to the dishwashing room, I do not remember. We were ambitious to do as the grown folks did, but I suppose we were obliged to wait at least until we were tall enough to lift the dishes to the high tables surrounding those great copper vats in which they were washed.

My memory is not clear as to our early sleeping arrangements; there must have been some regular progression governed by age. I remember sleeping with Dick and I remember that he snored annoyingly. At a later time I slept in Mr. Towner's room up in the mansard. Paul, then only one stage removed from babyhood, slept near me in a trundle bed, one of those low, square, boxlike cribs which in the daytime disappeared under larger beds. Often when the grown folks were gathered in evening meeting, Paul would start crying and his crying there in the darkness was, for me, a tragedy. When I could stand it no longer, I used to peep in at the door of the gallery which ran around three sides of the great meeting hall and try to attract the attention of someone. I say peep because the Big Meeting seemed to the children a solemn affair, and those peepings were undertaken with many misgivings and only as a last resort.

It was through the crack of the gallery door that I got my first glimpse of the Community assembled. I was greatly impressed. I remember that the hall below seemed filled with people; men were sitting bolt upright with solemn faces and arms folded; women were sewing or knitting at little tables where the cheerful yellow light from kerosene lamps with green paper shades competed with the general illumination. I had a momentary view of my father sitting near the stage — not on it — with his eyes closed. Uncle Frank was explaining to him in a loud voice — for he was then quite deaf — some question a member had asked. At another time I heard my father talking and could get no one in the gallery to pay any attention to me until he stopped.

Those were harrowing experiences, pattering barefooted down the long hallway, clad only in a nightgown, to a door I hardly dared open. The worst of it was that after some good Samaritan had come to my rescue and frightened or cajoled Paul into silence and had returned to the meeting, his crying often began again.

I remember sleeping in the drawing room with five other boys. We were forbidden to get out of bed, but managed to gratify our passion for sociability, without too greatly searing our consciences, by fastening a rope to a baby basket — a wicker affair which rolled on wooden wheels — and ferrying each other from bed to bed in this.

Still later — it must have been later because the ban on roaming had evidently become a dead letter — we had that adventure and committed that classic blunder which has become a tradition of Children's House days.

It happened thus: In the Nursery Kitchen closet was kept a fascinating assortment of supplies. I can still smell the odor of that closet — sage and catnip and strawberry leaves for making tea, peppermint for tummy-aches, and what was of greatest interest to boys, two wooden firkins, one filled with oyster crackers and the other with sugar. One night, when all grown folks were in Big Meeting, we decided on an expedition to the Nursery Kitchen for sugar. Unfortunately, the shelf was high and the firkin heavy, and by some mischance it slipped from our hands. There was a crash and a scattering of sugar over the floor.

We were panic-stricken. Hastily sweeping the sugar into a pile, we retreated to our beds where a council of war evolved a very stupid plan of action. Clifton, then a baby or nearly so, was sleeping in an adjoining room with Mrs. Waite. When that worthy woman came down from the meeting we sent one of the boys to inform her that we thought Clifton had been stealing sugar and had spilled some on the floor. It goes without saying that we were convicted of the crime. . . .

My cousin Dick is, perhaps, the most vivid memory of my childhood. We were by choice inseparable; so much so that often we were "separated" for falling into the spiritual error of "partiality." That verbal noun had a definite and serious, not to say sinister, significance in the Children's House. The penalty, upon conviction of partiality, was a sentence of separation for several days. The sentence usually ran like this: "Richard and Pierrepont must not speak to each other for three days." . . .

The etiquette — if I may use that word — of the Children's House was as definite and fixed as its moral code. We said "Yes, sir" and "No, sir" to our elders or were reported to Papa Kelly as "saucy." We addressed all grown folks as "Mr." or "Miss" excepting our parents and those who by reason of relationship or custom we could call "Uncle" or "Aunt." Even in conversation among ourselves we were expected to use these "respectful" titles.

The human aversion for obeying rules was sometimes in evidence among the usually well-disciplined Community children. My brother Holton often dropped the "Mr." or mumbled it unintelligibly in speaking of men he disliked, while both he and Karl, when telling their inimitable stories in the sanctity of an all-child audience, dramatized their victims as "Old Perry" or "Old Randolph." Those were daring adventures in lawlessness. . . .

There was another much-criticized error which, of course, violated the code of morals rather than manners; it was called in the Community "stickiness," more especially being "sticky" to one's parents. I think that this sin was more prevalent among the girls than the boys. My wife remembers an occasion when the sight of her mother led to a violent and, from Papa Kelly's point of view, disagreeable exhibition of "stickiness to her mother."

When I was six years old my mother was allowed to arrange a birthday party for me. I remember two little chairs and a low table set out under the tulip tree in the Quadrangle. There were only two at the party, Dick and I, but it was a real party and we had cake.

I think my mother got even more pleasure than I did out of that party. The Community system was harder on mothers than on their children. Whenever I was permitted to visit my mother in her mansard room — once a week or twice (I have forgotten which) — she always seemed trying to make up for lost opportunity, lavishing affection on me until, much as I loved her, I half grudged the time taken from play with those toys which she had — I think somewhat surreptitiously — collected for my visits.

Hers was a pleasant room, lighted by two windows set deep in an embrasure made necessary by the slant of the mansard roof. In the broad window seat I played that I was on a stage or, with the sky and clouds outside as my sea, imagined I was steering a boat as I had seen Mr. Inslee steer the boat he kept above the dam. My stage or boat was reached by climbing a coil — when it was not too hot. The Mansion House was a steam-heated at a time when central heating was rare, and every room had a homemade coil consisting of many horizontal lengths of iron pipe connected at their ends by curved "unions."

At one side of my mother's room was a wardrobe with ample drawers below. In addition, there was a desk and desk chair where she did her writing, a comfortable rocker, and a bed. Hanging on the wall was a whatnot. I especially remember this because on its three shelves, of diminishing size, were many articles that I used to tease my mother to let me take — figurines, little boxes, sparkling cards, daguerreotypes in marvelous frames, and a miscellaneous collection of little mementos. Hanging also on the walls were several pictures and a mirror in an old-fashioned wooden frame.

The afternoons with my mother meant a great deal to me, and it is no disparagement of my filial affection to add that freedom from departmental oversight as well as the petting and peppermints to be expected on such occasions enhanced their attractiveness. Certain it is that I often wept bitterly when the time came to return to the Children's House. I remember my mother's terror lest my crying be heard. She knew that Father Noyes frowned on any excess of parental affection as he did on all forms of "special love," and she feared that such demonstrations might deprive her of some of my regular visits.

As a matter of fact, she had concrete evidence of this danger. Once, as a punishment for some childish sin, Papa Kelly forbade my weekly visit to the mansard. I promptly went berserk. Forgetting my Children's House training and my fear of its head, I raged; I howled, I kicked, I lay down on the sinkroom floor and exhausted my infantile vocabulary in vehement protestations and accusations. Whereupon Papa Kelly seized me and shook me and commanded in a voice charged with indignation and authority — just such a voice as I imagined Jesus Christ used when casting out devils, "Be still, Pip, be still!" Then, firmly, "You have evidently got sticky to your mother. You may stay away from her another week." The turbulence was mine, but the greater tragedy was my mother's.

A child avid for play forgets easily; but whenever, as I played on the floor, she bent over me, her dark eyes appealing, and asked, "Darling, do you love me?" I always melted. My marbles and blocks were forgotten. I would reach up and put my arms about her neck. I remember how tightly she held me and how long, as though she would never let me go.

Lincoln Steffens

At the end of the nineteenth century, there were not many native-born Californians, but Joseph Lincoln Steffens (1866–1936) was one of them. Born in the Mission District of San Francisco and raised in Sacramento, Lennie — as he was called then — was the grandson of a Canadian farmer who had headed west with his wife in a wagon. He got as far as Illinois, where he settled and produced a family of sixteen or seventeen children (the count seems to have become confused). Steffens's father lived out the old man's dream by coming to California on horseback, but not as a traditional pioneer or gold-seeker. He was a bookkeeper, and he got a job with a paint and hardware company that had a branch in Sacramento, by then a quiet little town on a busy river — a place closer in spirit to Mark Twain's Hannibal than to the gold-rush camp it had once been.

"From the Sacramento valley on a clear day," Steffens later recalled, after becoming one of the most famous journalists of his age, "one can see the snow-capped peaks of the Sierras, and when the young summer wheat is stretching happily in the heat of the sun, when men and animals and boys are stewing and steaming, it is good to look up through the white-hot flames at the cool blue of the mountains and let your eyes skate over the frost."

The most important event of young Lennie's life came when he was eight: he was given a horse. "A Boy on Horseback" is a chapter from Steffens's Autobiography, which is one of the monumental works of American memoir writing.

"A Boy on Horseback,"
The Autobiography of Lincoln Steffens

MY LIFE ON HORSEBACK from the age of eight to fifteen was a happy one, free, independent, full of romance, adventure, and learning, of a sort. Whether my father had any theory about it or was moved only by my prayers I do not know. But he did have some ideas. He took away my saddle, for example. My mother protested that I had suffered enough, but he insisted and he gave me reasons, some for himself, some for me. He said I would be a better horseman if I learned to ride without stirrups and a saddle-horn to keep my balance. The Indians all rode bareback, and the Comanches, the best horsemen on the plains, used to attack, clinging out of sight to the far side of their horses and shooting under their necks.

"We had to shoot a Comanche's horse to get the fellow," he said, "and even then the devil would drop behind his dead pony and shoot at us over the carcass."

I consented finally to having my beautiful saddle hung high in the harness room until I could sit my horse securely. The result was that I came to prefer to ride bareback and used the saddle only for show or for games and work that needed stirrups and a horn, as in picking up things off a box on the ground or handling cattle (calves) with a rope.

That, however, was but one detail. I had begun about that time to play boys' games: marbles, tops, baseball, football, and I can see now my father stopping on his way home to watch us. He used to wag his head; he said nothing to me, but I knew he did not like those games. I think now that he thought there was some gambling in them, and he had reason to dread gambling. It was a vice that hung over from the mining days in California, and the new business men were against it. They could not have it stopped because "Frank" Rhodes, the political boss, was the keeper of a famous gambling-house; he protected business men, but also he protected his own business. They could not fight Frank too openly, but they lost money and they lost clerks and cashiers through the gambling hells. My father had had to discharge a favorite bookkeeper on account of his heavy play at the gaming-tables. He may have given me the pony to keep me from gambling games or to get me up off the streets and out into the country. There was another result, however, which he did not foresee.

After that blessed pony loped into my life, I never played those trading games which, as I see them now, are the leads not merely to gambling but to business. For there goes on among boys an active trade in marbles, tops, knives, and all the other tools and properties of boyhood. A born trader finds himself in them, and the others learn to like to trade. My theory is that those games are the first lessons in business: they cultivate the instinct to beat the other fellows on 'Change and so quicken their predatory wits. Desirable or no, I never got that training; I never had any interest in, I have always had a distaste for, business, and this my father did not intend. I remember how disappointed he was later when he offered to stay in his business till I could succeed him and I rejected the "great opportunity" with quick scorn — "Business! Never."

My pony carried me away not only from business but from the herd also and the herding habits of mind. The tendency of the human animal to think what others think, say what the mob says, do what the leaders do or command, and, generally, go with the crowd, is drilled in deep at school, where the playground has its fashions, laws, customs and tyrannies just as Main Street has. I missed that. I never played "follow the leader," never submitted to the ideals and the discipline of the campus or, for that matter, of the faculty; and so, ever since, I have been able to buy stocks during a panic, sell when the public was buying; I could not always face, but I could turn my back on, public opinion. I think I learned this when, as a boy on horseback, my interest was not in the campus; it was beyond it; and I was dependent upon, not the majority of boys, but myself and the small minority group that happened to have horses.

I began riding alone. When I mounted my pony the morning after I got him I knew no other boys that had horses, and I did not think of anybody else. I had a world before me. I felt lifted up to another plane, with a wider range. I could explore regions I had not been able to reach on foot. Sacramento is protected from high water in the rivers by levees which send the overflow off to flood other counties. I had visited these levees on foot and wondered what was beyond them. Now I could ride over them and the bridges to — anywhere, I thought. The whole world was open to me. I need not imagine it any more, I could go and see.

I was up early to water, feed, and clean the pony before breakfast. That meal, essential for the horse, was of no importance to me. I slighted it. My father, cautioning me not to work a horse till he had fed fully, said I had plenty of time to eat myself. But I could not eat. I was too excited, too eager, and when I was free to rise from the table I ran out to see if the pony was through his breakfast. He wasn't. I watched him; he was in no hurry. I urged him a bit, but he only lost time looking around at me curiously, and then slowly resumed his meal. My sisters came out to see me off, and one of them rebuked my impatience with a crude imitation of a grown-up.

"The *pony* eats like a gentleman," she said, as if I cared about gentlemen. Something my father had said hit me harder. He said that teamsters, vaqueros, and Indians fed more and longer when they were in a hurry to get off on a long, hard run than on other days; they foresaw that they must be "fortified with food." It took nerve, he admitted, to eat that way, but those fellows had nerve. They could control their animals so perfectly because they had self-control. They didn't force a horse, even in a pursuit. They changed the gait often and went long stretches at a walk. And they could shoot straight, especially in a fight or a battle, because they never became fidgety.

I didn't know it then, but I can see now, of course, that my father was using my horse to educate me, and he had an advantage over the school teachers; he was bringing me up to my own ideals; he was teaching me the things my heroes knew and I wanted to learn. My mother did not understand that. When she came out to the stable, I was anticipating the end of the pony's meal by putting on his saddle blanket and surcingle, and telling my sisters where I was going.

"Don't ride too far the first day," she said. "You will get hungry and sore."

Awful! But I got away at last, and I rode — in all directions. Intending to do one levee that day, and the others in succession the next two days, I rode over them all that morning. I rode over the first one to the American River, and I was disappointed. The general character of the earth's surface did not change much even in the great distance and the change was for the worse — sand and muddy brush. I turned back and rode over the opposite levee, and I could hardly believe it — the land on the other side was like the land on this side. I rode into town again and went across the bridge over the Sacramento River to Yolo County, and that was not different. By that time I was hungry, very hungry, and I came home. Also I was a little hot and uncomfortable in the seat. I was late for lunch, but my mother had kept things warm for me, good things, and she did not ask me very bad questions. Where had I gone? I told her that. What had I seen? I could not tell her that. I had gone to the horizon and seen nothing new, but I did not know that myself well enough to report it to anybody else. Nor could I answer her inquiry for the cause of my depression. Only I denied that I was sore, as she suggested. No, no, not that. I had fed my horse and rubbed him down; when I had eaten I went out and watered and walked him. Then I cleaned him till my sisters came home, and then we all cleaned him.

The next day I was sore, so sore I could hardly sit or walk, but having lied about it, I had to prove it; so I rode off again, in pain, but bravely as a cowboy or an Indian taking torture; only I did not go far. I stopped, dismounted, and let my pony feed on some grass under the trees of East Park. I lay there, and no, I did not think; I imagined things. I imagined myself as all sorts of persons, a cowboy, a trapper, a soldier, a knight, a crusader — I fancied myself as the hero of every story I had read. Not all on this one day. From the day my pony came to me I seem to have spent many, many hours, playing around in my imagination, which became the most active faculty of my mind. For, as I say, I was alone much of the time. I learned to like to be alone, and that pleasure I come back to always, even now. When I am tired of the crowd I go off somewhere by myself and have a good time inside my mind.

As a boy I would ride far, far away to some spot, give my pony a long rope to swing round on, and let him feed on the grass, while I sat and did nothing but muse. I read a great deal. Finding that books fed my fancies, I would take one along, and finding a quiet nook, I read. And my reading always gave me something to be. I liked to change the hero I was to the same thing on horseback, and once wholly in the part, I would remount my pony and be Napoleon, or Richard the Lion-hearted, or Byron, so completely that any actual happening would wake me up dazed as from a dreaming sleep. Dream people lived or lay in wait for me in the brush across the river, so that the empty spaces beyond my old horizon, the levee, became not only interesting but fascinating with dread or glory, and populated with Persons.

"Hey, kid! Don't swim the river there. The rapids'll sweep you clean to San Francisco."

I looked up. It was the bridge-tender, the man that walked the trestle over the American River after every train to put out fires started on the dry sleepers by live coals dropped from the locomotives. I respected the man that filled a responsible place like his, but I slid into the water, swam along shore, came out, and dressed. I could not tell him that Byron swam the Hellespont, which was harder to do than to cross the American at that point; and I did not like to confess that I had a trap set on the other side where the Chinamen had their peanut farm and represented the Saracens to me. When I was dressed, the trestle-walker bade me meet him at the end of the trestle. I did, and a friendship was well started. He didn't scold me, he praised my swimming, but he said that the current was strong at that place and that it wasn't brave, it was foolish, to go in there. "A boy oughtn't to do what a man wouldn't do." He asked me some questions, my name, age, where I lived, where my father's business was. He felt over and approved my pony. I asked him how he could walk so fast on the trestle, having no planks to go on, and stepping from one sleeper to the other.

"Oh," he said, "I can walk 'em fast now because I walked 'em slow at first."

I wanted to try. He took my hand and made me walk slowly, one by one, until I was over my nervousness. When I could do it alone, he invited me to his watchman's cabin, about one-third of the way across. I went, he following. When we reached his little house we sat down, and we had, man to man, a nice, long talk, which became so confidential that I trusted him with the information that I was a trapper and had my traps set for beavers all up and down the river. And my faith was not misplaced. He didn't say that there were no beavers in that river; we both knew there weren't, and we both knew that that didn't matter. All he said was that he was a gold miner himself — and expected to strike it rich some day.

"I don't work at it much," he admitted. "Mostly I tend bridge. But in between trains, when I ain't got a thing to do, I think about it. I think how I came west to find a fat claim and work it and get rich, so I write home that that's what I'm doing, prospectin', and I am, too, and sometimes I play I have struck it and I go home and I spend my money."

After that I caught more beavers, and he and I spent my profits my way. Yes, and after that he struck it richer than ever, and him and me, we went back east and we just blew in his money his way. It was fun. I got a bad name from this. There were grown-ups who said I was a "fearful liar," and no doubt I was unconvincing sometimes. My father asked me questions, and I told him about my bridge-tender. I said that my bridge-tender could run as fast as a train on the trestle, and my father gave me a talking-to for telling such a whopper. I felt so bad about it that I told the bridge-tender.

He thought a moment and then he said, "The next time your father is to take a train out this way, tell me, and tell him to be on the rear platform."

The next time my father was to take a train that crossed the trestle, I told him what to do, and I went out to my bridge-tender. He climbed down off the trestle, disappeared into the brush, and came back with a few ripe cantaloupes. We waited till the train came. Now trains had to go slow on that trestle, and as the locomotive passed, the bridge-tender held up a melon to the engineer and said something about "easy does it." So when the train passed, the bridge-tender jumped out after it and ran and ran; and he caught up to the rear car and he handed that melon to my father, who waved to him and then took off his hat to me.

The bridge-tender and me, we were awful proud. We talked about it and laughed. "That'll fix him," the bridge-tender said, and he wished we could get just one beaver to show 'em. "I'd give good money if I could buy one somewheres."

But I had no trouble about the beavers. Men scoffed, and some boys did at first, but I soon had all my crowd setting and watching traps in the river. And we had a war, too. There was that peanut farm run by the Chinamen who were Turks and Saracens. We boys were crusaders, knights. So when we used to swim over to steal the peanuts, we either got peanuts, which were good, or we had a battle with the Saracens, which was better. They came at us with clods of earth, which they threw. We fired back, and when they came too near we dived into the river, and ducking and diving, swam home to the Christian shore.

My crowd was small and of very slow growth. They were all fellows I met on horseback, an odd lot. First — and last — there was Hjalmar Bergman, a Swedish boy. His father, a potter, and his mother lived in a hut out on the outskirts of the town; they spoke no English and were very poor. Hjalmar had a horse because his father, who had received it in payment of a debt, had no use for it. Black Bess, as I renamed her, was a big mare, high spirited, but well trained in the cattle game. Whenever any dangerous work had to be done the vaqueros would borrow Black Bess, and we boys would go with her and see the fun. Jake Short, who was the best cowboy in town those days, knew Bess well; and she knew him or his business. Once there was a "loco" (mad) steer in a field that had to be shot. We sat on the fence and watched Jake ride out on Bess with his big Colt revolver ready. When Bess caught sight of the steer coming head down at them, she halted, braced herself, and stood fast, moving only to keep facing the crazy beef. Jake dropped the reins, settled his hips to the left in his saddle, and leaned forward on the right side. The steer came madly on till he was within ten feet of them; then Jake fired and Black Bess leaped bodily to the left, letting the steer fall upon the spot where she had stood. Jake jumped down and finished the steer, and there stood Bess just where he had left her.

"That's what I call a hoss," he said to Hjalmar, and I was proud. Bess was Hjalmar's hoss, but she was in our crowd.

There were other boys with horses, all sorts of boys and all sorts of horses, but mostly they were boys and horses that belonged in one way or another to the cattle and the butchering business. Will Cluness, the doctor's son, had a pony "just to ride," but he didn't go with us much; he preferred marbles, tops, and the other games on the ground. I invented or adapted games to horse play; Will liked some of them. Hide-and-seek, for example. We found a long, straight stretch of road in old East Park, with paths and brush and trees beside it. There, at the end of a run of, say, an eighth of a mile, we drew a line across the road. The boy who was "it" held his horse on the line while the rest of us scattered into the woods. "It" called out now and then — "Ready?" — until there was no answer; then he rode where he thought we might be. He took care to keep behind him a clear run to the home line, but he had to hunt for us or the sight of us on our horses. Our game was to ride out of sight around him and make a dash for home. If he saw one of us or a horse he recognized he shouted the rider's name, pointed, and, turning, ran his horse for home base. The named rider would start at the same instant, and there was a race.

The horses soon learned this game and would start for home so suddenly at the sight of "it" that their boy was sometimes left behind. I was hiding under a tree one day when my pony saw the white horse of Ernie Southworth, who was "it"; he leaped forward, banging me against a limb of the tree; I clutched the limb, and the pony darted out of the woods, met "it" on the road, raced him, and won. We had a dispute whether the rider had to be on his horse at the finish, and it happened so often that the horse came in alone that we made a rule: a horse, with or without his rider, won or lost the race.

But Will soon tired of this and our other games. He could not fight Saracens that were really only Chinamen, and he held it in great contempt to set traps for beavers that did not exist. There were other boys like that. They were realists, I would say now; practical men. I learned to play with such boys, too, but I preferred the fellows that were able to help create a world of our own and live in it.

I took men into my crowd, too; especially horsemen. The other fellows did not; they said that grown-ups laughed at and spoiled every game. And that was true in the main. But I knew men like the bridge-tender who could play, and there was Jake Stortz, a German who lived and had his barn on the block back of my stable. Jake had the city street-cleaning contract, and he was a fireman and a truck-man. He had lots of horses. His wife, a barefooted peasant woman, took care of the horses, and she and Jake were my advisers in the care, feeding, and handling of my pony. Jake let me be a fireman. He put a bit on my pony's halter, as he did on one of his own horses, arranged it so that you could with one movement snap it into the horse's mouth, untie, clear, mount him bareback, and so start for a fire the moment the whistle blew. At first I had to ride to the fire with Jake, and he would not wait a second for me, but I soon learned the signals and where to head for. I beat Jake to the fire sometimes, and the firemen knew it. "Where's Jake?" they'd call to me when I dashed up alone.

The first time there was a fire when I was at the dinner table, I upset my chair and frightened the whole family, but I got out and away so fast that nobody could say a word till I came home an hour or so later. Then I had to explain; my father spoke to Jake, and there was no trouble. I could go to fires any time except when I was in school or in bed, and my mother made me a fireman's red shirt.

But there was some unnecessary trouble about a stallion. Mrs. Stortz, who had charge of all the breeding of their animals, took me into all the technique of having colts. I held the mare while she steered the stallion. It was difficult work. The stallion got excited; he never wanted to wait till the mare was ready, and Mrs. Stortz had to hold him off. If the mare was restive and kicked, I had to hang on and make her stand. But we did this so often that we soon had it all down pat. And I had to "watch out" when the foal was due. Mrs. Stortz was responsible but busy, so I had to help; keep my eye on the mare who was left in the pasture field, with instructions to call her at the first sign of the birth.

One day as I was riding out on my pony I saw a mare down and the colt half out, and I couldn't make Mrs. Stortz hear. I let my pony go home; I ran to the mare, and she seemed to have given up. I patted her head, urged her to try again, and then ran and myself pulled out the baby horse. I did it all alone. Meanwhile I had been calling, "Mrs. Stortz, Mrs. Stortz." She came, and when she saw that all was well, she kissed me. And she told Jake and everybody. Jake was so glad. He said that that colt was to be the best horse he ever had and he'd name him after me. And he did. And I watched my colt grow with great impatience. Which was all all right. My father heard of it, and he spoke of it, but while there was some doubt about something — he wagged his head over it — he did not forbid anything. A couple of years later he

came home with a handbill in his hand, and he was very angry. I
didn't see why. I had seen the bill myself; it was posted up on Jake's
barn; I had one in our stable; and it was in every blacksmith's shop
and at the race track. It carried a picture of my colt, full grown and
with my name. It was an announcement that "this splendid, high-bred
stallion Lennie S. would stand the season for all mares at $50 a throw."
My father had a talk with Jake and the handbills were all called in;
another bill, with the same horse and the same price, but another
name, was put out.

Edith Wharton

Edith Wharton (1862–1937) was probably the best-known American fiction writer of the 1920s. She was born into a comfortable New York family (her father's actual worth was based on the fluctuating real-estate market, so some times were more comfortable than others) and was related to what were considered all the best people.

To escape the real-estate crash after the Civil War, her family went off to Europe, and until Edith was ten lived in France or Italy, with side trips to Germany and Spain. Seeing New York freshly in 1872 proved to be quite a shock for young Edith. Educated both at home and abroad only by tutors, she described herself as a "much governessed and guarded little girl."

This portrait of New York in the 1870s was written late in Mrs. Wharton's life — at the end of a career that saw the publication of more than fifty books (including The House of Mirth, The Age of Innocence, *and* Ethan Frome*) — and appeared in* Harper's *after her death. It reflects the somewhat crotchety opinions of a woman who had been born during the presidency of Lincoln and lived to see, much to her displeasure, the reelection of her fellow New Yorker Franklin Roosevelt, a man she considered a possibly dangerous socialist. It also reflects the decorative taste of the author of one of the first books published on American interior design.*

From "A Little Girl's New York"

IN THOSE DAYS the little "brownstone" houses (I never knew the technical name of that geological horror) marched up Fifth Avenue (still called "the Fifth Avenue" by purists) in an almost unbroken procession from Washington Square to the Central Park. Between them there passed up and down, in a leisurely double line, every variety of horse-drawn vehicle, from Mrs. Belmont's or Mrs. Astor's C-spring barouche to a shabby little covered cart drawn by a discouraged old horse and labelled in large letters: *Universal Exterminator* — which suggested collecting souls for the *Dies Irae,* but in reality designated a patent appliance for ridding kitchens of cockroaches.

The little brownstone houses, all with Dutch "stoops" (the five or six steps leading to the front door), and all not more than three stories high, marched Parkward in an orderly procession, like a young ladies' boarding school taking its daily exercise. The facades varied in width from twenty to thirty feet and here and there, but rarely, the line was broken by a brick house with brownstone trimmings; but otherwise they were all so much alike that one could understand how easy it would be for a dinner guest to go to the wrong house — as once befell a timid young girl of eighteen, to whom a vulgar *nouveau-riche* revealed her mistake, turning her out carriageless into the snow — a horrid adventure which was always used to point the rule that one must never allow a guest, even totally unknown, to discover such a mistake, but must immediately include him or her in the party. Imagine the danger of entertaining gangsters to which such social rules would expose the modern hostess! But I am probably the last person to remember that Arcadian code of hospitality.

Those were the days à propos of Fifth Avenue — when my mother used to say: "Society is completely changed nowadays. When I was first married we knew everyone who kept a carriage."

And this tempts me to another digression, sending me forward to my seventeenth year, when there suddenly appeared in Fifth Avenue a very small canary yellow brougham with dark trimmings, drawn by a big high stepping bay and driven by a coachman who matched the brougham in size and the high-stepper in style. In this discreet yet brilliant equipage one just caught a glimpse of a lady whom I faintly remember as dark haired, quietly dressed, and enchantingly pale, with a hat-brim lined with cherry color, which shed a lovely glow on her cheeks. It was an apparition surpassing in elegance and mystery any that Fifth Avenue had ever seen; but when our dark-blue brougham encountered the yellow one, and I cried: "Oh, Mamma, look — what a smart carriage! Do you know the lady?" I was hurriedly drawn back with the stern order not to stare at strange people and to remember that whenever our carriage passed the yellow one I was to turn my head away and look out of the other window.

For the lady in the canary colored carriage was New York's first fashionable hetaera. Her name and history were known in all the clubs, and the name of her proud proprietor was no secret in New York drawing-rooms. I may add that, being an obedient daughter, I always thereafter *did* look out of the other window when the forbidden brougham passed; but that one and only glimpse of the loveliness within it peopled my imagination with images of enchantment from Broceliande and Shalott (we were all deep in the "Idylls of the King"), and from the Cornwall of Yseult. She was, in short, sweet unsuspecting creature, my first doorway to romance, destined to become for me successively Guinevere and Francesca da Rimini, Beatrix Esmond and the *Dame aux Camelias*. And in the impoverished emotional atmosphere of old New York such a glimpse was like the mirage of palm trees in the desert.

I have often sighed, in looking back at my childhood, to think how pitiful a provision was made for the life of the imagination behind those uniform brownstone facades, and then have concluded that since, for reasons which escape us, the creative mind thrives best on a reduced diet, I probably had the fare best suited to me. But this is not to say that the average well-to-do New Yorker of my childhood was not starved for a sight of the high gods. Beauty, passion, and danger were automatically excluded from his life (for the men were almost as starved as the women); and the average human being deprived of air from the heights is likely to produce other lives equally starved — which was what happened in old New York, where the tepid sameness of the moral atmosphere resulted in a prolonged immaturity of mind.

But we must return to the brownstone houses, and penetrate from the vestibule (painted in Pompeian red, and frescoed with a frieze of stencilled lotus-leaves, taken from Owen Jones's *Grammar of Ornament*) into the carefully guarded interior. What would the New Yorker of the present day say to those interiors, and the lives lived in them? Both would be equally unintelligible to any New Yorker under fifty.

Beyond the vestibule (in the average house) was a narrow drawing-room. Its tall windows were hung with three layers of curtains: sash-curtains through which no eye from the street could possibly penetrate, and next to these, draperies of lace or embroidered tulle, richly beruffled, and looped back under the velvet or damask hangings which were drawn in the evening. This window garniture always seemed to me to symbolize the superimposed layers of under-garments worn by the ladies of the period — and even, alas, by the little girls. They were in fact almost purely a symbol, for in many windows even the inner "sash-curtains" were looped back far enough to give the secluded dwellers a narrow glimpse of the street; but no self-respecting mistress of a house (a brownstone house) could dispense with this triple display of window-lingerie, and among the many things I did which pained and scandalized my Bostonian mother-in-law, she was not least shocked by the banishment from our house in the country of all the thicknesses of muslin which should have intervened between ourselves and the robins on the lawn.

The brownstone drawing-room was likely to be furnished with monumental pieces of modern Dutch marquetry, among which there was almost always a cabinet with glazed doors for the display of "bric-a-brac." Oh, that bric-a-brac! Our mothers, who prided themselves on the contents of these cabinets, really knew about only two artistic productions — old lace and old painted fans. With regard to these the eighteenth-century tradition was still alive, and in nearly every family there were yards and yards of precious old lace and old fans of ivory, chicken-skin, or pale tortoise-shell, exquisitely carved and painted. But as to the other arts a universal ignorance prevailed, and the treasures displayed in the wealthiest houses were no better than those of the average brownstone-dweller. . . .

I have said that the little brown houses, marching up Fifth Avenue like disciplined schoolgirls, now and then gave way to a more important facade, sometimes of their own chocolate hue, but with occasional pleasing alternatives in brick. Many successive Fifth Avenues have since been erected on the site of the one I first knew, and it is hard to remember that none of the "new" millionaire houses which, ten or fifteen years later, were to invade that restless thoroughfare (and all of which long ago joined the earlier layers of ruins) had been dreamed of by the boldest innovator. Even the old families, who were subsequently to join the newcomers in transforming Fifth Avenue into a street of would-be palaces, were still content with plain wide-fronted houses, mostly built in the 'forties or 'fifties. In those simple days one could count on one's two hands the New York houses with ballrooms. . . .

The Assemblies [held at Delmonico's] were the most important of the big balls — if the word "big" as now understood could be applied to any social event in our old New York! There were, I think, three Assemblies in the winter, presided over by a committee of ladies who delegated three of their number to receive the guests at the ballroom door. The evening always opened with a quadrille, in which the ladies of the committee and others designated by them took part; and there followed other square dances, waltzes and polkas, which went on until the announcement of supper. A succulent repast of canvasback ducks, terrapin, foie-gras, and the best champagnes was served at small tables below stairs, in what was then New York's only fashionable restaurant; after which we re-ascended to the ballroom (in a shaky little lift) to begin the complicated maneuvers of the cotillion.

The "Thursday Evening Dances," much smaller and more exclusive, were managed by a committee of the younger married women — and how many young and pretty ones there were in our little society! I cannot, oddly enough, remember where these dances were held — and who is left, I wonder, to refresh my memory? There was no Sherry's restaurant as yet, and no Waldorf-Astoria, or any kind of modern hotel with a suite for entertaining; yet I am fairly sure we did not meet at "Del's" for the "Thursday Evenings."

At all dances large or small, a custom prevailed which caused untold misery to the less popular girls. This was the barbarous rule that if a young man asked a girl for a dance or, between dances, for a turn around the ballroom, he was obliged to keep her on his arm until another candidate replaced him; with the natural result that "to him (or rather her) that hath shall be given," and the wily young men risked themselves only in the vicinity of young women already provided with attendant swains. To remedy this embarrassing situation the more tactful girls always requested their partners, between dances, to bring them back to their mothers or "chaperons," a somnolent row of stout ladies in velvet and ostrich feathers enthroned on a row of settees against the ballroom walls.

The custom persisted for some years, and spoilt the enjoyment of many a "nice" girl not attractive enough to be perpetually surrounded by young men, and too proud to wish to chain at her side a dancer who might have risked captivity out of kindness of heart. I do not know when the fashion changed, and the young men were set free, for we went back to Europe when I was nineteen, and I had only brief glimpses of New York until I returned to it as a married woman.

The most conspicuous architectural break in the brownstone procession occurred when its march ended, at the awkwardly shaped entrance to the Central Park. Two of my father's cousins, Mrs. Mason Jones and Mrs. Colford Jones, bought up the last two blocks on the east side of Fifth Avenue, facing the so-called "Plaza" at the Park gates, and built thereon their houses and their children's houses; a bold move which surprised and scandalized society. Fifty-seventh

Street was then a desert, and ball goers anxiously wondered whether even the ubiquitous "Brown coupes" destined to carry home belated dancers would risk themselves so far a-field. But old Mrs. Mason Jones and her submissive cousin laughed at such apprehensions, and presently there rose before our astonished eyes a block of pale green-ish limestone houses (almost uglier than the brownstone ones) for the Colford Jones cousins, adjoining which our audacious Aunt Mary, who had known life at the Court of the Tuileries, erected her own white marble residence and a row of smaller dwellings of the same marble to lodge her progeny. The "Jones blocks" were so revolution-ary that I doubt whether any subsequent architectural upheavals along that historic thoroughfare have produced a greater impression. In our little provincial town (without electricity, telephones, taxis, or cab-stands) it had seemed inconceivable that houses or habits should ever change; whereas by the time the new millionaires arrived with their palaces in their pockets Fifth Avenue had become cosmopolitan, and was prepared for anything.

The lives led behind the brownstone fronts were, with few excep-tions, as monotonous as their architecture. European travel was grow-ing more frequent, though the annual holiday abroad did not become general until I grew up. In the brownstone era, when one crossed the Atlantic it was for a longer stay; and the returned traveler arrived with a train of luggage too often heavy with works of art and "an-tiques." Our mothers, not always aware of their aesthetic limitations, seldom restricted their purchases to lace and fans; it was almost a point of honor to bring back an "Old Master" or two and a few monsters in the way of modern Venetian furniture. For the traveler of moderate means, who could not soar to Salvator Rosa, Paul Potter, or Carlo Dolci (prime favorites of the day), facsimiles were turned out by the million by the industrious copyists of Florence, Rome or Amsterdam; and seldom did the well-to-do New Yorker land from a European tour unaccompanied by a Mary Magdalen cloaked in care-fully waved hair, or a swarth group of plumed and gaitered gamblers doing a young innocent out of his last sequin. One of these "awful warnings," a Domenichino, I think, darkened the walls of our dining room, and Mary Magdalen, minutely reproduced on copper, graced the drawing-room table (which was of Louis Philippe *buhl,* with ornate brass heads at the angles).

In our country houses, collections of faience, in which our mothers also flattered themselves that they were expert, were thought more suitable than pictures. Urbino, Gubbio, and various Italian luster wares, mostly turned out by the industrious Ginori of Florence, abounded in Newport drawing-rooms. I shall never forget my mother's mortification when some ill-advised friend arranged for a newly arrived Italian Minister — Count Corti, I think — to visit her supposed "collection" of "china" (as all forms of porcelain and pottery were then indifferently called). The diplomatist happened to be a collector of some repute, and after one glance at the Ginori output crowding every cabinet and table, he hurriedly draped his surprise in a flow of compliments which did not for a moment deceive my mother. I still burn with the humiliation inflicted by that salutary visit, which had the happy effect of restricting her subsequent purchases to lace, fans, or old silver — about which, incidentally, she also knew a good deal, partly, no doubt because she and my father had inherited some very good examples of Colonial silver from their respective forebears. . . .

We had returned when I was ten years old from a long sojourn in Europe, so that the New York from which I received my most vivid impressions was only that tiny fraction of a big city which came within the survey of a much governessed and guarded little girl — hardly less of a little girl when she "came out" (at seventeen) than when she first arrived on the scene at ten.

Perhaps the best way of recapturing the atmosphere of my little corner of the metropolis is to try to remember what our principal interests were — I say "our" because being virtually an only child, since my big brothers had long since gone forth into the world, I shared either directly or indirectly in most of the household goings-on.

My father and mother entertained a great deal and dined out a great deal; but in these diversions I shared only to the extent of hanging over the stair-rail to see the guests sweeping up to our drawing-room or, conversely, my mother sweeping down to her carriage, replendent in train, aigrette, and opera cloak. But though my parents were much invited, and extremely hospitable, the *tempo* of New York society was so moderate that not infrequently they remained at home in the evening. After-dinner visits were still customary, and on these occasions old family friends would drop in, ceremoniously arrayed in white gloves and white tie, with a tall hat, always carried up to the drawing-room and placed on the floor beside the chair of the caller — who, in due course, was regaled with the ten o'clock cup of tea which followed the heavy repast at seven-thirty. On these occasions the lonely little girl that I was remained in the drawing-room later than her usual bedtime, and the kindly whiskered gentlemen encouraged her to join in the mild talk. It was all very simple and friendly, and the conversation ranged safely from Langdons, Van Rensselaers, and Lydigs to Riveses, Duers, and Schermerhorns, with an occasional allusion to the Opera (which there was some talk of transplanting from the old Academy of Music to a "real" Opera House, like Covent Garden or the Scala), or to Mrs. Scott-Siddons's readings from Shakespeare, or Aunt Mary Jones's evening receptions, or my uncle Fred Rhinelander's ambitious dream of a Museum of Art in the Central Park, or cousin John King's difficulty in housing in the exiguous quarters of the New-York Historical Society a rather burdensome collection of pictures bequeathed to it by an eccentric young man whose family one did not wish to offend — a collection which Berenson, visiting it many years later, found to be replete with treasures, both French and Italian.

But the events in which I took an active part were going to church — and going to the theater. I venture to group them together because, looking back across the blurred expanse of a long life, I see them standing up side by side, like summits catching the light when all else is in shadow. Going to church on Sunday mornings was, I fear, no more than an unescapable family duty; but in the afternoon my father and I used to return alone together to the second service. Calvary Church, at the corner of Gramercy Park, was our parish church, and probably even in that day of hideous religious edifices, few less aesthetically pleasing could have been found. The service was "low," the music indifferent, and the fuliginous chancel window of the Crucifixion a horror to alienate any imaginative mind from all Episcopal forms of ritual; but the Rector, the Reverend Dr. Washburn, was a man of great learning, and possessed of a singularly beautiful voice — and I fear it was chiefly to hear Dr. Washburn read the Evening Lessons that my father and I were so regular in our devotions. Certainly it is to Dr. Washburn that I owe the discovery of the matchless beauty of English seventeenth-century prose; and the organ-roll of Isaiah, Job, and above all, of the lament of David over the dead Absalom, always come back to me in the accents of that voice, of which I can only say that it was worthy to interpret the English Bible.

The other great emotion of my childhood was connected with the theater. Not that I was, even at a tender age, an indiscriminate theater-lover. On the contrary, something in me has always resisted the influence of crowds and shows, and I have hardly ever been able to yield myself unreservedly to a spectacle shared with a throng of people. But my distrust of theatrical representation goes deeper than that. I am involuntarily hypercritical of any impersonation of characters already so intensely visible to my imagination that anyone else's conception of them interferes with that inward vision. And this applies not only to plays already familiar to me by reading, but to any stage representation — for, five minutes after I have watched the actors in a new play, I have formed an inner picture of what they ought to look like and speak like, and as I once said, in my rash youth, to someone who had asked me if I enjoyed the theater: "Well, I always want to get up on the stage and show them how they ought to act" — a reply naturally interpreted as a proof of intolerable self-assurance.

However, in spite of my inability to immerse myself in the play, I did enjoy the theater in my childhood, partly because it was something new, a window opening on the foam of faeryland (or at least I always hoped to see faeryland through that window), and partly, I still believe, because most of the acting I saw in those early days in New York was really much better than any I have seen since. The principal theaters were, in fact, still in possession of good English companies, of whom the elders had played together for years, and preserved and handed on the great tradition of well trained repertory companies, versus the evil "star" system which was so soon to crowd them out of business.

At Wallack's Theatre, still ruled by the deeply dyed and undoubtedly absurd Lester Wallack, there were such first-rate actors as old Mrs. Ponisi, Beckett, Harry Montague, and Ada Dyas; and when they deserted the classic repertory (Sheridan, Goldsmith, etc.) for the current drama, the average play they gave was about as good as the same type of play now acted by one or more out-of-focus stars with a fringe of obscure satellites.

But our most exciting evenings came when what the Germans call "guest-players" arrived from London, Berlin, or Rome with good repertory companies. Theater-going, for me, was in fact largely a matter of *listening to voices,* and never shall I forget the rapture of first hearing

> *And gentlemen in England, now abed*
> *Shall think themselves accursed they were not here,*

in George Rignold's vibrant barytone, when he brought *Henry V* to New York. . . .

In the way of other spectacles New York did not as yet provide much. There was in fact only the old Academy of Music, where Campanini, in his prime, warbled to an audience still innocently following the eighteenth-century tradition that the Opera was a social occasion, invented to stimulate conversation; but my recollection of those performances is not clear, for, by the time I was judged old enough to be taken to the Opera, the new Opera House was inaugurated, and with it came Wagner; and with Wagner a cultivated and highly musical German audience in the stalls, which made short work of the chatter in the boxes. I well remember the astonishment with which we learned that it was "bad form" to talk during the acts, and the almost immediate compliance of the box-audience with this new rule of politeness, which thereafter was broken only by two or three thick-skinned newcomers in the social world.

Apart from the Opera, the only popular entertainments I can recall were Barnum's three-ring circus (a sort of modern ocean liner before the letter) — and Moody and Sankey's revivalist meetings. I group the two in no spirit of disrespect to the latter, but because both were new and sensational, and both took place in the old Madison Square Garden, at that time New York's only large auditorium, where prize fights and circuses placidly alternated with religious revivals, without any sign of public disapproval. But I must add that, sincere as no doubt the protagonists were, there was a theatrical element in their call to religion which, in those pre-Eddyan days, deeply offended the taste of many people; and certainly, among the throngs frequenting their meetings many avowedly went for the sake of Sankey's singing rather than of his companion's familiar chats with the Almighty. Though America has always been the chosen field of sensational religious performances, the New York of my childhood was still averse to any sort of pious exhibitionism; but as I was never allowed to assist at the Moody and Sankey meetings, my impression of them is gathered entirely from the comments of my father's friends, from whom I fear Saint Francis of Assisi and Savonarola would have received small encouragement. My mother, at any rate, gave none to the revivalists; and my father and I had to content ourselves with the decorous beauty of Evening Prayer at Calvary Church.

From all this it will be seen that the New York of those days was a place in which external events were few and unexciting, and little girls had mostly to

> *be happy and building at home.*

"Yet" (as Stevenson's poem continues)

> *Yet as I saw it, I see it again.*
> *The kirk and the palace, the ships and the men,*
> *And as long as I live, and where'er I may be,*
> *I'll always remember my town by the sea —*

a town full indeed for me of palaces and ships, though the palaces came out of the "Tempest," "Endymion," and "Kubla Khan," and the ships were anchored on the schoolroom floor, ready to spread their dream-sails to all the winds of my imagination.

H. L. Mencken

There is a theory that people who remember, or at least talk about, their childhoods are those who had unhappy ones. Henry Louis Mencken (1880–1956), the gleeful iconoclast who delighted in attacking anything that struck him as middle-class ("the booboisie"), sentimental, or pretentious, single-handedly refutes that with his memoirs of growing up in Baltimore. Even the title gives him away. As an editor of Smart Set *and other magazines of the 1920s, he had a knack for titles, one of his best being* Damn! A Book of Calumny. *But when it came time to give a name to the book that covered his first twelve years he came up with* Happy Days.*

In fact he is so mellow about the whole subject that in his preface he calls the "comfortable and complacent bourgeoisie" from which he came a "great order of mankind" and with a certain drollery regrets that it has fallen into such ill repute. "I still maintain my dues-paying membership in it, and continue to believe that it was and is authentically human, and therefore worthy of the attention of philosophers, at least to the extent that the Mayans, Hittites, Kallikuks and so on are worthy of it."

Happy Days *was published when Mencken was sixty. A decade later he wrote that he was surprised that so many women had written to him saying how similar their childhoods had been to his. "It never occurred to me in my youth, or to any other normal American boy, that creatures in skirts and pigtails saw the world as we did."*

"Introduction to the Universe," *Happy Days*

AT THE INSTANT I first became aware of the cosmos we all infest I was sitting in my mother's lap and blinking at a great burst of lights, some of them red and others green, but most of them only the bright yellow of flaring gas. The time: the evening of Thursday, September 13, 1883, which was the day after my third birthday. The place: a ledge outside the second-story front windows of my father's cigar factory at

368 Baltimore street, Baltimore, Maryland, U. S. A., fenced off from space and disaster by a sign bearing the majestic legend: AUG. MENCKEN & BRO. The occasion: the third and last annual Summer Nights' Carnival of the Order of Orioles, a society that adjourned *sine die,* with a thumping deficit, the very next morning, and has since been forgotten by the whole human race.

At that larval stage of my life, of course, I knew nothing whatever about the Order of Orioles, just as I knew nothing whatever about the United States, though I had been born to their liberties, and was entitled to the protection of their army and navy. All I was aware of, emerging from the unfathomable abyss of nonentity, was the fact that the world I had just burst into seemed to be very brilliant, and that peeping at it over my father's sign was somewhat hard on my still gelatinous bones. So I made signals of distress to my mother and was duly hauled into her lap, where I first dozed and then snored away until the lights went out, and the family buggy wafted me home, still asleep.

The latter details, you will understand, I learned subsequently from historians, but I remember the lights with great clarity, and entirely on my own. They constitute not only the earliest of all my earthly recollections, but also one of my most vivid, and I take no stock in the theories of psychologists who teach that events experienced so early in life are never really recalled, but only reconstructed from family gossip. To be sure, there is a dead line beyond which even the most grasping memory does not reach, but I am sure that in my own case it must have run with my third birthday. Ask me if I recall the occasion, probably before my second, when I was initiated into the game of I-spy by a neighbor boy, and went to hide behind a wire screen, and was astonished when he detected me — ask me about that, and I'll admit freely that I recall nothing of it whatever, but only the ensuing anecdote, which my poor mother was so fond of telling that in the end I hid in the cellar every time she started it. Nor do I remember anything on my own about my baptism (at which ceremonial my father, so I have heard, made efforts to get the rector tight, and was hoist by his own petard), for I was then but a few months old. But not all the psychologists on earth, working in shifts like coal-miners, will ever convince me that I don't remember those lights, and wholly under my own steam.

They made their flash and then went out, and the fog again closed down. I don't recall moving to the new house in Hollins street that was

to be my home for so many years, though we took possession of it only
a few weeks later. I don't recall going into pants at about a quarter to
four years, though it must have been a colossal experience, full of
pride and glory. But gradually, as my consciousness jelled, my days
began to be speckled with other events that, for one reason or another, stuck. I recall, though only somewhat vaguely, the deck of an
excursion-boat, *circa* 1885, its deafening siren, and the wide, gray
waters of Chesapeake Bay. I recall very clearly being taken by my
father to a clothing-store bright with arc-lights, then a novelty in the
world, and seeing great piles of elegant Sunday suits, and coming
home with one that was tight across the stern. I recall a straw hat with
flowing ribbons, a cat named Pinkie, and my brother Charlie, then still
a brat in long clothes, howling like a catamount one hot Summer
night, while my mother dosed him with the whole pharmacopoeia of
the house, and frisked him for outlaw pins. I recall, again, my introduction to the wonderland of science, with an earthworm (*Lumbricus
terrestris*) as my first subject, and the experiment directed toward
finding out how long it would take him, laid out in the sun on the
backyard walk, to fry to death. And I recall my mother reading to me,
on a dark Winter afternoon, out of a book describing the adventures
of the Simple Simon who went to a fair, the while she sipped a cup of
tea that smelled very cheerful, and I glued my nose to the frosty
window pane, watching a lamplighter light the lamps in Union Square
across the street and wondering what a fair might be. It was a charming, colorful, Kate Greenaway world that her reading took me into,
and to this day I can shut my eyes and still see its little timbered
houses, its boys and girls gamboling on village greens, and its
unclouded skies of pale blue.

I was on the fattish side as an infant, with a scow-like beam and
noticeable jowls. Dr. C. L. Buddenbohn, who fetched me into sentience at 9 p.m., precisely, of Sunday, September 12, 1880, apparently
made a good (though, as I hear, somewhat rough) job of it, despite the
fact that his surviving bill, dated October 2, shows that all he charged
"to one confinement" was ten dollars. The science of infant feeding,
in those days, was as rudimentary as bacteriology or social justice, but
there can be no doubt that I got plenty of calories and vitamins, and
probably even an overdose. There is a photograph of me at eighteen
months which looks like the pictures the milk companies print in the
rotogravure sections of the Sunday papers, whooping up the zeal of

their cows. If cannibalism had not been abolished in Maryland some years before my birth I'd have butchered beautifully.

My mother used to tell me years afterward that my bulk often attracted public notice, especially when it was set off dramatically against her own lack of it, for she was of slight frame and less than average height, and looked, in her blue-eyed blondness, to be even younger than she actually was. Once, hauling me somewhere by horse-car, she was confronted by an old man who gaped at her and me for a while with senile impertinence, and then burst out: "Good God, girl, is that baby *yours?*" This adiposity passed off as I began to run about, and from the age of six onward I was rather skinny, but toward the end of my twenties my cross-section again became a circle, and at thirty I was taking one of the first of the anti-fat cures, and beating it by sly resorts to malt liquor.

My gradually accumulating and clarifying memories of infancy have to do chiefly with the backyard in Hollins street, which had the unusual length, for a yard in a city block, of a hundred feet. Along with my brother Charlie, who followed me into this vale when I was but twenty months old, I spent most of my pre-school leisure in it, and found it a strange, wild land of endless discoveries and enchantments. Even in the dead of Winter we were pastured in it almost daily, bundled up in the thick, scratchy coats, overcoats, mittens, leggings, caps, shirts, over-shirts and under-drawers that the young then wore. We wallowed in the snow whenever there was any to wallow in, and piled it up into crude houses, forts and snow-men, and inscribed it with wavering scrolls and devices by the method followed by infant males since the Würm Glaciation. In Spring we dug worms and watched for robins, in Summer we chased butterflies and stoned sparrows, and in Autumn we made bonfires of the falling leaves. At all times from March to October we made a Dust Bowl of my mother's garden.

The Hollins street neighborhood, in the eighties, was still almost rural, for there were plenty of vacant lots nearby, and the open country began only a few blocks away. Across the street from our house was the wide green of Union Square, with a fishpond, a cast-iron Greek temple housing a drinking-fountain, and a little brick office and tool-house for the square-keeper, looking almost small enough to have been designed by Chick Sale. A block to the westward, and well within range of our upstairs windows, was the vast, mysterious compound of the House of the Good Shepherd, with nuns in flapping habits flitting along its paths and alleys, and a high stone wall shutting it in from the world. In our backyard itself there were a peach tree, a cherry tree, a plum tree, and a pear tree. The pear tree survives to this day, and is still as lush and vigorous as it was in 1883, beside being thirty feet higher and so large around the waist that its branches bulge into the neighboring yards. My brother and I used to begin on the cherries when they were still only pellets of hard green, and had got through three or four powerful bellyaches before the earliest of them was ripe. The peaches, pears and plums came later in the year, but while we were waiting for them we chewed the gum that oozed from the peach-tree trunk, and practised spitting the imbedded flies and June bugs at Pinkie the cat.

There was also a grape-arbor arching the brick walk, with six vines that flourished amazingly, and produced in the Autumn a huge crop of sweet Concord grapes. My brother and I applied ourselves to them diligently from the moment the first blush of color showed on them, and all the sparrows of West Baltimore helped, but there was always enough in the end to fill a couple of large dishpans, and my mother and the hired girl spent a hot afternoon boiling them down, and storing them away in glass tumblers with tin tops. My brother and I, for some reason or other, had no fancy for the grape jelly thus produced with so much travail, but we had to eat it all Winter, for it was supposed, like camomile tea, to be good for us. I don't recall any like embalming of the peaches, plums and pears; in all probability we got them all down before there were any ripe enough to preserve. The grapes escaped simply because some of them hung high, as in the fable of the fox. In later years we collared these high ones by steeple-jacking, and so paid for escape from the jelly with a few additional bellyaches.

But the show-piece of the yard was not the grape-arbor, nor even the fruit-trees; it was the Summer-house, a rococo structure ten feet by ten in area, with a high, pointed roof covered with tin, a wooden floor, an ornate railing, and jig-saw spirals wherever two of its members came together. This Summer-house had been designed and executed by my mother's father, our Grandfather Abhau, who was a very skillful cabinet-maker, and had also made some of the furniture of the house. Everything of his construction was built to last, and when, far on in the Twentieth Century, I hired a gang of house-wreckers to demolish the Summer-house, they sweated half a day with their crowbars and pickaxes. In the eighties it was the throne-room and justice-seat of the household, at least in Summer. There, on fair Sunday mornings, my father and his brother Henry, who lived next door, met to drink beer, try out new combinations of tobacco for their cigar factory, and discuss the credit of customers and the infamies of labor agitators. And there, on his periodical visitations as head of the family, my Grandfather Mencken sat to determine all the delicate questions within his jurisdiction.

My mother was an active gardener, and during her forty-two years in Hollins street must have pulled at least a million weeds. For this business, as I first recall her, she had a uniform consisting of a long gingham apron and an old-time slat-bonnet — a head-dress that went out with the Nineteenth Century. Apron and slat-bonnet hung on nails behind the kitchen door, and on a shelf adjoining were her trowels, shears and other such tools, including always a huge ball of twine. My brother Charlie and I, as we got on toward school age, were drafted to help with the weeding, but neither of us could ever make out any difference between weeds and non-weeds, so we were presently transferred to the front of the house, where every plant that came up between the cobblestones of Hollins street was indubitably verminous. The crop there was always large, and keeping it within bounds was not an easy job. We usually tackled it with broken kitchen knives, and often cut our hands. We disliked it so much that it finally became convict labor. That is to say, it was saved up for use as punishment. I recall only that the maximum penalty was one hour, and that this was reserved for such grave offenses as stealing ginger-snaps, climbing in the pear-tree, hanging up the cat by its hind leg, or telling lies in a gross and obvious manner.

Charlie was somewhat sturdier than I, and a good deal fiercer. During most of our childhood he could lick me in anything approximating a fair fight, or, at all events, stall me. Civil war was forbidden in Hollins street, but my Grandfather Mencken, who lived in Fayette street, only three blocks away, had no apparent objection to it, save of course when he was taking his afternoon nap. I remember a glorious day when eight or ten head of his grandchildren called on him at once, and began raising hell at once. The affair started as a more or less decorous pillow-fight, but proceeded quickly to much more formidable weapons, including even bed-slats. It ranged all over the house, and must have done a considerable damage to the bric-a-brac, which was all in the Middle Bismarck mode. My grandmother and

Aunt Pauline, fixed by my grandfather's pale blue eye, pretended to be amused by it for a while, but when a large china thunder-mug came bouncing down the third-story stairs and a black hair-cloth sofa in the parlor lost a leg they horned in with loud shrieks and lengths of stove-wood, and my grandfather called time.

Charlie and I were very fond of Aunt Pauline, who was immensely hospitable, and the best doughnut cook in all the Baltimores. When the creative urge seized her, which was pretty often, she would make enough doughnuts to fill a large tin wash-boiler, and then send word down to Hollins street that there was a surprise waiting in Fayette street. It was uphill all the way, but Charlie and I always took it on the run, holding hands and pretending that we were miraculously dashing car-horses. We returned home an hour or so later much more slowly, and never had any appetite for supper. The immemorial tendency of mankind to concoct rituals showed itself in these feasts. After Charlie had got down his first half dozen doughnuts, and was taking time out to catch his breath and scrape the grease and sugar off his face, Aunt Pauline would always ask "How do they taste?" and he would always answer "They taste like more." Whether this catechism was original with the high contracting parties or had been borrowed from some patent-medicine almanac or other reference-work I don't know, but it never varied and it was never forgotten.

There were no kindergartens, playgrounds or other such Devil's Islands for infants in those innocent days, and my brother and I roved and rampaged at will until we were ready for school. Hollins street was quite safe for children, for there was little traffic on it, and that little was slow-moving, and a cart approaching over the cobblestones could be heard a block away. The backyard was enough for us during our earliest years, with the cellar in reserve for rainy days, but we gradually worked our way into the street and then across it to Union Square, and there we picked up all the games then prevailing. A few years ago, happening to cross the square, I encountered a ma'm in horn-rimmed spectacles teaching a gang of girls ring-around-a-rosy. The sight filled me suddenly with so black an indignation that I was tempted to grab the ma'm and heave her into the goldfish pond. In the days of my own youth no bossy female on the public payroll was needed to teach games to little girls. They taught one another — as they had been doing since the days of Neanderthal Man.

Nevertheless, there was a constant accretion of novelty, at least in detail. When we boys chased Indians we were only following the Sumerian boys who chased Akkadians, but the use of hatchets was certainly new, and so was the ceremony of scalping; moreover, our fiends in human form, Sitting Bull and Rain-in-the-Face, had been as unknown and unimagined to the Sumerian boys as Henry Ward Beecher or John L. Sullivan. The group songs we sang were mainly of English provenance, but they had all degenerated with the years. Here, precisely, is what we made of "King William" in Hollins street, *circa* 1885:

> *King William was King James's son;*
> *Upon a ri' a race he won;*
> *Upon his breast he wore a star,*
> *The which was called the life of war.*

What a *ri'* was we never knew and never inquired, nor did we attach any rational concept to *the life of war.* A favorite boys' game, called "Playing Se*bast*apool" (with a heavy accent on the *bast*), must have been no older in its outward form than the Crimean War, for Sebastapool was plainly Sevastopol, but in its essence it no doubt came down from Roman times. It could be played only when building or paving was going on in the neighborhood, and a pile of sand lay conveniently near. We would fashion this sand into circular ramparts in some friendly gutter, and then bristle the ramparts with gaudy tissue-paper flags, always home-made. Their poles were slivers of firewood, and their tissue-paper came from Newton's toy-store at Baltimore and Calhoun streets, which served the boys and girls of West Baltimore for seventy years, and did not shut down at last until the Spring of 1939. The hired girls of the block cooked flour paste to fasten the paper to the poles.

To the garrison of a Sebastapool all the smaller boys contributed tin soldiers, including Indians. These soldiers stood in close and peaceful ranks, for there was never any attempt at attack or defense. They were taken in at night by their owners, but the flags remained until rain washed the Sebastapool away, or the milkman's early morning horse squashed it. There were sometimes two or three in a block. Girls took a hand in making the flags, but they were not allowed to pat the ramparts into shape, or to touch the tin soldiers. Indeed, for a little girl of that era to show any interest in military affairs would have been as indecorous as for her to play leap-frog or chew tobacco. The older boys also kept rather aloof, though they stood ready to defend a Sebastapool against raiders. Tin soldiers were only for the very young. The more elderly were beyond such inert and puerile simulacra, which ranked with rag dolls and paper boats. These elders fought in person, and went armed.

In the sacred rubbish of the family there is a specimen of my hand-writing dated 1883 — two signatures on a sheet of paper now turned a dismal brown, the one small and rather neat and the other large and ornamented with flourishes. They seem somehow fraudulent, for I was then but three years old, but there they are, and the date, which is in my mother's hand, is very clear. Maybe she guided my stubby fingers. In the same collection there is another specimen dated January 1, 1887. It shows a beginning ease with the pen, though hardly much elegance. My mother also taught me many other humble crafts — for example, how to drive a nail, how to make paper boats, and how to sharpen a lead pencil. She even taught me how to thread a needle, and for a time I hoped to take over darning my own stock-ings and patching the seats of my own pants, but I never managed to master the use of the thimble, and so I had to give up. Tying knots was another art that stumped me. To this day I can't tie a bow tie, though I have taken lessons over and over again from eminent mas-ters, including such wizards as Joe Hergesheimer and Paul Patterson. When I go to a party someone has to tie my tie for me. Not in-frequently I arrive with the ends hanging, and must appeal to my hostess.

This incapacity for minor dexterities has pursued me all my life, often to my considerable embarrassment. In school I could never learn to hold a pen in the orthodox manner: my handwriting satisfied the professors, but my stance outraged them, and I suffered some rough handling until they finally resigned me to my own devices. In later life I learned bricklaying, and also got some fluency in rough carpentering, but I could never do anything verging upon cabinet-work. Thus I inherited nothing of the skill of my Grandfather Abhau. All my genes in that field came from my father, who was probably the most incompetent man with his hands ever seen on earth. I can't recall him teaching me anything in my infancy, not even marbles. He would sometimes brag of his youthful virtuosity at all the customary boys' games, but he always added that he had grown so old (he was thirty-one when I was six) and suffered so much from dead beats, noisy children and ungrateful cigarmakers, drummers and bookkeepers that he had lost it. Nor could he match the endless stories that my mother told me in the years before I could read, or the many songs. The only song I ever heard him sing was this one:

> *Rain forty days,*
> *Rain forty nights,*
> *Sauerkraut sticking out the smokestack.*

Apparently there were additional words, but if so he never sang them. The only *Märchen* in his répertoire had to do with a man who built a tin bridge. I recall nothing of this tale save the fact that the bridge was of tin, which astonished my brother and me all over again every time we heard of it. We tried to figure out how such a thing was possible, for the mention of tin naturally made us think of tomato-cans. But we never learned.

William Alexander Percy

When the novelist Walker Percy was fifteen, his widowed mother died and he and his two brothers were sent off to Greenville, Mississippi, to live with their "Uncle Will," William Alexander Percy (1885–1942), who was actually a second cousin. "He was a fabled relative," Walker Percy recalled,

> *the one you liked to speculate about. His father had been a United States senator and he had been decorated as an infantry officer in World War I. Beside that, he was a poet. The fact that he was also a lawyer and a planter didn't cut much ice — after all, the South was full of lawyer-planters. But how many people did you know who were war heroes and wrote books of poetry?*

The boys were adopted by their "uncle" and Walker lived in his all-male household for the next twelve years. It was a place full of visitors, Walker remembered, "poets, politicians, psychiatrists, sociologists, black preachers, folk singers, itinerant harmonica players" — a standard way station for any northerner who was trying to "understand the South." And when William Alexander Percy's Lanterns on the Levee: Recollections of a Planter's Son *was published in 1941, it was considered, for good or ill, the ultimate statement of the aristocratic South.*

In this excerpt, Percy deals with the heritage — both real and mythic — of grandparents.

"Mère and Père," *Lanterns on the Levee: Recollections of a Planter's Son*

ALTHOUGH Mère and Père, Mother's parents, were born in New Orleans, they were just as French as if they had landed day before yesterday from Lyon or Tours. Mère was plump, squat, and blue-eyed, with a soft face that never learned wrinkles or unlearned its miraculous pink and white. She wore pretty things, light in color, and little bonnets with forget-me-nots and pink rose-buds, and she always managed to look cool, in crises or midsummer. Père would not have had any particular look at all except for his beard, which was so long and silky it could be plaited into one, two, or three plaits and when hooked under and over his ears produced an amazing effect of benign ferocity. The year of fifty-cent cotton Père bought a Delta plantation on Deer Creek and bid adieu to crêpes suzette, absinthe, the old French Opera House, and all his kin except Uncle Alfred, whom no one spoke to or of because he had sold out to Ben Butler. He loaded Mère's nice French furniture, her Pleyel piano, and four little girls, of whom the blondest and prettiest was my mother, on the boat bound for Greenville, and launched forth to make his fortune in the un-French, uncivilized, undeveloped Delta country.

Père was merely bon bourgeois. But through Mère's veins coursed the blood of the Générelly de Rinaldis. Having somehow failed to stumble on this truly magnificent name in song, story, or archive, I recall the tentative inquiry I once made of Mère concerning her forebears. I was told positively, though a bit vaguely, it seemed to me, that the original old Rinaldi from his castle in thirteenth-century Italy had descended on a lovely lady in a neighboring castle and made her, in disregard of her wishes, his consort, and that this exploit satisfied the family's yen for romance and heroism for five or six centuries — in fact, until Mère's grandfather, a dashing and aristocratic youth, was hustled out of revolutionary France by a faithful servant after untold hardships and escapes, and turned up in New Orleans with a few charming water-colors of tulips and roses and a deep sense of wrong. A trifle tenuous, perhaps, as proof of glorious lineage, but Mère was calmly adamant in the conviction that her blood was blue, which gave her the upper hand over Père right from the outset. This was rather sad, because he was a sweet and infinitely polite soul and had been a Captain under Beauregard. Nor did he improve his status with Mère by acquiring this outlandish Delta property. Though she could pioneer, she had neither admiration nor liking for the role — no French woman ever has — and I suspect he rather misrepresented its charm and elegance, being as he was on the poetic and sentimental side. Even naming the place Camelia after her did not pacify her or compensate for its living-quarters, which, far from being a mansion with white columns, were, I must confess, a log cabin, though a commodious one and fairly comfortable for those days. No, Mère never forgave him; you could tell it when she said "Mais, Ernest"; and even when with an "Ach" she tapped me on the head with her thimbled first finger, I suspected the correction was meant for him as much as for myself. Père was not lazy or even fundamentally incompetent, but his competency never got itself focused. He lost the plantation, moved his family to town, started one business venture after another, and failed in all of them. When Father married his daughter she was a very poor girl who made her own clothes — pretty ones I am told — and had never seen more of the outer world than New Orleans and the Sacré Coeur Convent, where Père somehow managed to have her educated. Père was miscast; besides having little girls, his only accomplishment was raising roses. His Maman Cochets and Malmaisons and Maréchal Niels were famous, or should have been in any civilized community. He should have been provided with dominoes, a desiccated crony or two, a siphon, a bottle of Amer Picon, and a corner in a dingy café where some broad-bosomed madame queened it behind an elevated guichet — and of course he should have had seats for the opera twice a week, including Sunday night.

Instead, his life petered out in a drab little country town, very Protestant and very Anglo-Saxon. In such a setting the French family must have seemed an oddity, but it never tried to be less odd or less French. The little girls continued to play croquet on Sunday, to the scandal of everyone, and to enliven shamelessly that dour and boring day by dance tunes on their little French piano, while their betters attended divine services. Their trouble, and their strength, was that they recognized no betters. Not that they minded Anglo-Saxons or took their own religion hard, but they regarded their poverty as an incident and their position as an immutability. Mère would never have sought the advice of a priest, or anyone else, but she could not have imagined herself anything but a Catholic — it was a habit, a good one, she was sure, but not interesting and distinctly not a subject for conversation. Nor would she have called on members of the congregation whom she considered excellent in everything except social standing, or on anyone in this semi-civilized community, first. As the little French girls grew up they were attractive and popular, which made things easier for everybody, yet Mère permitted courting only within the strict French convention. She was a pain to suitors, chaperoning her daughters everywhere and sitting in her corner of the parlor, playing solitaire, when they came courting. She maintained this observation post — half dragon and half Brangäne — even after Mother was engaged to Father, and his only revenge was occasionally to swipe a card from her deck so she couldn't make it. Father was the catch of the town, but Mère had no enthusiasm for the match: she knew he was what Aunt Nana would call "something of a gay blade," and it never crossed her mind that the Percys were any better than the Bourges.

Were they? In the South a question of that kind is apt to fling family skeletons from their closets into the middle of the parlor floor and to set extant sibs and collaterals shrieking like mandrakes. Even today from Virginia to Texas, from Charleston to Natchez, ten thousand crepuscular old maids and widows in ghostly coveys and clusters are solving such unsolvable issues. They are our Southern Norns, keepers of family Bibles, pruners of family trees, whose role is to remember and foretell — to remember glory and to foretell disaster — while in the gaudy day outside the banker's daughter, Brunhilde, elopes with the soda-water jerker. Père had he been less polite, Mère had she been less assured, might have introduced such devastating evidence into the Bourges-Percy controversy as would have titillated Norn circles for months. They must have known the bleak facts of my paternal ancestry, which confidentially were these:

The first Percy in our part of the South, my great-great-grandfather, was Charles. He blew in from the gray or blue sea-ways with a ship of his own, a cargo of slaves, and a Spanish grant to lands in the Buffalo country south of Natchez. Court records show that he was made an Alcalde and called Don Carlos by the Spaniards, and his house was known as Northumberland Place. This was shortly after the Revolution. Where did he come from? How came he by a Spanish grant? What were his antecedents and station? To such questions climbers in the family tree have found no answers: Don Carlos came from nowhere, he issued suddenly from the sea like the Flying Dutchman or Aphrodite — though Mrs. Dana once darkly confided to me that on his westerly flight he had landed at one of the Caribbean Isles and left a record behind him there nothing short of "lamentable, lamentable." Was he a pirate? Or the lost heir of the earls of Northumberland? Or a hero of the Spanish wars? Silence. Mystery.

Don Carlos settled down on his plantation and married him an intelligent French lady from the other side of the river. The Lord blessed them with progeny, and things seemed to be going well and quite respectably when a lady suddenly appeared from England and said to Don Carlos: "I am the long lost wife of your bosom." As if that was not enough, she added: "Behold, your son and heir!" Whereupon she tendered him, not a wee bairn, but a full-grown Captain in the

English Navy, also yclept Charles. Certainly a discouraging business all round. It is not recorded that Don Carlos slapped the lady, but of course he was thoroughly provoked and everybody immediately began suing everybody else. Somewhere during the commotion Don Carlos walked down to the creek with a sugar kettle, tied it round his neck, and hopped in. The creek is still there and is called Percy's Creek to this good day. His will left his holdings, not to his English, but to his American family, whether from pique, outrage, or affection I can only surmise. The wives continued their litigation for a while, wrote eloquent letters to the Governor, and acted as outraged gentlewomen usually act. Then everything was hushed up or patched up without a court decision; both families calmly settled down in the same neighborhood and lived happily ever afterwards. Need I say the English lady was not my ancestress? I have a tender feeling for Don Carlos and wish I could ask him confidentially a few leading questions. He was not exactly a credit to anybody, but, as ancestors go, he had his points.

I once drove to Woodville, a little town which has grown up near the old Percy place, to see if I could discover the grave of Don Carlos. I thought his dates might be clarifying, and once in a while an inscription on a headstone is penetrating to the point of cruelty, if you know half the story. Of the usual engaging youth at the filling station I inquired: "Can you tell me where Charles Percy is buried?" "No," he replied, "didn't know he was dead." I elucidated vaguely. He laughed. "Maybe he'll know, he's a Percy," he said, pointing to a pleasant-looking, countryfied man sitting on the ditch bank, spitting tobacco juice. "No," drawled my half cousin, "we never could find where the old bird was buried. I reckon it was on the creek bank, and the creek's changed its course."

Playing Tarzan in the family tree is hazardous business; there are too many rotten branches. Mère and Père would have put such irrelevancies in the class with religion, as distinctly not a subject for conversation. The Percys were nice people; the Bourges were nice people — voilà tout! But I cannot help wondering what were the qualifications that admitted to the post-Civil-War aristocracy. Apparently not pedigree, certainly not wealth. A way of life for several generations? A tradition of living? A style and pattern of thinking and feeling not acquired but inherited? No matter how it came about, the Bourges and Percys were nice people — that is what I breathed in as a child, the certainty I was as good as anyone else, which, because of the depth of the conviction, was unconscious, never talked of, never thought of. Besides Southerners, the only people I have ever met graced with the same informal assurance were Russian aristocrats.

I suspect, however, that no pair ever looked less aristocratic than Père and I, he in his neat but well-worn and out-of-style sack suit, I barefooted and hatless, as we rushed up the levee to see the *Floating Palace* come round the bend. The blast of the calliope way up the river had electrified the countryside. All the Negroes, all the children, and half the adults were swarming to the levee. From the thick of the laughter and shoving and pointing, he and I would watch the magnificent apparition sweep down the center of the stream, black smoke pouring from its funnel and white plumes of steam from the calliope, whose stentorian cacophonies were like the laughter of the gods at some pranks of Hebe's, only off key. Waiting for dark and the show to begin was unbearable. At last the calliope would hit a high note and hold it, until you almost burst, then dash into "Dixie," and we would rush down the levee, squeeze on to the gangplank, buy our tickets, and at last, at last, enter — Elysium. Such a grand, exciting smell of sweating people, everybody eating pink popcorn and drinking pop, such a dazzle of lights, such getting stepped on and knocked over and picked up, and at last the show, the beautiful, incredible show! A little Japanese with jerky angular gyrations climbed a ladder of sharp swords on feet as bare as mine; an adorable lady in pink tights floated through the air with ravishing grace while an elegant gentleman in full evening dress explained she came from the Garden of Eden; a baker's daughter hid seven suitors from her father in his oven and when he returned he built up the fire and they were baked to a crisp; in fact, the baker took them out of the oven for you to see and they were flat and brown, exactly like gingerbread men. This last was surpassingly horrible and gave me nightmares for a solid week, to the confusion of the family, who finally in desperation administered castor oil followed by raspberry jam. But all the rest was divinely beautiful. Show-boat! I never heard of such a name in my time. Everybody knew it was the *Floating Palace* and worthy, a thousand times, of its title.

Mère and Père were at their best, I think, at Roxbury, Aunt Nana's place in Virginia, or possibly I saw them there less interruptedly and less flurried by such incidents as beset those who can't quite make both ends meet. It was an old run-down place, far out in the country, and Mère's corner room was full of sunlight and breeze. On afternoons when it was too hot for me to go on expeditions with the little darkies, the three of us would convene there and Mère would bring out her quilting materials, needle and thread, and that thimble of hers. Aunt Nana might rustle in with glasses of blackberry vinegar, which apparently went out when cocktails came in. It had a kingly color and when chilled with ice, which Uncle George had harvested last winter from the pond and stored in sawdust against such occasions, it tasted like those snow and honey concoctions of the Greeks, just sweet enough and just sour enough and altogether Olympian. Mère's quilts were marvels of skill and took months and months to make. They were born from the tails of neckties and scraps of velvet and silk from petticoats, bustles, and linings. She first sewed the scraps into squares, then she sewed the squares on each side of a panel of watered silk into a quilt shape; next she bordered the whole with a hand's width of velvet, and last she embroidered all of it with wonderful flowers and birds and vines and bows and even little baskets. The result was as personal as that web of Penelope's and as French as the illegitimate daughters of Louis XIV. In the making the vexatious aesthetic problem was to match the colors of the scraps. She tried them out this way and that, sometimes even consulting Père and me on the effect, though this I fancy was mere affability. Pink, of course, matched with blue or lavender or even light green, but never with red. It was unthinkable to set green and blue side by side, or blue and lavender. Red was always difficult, but yellow could be sprinkled nearly haphazard. I would watch with deep interest and so received my first lesson in color-consciousness. Perhaps I should thank her for later hours of delight with Rembrandt and Titian, and blame her perhaps for my being still a little scared and shocked by El Greco.

Meanwhile Père would start humming, and that would be my cue to ask him what opera the tune was from, was it grand or comic, heavy or light, what was the plot, was it as good as *Les Huguenots? Les Huguenots* was his classic example of a heavy opera, into which category fell *Aïda, Faust,* and an opera new to New Orleans called *Lohengrin,* which he had been told was *very* heavy. *Les Huguenots* was also grand opera. Grand opera always ended with a death or a suicide, usually two or three of each. Then why was not *Carmen* a grand opera? Well, it was heavy but not grand, because they gave it on Sunday nights in New Orleans, and at the Comique, not the Opéra, in Paris. What! *Carmen* on Sunday nights, like *La Belle Hélène* and *La Fille de Madame*

Angot and *Giroflé-Girofla?* Why did they do that? As these distinctions became more tenuous and Père more hard-pressed, Aunt Nana, who loved peace though she never abandoned an argument, would cough and observe that everybody said the New Orleans Opera House really was more beautiful than the Paris Opéra. Mère would observe: "Évidemment," since the Paris Opéra had no loges découvertes. Père out of the exuberance of his memories would start singing "O mon fils" from *La Juive* and go on louder and louder until he came to shocking grief on the high C of the climax. Mère would look over her glasses and exclaim: "Mais, Ernest," but not in her usual Fricka-to-Wotan manner, indeed so sympathetically that in a distrait moment she would sew crimson next to shrimp pink.

The French do actually love music, but in a maddening way. When a favorite passage is well sung the thing to do is to cheer and cry "Bravo! Bis!"; you do not swoon. Mère would have had no patience with swooning for any cause, or with ecstasy as a result of music any more than as a result of religion. Music was a charming décor, a delightful adjunct to living, in the same category as chic clothes and a considered cuisine. The great French artists felt the same way about it: Clouet, Poussin, Chardin, Renoir never attempted ecstasy. If you wish to express sentiment, that is permissible, in the manner of Greuze and Massenet, but ecstasy, no, ecstasy is too much. Verlaine and Debussy tried it, but they were more neurotic than French, and their success lay not in content but in style, which in its perfection was absolutely French. It is a rare Frenchman who really prefers *Pelléas* to *Hérodiade,* or Verlaine to de Musset. Mère and Père wouldn't have done so; that I do only proves, I suppose, that moony strain of Don Carlos.

Music would be continued on a less exalted plane by Aunt Nana and me after supper. We would open the parlor, always shuttered and musty and cool by day, light the candles on each side of the black upright piano, and sing duets. "Just a Song at Twilight" and "Love's Old Sweet Song" were out favorites, and we liked a new piece, "After the Ball," which was very sad, almost as sad as the tune Mother used to sing to herself while sewing, "Tit Willow, Tit Willow, Tit Willow." I cannot explain why I so completely misinterpreted Gilbert and Sullivan's intention. I have made such mistakes all my life, and it's too late now to change. It was too late from the beginning. The color of our temperament, our chief concern, is nothing of our making. If we are pink, we can only hope that fate will not set us cheek by jowl with red. If we see the world through mauve glasses, there's no sort of sense in wishing they were white. We may only console ourselves by noting that a certain opalescence, like sun through the misty mornings of London, is not without a loveliness denied the truer and cruder white noons of the desert.

Mary Antin

Not all American childhoods begin in America, and for many the journey to the New World is the most important event in growing up. Mary Antin (1881–1949) was born in Russia. When she was thirteen she traveled across Europe and the Atlantic Ocean with her mother, two sisters, and a young brother to Boston, where they were met by her father, who had gone on ahead three years before.

Not long after their arrival in America, Mary wrote an account of the trip in Yiddish, and in 1889 From Polotzk to Boston *was published in English. Later she went to Barnard and to Columbia Teachers College, married a professor of paleontology, and become a settlement worker at Hale House in Boston. Her subsequent books, both of them on immigrants and immigration, were* The Promised Land *and* They Who Knock at Our Gates.

This excerpt, from the conclusion to From Polotzk to Boston, *begins with the five Antins waiting on the Hamburg docks for a ship to take them to America. They are staying in a section for women and young children called Number Five.*

From *From Polotzk to Boston*

THE GREATEST EVENT was the arrival of some ship to take some of the waiting passengers. When the gates were opened and the lucky ones said good bye, those left behind felt hopeless of ever seeing the gates open for them. It was both pleasant and painful, for the strangers grew to be fast friends in a day and really rejoiced in each other's fortune, but the regretful envy could not be helped.

Amid such events as these a day was like a month at least. Eight of these we had spent in quarantine when a great commotion was noticed among the people of Number Five and those of the corresponding number in the men's division. There was a good reason for it. You remember that it was April and Passover was coming on; in fact, it began that night. The great question was, would we be able to keep it exactly according to the host of rules to be obeyed? You who know all about the great holiday can understand what the answer to that question meant to us. Think of all the work and care and money it takes to supply a family with all the things proper and necessary and you will see that to supply a few hundred was no small matter. Now, were they going to take care that all was perfectly right, and could we trust them if they promised, or should we be forced to break any of the laws that ruled the holiday?

All day long there was talking and questioning and debating and threatening that "we would rather starve than touch anything we were not sure of." And we meant it. So some men and women went to the overseer to let him know what he had to look out for. He assured them that he would rather starve along with us than allow anything to be in the least wrong. Still, there was more discussing and shaking of heads, for they were not sure yet.

There was not a crumb anywhere to be found, because what bread we received was too precious for any of it to be wasted; but the women made a great show of cleaning up Number Five, while they sighed and looked sad and told one another of the good hard times they had at home getting ready for Passover. Really, hard as it is, when one is used to it from childhood, it seems part of the holiday, and can't be left out. To sit down and wait for supper as on other nights seemed like breaking one of the laws. So they tried hard to be busy.

At night we were called by the overseer (who tried to look more important than ever in his holiday clothes — not his best, though) to the feast spread in one of the unoccupied rooms. We were ready for it, and anxious enough. We had had neither bread nor matzo for dinner, and were more hungry than ever, if that is possible. We now found everything really prepared; there were the pillows covered with a snow-white spread, new oilcloth on the newly scrubbed tables, some little candles stuck in a basin of sand on the window-sill for the women, and — a sure sign of a holiday — both gas lamps burning. Only one was used on other nights.

Happy to see these things, and smell the supper, we took our places and waited. Soon the cook came in and filled some glasses with wine from two bottles — one yellow, one red. Then she gave to each person — exactly one and a half matzos; also some cold meat, burned almost to a coal for the occasion. The young man — bless him — who had the honor to perform the ceremonies, was, fortunately for us all, one of the passengers. He felt for and with us, and it happened — past a coincidence — that the greater part of the ceremony escaped from his book as he turned the leaves. Though strictly religious, nobody felt in the least guilty about it, especially on account of the wine, for, when we came to the place where you have to drink the wine, we found it tasted like good vinegar, which made us all choke and gasp, and one little girl screamed "Poison!" so that all laughed, and the leader, who tried to go on, broke down too at the sight of the wry faces he saw; while the overseer looked shocked, the cook nearly set her gown on fire by overthrowing the candles with her apron (used to hide her face) and all wished our Master Overseer had to drink that "wine" all his days.

Think of the same ceremony as it is at home, then of this one just described. Do they even resemble each other?

Well, the leader got through amid much giggling and sly looks among the girls who understood the trick, and frowns of the older people (who secretly blessed him for it). Then, half hungry, all went to bed and dreamed of food in plenty.

No other dreams? Rather! For the day that brought the Passover brought us — our own family — the most glorious news. We had been ordered to bring our baggage to the office!

"Ordered to bring our baggage to the office!" That meant nothing less than that we were "going the next day!"

It was just after supper that we received the welcome order. Oh, who cared if there wasn't enough to eat? Who cared for anything in the whole world? We didn't. It was all joy and gladness and happy anticipation for us. We laughed, and cried, and hugged one another, and shouted, and acted altogether like wild things. Yes, we were wild with joy, and long after the rest were asleep, we were whispering together and wondering how we could keep quiet the whole night. We couldn't sleep by any means, we were so afraid of oversleeping the great hour; and every little while, after we tried to sleep, one of us would suddenly think she saw day at the window, and wake the rest, who also had only been pretending to sleep while watching in the dark for daylight.

When it came, it found no watchful eye, after all. The excitement gave way to fatigue, and drowsiness first, then deep sleep, completed its victory. It was eight o'clock when we awoke. The morning was cloudy and chilly, the sun being too lazy to attend to business; now and then it rained a little, too. And yet it was the most beautiful day that had ever dawned on Hamburg. We enjoyed everything offered for breakfast, two matzos and two cups of tea apiece — why it was a banquet. After it came the good-byes, as we were going soon. As I told you before, the strangers became fast friends in a short time under the circumstances, so there was real sorrow at the partings, though the joy of the fortunate ones was, in a measure, shared by all.

About one o'clock (we didn't go to dinner — we couldn't eat for excitement) we were called. There were three other families, an old woman, and a young man, among the Jewish passengers, who were going with us, besides some Polish people. We were all hurried through the door we had watched with longing for so long, and were a little way from it when the old woman stopped short and called on the rest to wait.

"We haven't any matzo!" she cried in alarm. "Where's the overseer?"

Sure enough we had forgotten it, when we might as well have left one of us behind. We refused to go, calling for the overseer, who had promised to supply us, and the man who had us in charge grew angry and said he wouldn't wait. It was a terrible situation for us.

"Oh," said the man, "you can go and get your matzo, but the boat won't wait for you." And he walked off, followed by the Polish people only.

We had to decide at once. We looked at the old woman. She said she wasn't going to start on a dangerous journey with such a sin on her soul. Then the children decided. They understood the matter. They cried and begged to follow the party. And we did.

Just when we reached the shore, the cook came up panting hard. She brought us matzo. How relieved we were then!

We got on a little steamer (the name is too big for it) that was managed by our conductor alone. Before we had recovered from the shock of the shrill whistle so near us, we were landing in front of a large stone building.

Once more we were under the command of the gendarme. We were ordered to go into a big room crowded with people, and wait till the name of our ship was called. Somebody in a little room called a great many queer names, and many passengers answered the call. At last we heard,

"Polynesia!"

We passed in and a great many things were done to our tickets before we were directed to go outside, then to a larger steamer than the one we came in. At every stop our tickets were either stamped or punched, or a piece torn off of them; till we stepped upon the steamer's deck. Then we were ordered below. It was dark there, and we didn't like it. In a little while we were called up again and then we saw before us the great ship that was to carry us to America.

I only remember, from that moment, that I had only one care till all became quiet: not to lose hold of my sister's hand. Everything else can be told in one word — noise. But when I look back, I can see what made it. There were sailors dragging and hauling bundles and boxes from the small boat into the great ship, shouting and thundering at their work. There were officers giving out orders in loud voices, like trumpets, though they seemed to make no effort. There were children crying, and mothers hushing them, and fathers questioning the officers as to where they should go. There were little boats and steamers passing all around, shrieking and whistling terribly. And there seemed to be everything under heaven that had any noise in it, come to help swell the confusion of sounds. I know that, but how we ever got in that quiet place that had the sign "For Families" over it, I don't know. I think we went around and around, long and far, before we got there.

But there we were, sitting quietly on a bench by the white berths.

When the sailors brought our things, we got everything in order for the journey as soon as possible, that we might go on deck to see the starting. But first we had to obey a sailor, who told us to come and get dishes. Each person received a plate, a spoon and a cup. I wondered how we could get along if we had no things of our own.

For an hour or two more there were still many noises on deck, and many preparations made. Then we went up, as most of the passengers did.

What a change in the scene! Where there had been noise and confusion before, peace and quiet were now. All the little boats and steamers had disappeared, and the wharf was deserted. On deck the "Polynesia" everything was in good order, and the officers walked about smoking their cigars as if their work was done. Only a few sailors were at work at the big ropes, but they didn't shout as before. The weather had changed, too, for the twilight was unlike what the day had promised. The sky was soft gray, with faint streaks of yellow on the horizon. The air was still and pleasant, much warmer than it had been all the day; and the water was as motionless and clear as a deep, cool well, and everything was mirrored in it clearly.

This entire change in the scene, the peace that encircled everything around us, seemed to give all the same feeling that I know I had. I fancied that nature created it especially for us, so that we should be allowed, in this pause, to think of our situation. All seemed to do so; all spoke in low voices, and seemed to be looking for something as they gazed quietly into the smooth depths below, or the twilight skies above. Were they seeking an assurance? Perhaps; for there was something strange in the absence of a crowd of friends on the shore, to cheer and salute, and fill the air with clouds and last farewells.

I found the assurance. The very stillness was a voice — nature's voice; and it spoke to the ocean and said,

"I entrust to you this vessel. Take care of it, for it bears my children with it, from one strange shore to another more distant, where loving friends are waiting to embrace them after long partings. Be gentle with your charge."

And the ocean, though seeming so still, replied, "I will obey my mistress."

I heard it all, and a feeling of safety and protection came to me. And when at last the wheels overhead began to turn and clatter, and the ripples on the water told us that the "Polynesia" had started on her journey which was not noticeable from any other sign, I felt only a sense of happiness. I mistrusted nothing.

But the old woman who remembered the matzo did, more than anybody else. She made great preparations for being seasick, and poisoned the air with garlic and onions.

When the lantern fixed in the ceiling had been lighted, the captain and the steward paid us a visit. They took up our tickets and noticed all the passengers, then left. Then a sailor brought supper — bread and coffee. Only a few ate it. Then all went to bed, though it was very early.

Nobody expected seasickness as soon as it seized us. All slept quietly the whole night, not knowing any difference between being on land or at sea. About five o'clock I woke up, and then I felt and heard the sea. A very disagreeable smell came from it, and I knew it was disturbed by the rocking of the ship. Oh, how wretched it made us! From side to side it went rocking, rocking. Ugh! Many of the passengers are very sick indeed, they suffer terribly. We are all awake now, and wonder if we, too, will be so sick. Some children are crying, at intervals. There is nobody to comfort them — all are so miserable. Oh, I am so sick! I'm dizzy; everything is going round and round before my eyes — Oh-h-h!

I can't even begin to tell of the suffering of the next few hours. Then I thought I would feel better if I could go on deck. Somehow, I got down (we had upper berths) and, supporting myself against the walls, I came on deck. But it was worse. The green water, tossing up the white foam, rocking all around, as far as I dared to look, was frightful to me then. So I crawled back as well as I could, and nobody else tried to go out.

By and by the doctor and the steward came. The doctor asked each passenger if they were well, but only smiled when all begged for some medicine to take away the dreadful suffering. To those who suffered from anything besides seasickness he sent medicine and special food later on. His companion appointed one of the men passengers for every twelve or fifteen to carry the meals from the kitchen, giving them cards to get it with. For our group a young German was appointed, who was making the journey for the second time, with his mother and sister. We were great friends with them during the journey.

The doctor went away soon, leaving the sufferers in the same sad condition. At twelve, a sailor announced that dinner was ready, and the man brought it — large tin pails and basins of soup, meat, cabbage, potatoes, and pudding (the last was allowed only once a week); and almost all of it was thrown away, as only a few men ate. The rest couldn't bear even the smell of food. It was the same with the supper at six o'clock. At three milk had been brought for the babies, and brown bread (a treat) with coffee for the rest. But after supper the daily allowance of fresh water was brought, and this soon disappeared and more called for, which was refused, although we lived on water alone for a week.

At last the day was gone, and much we had borne in it. Night came, but brought little relief. Some did fall asleep, and forgot suffering for a few hours. I was awake late. The ship was quieter, and everything sadder than by daylight. I thought of all we had gone through till we had got on board the "Polynesia"; of the parting from all friends and things we loved, forever, as far as we knew; of the strange experience at various strange places; of the kind friends who helped us, and the rough officers who commanded us; of the quarantine, the hunger, then the happy news, and the coming on board. Of all this I thought, and remembered that we were far away from friends, and longed for them, that I might be made well by speaking to them. And every minute was making the distance between us greater, a meeting more impossible. Then I remembered why we were crossing the ocean, and knew that it was worth the price. At last the noise of the wheels overhead, and the dull roar of the sea, rocked me to sleep. . . .

On the eighth day out we are again able to be about. I went around everywhere, exploring every corner, and learning much from the sailors; but I never remembered the names of the various things I asked about, they were so many, and some German names hard to learn. We all made friends with the captain and other officers, and many of the passengers. The little band played regularly on certain days, and the sailors and girls had a good many dances, though often they were swept by a wave across the deck, quite out of time. The children were allowed to play on deck, but carefully watched. Still the weather continued the same, or changing slightly. But I was able now to see all the grandeur of my surroundings, notwithstanding the weather.

Oh, what solemn thoughts I had! How deeply I felt the greatness, the power of the scene! The immeasurable distance from horizon to horizon; the huge billows forever changing their shapes — now only a wavy and rolling plain, now a chain of great mountains, coming and going farther away; then a town in the disance, perhaps, with spires and towers and buildings of gigantic dimensions; and mostly a vast mass of uncertain shapes, knocking against each other in fury, and seething and foaming in their anger; the grey sky, with its mountains of gloomy clouds, flying, moving with the waves, as it seemed, very near them; the absence of any object besides the one ship; and the deep, solemn groans of the sea, sounding as if all the voices of the world had been turned into sighs and then gathered into that one mournful sound — so deeply did I feel the presence of these things, that the feeling became one of awe, both painful and sweet, and stirring and warming, and deep and calm and grand. . . .

In this way the days went by. I thought my thoughts each day, as I watched the scene, hoping to see a beautiful sunset some day. I never did, to my disappointment. And each night, as I lay in my berth, waiting for sleep, I wished I might be able even to hope for the happiness of a sea voyage after this had been ended.

Yet, when, on the twelfth day after leaving Hamburg, the captain announced that we should see land before long, I rejoiced as much as anybody else. We were so excited with expectation that nothing else was heard but the talk of the happy arrival, now so near. Some were even willing to stay up at night, to be the first ones to see the shores of America. It was therefore a great disappointment when the captain said, in the evening, that we would not reach Boston as soon as he expected, on account of the weather.

A dense fog set in at night, and grew heavier and heavier, until the "Polynesia" was closely walled in by it, and we could just see from one end of the deck to the other. The signal lanterns were put up, the passengers were driven to their berths by the cold and damp, the cabin doors closed, and discomfort reigned everywhere.

But the excitement of the day had tired us out, and we were glad to forget disappointment in sleep. In the morning it was still foggy, but we could see a little way around. It was very strange to have the boundless distance made so narrow, and I felt the strangeness of the scene. All day long we shivered with cold, and hardly left the cabin. At last it was night once more, and we in our berths. But nobody slept. . . .

It was day again, and a little calmer. We slept now, till the afternoon. Then we saw that the fog had become much thinner and later on we even saw a ship, but indistinctly.

Another night passed, and the day that followed was pretty fair, and towards evening the sky was almost cloudless. The captain said we should have no more rough weather, for now we were really near Boston. Oh, how hard it was to wait for the happy day! Somebody brought the news that we should land tomorrow in the afternoon. We didn't believe it, so he said that the steward had ordered a great pudding full of raisins for supper that day as a sure sign that it was the last on board. We remembered the pudding, but didn't believe in its meaning.

I don't think we slept that night. After all the suffering of our journey, after seeing and hearing nothing but the sky and the sea and its roaring, it was impossible to sleep when we thought that soon we should see trees, fields, fresh people, animals — a world, and that world America. Then, above everything, was the meeting with friends we had not seen for years; for almost everybody had some friends awaiting them.

Morning found all the passengers up and expectant. Someone

questioned the captain, and he said we would land tomorrow. There was another long day, and another sleepless night, but when these ended at last, how busy we were! First we packed up all things we did not need, then put on fresh clothing, and then went on deck to watch for land. It was almost three o'clock, the hour the captain hoped to reach Boston, but there was nothing new to be seen. The weather was fair, so we would have seen anything within a number of miles. Anxiously we watched, and as we talked of the strange delay, our courage began to give out with our hope. When it could be borne no longer, a gentleman went to speak to the captain. He was on the upper deck, examining the horizon. He put off the arrival for the next day!

You can imagine our feelings at this. When it was worse the captain came down and talked so assuringly that, in spite of all the disappointments we had had, we believed that this was the last, and were quite cheerful when we went to bed.

The morning was glorious. It was the eighth day of May, the seventeenth day after we left Hamburg. The sky was clear and blue, the sun shone brightly, as if to congratulate us that we had safely crossed the stormy sea, and to apologize for having kept away from us so long. The sea had lost its fury; it was almost as quiet as it had been at Hamburg before we started, and its color was a beautiful greenish blue. Birds were all the time in the air, and it was worthwhile to live merely to hear their songs. And soon, oh joyful sight! we saw the tops of two trees!

What a shout there rose! Everyone pointed out the welcome sight to everybody else, as if they did not see it. All eyes were fixed on it as if they saw a miracle. And this was only the beginning of the joys of the day!

What confusion there was! Some were flying up the stairs to the upper deck, some were tearing down to the lower one, others were running in and out of the cabins, some were in all parts of the ship in one minute, and all were talking and laughing and getting in somebody's way. Such excitement, such joy! We had seen two trees!

Then steamers and boats of all kinds passed by, in all directions. We shouted, and the men stood up in the boats and returned the greeting, waving their hats. We were as glad to see them as if they were old friends of ours.

Oh, what a beautful scene! No corner of the earth is half so fair as the lovely picture before us. It came to view suddenly, — a green field, a real field with grass on it, and large houses, and the dearest hens and little chickens in all the world, and trees, and birds, and people at work. The young green things put new life into us, and are so dear to our eyes that we dare not speak a word now, lest the magic should vanish away and we should be left to the stormy scenes we know.

But nothing disturbed the fairy sight. Instead, new scenes appeared, beautiful as the first. The sky becomes bluer all the time, the sun warmer; the sea is too quiet for its name, and the most beautiful blue imaginable.

What are the feelings these sights awaken! They cannot be described. To know how great was our happiness, how complete, how free from even the shadow of a sadness, you must make a journey of sixteen days on a stormy ocean. Is it possible that we will ever again be so happy?

It was about three hours since we saw the first landmarks, when a number of men came on board, from a little steamer, and examined the passengers to see if they were properly vaccinated (we had been vaccinated on the "Polynesia"), and pronounced everyone all right. Then they went away, except one man who remained. An hour later we saw the wharves.

Before the ship had fully stopped, the climax of our joy was reached. One of us espied the figure and face we had longed to see for three long years. In a moment five passengers on the "Polynesia" were crying, "Papa," and gesticulating, and laughing, and hugging one another, and going wild altogether. All the rest were roused by our excitement, and came to see our father. He recognized us as soon as we him, and stood apart on the wharf not knowing what to do, I thought.

What followed was slow torture. Like mad things we ran about where there was room, unable to stand still as long as we were on the ship and he on shore. To have crossed the ocean only to come within a few yards of him, unable to get nearer till all the fuss was over, was dreadful enough. But to hear other passengers called who had no reason for hurry, while we were left among the last, was unendurable.

Oh, dear! Why can't we get off the hateful ship? Why can't papa come to us? Why so many ceremonies at the landing?

We said good-bye to our friends as their turn came, wishing we were in their luck. To give us something else to think of, papa succeeded in passing us some fruit; and we wondered to find it anything but a great wonder, for we expected to find everything marvellous in the strange country.

Still the ceremonies went on. Each person was asked a hundred or so stupid questions, and all their answers were written down by a very slow man. The baggage had to be examined, the tickets, and a hundred other things done before anyone was allowed to step ashore, all to keep us back as long as possible.

Now imagine yourself parting with all you love, believing it to be a parting for life; breaking up your home, selling the things that years have made dear to you; starting on a journey without the least experience in travelling, in the face of many inconveniences on account of the want of sufficient money; being met with disappointment when it was not to be expected; with rough treatment everywhere, till you are forced to go and make friends for yourself among strangers; being obliged to sell some of our most necessary things to pay bills you did not willingly incur; being mistrusted and searched, then half starved, and lodged in common with a multitude of strangers; suffering the miseries of seasickness, the disturbances and alarms of a stormy sea for sixteen days; and then stand within a few yards of him for whom you did all this, unable to even speak to him easily. How do you feel?

Oh, it's our turn at last! We are questioned, examined and dismissed! A rush over the planks on one side over the ground on the other, six wild beings cling to each other, bound by a common bond of tender joy, and the long parting is at an END.

Wanda Gág

Wanda Gág (1893–1946), the writer and illustrator of Millions of Cats *and dozens of other children's books, once observed:*

> *I was born in this country, but often feel as though I had spent my early years in Europe. My father was born in Bohemia, as were my mother's parents. My birthplace — New Ulm, Minnesota — was settled by Middle-Europeans, and I grew up in an atmosphere of Old World customs and legends, of Bavarian and Bohemian folk songs, of German* Märchen *and* Turnverein *activities. I spoke no English until I went to school.*

Her father, an artist, died when she was fifteen, leaving behind a wife, seven children, and very little money. On his deathbed he told Wanda, "Was der Papa nicht thun konnt', muss die Wanda halt fertig machen" ("What Papa couldn't do, Wanda will have to finish"). She took him literally and decided to help support the family by selling drawings to the local newspapers.

In October 1908, Wanda began a diary that would include not only the record of her business transactions, but also a portrait of life in her busy family and a collection of naive sketches of her brothers and sisters that almost look as though they could have been torn from the notebook of the turn-of-the-century Swedish painter Carl Larsson.

From "New Ulm, Minnesota,"
Growing Pains

Monday, Oct. 12, 1908

I sent one of my pictures to the Journal Junior, "Toddie's Hanged Our Dollies," and forgot to put my address on it so I sent another envelope with my address on it. The same day I sent a story, "Lou's Soap Bubble Party," and a picture to illustrate it, to McCall's. Some time ago I sent these three articles to the Youth's Companion —

> Story — Golden Brooch
> Picture — Great Grandmother's Chest
> Poem —   "   "   "

I wonder how the whole thing will turn out.

A few days ago Margaret Kelly told me that Marsha Schmid didn't believe I drew free hand. She thinks I trace. Trace indeed! When I don't even care much for copying.

Tuesday, Oct. 13

Some time ago I got a check for $1.00 prize from the Woman's Home Companion for a drawing. It had 14 children on it. I got the dollar at the Citizen's Bank.

I'm thru reading "Kristy's Rainy Day Party" and quite done with the Orange Fairy Book.

It is a beautiful day.

I do hope Mae Harris Anson [editor of the Journal Junior] will not throw away my picture before my second letter with my address reaches her.

The baby can say Deya for Stella, Dudi for Tussy, Adda for Asta, Deyi for Dehli, and all kinds of other words that she learns every day.

The same day I was at the bank I got our Fair money for this and last year, $3.25 in all.

1907	Wanda drawing — 1st	$.50
	Dehli and Asta drawing — 1st	$.50
	Tussy pillow slip — 2nd	$.25
1908	Wanda drawing — 1st	$.50
	Dehli " — 1st	$.50
	Wanda " — 3rd	$.25
	Stella Splasher — 2nd	$.25
	Tussy centerpiece — 1st	$.50

My money from the Fair and the one dollar from the Women's Home Companion will go for shoes, I think.

School is going out now. We'll have pot pie for dinner.

Wednesday, Oct. 14. A fine day.

Mama went to Hasenclever's today.

Tussy, Asta, and Dehli made some pictures yesterday evening but

Asta only carried out her idea on paper, "Taking a picture with a Kodak." It's as cute as it can be, and if she gets it as nice on the drawing paper I'm sure it'll be pretty good, for her at least. I didn't know she could do so well. Dehli and Tussy have theirs on drawing paper already, in India ink. Tussy's is called "Getting ready for Hallow e'en," and Delhi's is called "Eating Egg-O-See."

I started a story last night and I'm going to write some of it now——

Thursday, Oct. 15. A splendid day.

I finished the story yesterday and started another one.

Mama lay down this afternoon, and is still in bed.

The baby can say these words: Bugga for buggy, baba for baby, plll for please, Oh Gaka for Oh jiminy cracker, mama, bu for *bub*, mi for *mich; heis, horch,* and *guck da,* and can smack for driving. Abba for apple, gaggak for duck, *ch ch* and *doot doot* for a train, and a great many more.

I made supper tonight. We had fried potatoes, left over cabbage, and a little bit of veal-stew. We took mama's supper up on the waiter. The baby slept twice. I ironed a little today.

Saturday, Oct. 17. A dreary day.

Made another picture, "When sister makes the candy."

Yesterday grandma sent up two chickens, some cabbage, carrots and three cheese-cakes.

Stella made up a poem about a leaf last night, and Thursday night I wrote 2 poems, "The Snowstorm" and "A Mother Goose Party." Here is "The Snowstorm."

>   *1. I go to bed with my candle-light.*
>   *Outside the world is solemn and white,*
>   *And quietly, softly, hushed and slow,*
>   *Come the pretty, white little flakes of snow.*
>   *And leaving the world so calm and so white,*
>   *I creep to bed in the peaceful night.*
>   *2. In the morning when I get up. Oh ho!*
>   *The world is full of the drifting snow!*
>   *The little red house way down by the hills,*
>   *Is drifted with snow to its window sills.*
>   *I meet the world in the early morn,*
>   *In a jolly, frollicky wild snowstorm!*

I'm making an everyday jumper out of one of mama's wrappers. It isn't going to be pretty, I think. As far as I know it's going to be *horrid*. I'll have to get new shoes. My others are too small. We gave Ritschl's grandmother a picture of herself and her husband which papa painted.

I was at Ione Dekker's and got the Oct. Woman's Home Companion. Am writing the story of a Hollowe'en party to send them. Asta wrote a story too. It's just too funny! The baby is still up. She isn't sleepy yet. We have to laugh so much at her. She can say book, Aggaga for Egg-O-See and wawa for water. She can chew gum nicely.

Tussi, Stella + Asta   Bobbing for Apples.

Monday, Oct. 19. Sunny at times but smoky and windy.

They say the biggest mill in Minneapolis is burning. They also say that the woods in Michigan are burning.

I sketched the baby tonight after school, and just a little while before, I sketched Asta 4 times and Dehli 3 times. I sketched them in a dark room. They wore a night gown and held a candle. I want one for "The Snowstorm." 2 of them are in India Ink. The others are in pencil. I wish I had a decent pencil. The one I got from Karl Ritschl has disappeared. I have a faint Idea of seeing it in the desk-drawer last but search as I will, I can't find it.

Today was "leaf-searching" day. I got the *most* leaves and the prettiest ones, too; plum leaves, apple tree leaves, raspberry bush leaves, rose bush leaves, maple leaves and any number of other kinds. I have two shoe boxes full and a capful, and one of the buggy pockets is full too. Aunt Magdalene was here.

I like "Merrylips" but "Roberta & her brothers" isn't as good as I thought. Had sago pudding tonight. Good night.

Oct. 21, Wednesday. Rainy, dark day.

Aunt Mary was here yesterday and brought me 2 waists and a skirt. She told me Erna Rosen wants half a dozen postals. That makes a dozen I've got to make because Miss Brown wants 6.

Rec'd (for painting postals) $3.95		1907 Fair Money	$ .50
Cost 51½		1908 Fair Money	.75
Gain 3.43½		Prize from W. H. Companion	1.00
$1.69			$1.75
3.43½		6 cts. stamps for sending . . .	.06
.10 for stamping table cover			$1.69
Total gain $5.22½			

The baby thinks she can draw! — "ma guck grrrrr," she says.

Oct. 23. Rain, Rain, Rain.

Fern Fischer and Judy Dekker were over here last night. I made Judy a paper doll and Fern a picture. Washed and dried the breakfast dishes today and washed the dinner dishes. Today is ironing day and ironing night too it seems.

I made the first illustration to "The Snowstorm" tonight, that is, put in the shadings, etc. Wish I had somebody to tell me what they think about it. Somebody that knows about art. Stella is too young to criticise. No mail for me. It's perfectly discouraging. Wish I could draw like Mary True Ayer.

Oct. 26, Monday. Rain, Rain, Rain.

Rain since Friday *more* or *less*. Saturday we worked most of the time. Not much time for reading, drawing or anything like that. Yesterday I was over at Dekker's in the evening with Stella. Wore the white and pink lawn dress. We had apple dumplings for our Sunday dinner, and sour fish for supper tonight. We bought him of Mr. Schmid for 15 cents. For dinner we had beef steak fried in the furnace. Copied pretty many stories and poems* the day before yesterday, and Sunday I started to copy a fairy story.* No drawing worth mentioning.

Mama was up at Helk's today. I cleaned up part of the children's side of the attic today. They've mussed it all up. I gave Tussy a bundle of cloth to sew with today.

Nov. 2. A fine, warm, sunny day.

My hopes are shattered some. Got a letter from the Youth's Companion with my stuff in it & a letter from one of the Co.

Fern Fischer was here yesterday and she said that somebody told her that I don't do anything but read and draw. I guess so! I wonder if washing dishes, sweeping about 6 times a day, picking up things the baby and Howard throw around are reading. And I've never heard of taking care of babies, combing little sisters, cleaning bed rooms & attics as being classed as drawing! I wonder what else people will say about me.

Yesterday night I drew and inked 12 postals and today I colored them. They are all for Thanksgiving & I think I'll ask Eggen's Drug Store if they don't want to buy any of me.

* My own.

Made a picture not long ago called "The Bonfire."

I've got my new shoes now. They cost $1.75.

I've read "Betty Wales Junior" and it's splendid! Stella got "Miss Petticoats" but I didn't read it because I haven't much time & I've read it when I was in the 8th grade.

Dehli's drawing pictures all the time for her friends.

Nov. 11, Wed. A cold, bright day.

Miss Meadows* asked me whether I was going somewhere to study art later, and I told her I'd like to go to high school first. "All right, come in January," she said. But I don't know whether I can. To be sure I'd like to but —. Ione Dekker said that I should take 4 half subjects & so get 2 credits.

I've got Tussy's Christmas presents done — two of them — bookmarks.

I and Stella and Asta were out at Aunt Klaus's. We got a lot of pretty milkweeds & rose berries & autumn leaves, besides some apples which Aunt Klaus gave us along. We had a splendid time.

I drew a heading in india ink for Aunt Janet's Pages† but I don't know whether I'll send it — the stamps are giving out, that's why. My india ink is quite gone too. I don't see how I'm to get some when it's gone.

I phoned to Eggen's Drug Store several days ago and asked what they intended to do about the postals and they said they'd keep them. He said they'd sold quite a number already.

* A high-school teacher.

† A juvenile feature of the *Woman's Home Companion*.

November 12. A cold day. It's snowing.

Mama didn't feel well so I made supper. We didn't have much to make anyway, just bacon and potatoes to fry. Made a Fireplace Picture last night. I'd like to send it to the Journal Junior, but the stamps —.

Nov. 13. A cold snowy day. Friday.

Great good luck! I found an old book with 5 stamps — 2 cent stamps — in it! I'm so glad. Now I'm going to send the Heading for Aunt Janet's Pages, and one or two pictures to the Journal Junior. I sorted all our labels today. We've got 90 covers of Fleischmann's Compressed Yeast — 50 of Lion Coffee heads — 30 of 9 O'clock Washing Tea. That's how I found the stamps. The baby can say *dümp* for *strümpf*. Asta is copying a story tonight which she wrote some time ago. It's called "The Girl who didn't Obey her Mother." I found the big eraser again today.

Nov. 15, Sunday

Good luck!!!!!!!!

I just got the Journal Junior from Fern, and my picture, "Toddie's Hanged Our Dollies," is in it! I suppose the dollar prize will come pretty soon. Oh I'm so glad. That makes another dollar for mama.

I promised to draw Miss Brown a picture and she promised to give me a 2 cent stamp to send the Heading for Aunt Janet's Pages away. I'm glad. Asta's drawing a picture tonight. The baby can hug, kiss, show us where her heart is, and show us her tongue.

"Toddie has hanged our dollies"

Nov. 16, Monday

I got the check for one dollar from the J.J. today. Otherwise no mail. I got the stamp from Miss Brown today. Copied Miss Brown's sheet music called "Dreaming." It's a pretty piece.

Nov. 17, Tuesday

I got a letter from a little eight year girl in Minneapolis complimenting me on my picture in the J.J. Stella got the "Prisoner of Zenda" today. I've read over half. It's splendid. We had our storm windows made on today. I found the pencil I got from Karl Ritschl, today. I'm writing with it. It was a beautiful day.

Nov. 18

A beautiful day but oh! so twisted! Mama bought wood today — $8½ a cord. I wasn't good today, I read too much and didn't work enough. But really I wish I hadn't been so bad.

Stella, Tussy & Asta are over by Fischer's this evening, and I and mama cried.

November 19. A nice day. Thursday.

Today was wash day. I and Stella rung out and hung up nearly all the wash (which was not so very much). The baby is getting cuter all the time.

Nov. 27

I have been down at grandma's. We came home yesterday in time for the Thanksgiving dinner. We had pumpkin pie, potatoes, goose & apples. Oh I was homesick the last day I was at grandma's.

Vivian Ritschl wants 2 dozen place cards painted, a cupid holding a package of rice. She's going to marry soon and I think her mama gives her a party next Tuesday.

I went down to Eggen's to get some paints. I got *Devoe* with 2 yellow, 1 blue, 1 red, & also 5 Calendars at 1 cent a piece. I sell postals to Eggen's, 6 for 25 cents & they sell them for 5 cents straight thru. That makes $.75 credit for our school books, the cost of all was $1.13 I believe. I'll have that paid off pretty soon.

Aunt Magdalene was here. She brought me a blue velvet hat and promised me a black and white checked jumper. I'm so glad!

No mail! We've got the baby up quite late tonight & she's so foxy! She mocks just everything we do. I was at Ione's tonight & she gave me 2 great sheets of drawing paper. I'm glad of that too.

November 30. A cold windy day.

Fern Fischer came over in the afternoon and brought the Journal Junior. Ione's story is in it. That's the second one she has had in. Perhaps I'll send one pretty soon too.

December 1. A cold, windy, sunny day.

It was zero this morning. Inked 6 postals while the baby was sleeping this afternoon and inked 4 tonight. No mail for me. I wonder when I'm going to hear from McCall's? Stella got "Dotty Dimple at School" today. I've read nearly all of it. It's good.

Dehli's wearing Asta's coat, Asta's wearing Tussy's, and Tussy's wearing the one which used to be Stella's. All of us have coats now except I & mama.

December 2, Wednesday

The baby can say gatz for *katz* which means cat. Sometimes when she has something she oughtn't to have, then we try to take it from her, she says, "Da bow-wow gomt da," for "*Der bow-wow kommt da,*" meaning "There comes the dog." She tries to scare us that way but we can't scare her. She simply isn't afraid of anything.

The baby slept in the morning. In the afternoon I went down to Eggen's to bring a dozen postals down. I took some pretty heavy drawing paper along home too. You get 2 great big sheets for a nickel so I got a nickel's worth. I asked Eggen's clerk whether they had any India Ink in bottles and he told me they had only the sticks. He asked me what kind of bottles they were and I described them to him and he said he could write it down on the order list and get one for me. He is very nice and obliging to customers. I had on my hat that I got from Aunt Magdalene. Eggen's have a great many nice books that I'd like to have. I wish I had a little more money. I hope I'll get a book for Christmas.

No mail at all for me. I do hope McCall's got my story and illustrations, but it almost seems as if they didn't because I haven't heard from them for so long.

We had chicken pot pie for supper. I'm drawing postals again tonight.

December 7, Monday. A cold but bright day.

December 4th was Dehli's birthday. She didn't get anything from us because we didn't have enough time & money to give her anything. Perhaps Asta and Tussy made her some pictures or cards tho.

Oh but I worked this afternoon. I was pegging away at copying a story with the *most horrid* pen. It scratched just like everything. It made me so cross and it was almost a thousand words long, too. I had the baby upstairs with me, too, while I was writing it. She kept climbing on my chair and begging for candy. Finally I had it done, it was the story about the "Punken Hunt" with two boys in it called Fletcher and Buster.

I sent it to the J.J. I wanted to illustrate it at first — because several years ago I sent one too, illustrated & the Editor said I should send another one illustrated on unruled paper (I had my picture on ruled

ink paper) but I've never tried it since then — but I didn't have time enough so I sent it off without.

Dear! I've such a lot to do! Xmas presents! (to make without any money at all, as may be said) Miss Brown's picture! Postals! etc.! etc.!

In the afternoon Stella went up to Hasenclever's. She got two big pieces of cloth to choose from for the bag which they make in school. Mama couldn't afford it so Mrs. Hasenclever was kind enough to give her some. One is a piece of silk crepe and the other is cashmere or imitation. Stella will use the silk, I think, and mama gets the cashmere.

Saturday the *Stroh zempra** was at our house. Mama went (?) to the butcher shop and suddenly a great rattling and clattering was heard outside the door. The smaller children, (except baby) were in bed but they came down thinking it was music. I & Stella made believe holding the door so he (or she!) couldn't get in. Then all at once some candy came dashing into the room by way of the door and we picked it up. They were all so scared that they wanted to eat the candy next day! and Tussy got a nigger baby without a head without noticing or caring in the least, which she otherwise would have noticed. They were all very anxious to get to bed (except I & Stella & the baby, of course) but soon there was a knocking at the window too. Soon mama came with some meat which, by the way, had been bought the other day, and of course Tussy, Asta, Dehli and Howard were very glad to have her there again. They promised to be good. They were too scared to sing.

Tussy is to be a fairy in School for Christmas. We have some wings, twisted wire with cloth sewed over it. Stella had them once when she was in the 4th grade. Papa had painted them then. They are so pretty! Just like real wings.

December 13, Sunday. A fine warm day.

This is Howard's birthday. We had cookies for supper — a special treat — and he got some pictures from us children.

I was up at Dekker's today but Ione wasn't home. Tussy & the baby were with me. We stayed by Dekker's for a while and then I went up to Hasenclever's. None of the Hasenclevers were home either, so I

---

* Visits from the *Stroh zempra* were always expected at our house around Christmas time. He carried candy for good children, and iron chains which he rattled ominously in order to scare the naughty ones. For very bad children he had a sack full of straw with which to stuff their insides after they had been cut open. Some adult played this role much as an American father plays the part of Santa Claus. I do not know the origin of this custom.

went to Birnbaum's but Lieschen wasn't home either, so I went home again.

When I came home Aunt Magdalene was there. She had been up several days this week. She sewed Dehli and Asta a dress. She didn't quite finish them tho. She finished them down at grandma's and brought them up today, finished. She bought Dehli's cloth. It's a light blue and is a sort of Danish Cloth. Aunt Magdalene slept by us that night.

I've got quite a lot of Xmas Presents done. I've got Dr. Haftel's, Dr. Fraade's, Mr. Harrington's, Ritschl's, and some more are done.

Aunt Magdalene and I went to Eggen's. I asked whether they needed any more postals because if they had some yet I'd wait a while yet, and Mr. Eggen told me that they didn't need any just now, but perhaps later they'd need pretty many later, because there's usually quite a rush for Xmas postals when Xmas draws near.

Cousin Clara was here tonight with her little girl. She gave Howard a nickel & baby a nickel. She bought 2 postals of me too, so I got another 10 cents.

December 18, Friday. A bright sunny day.

It has snowed, and a great deal too, and it was cold, too, for several days. There are not very many wagons to be seen now, there are mostly sleighs. Today is the last day of school this year. Now come the Xmas holidays. They will have no school until January 4th, I think. I've got an order for 2 dozen postals from the Turn-verein and an order for 25 from Mrs. Schmiff.

December 23, Wednesday

Oh goody! goody! goody! We've gotten so many Xmas presents. Monday they started in coming. In the forenoon Henry Hack came over with about 15 cents worth of nuts, a nickel doll with 2 braids for Tussy, and a lot of ribbon "to make doll dresses," he said. But we are going to use the ribbon for hair-ribbons. I made a Christmas present for Mrs. Hack and sent it over with the children.

The same day I went down town to send Ritschl's Xmas presents off. On Monday, too, we got some apples but we haven't the least idea where they came from. The next day we got more apples, almost a bushel, from the Turn-verein and a great big box of underwear from Mrs. Graf. I had sent a present to her too. Today we got 100 lbs. flour from the Ladies' Turner Society. Yesterday I was downtown with

Aunt Mary and she bought just piles of things for us. The others didn't see them tho, yet.

Afterwards I went to Eggen's. I bought 10 cents nuts and 15 cents candy. Oh yes, I forgot to say I bought 4 ink tablets and 3 pencil tablets at 3 cents each. Nobody saw these except Stella, I and mama. When I came home again, Mrs. Harrington rang up by phone. Stella went to the phone and Mrs. Harrington told her that I should come down Wednesday afternoon. I went to bed very happy.

Today we washed dishes and cleaned up a little and off I started for Mrs. Harrington's. Mrs. Joliffe was there when I came. Mrs. Harrington just wants me to go to school. It was almost noon when Mrs. Joliffe went so Mrs. Harrington asked me to stay to lunch. She told me to go to the music room. I went in and sat on the couch. Mr. Harrington came in too, and he asked me how old I was and other things. I had noticed several pretty oil paintings in the room and was quite sure that papa had made them. Mr. Harrington told me that papa had made them, and the decorations of the room too. He said he was sorry that papa was not living. He said it was so hard to get anyone to do the decorating. Of course I had to cry. I tried to keep the tears from coming but I couldn't. I sat as if in a dream. I don't know, I felt so funny, but I found Mr. Harrington leading me into the dining room with his arm around me. I managed to stop crying just enough that I could see straight but it took pretty long for the tears to clear away. Mr. Harrington didn't eat anything, I think. Mrs. Harrington said he wasn't feeling well, and he looked as if he were sick. They had mince pie but I didn't care for any. I liked the honey bread best of all.

Oh yes, before lunch I phoned to mama telling her that Mrs. Harrington wanted me to stay for lunch & that she wanted to buy me a coat. After dinner we went off. We got a nice red coat, half tight-fitting & butterfly sleeves. Then Mrs. Harrington got me a skirt, a woolen one to make shorter, 6 linen handkerchiefs, the baby a go-cart for 75 cents, and hair ribbons, a whole lot. She also got some outing-flannel, pink and blue, for petticoats for me. Then we went to Eggen's where Mrs. Harrington bought a wagon and horse for Howard. It cost 25 cents.

Coming out of Eggen's store I said to Mrs. Harrington, "How can we ever thank you enough?" And she said, "Oh, be a good girl and study all you can and be neat, that'll pay for it." I told her I'd send some of my pictures down too. She told me to come down often and see her, and phone any time I want. I'm so happy!

Oh yes, and Aunt Klaus was here — and she brought a great pat of butter, some milk and 2 cheese cakes! We had pea soup today. Tussy has been down at Nora's for two days to take care of Cousin Dolores. She got six cents yesterday.

December 25

This is Christmas day at last and we have the most presents!

Asta, Dehli and Howard went to bed at 7 o'clock. They were very much excited. I & Stella fixed up the Christmas tree in the evening, and a good deal of trouble we had too. The tree was crooked and looked as if it would tumble over any minute. Finally we found some strong cord and got it all right. We put on apples, cookies, candy and candles. We hadn't hardly any ornaments but I like it better if the trees are decorated with eatables than all such things that can't be eaten.

December 30

Yesterday I took 12 postals for the Turnverein up to Hershl's. Paula Hershl showed me her presents. She's got some pretty ones.

Yesterday evening I sketched mine, Tussy's big doll, Asta's small

doll, Dehli's small doll and Tussy's small doll, and I & Stella were just admiring Tussy's ten-cent doll's jacket when down went the doll and off went a leg. Oh but I was scared! Tussy cried over it this morning but I gave her some blue velvet which Mrs. Hasenclever had given to me and she was quite satisfied.

The wind is roaring around the house like everything. No mail.

December 31. A Happy New Year!

This is Sylvester Eve, and we children have been dripping candle.

We got coal today and the whole house is black. In the cellar the whole table and floor are as black as ink.

I brought papa's oil painting of roses up to Hershl's for the Turnverein. It is a New Year's present. We had oysters, crackers, coffee, apple cake, and cinnamon cake for supper as a special New Year's treat. I don't know whether we'll stay up until midnight.

Li Ling Ai

Li Ling Ai was Third Daughter, the sixth child of Li Tai Heong and Li Khai Fai, a husband-and-wife team of doctors who had left Canton, China, in 1896 to practice medicine in Honolulu. They were twenty-one years old at the time, and over the next decade or so, during which the Li children were born, Ling Ai's busy father founded a hospital, a pro–Sun Yat-sen newspaper, the School for the Arrangement of the Self (to instruct young Chinese-Hawaiians in the philosophy of their ancestors), the Chinese Anti-Opium Society, and the All-Chinese Baseball Team. Her mother was an obstetrician who seems to have specialized in charity cases.

Ling Ai's memoirs of her childhood are at once stylish and self-effacing to the point that while she exists as "one of the little ones" she allows herself few touches of individuality. Instead she paints a passive, communal portrait of life in a large family that seems dominated in equal parts by two strong-willed parents and an equally determined cook, Ah Pak Po. Everyone, in fact, seems to have a voice but the children.

This excerpt from Li Ling Ai's autobiography, Life Is for a Long Time, *begins in 1913, when the Lis, having saved up three hundred dollars, build their first house in Honolulu.*

From "They Build Their House," *Life Is for a Long Time*

FATHER AND MOTHER . . . built their house on level ground on Kukui Street, the broad street of Light. On one side of the house ran a little lane, Kukui Lane, which started at one end of the main street of Light and ended on the other end. "A small lane with two mouths," mother said, "a happy little lane lined on each side with happy little homes, all with nice front yards filled with trees, flowers and children at play."

A huge mango tree, at least two hundred years old, stood guard at one side of the front entrance of the yard. A royal palm, at least thirty feet high, stood in the exact corner of the lot at the point where the little lane met the big street called Kukui. And by the gate of the back entrance there was a spreading breadfruit tree.

"Fruit at the front entrance, and fruit at the back entrance so that there will be no excuse for anyone to starve," explained our father to his children when he told us how he planned his and mother's first home in Hawaii built with their own earned money.

In the front yard, father had planted roses — golden yellow, crimson, pale pink and pure white — "like the first roses brought to Europe from China by the first Jewish and Arab traders before even Marco Polo's time," said father. And there were fuchsias, cassia blossoms and jasmine in porcelain pots hovering over rows of violets which bordered the slate walk from the front of the house around one side to the back entrance — "all the flowers of song and poetry from China across the sea," said father.

On the other side of the house, father had planted a straight row of tall ti-plants, "the ti-plant whose roots are used by the old Hawaiians to ferment into a drink stronger than the strongest corn whiskey manufactured in the stealth of some southern mountain retreat," he told us. "But the leaves of the ti, broad, green and shiny, are used by the Hawaiians to cover their tables when feasting, to cover their bodies as skirts when dancing, and to thatch the roofs of their homes. So you see the 'ti' plant is to the Hawaiians what the bamboo is to the Chinese." And to remind us of China too there were clumps of bamboo near the ti-plants. Father had also planted trees of loquats with their juicy wax-like pale yellow fruit and a carambola tree on the side near the lane, with its small purple and white star-like flower clusters bursting in season, and then turning into pale green and pale yellow fruit, smooth and shiny as satin, and ridged in the five points of the largest star in the sky. "Good for clearing the system of poisons," father said.

And then there were the lichee trees and their cousin, the dragon's eye tree. And father said that if we were good and patient, the trees might fruit in twenty years. For, the lichee and dragon's eye bloom only for good and patient people. And so, in all the years in growing up, we children tried to be good and patient so that the trees might some day bloom for us. But many of us children went far away before the trees bloomed, far away to the farthest end of Eastern America, or to China on the other side of the world, from whence father and mother had come. So never were we all home together to see the first bloom after twenty years of counting, twenty years of being good, of being patient. But father said it was as it should be, that it was for the children of the children to inherit the blessings, that if the children and their children were pure in heart and good in their souls, then the trees would fruit forever.

With all these trees and flowers and plants from near and far away, father and mother surrounded their house, for their family and friends. "For there must always be something to pick in a garden," said father, "there must always be something to eat, something to see and to smell to add spice to the senses, excitement and delicacy to the soul."

And too, father and mother built their house facing the high mountains in the distance, "For there must always be, too, something high and far to look at," they said. And it was indeed a house just as mother had wanted — "a house with a strong foundation in the ground, a roof pointing to the sky, and with many rooms for everything in living" including the privacy she said her children must learn to cherish.

With the new year of 1914, father and mother opened wide the doors of the new house to all their friends.

Many came bringing all their big and little children and big and small gifts from the heart — flower-embossed spittoons the shape of gourds and the colors of the rainbow, five dollar gold pieces wrapped in red paper for good luck, tributes in bold calligraphy, flower leis, live chickens, boxes of oranges, tangerines and peaches with wishes for long life, happiness and all the good thoughts that good people have for other good people.

"Many too came to see just what kind of house your father and mother had built for themselves," said Ah Pak Po. "And they meandered about upstairs and downstairs, one room into another room, knocking at walls to see if they were of hard wood or soft wood, looking out of the many windows from upstairs to see if they could see the head of Kukui Street, or the tail of Nuuanu Street, from the house.

"Some thought the walls too high and a waste of good lumber. But many agreed that high walls are wonderful, for the house would be cool all the year around in the tropical weather of the Hawaiian Islands. And, there were some who told your mother that renting a house was more sensible than owning a house — no worries about plumbing, termites, yards or repainting — let the landlord bother!"

Mother said that she was very proud of the restraint Ah Pak Po practiced that day. Ah Pak Po only clacked and bustled about the new kitchen, chopping and cooking and cooking and chopping — and yelling at this child, or that child running in or out of the kitchen to pilfer a piece of chicken, a small bit of ham. This old friend, or that old friend, would wander now and then into the kitchen to make one comment or another about father's and mother's house, but Ah Pak Po let out not one blast, said mother.

But whenever a remark sounded to her ears like the smell of old fish, Ah Pak Po chopped with all her might with her cleaver on the many gizzards and onions necessary for the tidbit dishes of the feast, as though she could not mince them fine enough to suit the devil. Or, she would grab one of the many live chickens she had waiting on the porch outside the kitchen, tied leg to leg by a string. And then, before the chicken could even begin to squawk out loud, she chopped off its head with her cleaver, as though she liked nothing better than to chop off the heads of chickens to make them good and dead!

The visiting hours were over at last. The front door of the new house was now wide open to friends as well as patients — and life went on as before for mother and father.

"The trees and flowers took root in our garden quickly," said mother. "Under the gentle suns and calm breezes of our islands, the children bloomed like the hibiscus and the lauhala trees on the mountainside. The wind-air of Hawaii blew softly through the many windows of our house. In spite of the chaos in the world outside of our door, we came to feel that Hawaii, daughterland of the United States of America and wifeland of our choice, was truly the Peach Garden sung of by the ancient sages of China."

There was much living in father's and mother's house and there was much learning too. As father's and mother's children, we had to learn every way that they thought was necessary — if we wanted to live what mother called the "full life of a whole person."

There were many ways to learn she told us: we had to learn the way of the mind, the way of the spirit, and the way of the body, she enumerated for us on her fingers. But with all the ways and all the things we had to learn, mother considered cooking a first and fundamental step toward "the full life of a whole person." Whether her children were boys or girls, or whether they had talent and desire, or none at all for cooking, she insisted that they must learn what she called "the art of cooking."

The good sisters at Ying Tong had trained her in the thoroughness and exactness necessary for a woman of medicine. And so mother insisted on thoroughness and exactness when she set out to teach us the art of cooking. Many were the times we children felt that the thoroughness and exactness demanded by our mother was too strict. And many were the times we complained loudly to our father about having to cook in mother's way. But father never gave us any sympathy. He always laughed his booming laughter and said, "It hasn't done your mother any harm."

And so, when any of the children grew to the ripe years of fourteen, it was always taken for granted in our house that that one was old enough to learn how to cook — "not just to boil an egg, or a pot of rice, or a few potatoes in the pot," said mother, "but to cook to suit the taste of a delicate tongue, to please the fastidious demands of a nervous stomach, to delight the gentle soul of a poet."

Mother always stood by our side to watch and see that we cut an onion into pieces the way she said we should, properly small, or properly wide for whichever dish she was teaching us to cook that day. Too, she insisted always that the chicken must be cut with sure clean strokes of the cleaver, with no wasted motions, no jagged edges, no torn flesh.

There were many ways to cut a piece of celery, she always pointed out. And she taught us all of them — in slants, in strips, in moonshaped pieces, in little bits of squares. Each shape, each strip must match the cut of fish or meat, she said, and all the bits in the dish, no matter how many, must blend to please the eye, tickle the palate and tease the nose.

Sometimes, in our impatience, we would cut the food any old way. But mother never scolded us too much. She would only put away the jagged pieces into a covered bowl carefully, to be saved and used another time. As carefully, she would take out more fresh meat and more raw vegetables and set us to cutting all over again, even though we grumbled much.

Not only was there the art of cutting to learn. There was also the art of cooking over the fire — the use of proper flame. "High flame or low flame, one must use the judgment and care of an astute ruler of a kingdom," she said. "Different vegetables and different meats — different timings. Some food must be sautéed fast, over high flame, some foods must be simmered slowly, over low flame. Others must be stirred slowly, while others must be fried quickly. Some must be plunged, some must be parched, and some must be red-burned." High flame or low flame, sautéeing or simmering, mother watched and instructed and insisted on exactness and thoroughness.

As if this were not enough, she insisted too that we must always wash the dishes and scrub the implements, after the chore of cooking. And even in this she insisted that we had to be exact and thorough.

"The water must be just right and boiling hot," she always said. "The soaping must be just right, bubbling frothy with suds." The rinse water had to be hot enough to rinse clean, and yet we were not to waste too much water while doing so. And when all were gleaming and clean and sanitary at last she watched carefully to see if we had put everything away properly — "the only way which is right," she said, "with each bowl in its proper place and each dish in its proper order."

There were times when many of her children thought that mother, in her strictness, did not love them truly. But when father's mother came from China to Hawaii, to see all of us she said that we were very capable and good cooks as well as good children, and that mother must have loved us truly to have taught us so well. We were very happy, then, that mother had been so strict with us. And never again after that did we ever doubt that mother truly loved us. For now we knew that mother, in her true love for us, only wanted us to learn to be whole persons, so that we would be assured of the full life she had herself — and we knew too that to be a whole person that one has first to learn how to cook!

Father never taught us the way mother did. No, he never taught us the way she did. He only loved so much of so many little things, and felt so much for so many dreams, that we children, loving and feeling, could not help but learn to love and feel too as he did. Perhaps his was another way to become the whole persons mother talked about!

There were so many things in living that father loved — riding in the wind with the rain falling from the heavens above, the soft petals of roses scented fresh with dew, the song of birds winging high in the sky, the pale gold of cassia blossoms from their dark leaves peeping shy — and he taught us to love them too.

There was climbing that he loved — climbing the high mountains of Hawaii overlooking the sea. And he would take us children climbing with him, climbing the high mountains, climbing. And when at last we stood breathless at the very top, he'd point to the waters shimmering from afar, shimmering through the lace of the trees; the waters in the distance — pale green, aquamarine, purple and gray, fading into the mist of the far islands, and, as father always said, fading even into the distant lands beyond, far beyond the sea. We'd look and look. And then, like our father, we would stand quietly, quietly stand looking, looking far beyond, far into the sea.

There were the other times when he took us little ones around the other side of the island to look, to look at the sea from boats with glass bottoms through which one could look way down into the sea. And father would point out to us a whole world of wonder and color — silver, jade, jet, shooting through coral trees and caves dark as spice! And here, a feathery anemone in the palest of pink, precariously close to a giant devilfish, spitting out ink! And there, slithering silently, a slippery black eel, mouth open wide, ready to snap and eat the tiny fish swarming in schools, daring and darting busily from danger! All of this father would show us to love.

After this, father would drive us further over to the other side of the island, to the place where lived old men still planting rice and taro on patches of land sweeping from the side of the roads and reaching out almost to the sea, old men from China who poured us big cups of tea. There were, too, whole families of Hawaiians — old Tutu, and her many cousins — a raft of them calling out loud, "Kauka Li, Doctor Li."

Father, laughing, would introduce us as his "Lili Keiki wahines," his small women children. And laughing gaily, they would give us coconuts and fresh papaya right off the trees.

Father would examine them carefully with his instruments from his small black bag. And finding nothing wrong, he'd laugh and tell them all in his voice, as booming as the sea, that they were as healthy and as happy as any man in the world could be. He'd laugh and laugh as low and rumbling as the seas, and they too laughed and laughed merrily and happily. I could tell from father's face that he was happy, for the smile on his face was soft, and the look in his eyes was gentle as the day.

Father loved the wind too, and many were the times he took us little ones out riding with him in his car — "to feel, to catch the wind," he said. Up Nuuanu, the street of Laughing Showers, he'd drive, up toward the foot of the Pali, cautioning us all the while to wrap ourselves warmly — while catching the wind. Up, up the gently winding road he drove stopping his car only at a particular spot to point out to us the knife-edged ridge towering high in the distance on the opposite side of the road, a ridge with a waterfall flowing down the sides and then blown upward — by the wind. We'd lift our heads high to look up at the cliffs with their waterfall blown upside down — by the wind.

And after we had had our fill of the wonder, father would again drive slowly round the bend, and another bend. And then he would stop again to point out to us the thick forest of Kamani trees, with their shiny green leaves the size of a man's palm, casting shadows over the dark trunks, twisted and coiled like huge black serpents, serpents sighing and moaning with each breath of the wind, moaning and sighing — a prayer to the wind, we said. And then he would tell us to look closely into the shadows below, and he'd point out to us where the pale gold and white of ginger blossoms peeped in clusters from behind huge leaves. He would tell us to breathe in deeply of their spicy scent — floated up from the shadows by the wind, he said.

And we'd breathe and breathe the spicy scent, forgetting the sinister shadows, the trees bent by the wind.

We'd come to the top of the road at last, high up over the valleys. We'd come to the top, just below the pointed peak of the Pali, reaching into the mists of the sky — And he'd hold us each by the hand to run against the winds, the winds where they met, at the top of the road, at the mouth of the pass, by the foot of the peak of the Pali overlooking the peaceful valleys.

Yes, father taught us to love so many things, so many things that he loved so deeply, and so far and so wide. But most of all, mother said, he loved his family, his friends and people and wanted others to learn too, his kind of loving.

Sanora Babb

In 1913, when Sanora Babb was seven years old, she and her mother and father and four-year-old sister left Oklahoma and took the train to the end of the line in Lamar, Colorado, and then went by cart to their new homestead. Waiting there in a sod house he had dug out of the prairie was her grandfather, her father's father, Alonzo. For simply paying the taxes for five years and improving the land by building a farm ("proving up," it was called), they would be given a government claim of 160 acres. In addition, her father had sold his bakery to buy outright 320 acres of grazing land — land on which it turned out there was no water.

Sanora's father had insisted that since they were beginning a new life they should leave all their old possessions behind. Her mother refused to abandon her piano, so it was dragged along, hauled overland from the railroad and established in all its highly polished glory in the dark, mud-walled house, which was little more than a roofed-over hole in the ground.

All this, it should be remembered, was happening in 1913, long after sod-busting had lost its popularity. Sanora Babb remembers, "While other parts of the United States moved swiftly ahead, the hopeful or desperate people who filed claims on these high western grazing lands were plunged a hundred years backward in our history, to live and struggle again like the early settlers in other states."

The homesteading scheme proved to be a disaster, and Grandfather Alonzo would eventually lose his land for nonpayment of taxes. The family moved on. Sanora would later marry the great cinematographer James Wong Howe. This chapter from her autobiography deals with the family's first winter in their new sod home.

From *An Owl on Every Post*

DURING OUR EVENING VISIT to the cane patch before going to bed, a soft snow was falling. The northern sky was heavy with winter storm. A cold wind rose, shaking the dry cane stalks, and the feathery snow turned to icy barbs and whirled up from the ground and away on the wind. We heard the dugout door rise and drop and Grandfather's long steps going toward the barn.

All night we heard the wind and felt it entering every crack and crevice, strong and freezing cold. It tugged at the dugout's slant door, threatened to break the windows, and lashed over the plain in long sorrowful howls. We woke from our bone-cold sleep at daybreak; the windows were dark.

"A blizzard," Grandfather said. He lighted the oil lamp and with cold stiff fingers built the fire in his penurious way, careful of wood so hard to obtain. From a kindling stick he cut shavings with his pocketknife until a small heap curled in the grate of the monkey stove, its two round lids and the center divider stacked on the iron rim. Over the shavings he laid a patterned network of cedar bark and twigs, and over these a piece of two-inch branch with another in readiness. He struck a match and lighted the shavings, blowing on the flame, fanning it with his long brown hand, directing the fire where he wished. When the flame caught well, he replaced the stove lids and turned the damper to adjust the draught in the black tin chimney that rose up through the roof. The burning made a pleasant small roar in the cold room.

We leaped from our beds and dressed quickly, each in his accustomed space so as not to be in the way of another. When the five of us were in the dugout, there was hardly a foot to spare.

Mama was already preparing the coffee in the granite pot, the coffee that would be warmed over, diluted, extended for days until no further extension was possible. This was a good morning when the coffee was fresh. As we had little else, Marcy and I were given hot water with coffee. We sat at the wooden table covered with oilcloth, our five tin cups and tin plates gleaming in the lamplight. The warmed flour-and-water hardtack occupied the center of the table and gave off a flat odor that nevertheless had its charms for our hunger. We each broke a piece from this pancake and poured over it thick brown sorghum molasses from a white china pitcher Mama had managed to bring along from our other life. That pitcher among the tin was a treasure that between meals rested on the piano and, in spring, held white soapweed blooms or branches of wild sage, and the blue, red, and yellow wild flowers that I always thought of as brave.

Grandfather glanced at the windows now and then, and when no light from dawn or sunup dimmed our lamp, he rose and went to examine the darkened glass.

"Snow," he said. "We're in a drift. Drifted over."

Papa put on his work coat and started up the stone steps.

"Where are you going, son?"

"To see about the horses."

Grandfather shook his head. "We're snowed in," he said quietly.

"Well, what if we are? I have to go to the barn, so I'm going."

"You can try."

Papa was irritated by this patient tone. Bracing himself with his hands against the narow walls of the entrance, he pressed a shoulder up against the door, which lay on a slant almost horizontal above his head. The door failed to open or make the slightest sound of giving. Papa hunched his great strength into his arched back, braced himself again and pushed. Nothing happened. He picked up a crowbar from among the tools there and began to pry at the door's edge. Still the door remained fast, and in his urgency he broke off a splinter of wood.

"Careful," Grandfather said with infinite calm.

"Careful, hell!" Papa glared at his father. "What are you going to do, stay in here all day?"

"We may. I have. Sometimes more than a day or two. I lost count."

"What about the horses?" Papa was more alarmed about the horses than about ourselves.

"They were snowed in too."

"They could have died of thirst for all you cared."

"Well, a little snow drifted in and they ate that. Better off than I was. I finally broke a window pane and got some snow for myself, but it was gloomy with the window boarded up till I got to town. That was some time."

"They must have been knee-deep in dung."

"They were."

"I suppose you were too."

"Well, now, we needn't discuss that."

"It's a fact we'll have to put up with if we can't get out. What do you say to that?"

"We can dig a hole in the floor — it's dirt — and take the soil out later and replace it with clean dirt."

Grandfather's calm reasoning, his voice of experience infuriated Papa. Our fastidiousness, already having suffered so many blows, was once more to be assailed. Mama appeared resigned to anything, but beneath her quiet mask something was stirring to emerge at a future time when we had forgotten this latest trial.

"I can't stay in this goddamned hole-in-the-ground all day!" Papa said as he came down the steps.

"Mama has to — lots," I said.

"Shut up," Papa told me.

"What shall we do?" Marcy asked in a frightened way and lunged from her perch on the bed into Papa's arms.

"We'll do something," he soothed her. "Your dad will take care of everything. Now, get down, Marcy, get under the covers and keep warm. I want to think."

"What do you suppose has happened to Bounce?" I too was concerned about the animals.

"He's in the barn with the horses. He's all right," Grandfather said. He put another piece of wood in the fire. "I brought this bridle in last night, so I may as well mend it now." He sat down on his cot and began to work on the worn leather.

"Well, I'll be damned," Papa said in amazement.

"We will have to wait for the sun to come out, hoping it will, and it may loosen the snow. Depends on how deep it is."

"What if it turns cold and freezes?" Papa demanded.

"We'll cross that bridge when we get to it."

"Well, I hope we get to it," Papa said meanly. "I want to see you get out of that one."

"I don't know any more than you do," Grandfather said rather sharply now. "But I'm trying to keep calm. Your temper hasn't opened the door yet."

That set Papa to new attempts to raise the door, but when he failed, he hunted up an old deck of cards and began to play solitaire on the kitchen table, apparently absorbed in the game, but it was clear to us that he was mapping a new strategy to defeat this powerful natural enemy.

"This snow will be good for the soil," Grandfather Alonzo said, "good for the soil and the buffalo grass."

Papa smacked his deck down on the table and swept all the cards together. "What the hell's happening to all those poor cattle out on the range, thousands of them?"

"By Jupiter! If you don't think of everything!" Grandfather looked at him and his eyes were black and fiery. He turned back to his harness-mending and said as if he had forgotten his flare at his son, "I feel right sorry for all those cattle; they can't get at the grass. If the men can get out, they'll scatter some cottonseed cake or hay; if they can't . . . well, maybe this won't last. The cattle are much worse off in a blizzard when the zero wind blows and freezes them."

We were used to the silence of the plains, but this snowed-in silence had a different quality. We got through the first day well enough and went to sleep hopeful of the next day's sun. Our lamp had burned all day against the darkness in the dugout, and Mama filled its glass bowl with coal oil in the evening while I shined the glass chimney with old newspaper. Filling and cleaning the lamp was a pleasant little task of every evening, but this day had not the character of others. We did not know whether the snow had ceased or whether it fell and buried us more deeply; but we were glad not to hear the wind.

The second day was more difficult. The men were used to being outdoors, and we were so crowded living every detail of our lives together that nothing mattered more now than our freedom from this tiny underground room.

On the second and third days and nights we heard the cattle bawling, a forlorn and desolated sound, a genuine lament painful to hear. They were hungry and their grass, the short gray curled grass of the high plains, was far beneath the snow, or they would have pawed down to a slight feeding at least. We felt the increased chill through the walls and knew that in spite of their heavier winter coats the cattle were cold.

We stayed in bed wearing our warmest clothing and burned as little wood as possible, but on the third day our wood gave out. That same afternoon we heard small crackling sounds in the snow and we knew the sun was shining, had been shining perhaps all day. Papa began to work at raising the door, and after two hours of trying all the ways he had thought of during those dark days, he managed to raise the door and prop it up enough to crawl through. There was no place to go except into the snow. He gathered his strength and plunged upward like a swimmer battling for the surface. We heard a loud blow of breath and a shout of honest delight.

"Say! It's deep! I've got my head out. The world is sure a pretty sight." He flailed about making a larger passage and called back, "Hand me up the shovel, Dad."

Grandfather pushed the shovel through the loosened snow already caved in over Papa's tunnel, and we soon heard the spirited whoosh and shush of digging.

"I can't get a swing on this," he shouted.

After a long while Papa had pitched enough snow above his head and trampled and packed enough down around him for Grandfather to crawl out with another shovel. When they had succeeded in opening a space for themselves to work, they were not long in uncovering the door. But they were a long time cutting a narrow path between five-foot walls of snow to the barn.

Mama, Marcy, and I came out. Walking in the white corridor was a new delight. In order to see our winter world we must find the woodpile and climb to its top. There we turned slowly around looking over the great circle of snow that for us began with our farm at the center and reached to the horizon. How tell its beauty? It lay white and silent, sparkling in the sun. We stood in awe of the purity laid upon the world giving respite from all that was not in harmony with the deepest yearnings of our souls. Over the earth lay this purest of days, its gentle beauty speaking to a part of us unspoken to, ignored by the hard land beneath.

We must take advantage of the light, so we climbed down and pulled out logs and carried them back to the dugout. None of us wished to enter that underground room until we were forced by the ending day. We followed the men to the barn.

An overhang on the east side made it easy to get in. There, with the patient acceptance of work animals, the horses were in their stalls, hungry but safe. A leak of snow had provided their water. Grandfather led them outside, where they snorted and stamped about in the limited space free of deep snow while Papa cleaned away the manure and filled their mangers with fodder and heads of feterita from the small granary attached to the north side of the barn. Our warm breath made clouds in the cold air, and a small fog rose from the great warm bodies of the horses.

When they were led back into the clean, good-smelling barn, Grandfather curried Dip and I curried Fred, my favorite, a large white horse with dappled hindquarters and a long white tail. His head was less handsome than Dip's, Dip being a big well-bred bay. Fred's wild pink eyes looked at me with trust, and when I laid my cheek against the enormous flat bone of his jaw and spoke to him, he swung his head around with care not to knock me off the stool on which I had to stand in order to curry his back, and nibbled at my arm with soft lips. Fred had under his skin on each shoulder a coin, the size of a quarter, placed there by someone who owned him before Grandfather, and for what reason we could not understand. A superstition, perhaps, or a crude joke of sorts. The skin must have been slit, the coins inserted, and the flesh healed over. These spots were not painful so they remained only a curiosity, but curiosity they were, a mark of man.

I touched one and Fred quivered his flesh as if to dislodge a fly. Then he shook his great head, his coarse mane striking against my face, a sign of tolerant impatience. I held his mane and swung up onto his back, moving about there as on a private continent, currying him, bringing him back to this comforting pleasure.

When we left the barn, we saw Bounce trying to run on top of the snow, hopeful of chasing a jackrabbit for his hunger, but he sank through the snow's soft crust time and again until he realized the uselessness of his efforts and returned sheepishly to the tunneled path. Mama brought him a piece of hardtack and he shared our common food.

Out on the range we could see the dark patterns on the snow — the herds of cattle pressed close together for warmth and protection against the gray wolves who in desperate hunger would attack a stray beast. Then seeing that the snow had blown deeper around the farm buildings than in the clear, we plunged into a journey to the gate, just to be going someplace, anyplace after the confinement indoors. At each step we were sinking into the snow, rising, lifting our legs for another step, falling, laughing, falling again. Bounce floundered about, joyous for our company and the sense of play.

But at the fence our laughter ceased, for there frozen stiff, caught in the barbed wire fence, were three dead steers who had strayed from the herd in the storm. We stared in fascination at this close sight and alien presence of death.

"Coyotes will clear them away," Grandfather Alonzo said, leading us back toward the dugout.

"Clear them away?" I asked.

"Eat them, child. Coyotes keep the plains clean, even if they do catch a few chickens now and then."

"But we have no chickens."

"In the spring we will," Papa said.

"Coyotes catch mostly prairie dogs, anyway," Grandfather said, "rabbits and rats. All great breeders; coyotes keep them down."

"You talk as if the coyotes are personal friends of yours," Papa said.

"Well, when you live here alone as long as I have, they'll be your friends too. I listen for them to yip and bark and sing, and I like to see them sitting around on their haunches looking at me in plain curiosity. They'll bear studying."

"No sheep rancher would listen to such talk," Papa said. "They kill too many lambs."

"Sick ones, maybe. Besides, we have no sheep ranches around here, thank God," Grandfather said. "Sheep ruin the pasture, eating down to the roots and cutting the rest with their sharp hoofs."

"Hell, I like all kinds of animals," Papa said, apparently irritated at somehow having got on the side opposing himself. "But a man living in the wilds has to protect himself from them."

"I'd say it is mostly the other way around," Grandfather said. "The Indians killed buffalo for food and hide and still the plains were black with them, millions of them. The white man slaughtered them all in just a few years. Goddang it, they're after the coyote now, poisoning, trapping, shooting. The wild horses are mostly gone already, hid out in the mountains. What's wrong with man that he can't think in a pattern? Everything has a purpose."

"Now, I'd like to break me a wild horse —" Papa said as if dreaming of this feat. "Break him to ride without breaking his spirit."

"That's the only true way," Grandfather agreed. "Listen —"

We heard the far-off wagon, its small sounds made smaller by our snow-softened world. Then we saw the wagon moving slowly along the road from the big ranch to the south. Cowboys riding to the rear came alongside and were handed sacks of cottonseed cakes. The cowboys rode off across the range to a herd of cattle, their horses plunging and struggling through the snow. Our hearts rose again from the frozen beasts tangled in our fence, from the slaughtered buffalo and the hunted coyote, to the sight of the surviving, living cattle being fed after days of hunger and cold.

Papa was looking at the dead ones in a thoughtful way, no longer interested in anything else. Then he turned on us as if he were angry. "I'm going to take one of those steers. We're just as hungry as the coyotes."

"Steal?" I whispered.

"Shut up! And don't let me ever hear you say a word about this, or I'll tan your bottom."

I knew he would; the experience was familiar. I remembered the first time well, when I had stolen a packet of flower seeds and, believing in magic, was certain that the beautiful colored blooms pictured could be shaken out of the envelope. The results were quite different. First, a spanking; next, a brief explanation of stealing, and last, the humiliation of returning the packet, telling the storekeeper I had stolen it, which was wrong, and that I was sorry. I determined never to steal again.

"But it's *stealing*." I dared to correct Papa as he had corrected me.

At times he spoke to me as an equal. "Now, listen here. These steers are no use to anybody now."

"Maybe their hides," Grandfather said.

"Damn it all! Stay out of this!"

"This is still my farm, son, and I don't want a stolen animal on it."

Papa walked away and came right back. "I'm not stealing! Will the coyotes be stealing?"

"I can't say they will be; no."

"After dark tonight we'll come out here and drag one of these steers in and I'll saw off some meat. We'll get a few square meals. When the weather starts thawing, we'll bury the rest."

"Best get out of sight then," Grandfather said, "so's not to attract the men up here looking for strays."

We went back to the dugout in an atmosphere of conspiracy. All the pure delight of our trip to the gate was gone. Only Marcy still played in the drifts.

"It's going to snow again tonight," Papa said, pointing to the gray northern sky. "The air is getting warmer. Snow will cover up our tracks when we drag him in."

Even the snow was in league with our covert doings.

Alfred Kazin

Alfred Kazin (b.1915) grew up in a section of Brooklyn called Brownsville, a place at the end of a subway line that had not deteriorated into a slum. It had been especially built by real-estate developers to be a slum — a ghetto for eastern-European Jews who had begun to arrive in New York in great numbers at the turn of the century. What the developers had not planned on was the neighborhood's becoming a hotbed of social reform. It was where Margaret Sanger opened her first birth-control clinic, where Emma Goldman ran an ice-cream parlor (briefly), and where the New York Anarchists Club once tried to hold a Yom Kippur Ball, until it was raided by the police.

Kazin's memoir A Walker in the City, *published in 1951, after he had become one of America's leading literary critics, is his story of a Brownsville boyhood. It may also be the finest American memoir this century has produced.*

From "From the Subway to the Synagogue" and "The Kitchen," *A Walker in the City*

WHEN I WAS A CHILD I thought we lived at the end of the world. It was the eternity of the subway ride into the city that first gave me this idea. It took a long time getting to "New York"; it seemed longer getting back. Even the I.R.T. got tired by the time it came to us, and ran up into the open for a breath of air before it got locked into its terminus at New Lots. As the train left the tunnel to rattle along the elevated tracks, I felt I was being jostled on a camel past the last way stations in the desert. Oh that ride from New York! Light came only at Sutter Avenue. First across the many stations of the Gentiles to the East River. Then clear across Brooklyn, almost to the brink of the ocean all our fathers crossed. All those first stations in Brooklyn — Clark, Borough Hall, Hoyt, Nevins, the junction of the East and West Side express lines — told me only that I was on the last leg home, though there was always a stirring of my heart at Hoyt, where the grimy subway platform was suddenly enlivened by Abraham and Straus's windows of ladies' wear. Atlantic Avenue was vaguely exciting, a crossroads, the Long Island railroad; I never saw a soul get in or out at Bergen Street; the Grand Army Plaza, with its great empty caverns smoky with dust and chewing-gum wrappers, meant Prospect Park and that stone path beside a meadow where as a child I ran off from my father one summer twilight just in time to see the lamplighter go up the path lighting from the end of his pole each gas mantle suddenly flaring within its corolla of pleated paper — then, that summer I first strayed off the block for myself, the steps leading up from the boathouse, the long stalks of grass wound between the steps thick with the dust and smell of summer — then, that great summer at sixteen, my discovery in the Brooklyn Museum of Albert Pinkham Ryder's cracked oily fishing boats drifting under the moon. Franklin Avenue was where the Jews began — but all middle-class Jews, *alrightniks,* making out "all right" in the New World, they were still Gentiles to me as they went out into the wide and tree-lined Eastern Parkway. For us the journey went on and on — past Nostrand, past Kingston, past Utica, and only then out into the open at Sutter, overlooking Lincoln Terrace Park, "Tickle-Her" Park, the zoo of our adolescence, through which no girl could pass on a summer evening without its being understood forever after that she was "in"; past the rickety "two-family" private houses built in the fever of Brownsville's last real-estate boom; and then into Brownsville itself — Saratoga, Rockaway, and home. For those who lived still beyond, in East New York, there was Junius, there was Pennsylvania, there was Van Siclen, and so at last into New Lots, where the city goes back to the marsh, and even the subway ends.

Yet it was not just the long pent-up subway ride that led me to think of Brownsville as the margin of the city, the last place, the car barns where they locked up the subway and the trolley cars at night. There were always raw patches of unused city land all around us filled with "monument works" where they cut and stored tombstones, as there were still on our street farmhouses and the remains of old cobbled driveways down which chickens came squealing into our punchball games — but most of it dead land, neither country nor city, with that look of prairie waste I have so often seen on my walks along the fringes of American cities near the freight yards. We were nearer the ocean than the city, but our front on the ocean was Canarsie — in those days the great refuse dump through which I made my first and grimmest walks into the city — a place so celebrated in New York vaudeville houses for its squalor that the very sound of the word was always good for a laugh. CAN-NARR-SIE! They fell into the aisles. But that was the way to the ocean we always took summer evenings — through silent streets of old broken houses whose smoky red Victorian fronts looked as if the paint had clotted like blood and had then been mixed with soot — past infinite weedy lots, the smell of freshly cut boards in the lumber yards, the junk yards, the marshland eating the pavement, the truck farms, the bungalows that had lost a window or a door as they tottered on their poles against the damp and the ocean winds. The place as I have it in my mind still reeks of the fires burning in the refuse dumps. Farms that had once been the outposts of settlers in Revolutionary days had crumbled and sunk like wet sand. Canarsie was where they opened the sluice gates to let the city's muck out into the ocean. But at the end was the roar of the Atlantic and the summer house where we stood outside watching through lattices the sports being served with great pitchers of beer foaming onto the red-checked tablecloths. Summer, my summer! Summer!

We were of the city, but somehow not in it. Whenever I went off on my favorite walk to Highland Park in the "American" district to the north, on the border of Queens, and climbed the hill to the old reservoir from which I could look straight across to the skyscrapers of Manhattan, I saw New York as a foreign city. There, brilliant and unreal, the city had its life, as Brownsville was ours. That the two were joined in me I never knew then — not even on those glorious summer nights of my last weeks in high school when, with what an ache, I would come back into Brownsville along Liberty Avenue, and, as soon as I could see blocks ahead of me the Labor Lyceum, the malted milk and Fatima signs over the candy stores, the old women in their house-dresses sitting in front of the tenements like priestesses of an ancient cult, knew I was home.

We were the end of the line. We were the children of the immigrants who had camped at the city's back door, in New York's rawest, remotest, cheapest ghetto, enclosed on one side by the Canarsie flats and on the other by the hallowed middle-class districts that showed the way to New York. "New York" was what we put last on our address, but first in thinking of the others around us. *They* were New York, the Gentiles, America; we were Brownsville — *Brunzvil,* as the old folks said — the dust of the earth to all Jews with money, and notoriously a place that measured all success by our skill in getting away from it. So that when poor Jews left, *even* Negroes, as we said, found it easy to settle on the margins of Brownsville, and with the coming of spring, bands of Gypsies, who would rent empty stores, hang their rugs around them like a desert tent, and bring a dusty and faintly sinister air of carnival into our neighborhood. . . .

It was the darkness and emptiness of the streets I liked most about Friday evening, as if in preparation for that day of rest and worship which the Jews greet "as a bride" — that day when the very touch of money is prohibited, all work, all travel, all household duties, even to the turning on and off of a light — Jewry had found its way past its tormented heart to some ancient still center of itself. I waited for the streets to go dark on Friday evening as other children waited for the Christmas lights. Even Friday morning after the tests were over glowed in anticipation. When I returned home after three, the warm odor of a coffee cake baking in the oven and the sight of my mother on her hands and knees scrubbing the linoleum on the dining-room floor filled me with such tenderness that I could feel my senses reaching out to embrace every single object in our household. One Friday, after a morning in school spent on the voyages of Henry Hudson, I returned with the phrase *Among the discoverers of the New World* singing in my mind as the theme of my own new-found freedom on the Sabbath.

My great moment came at six, when my father returned from work, his overalls smelling faintly of turpentine and shellac, white drops of silver paint still gleaming on his chin. Hanging his overcoat in the long dark hall that led into our kitchen, he would leave in one pocket a loosely folded copy of the New York *World;* and then everything that beckoned to me from that other hemisphere of my brain beyond the East River would start up from the smell of fresh newsprint and the sight of the globe on the front page. It was a paper that carried special associations for me with Brooklyn Bridge. They published the *World* under the green dome on Park Row overlooking the bridge; the fresh salt air of New York harbor lingered for me in the smell of paint and damp newsprint in the hall. I felt that my father brought the outside straight into our house with each day's copy of the *World.* The bridge somehow stood for freedom; the *World* for that rangy kindness and fraternalism and ease we found in Heywood Broun. My father would read aloud from "It Seems To Me" with a delighted smile on his face. "A very clear and courageous man!" he would say. "Look how he stands up for our Sacco and Vanzetti! A real social conscience, that man! Practically a Socialist!" Then, taking off his overalls, he would wash up at the kitchen sink, peeling and gnawing the paint off his nails with Gold Dust Washing Powder as I poured it into his hands, smacking his lips and grunting with pleasure as he washed himself clean of the job at last, and making me feel that I was really helping him, that I, too, was contributing to the greatness of the evening and the coming day.

By sundown the streets were empty, the curtains had been drawn, the world put to rights. Even the kitchen walls had been scrubbed and now gleamed in the Sabbath candles. On the long white tablecloth were the "company" dishes, filled for some with *gefillte* fish on lettuce leaves, ringed by red horseradish, sour and half-sour pickles, tomato salad with a light vinegar dressing; for others, with chopped liver in a bed of lettuce leaves and white radishes; the long white *khalleh*, the Sabbath loaf; chicken soup with noodles *and* dumplings; chicken, meat loaf, prunes, and sweet potatoes that had been baked all day into an open pie; compote of prunes and quince, apricots and orange rind; applesauce; a great brown nutcake filled with almonds, the traditional *lekakh;* all surrounded by glasses of port wine, seltzer bottles with their nozzles staring down at us waiting to be pressed; a samovar of Russian tea, *svetouchnee* from the little red box, always served in tall glasses, with lemon slices floating on top. My father and mother sipped it in Russian fashion, through lumps of sugar held between the teeth.

Afterwards we went into the "dining room" and, since we were not particularly orthodox, allowed ourselves little pleasures outside the Sabbath rule — an occasional game of Casino at the dining-room table where we never dined; and listening to the victrola. The evening was particularly good for me whenever the unmarried cousin who boarded with us had her two closest friends in after supper.

They were all dressmakers, like my mother; had worked with my mother in the same East Side sweatshops; were all passionately loyal members of the International Ladies Garment Workers Union; and were all unmarried. We were their only family. Despite my mother's frenzied matchmaking, she had never succeeded in pinning a husband down for any of them. As she said, they were all too *particular* — what a calamity for a Jewish woman to remain unmarried! But my cousin and her friends accepted their fate calmly, and prided themselves on their culture and their strong *progressive* interests. They felt they belonged not to the "kitchen world," like my mother, but to the enlightened tradition of the old Russian intelligentsia. Whenever my mother sighed over them, they would smile out of their greater knowledge of the world, and looking at me with a pointed appeal for recognition, would speak of novels they had read in Yiddish and Russian, of *Winesburg, Ohio,* of some article in the *Nation.*

Our cousin and her two friends were of my parents' generation, but I could never believe it — they seemed to enjoy life with such outspokenness. They were the first grown-up people I had ever met who used the word *love* without embarrassment. "*Libbe! Libbe!*" my mother would explode whenever one of them protested that she could not, after all, marry a man she did not love. "What is this love you make such a stew about? You do not like the way he holds his cigarette? Marry him first and it will all come out right in the end!" It astonished me to realize there was a world in which even unmarried women no longer young were simply individual human beings with lives of their own. *Our* parents, whatever affection might offhandedly be expressed between them, always had the look of being committed to something deeper than *mere* love. Their marriages were neither happy nor unhappy; they were arrangements. However they had met — whether in Russia or in the steerage or, like my parents, in an East Side boarding house — whatever they still thought of each other, *love* was not a word they used easily. Marriage was an institution people entered into — for all I could ever tell — only from immigrant loneliness, a need to be with one's own kind that mechanically resulted in the *family*. The *family* was a whole greater than all the individuals who made it up, yet made sense only in their untiring solidarity. I was perfectly sure that in my parents' minds *libbe* was something exotic and not wholly legitimate, reserved for "educated" people like their children, who were the sole end of their existence. My father and mother worked in a rage to put us above their level; they had married to make *us* possible. We were the only conceivable end to all their striving; we were their America. . . .

In Brownsville tenements the kitchen is always the largest room and the center of the household. As a child I felt that we lived in a kitchen to which four other rooms were annexed. My mother, a "home" dressmaker, had her workshop in the kitchen. She told me once that she had begun dressmaking in Poland at thirteen; as far back as I can remember, she was always making dresses for the local women. She had an innate sense of design, a quick eye for all the subtleties in the latest fashions, even when she despised them, and great boldness. For three or four dollars she would study the fashion magazines with a customer, go with the customer to the remnants store on Belmont Avenue to pick out the material, argue the owner down — all remnants stores, for some reason, were supposed to be shady, as if the owners dealt in stolen goods — and then for days would patiently fit and baste and sew and fit again. Our apartment was always full of women in their housedresses sitting around the kitchen table waiting for a fitting. My little bedroom next to the kitchen was the fitting room. The sewing machine, an old nut-brown Singer with golden scrolls painted along the black arm and engraved along the two tiers of little drawers massed with needles and thread on each side of the treadle, stood next to the window and the great coal-black stove which up to my last year in college was our main source of heat. By December the two outer bedrooms were closed off, and used to chill bottles of milk and cream, cold borscht and jellied calves' feet.

The kitchen held our lives together. My mother worked in it all day long, we ate in it almost all meals except the Passover *seder*, I did my homework and first writing at the kitchen table, and in winter I often had a bed made up for me on three kitchen chairs near the stove. On the wall just over the table hung a long horizontal mirror that sloped to a ship's prow at each end and was lined in cherry wood. It took up the whole wall, and drew every object in the kitchen to itself. The walls were a fiercely stippled whitewash, so often rewhitened by my father in slack seasons that the paint looked as if it had been squeezed and cracked into the walls. A large electric bulb hung down the center of the kitchen at the end of a chain that had been hooked into the ceiling; the old gas ring and key still jutted out of the wall like antlers. In the corner next to the toilet was the sink at which we washed, and the square tub in which my mother did our clothes. Above it, tacked to the shelf on which were pleasantly ranged square, blue-bordered white sugar and spice jars, hung calendars from the Public National Bank on Pitkin Avenue and the Minsker Progressive Branch of the Workman's Circle; receipts for the payment of insurance premiums, and household bills on a spindle; two little boxes engraved with Hebrew letters. One of these was for the poor, the other to buy back the Land of Israel. Each spring a bearded little man would suddenly appear in our kitchen, salute us with a hurried Hebrew blessing, empty the boxes (sometimes with a sidelong look of disdain if they were not full), hurriedly bless us again for remembering our less fortunate Jewish brothers and sisters, and so take his departure until the next spring, after vainly trying to persuade my mother to take still another box. We did occasionally remember to drop coins in the boxes, but this was usually only on the dreaded morning of "mid-terms" and final examinations, because my mother thought it would bring me luck. She was extremely superstitious, but embarrassed about it, and always laughed at herself whenever, on the morning of an examination, she counseled me to leave the house on my right foot. "I know it's silly," her smile seemed to say, "but what harm can it do? It may calm God down."

The kitchen gave a special character to our lives; my mother's character. All my memories of that kitchen are dominated by the nearness of my mother sitting all day long at her sewing machine, by the clack-ing of the treadle against the linoleum floor, by the patient twist of her right shoulder as she automatically pushed at the wheel with one hand or lifted the foot to free the needle where it had got stuck in a thick piece of material. The kitchen was her life. Year by year, as I began to take in her fantastic capacity for labor and her anxious zeal, I realized it was ourselves she kept stitched together. I can never re-member a time when she was not working. She worked because the law of her life was work, work and anxiety; she worked because she would have found life meaningless without work. She read almost no English; she could read the Yiddish paper, but never felt she had time to. We were always talking of a time when I would teach her how to read, but somehow there was never time. When I awoke in the morn-ing she was already at her machine, or in the great morning crowd of housewives at the grocery getting fresh rolls for breakfast. When I returned from school she was at her machine, or conferring over *McCall's* with some neighborhood woman who had come in pointing hopefully to an illustration — "Mrs. Kazin! Mrs. Kazin! Make me a dress like it shows here in the picture!" When my father came home from work she had somehow mysteriously interrupted herself to make supper for us, and the dishes cleared and washed, was back at her machine. When I went to bed at night, often she was still there, pounding away at the treadle, hunched over the wheel, her hands steering a piece of gauze under the needle with a finesse that always contrasted sharply with her swollen hands and broken nails. Her left hand had been pierced through when as a girl she had worked in the infamous Triangle Shirtwaist Factory on the East Side. A needle had gone straight through the palm, severing a large vein. They had sewn it up for her so clumsily that a tuft of flesh always lay folded over the palm.

The kitchen was the great machine that set our lives running; it whirred down a little only on Saturdays and holy days. From my mother's kitchen I gained my first picture of life as a white, over-heated, starkly lit workshop redolent with Jewish cooking, crowded with women in housedresses, strewn with fashion magazines, patterns, dress material, spools of thread — and at whose center, so lashed to her machine that bolts of energy seemed to dance out of her hands and feet as she worked, my mother stamped the treadle hard against the floor, hard, hard, and silently, grimly at war, beat out the first rhythm of the world for me.

Every sound from the street roared and trembled at our windows — a mother feeding her child on the doorstep, the screech of the trolley cars on Rockaway Avenue, the eternal smash of a handball against the wall of our house, the clatter of *"der Italyéner"* 's cart packed with watermelons, the sing-song of the old-clothes men walking Chester Street, the cries *"Árbes! Árbes! Kinder! Kinder! Heyse gute árbes!"* All day long people streamed into our apartment as a matter of course — "customers," upstairs neighbors, downstairs neighbors, women who would stop in for a half-hour's talk, salesmen, relatives, insurance agents. Usually they came in without ringing the bell — everyone knew my mother was always at home. I would hear the front door opening, the wind whistling through our front hall, and then some familiar face would appear in our kitchen with the same bland, matter-of-fact inquiring look: no need to stand on ceremony: my mother and her kitchen were available to everyone all day long.

At night the kitchen contracted around the blaze of light on the cloth, the patterns, the ironing board where the iron had burned a black border around the tear in the muslin cover; the finished dresses looked so frilly as they jostled on their wire hangers after all the work my mother had put into them. And then I would get that strangely ominous smell of tension from the dress fabrics and the burn in the cover of the ironing board — as if each piece of cloth and paper crushed with light under the naked bulb might suddenly go up in flames. Whenever I pass some small tailoring shop still lit up at night and see the owner hunched over his steam press; whenever in some poorer neighborhood of the city I see through a window some small crowded kitchen naked under the harsh light glittering in the ceiling, I still smell that fiery breath, that warning of imminent fire. I was always holding my breath. What I must have felt most about ourselves, I see now, was that we ourselves were like kindling — that all the hard-pressed pieces of ourselves and all the hard-used objects in that kitchen were like so many slivers of wood that might go up in flames if we came too near the white-blazing filaments in that naked bulb. Our tension itself was fire, we ourselves were forever burning — to live, to get down the foreboding in our souls, to make good.

Twice a year, on the anniversaries of her parents' deaths, my mother placed on top of the ice-box an ordinary kitchen glass packed with wax, the *yortsayt*, and lit the candle in it. Sitting at the kitchen table over my homework, I would look across the threshold to that mourning-glass, and sense that for my mother the distance from our kitchen to *der heym*, from life to death, was only a flame's length away. Poor as we were, it was not poverty that drove my mother so hard; it was loneliness — some endless bitter brooding over all those left behind, dead or dying or soon to die; a loneliness locked up in her kitchen that dwelt every day on the hazardousness of life and the nearness of death, but still kept struggling in the lock, trying to get us through by endless labor.

With us, life started up again only on the last shore. There seemed to be no middle ground between despair and the fury of our ambition. Whenever my mother spoke of her hopes for us, it was with such unbelievingness that the likes of us would ever come to anything, such abashed hope and readiness for pain, that I finally came to see in the flame burning on top of the ice-box death itself burning away the bones of poor Jews, burning out in us everything but courage, the blind resolution to live. In the light of that mourning-candle, there were ranged around me how many dead and dying — how many eras of pain, of exile, of dispersion, of cringing before the powers of this world!

It was always at dusk that my mother's loneliness came home most to me. Painfully alert to every shift in the light at her window, she would suddenly confess her fatigue by removing her pince-nez, and then wearily pushing aside the great mound of fabrics on her machine, would stare at the street as if to warm herself in the last of the sun. "How sad it is!" I once heard her say. "It grips me! It grips me!" Twilight was the bottommost part of the day, the chillest and loneliest time for her. Always so near to her moods, I knew she was fighting some deep inner dread, struggling against the returning tide of darkness along the streets that invariably assailed her heart with the same foreboding — Where? Where now? Where is the day taking us now?

Yet one good look at the street would revive her. I see her now, perched against the windowsill, with her face against the glass, her eyes almost asleep in enjoyment, just as she starts up with the guilty cry — "What foolishness is this in me!" — and goes to the stove to prepare supper for us: a moment, only a moment, watching the evening crowd of women gathering at the grocery for fresh bread and milk. But between my mother's pent-up face at the window and the winter sun dying in the fabrics — "Alfred, see how beautiful!" — she has drawn for me one single line of sentience.

Eudora Welty

In her lectures at Harvard, which were published as One Writer's Beginnings, *Eudora Welty said: "Learning stamps you with its moments. Childhood's learning is made up of moments. It isn't steady. It's a pulse."*

*She was born in 1909 in Jackson, Mississippi, which is still her home. Over
the years her novels and short-story collections — which are notable for their
humor, the naturalness of their conversational rhythms, and their precise sense
of place — have included* The Robber Bridegroom, Delta Wedding,
Losing Battles, *and* The Optimist's Daughter.

*A clue to the uniqueness of Eudora Welty's special genius can be found not
only in her feeling for the Mississippi Delta, but also in her unabashed fondness
for American detective fiction, especially the ironically realistic stories of the
Ross Macdonald school. It is also worth noting that before she turned to writing
fiction, she was a skillful photographer. Her "snapshot album," as she called it,*
One Time, One Place, *is a collection of Depression photographs taken while
she was working with the WPA in Mississippi.*

"The Little Store"

Two BLOCKS AWAY from the Mississippi State Capitol, and on the
same street with it, where our house was when I was a child growing
up in Jackson, it was possible to have a little pasture behind your
backyard where you could keep a Jersey cow, which we did. My mother
herself milked her. A thrifty homemaker, wife, mother of three, she
also did all her own cooking. And as far as I can recall, she never set
foot inside a grocery store. It wasn't necessary.

For her regular needs, she stood at the telephone in our front hall
and consulted with Mr. Lemly, of Lemly's Market and Grocery downtown, who took her order and sent it out on his next delivery. And
since Jackson at the heart of it was still within very near reach of the
open country, the blackberry lady clanged on her bucket with a quart

measure at your front door in June without fail, the watermelon man rolled up to your house exactly on time for the Fourth of July, and down through the summer, the quiet of the early-morning streets was pierced by the calls of farmers driving in with their plenty. One brought his with a song, so plaintive we would sing it with him:

> *"Milk, milk,*
> *Buttermilk,*
> *Snap beans — butterbeans —*
> *Tender okra — fresh greens . . .*
> *And buttermilk."*

My mother considered herself pretty well prepared in her kitchen and pantry for any emergency that, in her words, might choose to present itself. But if she should, all of a sudden, need another lemon or find she was out of bread, all she had to do was call out, "Quick! Who'd like to run to the Little Store for me?"

I would.

She'd count out the change into my hand, and I was away. I'll bet the nickel that would be left over that all over the country, for those of my day, the neighborhood grocery played a similar part in our growing up.

Our store had its name — it was that of the grocer who owned it, whom I'll call Mr. Sessions — but "the Little Store" is what we called it at home. It was a block down our street toward the capitol and half a block further, around the corner, toward the cemetery. I knew even the sidewalk to it as well as I knew my own skin. I'd skipped my jumping-rope up and down it, hopped its length through mazes of hopscotch, played jacks in its islands of shade, serpentined along it on my Princess bicycle, skated it backward and forward. In the twilight I had dragged my steamboat by its string (this was homemade out of every new shoebox, with candle in the bottom lighted and shining through colored tissue paper pasted over windows scissored out in the shapes of the sun, moon and stars) across every crack of the walk without letting it bump or catch fire. I'd "played out" on that street after supper with my brothers and friends as long as "first-dark" lasted; I'd caught its lightning bugs. On the first Armistice Day (and this will set the time I'm speaking of) we made our own parade down that walk on a single velocipede — my brother pedaling, our little brother riding the handlebars, and myself standing on the back, all with arms wide, flying flags in each hand. (My father snapped that picture as we raced by. It came out blurred.)

As I set forth for the Little Store, a tune would float toward me from the house where there lived three sisters, girls in their teens, who ratted their hair over their ears, wore headbands like gladiators, and were considered to be very popular. They practiced for this in the daytime; they'd wind up the Victrola, leave the same record on they'd played before, and you'd see them bobbing past their dining-room windows while they danced with each other. Being three, they could go all day, cutting in:

> "Everybody ought to know-oh
> How to do the Tickle-Toe
> (how to do the Tickle-Toe)" —

they sang it and danced to it, and as I went by to the same song, I believed it.

A little further on, across the street, was the house where the principal of our grade school lived — lived on, even while we were having vacation. What if she would come out? She would halt me in my tracks — she had a very carrying and well-known voice in Jackson, where she'd taught almost everybody — saying, "Eudora Alice Welty, spell OBLIGE." OBLIGE was the word that she of course knew had kept me from making 100 on my spelling exam. She'd make me miss it again now, by boring her eyes through me from across the street. This was my vacation fantasy, one good way to scare myself on the way to the store.

Down near the corner waited the house of a little boy named Lindsey. The sidewalk here was old brick, which the roots of a giant chinaberry tree had humped up and tilted this way and that. On skates, you took it fast, in a series of skittering hops, trying not to touch ground anywhere. If the chinaberries had fallen and rolled in the cracks, it was like skating through a whole shooting match of marbles. I crossed my fingers that Lindsey wouldn't be looking.

During the big flu epidemic he and I, as it happened, were being nursed through our sieges at the same time. I'd hear my father and mother murmuring to each other, at the end of a long day, "And I wonder how poor little *Lindsey* got along today?" Just as, down the street, he no doubt would have to hear his family saying, "And I wonder how is poor *Eudora* by now?" I got the idea that a choice was going to be made soon between poor little Lindsey and poor Eudora, and I came up with a funny poem. I wasn't prepared for it when my father told me it wasn't funny and my mother cried that if I couldn't be ashamed for myself, she'd have to be ashamed for me:

> *There was a little boy and his name was Lindsey.*
> *He went to heaven with the influinzy.*

He didn't, he survived it, poem and all, the same as I did. But his chinaberries could have brought me down in my skates in a flying act of contrition before his eyes, looking pretty funny myself, right in front of his house.

Setting out in this world, a child feels so indelible. He only comes to find out later that it's all the others along his way who are making themselves indelible to him.

Our Little Store rose right up from the sidewalk; standing in a street of family houses, it alone hadn't any yard in front, any tree or flowerbed. It was a plain frame building covered over with brick. Above the door, a little railed porch ran across on an upstairs level and four windows with shades were looking out. But I didn't catch on to those.

Running in out of the sun, you met what seemed total obscurity inside. There were almost tangible smells — licorice recently sucked in a child's cheek, dill-pickle brine that had leaked through a paper sack in a fresh trail across the wooden floor, ammonia-loaded ice that had been hoisted from wet croker sacks and slammed into the icebox with its sweet butter at the door, and perhaps the smell of still-untrapped mice.

Then through the motes of cracker dust, cornmeal dust, the Gold Dust of the Gold Dust Twins that the floor had been swept out with, the realities emerged. Shelves climbed to high reach all the way around, set out with not too much of any one thing but a lot of things — lard, molasses, vinegar, starch, matches, kerosene, Octagon soap (about a year's worth of octagon-shaped coupons cut out and saved brought a signet ring addressed to you in the mail. Furthermore, when the postman arrived at your door, he blew a whistle). It was up to you to remember what you came for, while your eye traveled from cans of sardines to ice cream salt to harmonicas to flypaper (over your head, batting around on a thread beneath the blades of the ceiling fan, stuck with its testimonial catch).

Its confusion may have been in the eye of its beholder. Enchantment is cast upon you by all those things you weren't supposed to have need for, it lures you close to wooden tops you'd outgrown, boy's marbles and agates in little net pouches, small rubber balls that wouldn't bounce straight, frazzly kite-string, clay bubble-pipes that would snap off in your teeth, the stiffest scissors. You could contemplate those long narrow boxes of sparklers gathering dust while you waited for it to be the Fourth of July or Christmas, and noisemakers in the shape of tin frogs for somebody's birthday party you hadn't been invited to yet, and see that they were all marvelous.

You might not have even looked for Mr. Sessions when he came around his store cheese (as big as a doll's house) and in front of the counter looking for you. When you'd finally asked him for, and received from him in its paper bag, whatever single thing it was that you had been sent for, the nickel that was left over was yours to spend.

Down at a child's eye level, inside those glass jars with mouths in their sides through which the grocer could run his scoop or a child's hand might be invited to reach for a choice, were wineballs, all-day suckers, gumdrops, peppermints. Making a row under the glass of a counter were the Tootsie Rolls, Hershey Bars, Goo-Goo Clusters, Baby Ruths. And whatever was the name of those pastilles that came stacked in a cardboard cylinder with a cardboard lid? They were thin and dry, about the size of tiddlywinks, and in the shape of twisted rosettes. A kind of chocolate dust came out with them when you shook them out in your hand. Were they chocolate? I'd say rather they were brown. They didn't taste of anything at all, unless it was wood. Their attraction was the number you got for a nickel.

Making up your mind, you circled the store around and around, around the pickle barrel, around the tower of Cracker Jack boxes; Mr. Sessions had built it for us himself on top of a packing case, like a house of cards.

If it seemed too hot for Cracker Jacks, I might get a cold drink. Mr. Sessions might have already stationed himself by the cold-drinks barrel, like a mind reader. Deep in ice water that looked black as ink, murky shapes that would come up as Coca-Colas, Orange Crushes, and various flavors of pop, were all swimming around together. When you gave the word, Mr. Sessions plunged his bare arm in to the elbow and fished out your choice, first try. I favored a locally bottled concoction called Lake's Celery. (What else could it be called? It was made by a Mr. Lake out of celery. It was a popular drink here for years but was not known universally, as I found out when I arrived in New York and ordered one in the Astor bar.) You drank on the premises, with feet set wide apart to miss the drip, and gave him back his bottle.

But he didn't hurry you off. A standing scales was by the door, with a stack of iron weights and a brass slide on the balance arm, that would weigh you up to three hundred pounds. Mr. Sessions, whose hands were gentle and smelled of carbolic, would lift you up and set your feet on the platform, hold your loaf of bread for you, and taking his time while you stood still for him, he would make certain of what you weighed today. He could even remember what you weighed the last time, so you could subtract and announce how much you'd gained. That was goodbye.

Is there always a hard way to go home? From the Little Store, you could go partway through the sewer. If your brothers had called you a scarecat, then across the next street beyond the Little Store, it was possible to enter this sewer by passing through a privet hedge, climbing down into the bed of a creek, and going into its mouth on your knees. The sewer — it might have been no more than a "storm sewer" — came out and emptied here, where Town Creek, a sandy, most often shallow little stream that ambled through Jackson on its way to the Pearl River, ran along the edge of the cemetery. You could go in darkness through this tunnel to where you next saw light (if you ever did) and climb out through the culvert at your own street corner.

I was a scarecat, all right, but I was a reader with my own refuge in storybooks. Making my way under the sidewalk, under the street and the streetcar track, under the Little Store, down there in the wet dark by myself, I could be Persephone entering into my six-month sojourn underground — though I didn't suppose Persephone had to crawl, hanging onto a loaf of bread, and come out through the teeth of an iron grating. Mother Ceres would indeed be wondering where she could find me, and mad when she knew. "Now am I going to have to start marching to the Little Store for *myself*?"

I couldn't picture it. Indeed, I'm unable today to picture the Little Store with a grown person in it, except for Mr. Sessions and the lady who helped him, who belonged there. We children thought it was ours. The happiness of errands was in part that of running for the moment away from home, a free spirit. I believed the Little Store to be a center of the outside world, and hence of happiness — as I believed what I found in the Cracker Jack box to be a genuine prize, which was as simply as I believed in the Golden Fleece.

But a day came when I ran to the store to discover, sitting on the front step, a grown person, after all — more than a grown person. It was the Monkey Man, together with his monkey. His grinding-organ was lowered to the step beside him. In my whole life so far, I must have laid eyes on the Monkey Man no more than five or six times. An itinerant of rare and wayward appearances, he was not punctual like the Gipsies, who every year with the first cool days of fall showed up in the aisles of Woolworth's. You never knew when the Monkey Man might decide to favor Jackson, or which way he'd go. Sometimes you heard him as close as the next street, and then he didn't come up yours.

But now I saw the Monkey Man at the Little Store, where I'd never seen him before. I'd never seen him sitting down. Low on that familiar doorstep, he was not the same any longer, and neither was his monkey. They looked just like an old man and an old friend of his that wore a fez, meeting quietly together, tired, and resting with their eyes fixed on some place far away, and not the same place. Yet their romance for me didn't have it in its power to waver. I wavered. I simply didn't know how to step around them, to proceed on into the Little Store for my mother's emergency as if nothing had happened. If I could have gone in there after it, whatever it was, I would have given it to them — putting it into the monkey's cool little fingers. I would have given them the Little Store itself.

In my memory they are still attached to the store — so are all the others. Everyone I saw on my way seemed to me then part of my errand, and in a way they were. As I myself, the free spirit, was part of it too.

All the years we lived in that house where we children were born, the same people lived in the other houses on our street too. People changed through the arithmetic of birth, marriage and death, but not by going away. So families just accrued stories, which through the fullness of time, in those times, their own lives made. And I grew up in those.

But I didn't know there'd ever been a story at the Little Store, one that was going on while I was there. Of course, all the time the Sessions family had been living right overhead there, in the upstairs rooms behind the little railed porch and the shaded windows; but I think we children never thought of that. Did I fail to see them as a family because they weren't living in an ordinary house? Because I so seldom saw them close together, or having anything to say to each other? She sat in the back of the store, her pencil over a ledger, while he stood and waited on children to make up their minds. They worked in twin black eyeshades, held on their gray heads by elastic bands. It may be harder to recognize kindness — or unkindness, either — in a face whose eyes are in shadow. His face underneath his shade was as round as the little wooden wheels in the Tinker Toy box. So was her face. I didn't know, perhaps didn't even wonder: were they husband and wife or brother and sister? Were they father and mother? There were a few other persons, of various ages, wandering singly in by the back door and out. But none of their relationships could I imagine, when I'd never seen them sitting down together around their own table.

The possibility that they had any other life at all, anything beyond what we could see within the four walls of the Little Store, occurred to me only when tragedy struck their family. There was some act of violence. The shock to the neighborhood traveled to the children, of course; but I couldn't find out from my parents what had happened. They held it back from me, as they'd already held back many things, "until the time comes for you to know."

You could find out some of these things by looking in the un-abridged dictionary and the encyclopedia — kept to hand in our dining room — but you couldn't find out there what had happened to the family who for all the years of your life had lived upstairs over the Little Store, who had never been anything but patient and kind to you, who never once had sent you away. All I ever knew was its aftermath: they were the only people ever known to me who simply vanished. At the point where their life overlapped into ours, the story broke off.

We weren't being sent to the neighborhood grocery for facts of life, or death. But of course those are what we were on the track of, anyway. With the loaf of bread and the Cracker Jack prize, I was bringing home the intimations of pride and disgrace, and rumors and early news of people coming to hurt one another, while others prac-ticed for joy — storing up a portion for myself of the human mystery.

William Jay Smith

The poet William Jay Smith was an "Army brat." His father, a career corporal (he was once promoted to sergeant but that did not last long), was assigned to the Sixth Infantry Band at Jefferson Barracks, Missouri. Officially, he played the clarinet. He was also a serious gambler, drinker, and — in what proved to be a disastrous combination — amateur bootlegger. William was three and a half in 1921 when he and his mother and his younger brother came to live at "the Barracks," located on the west bank of the Mississippi River just south of Saint Louis.

Unlike most professional soldiers, Smith's father was not regularly transferred from post to post but stayed at Jefferson for twenty years. As a result, the younger Smith — who went on to Columbia University and Oxford (as a Rhodes Scholar), published a number of books of poetry and criticism, and spent two years in the Vermont House of Representatives — did not get to see the world as most army children do, but got to know one isolated community very well.

"The Bootleg Business" is from Smith's autobiography.

"The Bootleg Business," *Army Brat*

How it was that we entered what my father called the "Bootleg Business" I am not quite sure. But it began with our moving in the spring of 1930 from the Barracks to what was known as the Boston house. A sergeant named Boston, who had retired to St. Augustine, Florida, to manage a national cemetery, owned the sizeable two-story square frame structure which looked out on the North Gate entrance to Jefferson Barracks. The address, 9988 South Broadway, indicated that it was indeed the last house.

The North Gate, the main gate to the Barracks, consisted of two large gate posts made of square white limestone blocks topped with black-painted cannon balls. Next to the gate posts was the sentry box, where the guard on duty stopped each car as it approached the gate to inquire about the purpose of its visit, its destination, and then, usually without further ado, to wave it past. Although cars were rarely turned away, the guard made clear to each driver that he was entering a special domain. Even the Dinky or Toonerville Trolley, whose tracks into the Barracks curved past the North Gate opposite the Boston house, had to stop long enough for the guard to make sure that all was right on board before it could proceed.

We had been threatened for some time with having to move. Each time there was a post-wide inspection by the commanding officer or by an area commander, word would get out that the unsightly cantonment buildings were to be torn down. They were eyesores. But usually there would be a year's reprieve — until the next major white-glove inspection. But finally the ax fell, and we were told that we would have to move. Our next-door neighbors for several years on the Western Front had been Sergeant and Mrs. O'Hara and their three children, Billy, Marie, and Colleen. They were now our closest friends, and we did not want to lose touch with them. As Sergeant O'Hara had only two more years of service before retiring, he did not want to settle in any permanent way in the county. It was decided that we would occupy the Boston house together, the O'Haras in the three ground-floor rooms and we in the three upstairs rooms, all sharing the one bathroom on the second floor.

The front hallway was papered in a dark flowery paper, and the stairs led up to our living room, furnished with a fake leather divanet and a wicker chaise longue belonging to the O'Haras, who had spent some years in the Philippines and had many mementos to show for it. They did not have room for the chaise longue in their cramped quarters downstairs, and it became for me the most important and exotic piece that the house possessed. It had pockets on each side, and it seemed the height of luxury to be able to put up my feet and stretch out with books at my elbows and to imagine the gentle movement of palm fronds overhead; it was here that I wrote my first poems. The two books that I kept in the pockets of the chaise longue I had discovered in the Bostons' basement storeroom, *Poems of the Great War*, edited by J. W. Cunliffe, and *One Hundred and One Famous Poems*, compiled by Roy J. Cook. In the latter I discovered Wordsworth's "Ode: Intimations of Immortality," which became one of my favorites, and although I could not fully understand the meaning of the lines, I read them over and over:

> *Though nothing can bring back the hour*
> *Of splendor in the grass, of glory in the flower;*
> *We will grieve not, rather find*
> *Strength in what remains behind . . .*

Off our living room was the kitchen, which had a metal sink and a window looking out over the backyard. The front bedroom had windows right above the street, which opened on a large oak tree. Through the branches the lights of the sentry box at the gate shone all during the night. Because the ground fell away steeply from the street, the Boston house appeared to be perched on a high hill. A driveway led down beside the house, on the reservation side, to a garage at the bottom. In a corner next to it was an old outhouse, the remnant of an earlier era. A long back porch ran the length of the house, and stairs from it led up to our kitchen. In the middle of the backyard was a broken-down grape arbor.

The backyard did not look very promising when we first arrived; the previous tenants had left tin cans and rubbish everywhere. Within a short time, as self-appointed gardener, I would have the yard cleaned up with shovel and rake. Down in one corner was an open level spot which I would turn annually into a garden. While I began by planting several different kinds of vegetables, I settled in the end on string beans as being the easiest and really the most satisfying. I delighted in turning over the rich loam in the spring, putting in the seeds, and then watching the beans sprout and soon leap round their poles. In the summer heat there was a whole world of looping and tangled vines producing long, luscious beans.

On one side of the house were pear and cherry trees and a great clump of mock orange in one corner. There were lilacs in profusion right off the back porch and violets in clumps in the spring. We shared with the O'Haras the entire expense of the house, the rent of which was thirty dollars a month.

In the fall of 1931, after we had occupied the Boston house for more than a year, I began Cleveland High School in St. Louis, and soon afterward the O'Haras departed for Long Beach, California. Just as there was a rigid order to life on the reservation, so there was also a precise order to the retirement of both enlisted men and officers. There were certain enclaves in Florida and California to which they gravitated then as now. For years I had heard talk of Long Beach with its mild climate and sunshine as an ideal haven for retired enlisted men. The O'Haras packed up their car and were off, like many of their breed before them, to Long Beach, and we were faced with the difficult problem of having to move again.

My parents talked first of sharing the house with another couple in the Band, but my father opposed this. The O'Haras had to leave a number of pieces of furniture behind — an electric refrigerator (a Kelvinator, one of the early models) and a complete dining room outfit. My mother spent days making dresses for the O'Hara girls to pay for them.

My father then came up with the proposal that we go into the "Bootleg Business" and take over the entire house. His idea was to make some home brew and invite his fellow Bandsmen from the Barracks to share it with him and thus make a small profit which would take care of our increased rent and give us an easy and comfortable place to live in. My mother was not exactly enchanted by the plan, especially since she did not drink herself, but she did not oppose it on moral grounds. She was quite aware that there were bootleg joints all over St. Louis County and that most of them were frequented by my father. If the police cared that the law was being broken, they never gave any indication of it. As long as the establishments were quiet, they didn't object. And the Army itself would be the last to òbject. The bootlegger was after all only offering a needed service. There were so many bootleggers in Lemay that it was said that you could fall off one porch and onto another and never miss a round of drinks. A man named Singer ran a bootleg joint down the street from us in a large white frame house. He had been in business for years and raked in the money from his military customers. His place was their first stop off the base. My mother's frugal nature may have been attracted by the notion that some of my father's meager salary would not be going into someone else's pockets.

Liquor had always been available in one way or another on the post. When the regular ration of early days was discontinued, whiskey was provided by the sutler who ran the garrison's general store. When the sutler in turn was forbidden to sell spirits, the men would exchange provisions purchased from him for spirits obtained from civilians. My father was not the first enlisted man to engage in the production of home brew. Sergeant Daley, who produced home brew and wine, made the mistake of selling it at the rifle range at Arcadia and was caught. Sergeant Ailsworth, whose wife "Madam Queen" became celebrated throughout the garrison for her bright curly hennaed hair, had taken his own supply of home brew in a hay wagon and had hidden it at one point in the ammunition dump of a sinkhole to avoid detection.

My father may have been prompted in his decision to make his own beer by an article that appeared in the January 24, 1932, issue of the St. Louis *Post-Dispatch*. G. K. Chesterton, who was to speak a few days later at the Odeon Theater on "Culture and the Coming Peril," had this to say: "In one of the weekly articles I sent home, I suggested that we prohibit everything. It appears that if we can keep prohibition a while we may have a real revival of the ancient art of home brewing. It's merely a matter of time until everyone does it, and does it well. The devil, as usual working against his will, the will of God seems to be on the point of restoring some of the old arts of the household. Let the Government only prohibit everything — boots, shoes, coats, hats, tables, chairs — on high moral grounds, and man will once again start doing the old domestic crafts, to the vast increase of his intelligence and peace of mind."

The Noble Experiment was on its way out. The Wickersham Law Enforcement Commission had announced a few days before Chesterton's visit that it felt that it was impossible to ban beer and wine in homes. The report of the Commission had said: "Why home wine making should be lawful while home brewing of beer and home distilling of spirits are not; why home wine making for home use is less reprehensible than making the same wine outside the home for home use, and why it should be penal to make wine commercially for use in home and not penal to make in huge quantities the material for wine making and set up an elaborate selling campaign for disposing of them is not apparent." The report lashed out at the failure of prohibition forces to entrap the real leaders of the bootlegging business. "In place of the small still operated by the individual moonshiner, there are plants of a capacity fairly comparable to the old-time lawful distillery. . . . The business of maintaining and operating them is well-organized." Mindful that most operators, big or small, would not be harassed, we began. Probably from Singer or other bootlegging associates my father acquired all the equipment necessary for the business, a ten-gallon stone crock and several cases of bottles, and soon the first batch of home brew was ready for consumption.

The procedure for making it was simple. Two large cans of malt were needed for the ten-gallon crock. The cans of malt with their yellow labels — resembling yellow cans of Mexican tamales but bigger and fatter — covered with reproductions of medals won at various fairs and expositions had an appropriate plump German appearance. Water was heated on the gas range in the kitchen in a large kettle and two cans of malt were stirred in. When the mixture cooled and yeast had been added, it was taken to the cellar and poured into the crock, which was then covered over with cheese cloth and tied with a string to keep out gnats and bugs. The mixture was left overnight, and the next day a large Irish potato was cut into three pieces and tossed into the crock. The starch in the potato pieces would cause the yeast to settle to the bottom.

Although it was advisable to wait longer, our brew was ready for bottling in two or three days. A short piece of hose was dropped into the crock and the brew siphoned out into bottles that contained a small amount of sugar. You had to be careful not to drop the hose down too close to the bottom so as not to get the yeast all stirred up. Then you would draw in on the hose to get the brew started. Since Richie and I were designated to help with the bottling, we also had to siphon off the stuff to get it started. While I now think that there is nothing more refreshing than good cold beer, I then found the taste or even the smell of my father's abhorrent. I recall it as having the smell of old wet Army shoes and the taste of a soggy blanket.

When the bottles were filled, each one was set under the simple capper that brought down the cap on the bottle, sealing it airtight, and that was that. The bottles were put in cases, the cases stacked up, and the brew was ready for drinking.

The home brew was deposited in the Kelvinator in the kitchen, and it did not stay there long. The men on the post were ready to drink anything they could find. Soon there were any number of thirsty Bandsmen gathered around our dining table. The beer was priced at ten cents a pint. It was sometimes bottled in quart bottles and sold by the glass, at five cents a glass. Before long, men from all the other companies were arriving every evening, and, considering the amount of brew consumed, there should have been a profit. But from the beginning my father made the mistake of giving credit. He was forced to do so because most of the men had no cash whatever during the month: it all came on payday and disappeared at once. My father kept track of the glasses consumed by making marks on a pad, and then on on payday the men were supposed to come in and pay up. There were fewer poker games on the post in those days than there had been when the Sixth Infantry had first arrived and the men had saved up their money on the march across the country. But most of them were making a mere pittance anyway, and some of them were married. There was little money left to spend on drink.

Some of the men came regularly and paid up. There was Beerbaum, a thin blond horn player, a graduate of the University of Illinois. We were, of course, at the height of the Great Depression, and many of the men had turned to the military when there was no place else to turn. There was another college graduate, a full-blooded Indian, six feet four inches tall, "Big Ike," a Sioux, the star of the Band's basketball team. The men called him "Chief." He was a gentle, kind man, who from time to time brought his tall blonde wife, just as blonde as he was dark. She had a job in North St. Louis, and they came together usually only on weekends. Another Indian member of the Band and also a steady customer was "Little Ike," a Comanche. A Polish-American clarinetist named Trask sometimes brought his very attractive Polish girlfriend. Another young clarinetist from southern Illinois, Clyde Maynard, brought his pretty young wife Louise. She did not like Army life at all, and soon managed to persuade her husband to give it up. She and Clyde, who both were favorites of my mother's, became her life-long friends, and mine as well.

Although there were in general few women customers, there was one regular one — Adele Grimble, the wife of Sergeant Grimble. The Grimbles had been our next-door neighbors in the K.C. Building on the post, and now lived around the corner on Teddy Avenue. Dell Grimble had served for years as secretary to the supply officer of the post, and her husband was a barber. Together they knew all the gossip. Dell Grimble, a plumpish little woman with delicate doll-like features and a quick laugh, was a descendant of the original settlers of Carondelet who had deeded the land of the Barracks to the Army in 1826. She naturally took a proprietary interest in the reservation, and was a mine of information about it. Her mother, the wife of Pvt. "Pop" Stewart, who operated the hog ranch on the post, still spoke the French that her family had always spoken. I began to take weekly lessons with her when I was only eight or nine, and by the time I came to study French in high school, I already had a certain proficiency in the language. Mrs. Stewart was to me a grand old lady, and living as she did in a little house tucked away in the woods as in a fairy tale, it seemed to me absolutely natural that she should speak another language.

Most of our bootlegging customers were loners — men like

Holbrook, the snare drummer, a small man with a shriveled-up face. Or Sgt. "Cat" Collins of Service Company, a solid, red-faced, square-shouldered man in his fifties who had served in Panama and elsewhere overseas, an old-timer who had no end of stories to tell. "Cat" Collins took the part of Santa Claus every Christmas Eve in the Post Chapel. Then there was Upchurch, perhaps the steadiest customer. He was an emaciated, gray-haired wisp of a man with black horn-rimmed glasses and a roll-your-own, Bull Durham cigarette constantly dangling from his mouth. As prim and precise as a country school teacher, he took down the orders at the Commissary on regular printed forms.

"Nothing," Upchurch said emphatically, when he heard that I was interested in poetry, "is poetry if it does not rhyme." I knew perfectly well that there were many poems that did not rhyme, but I realized that it was hopeless to discuss the subject with Upchurch. His statement simply reinforced my basic distrust of him.

Upchurch became a permanent fixture, and his consumption of home brew did nothing to fatten him up, but he went on consuming it all the same. He would run up a bill of $100 or more and still be there every evening soon after retreat. He was deeply in debt to us when we closed down our bootlegging operation years later.

The greatest propriety was always observed. My mother did not drink at all, and she sat down with the men as if she had been receiving them in her parlor down South.

During the week no session in the evening lasted very late: most of the men had to be back on the post and in their bunks in time for reveille at 5:30 the next morning. That usually meant that, not having money for carfare, they would have to walk back the mile through the woods. My father had to be up and off at seven in the morning. The big gatherings took place on weekends, especially after payday. Because the men just came and stayed, my mother was persuaded to provide them with food. She cooked huge meals — baked ham, fried chicken, and turkey, with cornbread and her own hot rolls. A delicious dinner with all the fixings was priced at only fifty cents. The men were delighted to have all the benefits of home — and home as many of them had never known it — for so little.

It became clear as time went by that home brew and food were not bringing in much money. And so my father decided to begin dealing in hard liquor. A dark good-looking young man soon pulled up and parked his elegant black coupé in front of our house and brought from it a rectangular leather case, which he carried to the back of the house and up the long steps to our kitchen. His leather case, which he then opened, fitted neatly around a five-gallon can of pure alcohol. It was probably through old experienced bootlegging hands like Singer, whose customers all paid cash, that my father had found out how to get in touch with the charming, polite young man who also brought to our kitchen an oak barrel and cases of whiskey bottles, pints and half-pints. The oak barrel was soon installed on its side in a frame on the shelf of the closet in the middle room upstairs, which was the bedroom that Richie and I shared. My father would cut the alcohol in half, adding five gallons of water to five gallons of alcohol. This mixture was poured into the oak barrel, whose charcoal-lined interior would color the alcohol in due time. To speed up the process my father tried first putting prunes into the barrel, but the prunes gave the liquor a bitter taste. He again consulted the experts, and the gentleman caller brought, along with his next leather-encased delivery, an electric needle about six inches long. It was a steel rod like a soldering iron. The needle would be plugged in, and, when red, would be inserted in the hole in the barrel and remain there for two or three days. The alcohol would then absorb the flavor and the coloring from the barrel. And the whiskey, selling for forty cents a half-pint and seventy-five cents a pint, was as fine as any that could be acquired in the county. At least it was cut in a clean and decent way, and in those days that was just about all that anyone could ask.

In the process of the "cutting," the alcoholic vapors that emerged from my closet made me feel when I went to bed that I was about to be hauled off to an operating room. The room had been intended as a kitchen, and the large gunmetal gray sink that greeted me when I awoke gave me the sensation of being locked up in some evil and foul-smelling laboratory.

The alcoholic vapors that swept my room haunted me even when I left the house. I began to think of the entire business as not only extremely distasteful but also dangerously unlawful. At first, involved with my own activities at school, I had thought little about the business and even welcomed the visitors it brought to our house, which had previously had so few guests. In the early stages everything was discreet: only a handful of men came to the house, and they usually arrived after dark. Now that we sold hard liquor as well as home brew, a steady stream of men would dart in and out, especially on payday, just to pick up a bottle — right under the nose of the guard at the gate.

I now realize that the guard could probably not have cared less, even if brawls had taken place and men had been tossed out in front of him on the pavement. All this was not his concern: he was there to check the cars coming in and out of the Barracks. But then he seemed to me — as indeed he was — the symbol of authority, an authority which one day was sure to crack down on us. Our house was so close to the gate that from the windows of the front bedroom I could gaze down through the branches of the oak tree in our front yard right onto the gate. I could hear every word that the guard said and could almost make out what he was writing down on his pad. The lights of the passing cars, reflected upward, threw the oak branches into grotesque relief on the ceiling. The front bedroom was the one farthest from the noise of the drinkers down below, and I would frequently repair to it in the evening. Whenever a car drew up and parked in front of the house or across the street for any length of time, I would hold my breath: this was surely a private detective who was waiting for the police to arrive. The siren would sound momentarily, a police car would wheel in, making a U-turn and discharging its burly occupants right on our front steps. Then there would be a banging on the front door — I could hear it down below right then — and we would all be whisked off, hands high in the air, tears streaming down my mother's face, to spend years in jail. The scene that I pictured while the great beaked shadows came and went on the bedroom ceiling was straight out of one of the films that I had seen at the post picture show. The bootleggers in the films all traveled in big cars in big cities — but we were allied to them, I thought, and our alliance could only bring us to a bad end.

If the evenings made me apprehensive, the days were in their own way just as terrifying. A large World War I liberty truck picked up the Army children of the neighborhood to take them to school in the morning and bring them back in the afternoon. Our school bus had none of the amenities of the modern yellow pumpkin coach. Covered with heavy khaki canvas held hooped over us, it had no windows and three long benches, one on each side and one down the middle, along which we squeezed like so many lumps of dough or squirming fish. To help us on and off and to watch over us, we had a "bus sergeant." He was not a sergeant, but a private detailed for this not exactly delectable duty. The Barracks bus made several stops, first at Hancock School on South Broadway, then at Carondelet and Blow Elementary Schools in Carondelet, and then farther up in South St. Louis at

Cleveland High School. Our front porch was the gathering place each morning for the children of the neighborhood. Our parlor and dining room were still heavy with the smell of home brew and tobacco from the night before, and I lived in terror that one of my schoolmates would burst into the house one morning, discover a mass of empty beer glasses on the table or in the sink, and find us out. I hated the school bus anyway; its high metal gate pinned us in like animals, and like animals we behaved. Children can be cruel to one another, even under the best of circumstances, but caged up as we were, the brute element predominated.

In reality no one said anything to me directly about our bootlegging, but I found intimations of what many of them knew in much of what they said. In dreams at night I would hear the kids all singing:

> *We're going on a picnic,*
> *Who will be there?*
>> *George*
>>> *Cecile*
>>>> *Inett*
>>>>> *Luther*
>>>>>> *Tommy . . .*

In my dream I would call out the names of all my companions on the school bus, and then their song would conclude as all their fingers pointed to me:

> *I'll bring the sandwiches*
> *And* you *bring the beer . . .*

I would awake in a cold sweat and listen while in the still night a car would pull up at the North Gate, pause for a moment that seemed an eternity, and then continue on, its sound trailing off as it wound around the sinkholes toward the heart of the Barracks.

Jean Fritz

Not all American childhoods are lived in America. Jean Fritz, the children's book writer, was born in China, the daughter of missionaries, and went "home" to America for the first time when she was twelve. Although she lived in Hankow and attended a British school where they sang "God Save the King" every morning, her patriotism was never in doubt. Didn't her mother teach classes at the local Y.M.C.A. on American manners? Wasn't "home" a place called Washington, Pennsylvania?

In this excerpt from her autobiography, Jean, in the spirit of Lexington, Concord, and the "shot heard round the world," plots her own rebellion against British rule. The year is 1925, and she is ten.

From *Homesick*

IN MY FATHER'S STUDY there was a large globe with all the countries of the world running around it. I could put my finger on the exact spot where I was and had been ever since I'd been born. And I was on the wrong side of the globe. I was in China in a city named Hankow, a dot on a crooked line that seemed to break the country right in two. The line was really the Yangtse River, but who would know by looking at a map what the Yangtse River really was?

Orange-brown, muddy mustard-colored. And wide, wide, wide. With a river smell that was old and came all the way up from the bottom. Sometimes old women knelt on the riverbank, begging the River God to return a son or grandson who may have drowned. They would wail and beat the earth to make the River God pay attention, but I knew how busy the River God must be. All those people on the Yangtse River! Coolies hauling water. Women washing clothes. House-boats swarming with old people and young, chickens and pigs. Big crooked-sailed junks with eyes painted on their prows so they could see where they were going. I loved the Yangtse River, but, of course,

I belonged on the other side of the world. In America with my grand-mother.

Twenty-five fluffy little yellow chicks hatched from our eggs today, my grand-mother wrote.

I wrote my grandmother that I had watched a Chinese magician swallow three yards of fire.

The trouble with living on the wrong side of the world was that I didn't feel like a *real* American.

For instance. I could never be president of the United States. I didn't want to be president; I wanted to be a writer. Still, why should there be a *law* saying that only a person born in the United States could be president? It was as if I wouldn't be American enough.

Actually, I was American every minute of the day, especially during school hours. I went to a British school and every morning we sang "God Save the King." Of course the British children loved singing about their gracious king. Ian Forbes stuck out his chest and sang as if he were saving the king all by himself. Everyone sang. Even Gina Boss who was Italian. And Vera Sebastian who was so Russian she dressed the way Russian girls did long ago before the Revolution when her family had to run away to keep from being killed.

But I wasn't Vera Sebastian. I asked my mother to write an excuse so I wouldn't have to sing, but she wouldn't do it. "When in Rome," she said, "do as the Romans do." What she meant was, "Don't make trouble. Just sing." So for a long time I did. I sang with my fingers crossed but still I felt like a traitor.

Then one day I thought: If my mother and father were really and truly in Rome, they wouldn't do what the Romans did at all. They'd probably try to get the Romans to do what *they* did, just as they were trying to teach the Chinese to do what Americans did. (My mother even gave classes in American manners.)

So that day I quit singing. I kept my mouth locked tight against the king of England. Our teacher, Miss Williams, didn't notice at first. She stood in front of the room, using a ruler for a baton, striking each syllable so hard it was as if she were making up for the times she had nothing to strike.

(Miss Williams was pinch-faced and bossy. Sometimes I wondered what had ever made her come to China. "Maybe to try and catch a husband," my mother said.

A husband! Miss Williams!)

"Make him vic-tor-i-ous," the class sang. It was on the strike of "vic" that Miss Williams noticed. Her eyes lighted on my mouth and when we sat down, she pointed her ruler at me.

"Is there something wrong with your voice today, Jean?" she asked.

"No, Miss Williams."

"You weren't singing."

"No, Miss Williams. It is not my national anthem."

"It is the national anthem we sing here," she snapped. "You have always sung. Even Vera sings it."

I looked at Vera with the big blue bow tied on the top of her head. Usually I felt sorry for her but not today. At recess I might even untie that bow, I thought. Just give it a yank. But if I'd been smart, I wouldn't have been looking at Vera. I would have been looking at Ian Forbes and I would have known that, no matter what Miss Williams said, I wasn't through with the king of England.

Recess at the British School was nothing I looked forward to. Every day we played a game called prisoner's base, which was all running and shouting and shoving and catching. I hated the game, yet everyone played except Vera Sebastian. She sat on the sidelines under her blue bow like someone who had been dropped out of a history book. By recess I had forgotten my plans for that bow. While everyone was getting ready for the game, I was as usual trying to look as if I didn't care if I was the last one picked for a team or not. I was leaning against the high stone wall that ran around the schoolyard. I was looking up at a little white cloud skittering across the sky when all at once someone tramped down hard on my right foot. Ian Forbes. Snarling bulldog face. Heel grinding down on my toes. Head thrust forward the way an animal might before it strikes.

"You wouldn't sing it. So say it," he ordered. "Let me hear you say it."

I tried to pull my foot away but he only ground down harder.

"Say what?" I was telling my face please not to show what my foot felt.

"*God save the king.* Say it. Those four words. I want to hear you say it."

Although Ian Forbes was short, he was solid and tough and built for fighting. What was more, he always won. You had only to look at his bare knees between the top of his socks and his short pants to know that he would win. His knees were square. Bony and unbeatable. So of course it was crazy for me to argue with him.

"Why should I?" I asked. "Americans haven't said that since George the Third."

He grabbed my right arm and twisted it behind my back.

"Say it," he hissed.

I felt the tears come to my eyes and I hated myself for the tears. I hated myself for not staying in Rome the way my mother had told me.

"I'll never say it," I whispered.

They were choosing sides now in the schoolyard and Ian's name was being called — among the first as always.

He gave my arm another twist. "You'll sing tomorrow," he snarled, "or you'll be bloody sorry."

As he ran off, I slid to the ground, my head between my knees. *Oh, Grandma, I thought, why can't I be there with you? I'd feed the chickens for you. I'd pump water from the well, the way my father used to do.*

It would be almost two years before we'd go to America. I was ten years old now; I'd be twelve then. But how could I think about *years*? I didn't even dare to think about the next day. After school I ran all the way home, fast so I couldn't think at all.

Our house stood behind a high stone wall which had chips of broken glass sticking up from the top to keep thieves away. I flung open the iron gate and threw myself through the front door.

"I'm home!" I yelled.

Then I remembered that it was Tuesday, the day my mother taught an English class at the Y.M.C.A. where my father was the director.

I stood in the hall, trying to catch my breath, and as always I began to feel small. It was a huge hall with ceilings so high it was as if they would have nothing to do with people. Certainly not with a mere child, not with me — the only child in the house. Once I asked my best friend, Andrea, if the hall made her feel little too. She said no. She was going to be a dancer and she loved space. She did a high kick to show how grand it was to have room.

Andrea Hull was a year older than I was and knew about everything sooner. She told me about commas, for instance, long before I took punctuation seriously. How could I write letters without commas? she asked. She made me so ashamed that for months I hung little wagging comma-tails all over the letters to my grandmother. She told me things that sounded so crazy I had to ask my mother if they were true. Like where babies came from. And that someday the whole world would end. My mother would frown when I asked her, but she always agreed that Andrea was right. It made me furious. How could she know such things and not tell me? What was the matter with grown-ups anyway?

I wished that Andrea were with me now, but she lived out in the country and I didn't see her often. Lin Nai-Nai, my amah, was the only one around, and of course I knew she'd be there. It was her job to stay with me when my parents were out. As soon as she heard me come in, she'd called, "Tsai loushang," which meant that she was upstairs. She might be mending or ironing but most likely she'd be sitting by the window embroidering. And she was. She even had my embroidery laid out, for we had made a bargain. She would teach me to embroider if I would teach her English. I liked embroidering: the cloth stretched tight within my embroidery hoop while I filled in the stamped pattern with cross-stitches and lazy daisy flowers. The trouble was that lazy daisies needed French knots for their centers and I hated making French knots. Mine always fell apart, so I left them to the end. Today I had twenty lazy daisies waiting for their knots.

Lin Nai-Nai had already threaded my needle with embroidery floss. "Black centers," she said, "for the yellow flowers."

I felt myself glowering. "American flowers don't have centers," I said and gave her back the needle.

Lin Nai-Nai looked at me, puzzled, but she did not argue. She was different from other amahs. She did not even come from the servant class, although this was a secret we had to keep from the other servants who would have made her life miserable, had they known. She had run away from her husband when he had taken a second wife. She would always have been Wife Number One and the Boss no matter how many wives he had, but she would rather be no wife than head of a string of wives. She was modern. She might look old-fashioned, for her feet had been bound up tight when she was a little girl so that they would stay small, and now, like many Chinese women, she walked around on little stumps stuffed into tiny cloth shoes. Lin Nai-Nai's were embroidered with butterflies. Still, she believed in true love and one wife for one husband. We were good friends, Lin Nai-Nai and I, so I didn't know why I felt so mean.

She shrugged. "English lesson?" she asked, smiling.

I tested my arm to see if it still hurt from the twisting. It did. My foot too. "What do you want to know?" I asked.

We had been through the polite phrases — Please, Thank you, I beg your pardon, Excuse me, You're welcome, Merry Christmas (which she had practiced but hadn't had a chance to use since this was only October).

"If I meet an American on the street," she asked, "how do I greet him?"

I looked her straight in the eye and nodded my head in a greeting. "Sewing machine," I said. "You say, 'Sew-ing ma-chine.' "

She repeated after me, making the four syllables into four separate words. She got up and walked across the room, bowing and smiling. "Sew Ing Ma Shing."

Part of me wanted to laugh at the thought of Lin Nai-Nai maybe meeting Dr. Carhart, our minister, whose face would surely puff up, the way it always did when he was flustered. But part of me didn't want to laugh at all. I didn't like it when my feelings got tangled, so I ran downstairs and played chopsticks on the piano. Loud and fast. When my sore arm hurt, I just beat on the keys harder.

Then I went out to the kitchen to see if Yang Sze-Fu, the cook, would give me something to eat. I found him reading a Chinese newspaper, his eyes going up and down with the characters. (Chinese words don't march across flat surfaces the way ours do; they drop down cliffs, one cliff after another from right to left across a page.)

"Can I have a piece of cinnamon toast?" I asked. "And a cup of cocoa?"

Yang Sze-Fu grunted. He was smoking a cigarette, which he wasn't supposed to do in the kitchen, but Yang Sze-Fu mostly did what he wanted. He considered himself superior to common workers. You could tell because of the fingernails on his pinkies. They were at least two inches long, which was his way of showing that he didn't have to use his hands for rough or dirty work. He didn't seem to care that his fingernails were dirty, but maybe he couldn't keep such long nails clean.

He made my toast while his cigarette dangled out of the corner of his mouth, collecting a long ash that finally fell on the floor. He wouldn't have kept smoking if my mother had been there, although he didn't always pay attention to my mother. Never about butter pagodas, for instance. No matter how many times my mother told him before a dinner party, "No butter pagoda," it made no difference. As soon as everyone was seated, the serving boy, Wong Sze-Fu, would bring in a pagoda and set it on the table. The guests would "oh" and "ah," for it was a masterpiece: a pagoda molded out of butter, curved roofs rising tier upon tier, but my mother could only think how unsanitary it was. For, of course, Yang Sze-Fu had molded the butter with his hands and carved the decorations with one of his long fingernails. Still, we always used the butter, for if my mother sent it back to the kitchen, Yang Sze-Fu would lose face and quit.

When my toast and cocoa were ready, I took them upstairs to my room (the blue room) and while I ate, I began *Sara Crewe* again. Now there was a girl, I thought, who was worth crying over. I wasn't going to think about myself. Or Ian Forbes. Or the next day. I wasn't. I wasn't.

And I didn't. Not all afternoon. Not all evening. Still, I must have decided what I was going to do because the next morning when I started for school and came to the corner where the man sold hot chestnuts, the corner where I always turned to go to school, I didn't turn. I walked straight ahead. I wasn't going to school that day.

I walked toward the Yangtse River. Past the store that sold paper pellets that opened up into flowers when you dropped them in a glass of water. Then up the block where the beggars sat. I never saw anyone give money to a beggar. You couldn't, my father explained, or you'd be mobbed by beggars. They'd follow you everyplace; they'd never leave you alone. I had learned not to look at them when I passed and yet I saw. The running sores, the twisted legs, the mangled faces. What I couldn't get over was that, like me, each one of these beggars had only one life to live. It just happened that they had drawn rotten ones.

Oh, Grandma, I thought, we may be far apart but we're lucky, you and I. Do you even know how lucky? In America do you know?

This part of the city didn't actually belong to the Chinese, even though the beggars sat there, even though upper-class Chinese lived there. A long time ago other countries had just walked into China and divided up part of Hankow (and other cities) into sections, or concessions, which they called their own and used their own rules for governing. We lived in the French concession on Rue de Paris. Then there was the British concession and the Japanese. The Russian and German concessions had been officially returned to China, but the people still called them concessions. The Americans didn't have one, although, like some of the other countries, they had gunboats on the river. In case, my father said. In case what? Just in case. That's all he'd say.

The concessions didn't look like the rest of China. The buildings were solemn and orderly with little plots of grass around them. Not like those in the Chinese part of the city: a jumble of rickety shops with people, vegetables, crates of quacking ducks, yard goods, bamboo baskets, and mangy dogs spilling onto a street so narrow it was hardly there.

The grandest street in Hankow was the Bund, which ran along beside the Yangtse River. When I came to it after passing the beggars, I looked to my left and saw the American flag flying over the American consulate building. I was proud of the flag and I thought maybe today it was proud of me. It flapped in the breeze as if it were saying ha-ha to the king of England.

Then I looked to the right at the Customs House, which stood at the other end of the Bund. The clock on top of the tower said nine-thirty. How would I spend the day?

I crossed the street to the promenade part of the Bund. When people walked here, they weren't usually going anyplace; they were just out for the air. My mother would wear her broad-brimmed beaver hat when we came and my father would swing his cane in that jaunty way that showed how glad he was to be a man. I thought I would just sit on a bench for the morning. I would watch the Customs House clock, and when it was time, I would eat the lunch I had brought along in my schoolbag.

I was the only one sitting on a bench. People did not generally "take the air" on a Wednesday morning and besides, not everyone was allowed here. The British had put a sign on the Bund, NO DOGS, NO CHINESE. This meant that I could never bring Lin Nai-Nai with me. My father couldn't even bring his best friend, Mr. T. K. Hu. Maybe the British wanted a place where they could pretend they weren't in China, I thought. Still, there were always Chinese coolies around. In order to load and unload boats in the river, coolies had to cross the Bund. All day they went back and forth, bent double under their loads, sweating and chanting in a tired, singsong way that seemed to get them from one step to the next.

To pass the time, I decided to recite poetry. The one good thing about Miss Williams was that she made us learn poems by heart and I liked that. There was one particular poem I didn't want to forget. I looked at the Yangtse River and pretended that all the busy people in the boats were my audience.

" 'Breathes there the man, with soul so dead,' " I cried, " 'Who never to himself hath said, This is my own, my native land!' "

I was so carried away by my performance that I didn't notice the policeman until he was right in front of me. Like all policemen in the British concession, he was a bushy-bearded Indian with a red turban wrapped around his head.

He pointed to my schoolbag. "Little miss," he said, "why aren't you in school?"

He was tall and mysterious-looking, more like a character in my Arabian Nights book than a man you expected to talk to. I fumbled for an answer. "I'm going on an errand," I said finally. "I just sat down for a rest." I picked up my schoolbag and walked quickly away. When I looked around, he was back on his corner, directing traffic.

So now they were chasing children away too, I thought angrily. Well, I'd like to show them. Someday I'd like to walk a dog down the whole length of the Bund. A Great Dane. I'd have him on a leash — like this — (I put out my hand as if I were holding a leash right then) and he'd be so big and strong I'd have to strain to hold him back (I strained). Then of course sometimes he'd have to do his business and I'd stop (like this) right in the middle of the sidewalk and let him go to it. I was so busy with my Great Dane I was at the end of the Bund before I knew it. I let go of the leash, clapped my hands, and told my dog to go home. Then I left the Bund and the concessions and walked into the Chinese world.

My mother and father and I had walked here but not for many months. This part near the river was called the Mud Flats. Sometimes it was muddier than others, and when the river flooded, the flats disappeared underwater. Sometimes even the fishermen's huts were washed away, knocked right off their long-legged stilts and swept down the river. But today the river was fairly low and the mud had dried so that it was cracked and cakey. Most of the men who lived here were out fishing, some not far from the shore, poling their sampans through the shallow water. Only a few people were on the flats: a man cleaning fish on a flat rock at the water's edge, a woman spreading clothes on the dirt to dry, a few small children. But behind the huts was something I had never seen before. Even before I came close, I guessed what it was. Even then, I was excited by the strangeness of it.

It was the beginnings of a boat. The skeleton of a large junk, its ribs lying bare, its backbone running straight and true down the bottom. The outline of the prow was already in place, turning up wide and snub-nosed, the way all junks did. I had never thought of boats starting from nothing, of taking on bones under their bodies. The eyes, I supposed, would be the last thing added. Then the junk would have life.

The builders were not there and I was behind the huts where no one could see me as I walked around and around, marveling. Then I climbed inside and as I did, I knew that something wonderful was happening to me. I was a-tingle, the way a magician must feel when he swallows fire, because suddenly I knew that the boat was mine. No matter who really owned it, it was mine. Even if I never saw it again, it would be my junk sailing up and down the Yangtse River. My junk seeing the river sights with its two eyes, seeing them for me whether I was there or not. Often I had tried to put the Yangtse River into a poem so I could keep it. Sometimes I had tried to draw it, but nothing I did ever came close. But now, *now* I had my junk and somehow that gave me the river too.

I thought I should put my mark on the boat. Perhaps on the side of the spine. Very small. A secret between the boat and me. I opened my schoolbag and took out my folding penknife that I used for sharpening pencils. Very carefully I carved the Chinese character that was our name. Gau. (In China my father was Mr. Gau, my mother was Mrs. Gau, and I was Little Miss Gau.) The builders would paint right over the character, I thought, and never notice. But I would know. Always and forever I would know.

For a long time I dreamed about the boat, imagining it finished, its sails up, its eyes wide. Someday it might sail all the way down the Yangtse to Shanghai, so I told the boat what it would see along the way because I had been there and the boat hadn't. After a while I got hungry and I ate my egg sandwich. I was in the midst of peeling an orange when all at once I had company.

A small boy, not more than four years old, wandered around to the back of the huts, saw me, and stopped still. He was wearing a ragged blue cotton jacket with a red cloth, pincushion-like charm around his neck which was supposed to keep him from getting smallpox. Sticking up straight from the middle of his head was a small pigtail which I knew was to fool the gods and make them think he was a girl. (Gods didn't bother much with girls; it was boys that were important in China.) The weather was still warm so he wore no pants, nothing below the waist. Most small boys went around like this so that when they had to go, they could just let loose and go. He walked slowly up to the boat, stared at me, and then nodded as if he'd already guessed what I was. "Foreign devil," he announced gravely.

I shook my head. "No," I said in Chinese. "American friend." Through the ribs of the boat, I handed him a segment of orange. He ate it slowly, his eyes on the rest of the orange. Segment by segment, I gave it all to him. Then he wiped his hands down the front of his jacket.

"Foreign devil," he repeated.

"American friend," I corrected. Then I asked him about the boat. Who was building it? Where were the builders?

He pointed with his chin upriver. "Not here today. Back tomorrow."

I knew it would only be a question of time before the boy would run off to alert the people in the huts. "Foreign devil, foreign devil," he would cry. So I put my hand on the prow of the boat, wished it luck, and climbing out, I started back toward the Bund. To my surprise the boy walked beside me. When we came to the edge of the Bund, I squatted down so we would be on the same eye level.

"Good-bye," I said. "May the River God protect you."

For a moment the boy stared. When he spoke, it was as if he were trying out a new sound. "American friend," he said slowly.

When I looked back, he was still there, looking soberly toward the foreign world to which I had gone.

The time, according to the Customs House clock, was five after two, which meant that I couldn't go home for two hours. School was dismissed at three-thirty and I was home by three-forty-five unless I had to stay in for talking in class. It took me about fifteen minutes to write "I will not talk in class" fifty times, and so I often came home at four o'clock. (I wrote up and down like the Chinese: fifty "I's," fifty "wills," and right through the sentence so I never had to think what I was writing. It wasn't as if I were making a promise.) Today I planned to arrive home at four, my "staying-in" time, in the hope that I wouldn't meet classmates on the way.

Meanwhile I wandered up and down the streets, in and out of stores. I weighed myself on the big scale in the Hankow Dispensary and found that I was as skinny as ever. I went to the Terminus Hotel and tried out the chairs in the lounge. At first I didn't mind wandering about like this. Half of my mind was still on the river with my junk, but as time went on, my junk began slipping away until I was alone with nothing but questions. Would my mother find out about today? How could I skip school tomorrow? And the next day and the next? Could I get sick? Was there a kind of long lie-abed sickness that didn't hurt?

I arrived home at four, just as I had planned, opened the door, and called out, "I'm home!" Cheery-like and normal. But I was scarcely in the house before Lin Nai-Nai ran to me from one side of the hall and my mother from the other.

"Are you all right? Are you all right?" Lin Nai-Nai felt my arms as if she expected them to be broken. My mother's face was white. "What happened?" she asked.

Then I looked through the open door into the living room and saw Miss Williams sitting there. She had beaten me home and asked about my absence, which of course had scared everyone. But now my mother could see that I was in one piece and for some reason this seemed to make her mad. She took me by the hand and led me into the living room. "Miss Williams said you weren't in school," she said. "Why was that?"

I hung my head, just the way cowards do in books.

My mother dropped my hand. "Jean will be in school tomorrow," she said firmly. She walked Miss Williams to the door. "Thank you for stopping by."

Miss Williams looked satisfied in her mean, pinched way. "Well," she said, "ta-ta." (She always said "ta-ta" instead of "good-bye." Chicken language, it sounded like.)

As soon as Miss Williams was gone and my mother was sitting down again, I burst into tears. Kneeling on the floor, I buried my head in her lap and poured out the whole miserable story. My mother could see that I really wasn't in one piece after all, so she listened quietly, stroking my hair as I talked, but gradually I could feel her stiffen. I knew she was remembering that she was a Mother.

"You better go up to your room," she said, "and think things over. We'll talk about it after supper."

I flung myself on my bed. What was there to think? Either I went to school and got beaten up. Or I quit.

After supper I explained to my mother and father how simple it was. I could stay at home and my mother could teach me, the way Andrea's mother taught her. Maybe I could even go to Andrea's house and study with her.

My mother shook her head. Yes, it was simple, she agreed. I could go back to the British School, be sensible, and start singing about the king again.

I clutched the edge of the table. Couldn't she understand? I couldn't turn back now. It was too late.

So far my father had not said a word. He was leaning back, teetering on the two hind legs of his chair, the way he always did after a meal, the way that drove my mother crazy. But he was not the kind of person to keep all four legs of a chair on the floor just because someone wanted him to. He wasn't a turning-back person so I hoped maybe he would understand. As I watched him, I saw a twinkle start in his eyes and suddenly he brought his chair down slam-bang flat on the floor. He got up and motioned for us to follow him into the living room. He sat down at the piano and began to pick out the tune for "God Save the King."

A big help, I thought. Was he going to make me practice?

Then he began to sing:

"My country 'tis of thee,
Sweet land of liberty, . . ."

Of course! It was the same tune. Why hadn't I thought of that? Who would know what I was singing as long as I moved my lips? I joined in now, loud and strong.

"Of thee I sing."

My mother laughed in spite of herself. "If you sing that loud," she said, "you'll start a revolution."

"Tomorrow I'll sing softly," I promised. "No one will know." But for now I really let freedom ring.

Then all at once I wanted to see Lin Nai-Nai. I ran out back, through the courtyard that separated the house from the servants' quarters, and upstairs to her room.

"It's me," I called through the door and when she opened up, I threw my arms around her. "Oh, Lin Nai-Nai, I love you," I said. "You haven't said it yet, have you?"

"Said what?"

"Sewing machine. You haven't said it?"

"No," she said, "not yet. I'm still practicing."

"Don't say it, Lin Nai-Nai. Say 'Good day.' It's shorter and easier. Besides, it's more polite."

"Good day?" she repeated.

"Yes, that's right. Good day." I hugged her and ran back to the house.

The next day at school when we rose to sing the British national anthem, everyone stared at me, but as soon as I opened my mouth, the class lost interest. All but Ian Forbes. His eyes never left my face, but I sang softly, carefully, proudly. At recess he sauntered over to where I stood against the wall.

He spat on the ground. "You can be bloody glad you sang today," he said. Then he strutted off as if he and those square knees of his had won again.

And, of course, I was bloody glad.

Monica Sone

The Japanese word for "generation" is sei. *So, by adding a prefix — Is, Ni, or San, the numbers "one," "two," or "three" — one can count the number of generations a Japanese-American is from Japan. Monica Itoi Sone (b.1919), the daughter of a man who came to the United States in 1904 as a law student and became the proprietor of a Seattle skid-row hotel, titled her autobiography* Nisei Daughter.

In this excerpt, she provides a vivid picture of social life in the Seattle Japanese community in the 1920s. It was a large, concentrated neighborhood, numbering about 8,500 inhabitants in 1930, with its own newspapers, social clubs, sports events, and political and religious organizations (both Christian and Buddhist). Its center was Nippon Kan Hall, an old auditorium just outside the business district that was used for everything from political rallies to performances of shibai *plays to sumo matches.*

From "The Japanese Touch," *Nisei Daughter*

NEW YEAR'S, as my family observed it, was a mixture of pleasure and agony. I enjoyed New Year's eve which we spent together, waiting for midnight. On New Year's eve, no one argued when Mother marched us into the bathtub, one by one. We understood that something as important as a new year required a special sacrifice on our part. Mother said the bath was a symbolic act, that we must scrub off the old year and greet the new year clean and refreshed in body and spirit.

The rest of the evening we spent crowded around the table in the living room playing *Karuta*, an ancient Japanese game. It consisted of one hundred old classic poems beautifully brushed upon one hundred cards, about the size of a deck of cards. There was one set of cards on which were written the *shimo no ku*, the second half of the poems. These were laid out on the table before the players. A reader presided over a master set of one hundred cards which contained the *kami no ku*, the first half of the poem as well as the *shimo no ku*. As the reader read from the key cards, the players were to try to pick up the card on the table before anyone else could claim it. The player or the team who picked up the greatest number of cards was the winner. An expert player knew the entire one hundred poems by heart so that when the reader had uttered the first few words, he knew instantly which card was being called out. When several experts competed the game was exciting and stimulating. But in our family only Mother and Father knew the poems, and they slowed their paces to match ours.

Mother was always the reader, chanting out the poems melodically. Sumiko, being the baby of the family, was allowed to stand on a chair at Mother's elbow and get a preview of the card being read. Sumiko would look, jump off the chair, and scurry around the table to find the card while we waited impatiently for Mother to get to the second half of the poem. I howled with indignation, "Mama, make Sumiko stop cheating! It's not fair . . . I'll never find a card as long as she peeks at the *kami no ku!*"

Mother laughed indulgently, "Now, don't get so excited. Sumi-chan's just a little girl. She has to have some fun, too."

The evening progressed noisily as we fluttered about like anxious little moths, eyes riveted on the table. Anyone who found a card would triumphantly shout "*Hai!*" and slam down on it with a force that would have flattened an opponent's fingers. Promptly at midnight we stopped. Out in the harbor, hundreds of boats sounded their foghorns to herald the New Year. Automobiles raced by under our windows, their horns blowing raucously. Guns exploded, cowbells clanged, the factory whistle shrilled. Henry swept the cards off the table, leaped into the air in his billowing nightshirt and shouted "Happy New Year, everybody! Happy New Year!" We turned on the radio full blast so we could hear the rest of the city cheer and sing "Auld Lang Syne." Horrified, Father implored us, "Ohhh the guests, the guests. Lower that radio. We'll wake our guests."

Then Father and Mother slipped quietly down the hallway to the kitchen to prepare refreshments. Although the black-painted steampipe, running alongside one wall in the room, made energetic knocking noises which meant that it was piping hot, the parlor was chilly. I turned the tiny gas heater higher and Sumiko and I sat in front of it, pulling our voluminous flannel gowns over our knees and cold toes. We sat with our chins resting comfortably on our knees and huddled so close to the heater that our faces began to tighten and glow beet-red. I was floating in half sleep when I heard Mother and Father's voices murmuring gently. "*Sah,* who gets the smallest piece of pie?"

"Not me!" Sumiko jumped up defensively. Then she saw Father's eyes smiling.

Father had carried in a pot of hot coffee and fresh, honey-crusted apple pie with its golden juice bubbled through the slits. Mother brought in thick hot chocolate, with plump soft marshmallow floating on top, for us.

It was customary for the Japanese to eat buckwheat noodles on New Year's eve, but every year whenever Mother wondered aloud whether she should make some, we voted it down. Father said, "No noodles for me either, Mama. A good hot cup of coffee is what will please me most."

Father sliced the pie and as we let the flaky, butter-flavored crust melt in our mouths, we did not envy anyone eating noodles.

The next morning when we were breakfasting on fruit juice, ham and eggs, toast and milk, Mother said, "We really should be eating *ozoni* and *mochi* on New Year's morning."

We gagged, "Oh, no, not in the morning!"

"Well now, don't turn your nose up like that. It's a perfectly respectable tradition."

Ozoni was a sort of thick chicken stew with solid chunks of carrots, bamboo sprouts, giant white radishes and taro roots. Into this piping hot mixture, one dipped freshly toasted rice dumplings, puffed into white airy plumpness, in the same way one dunked doughnuts into coffee. But the rice dumpling had an annoying way of sticking to everything like glue . . . to the chopsticks, to the side of the bowl, and on the palate. It was enough to cause a panic when the thick, doughy dumpling fastened itself in the throat and refused to march on down to the stomach.

Father backed us up once more, "*Ozoni* is good, I admit, but I don't like to battle with my food so early in the morning. Let's have some more coffee, Mama."

"Well, having a whimsical family like this certainly saves me a lot of work."

Up to that moment the family was in perfect harmony about whether we would celebrate New Year's in the Japanese or the American way. But a few hours later our peace was shattered when Mother said, "*Sah,* now we must pay our respects to the Matsuis."

"Not again," Henry shuddered.

"Yes again, and I don't want to hear any arguments."

"But why must *we* go? Why can't you and Papa go by yourselves this time?"

"We are all going together for the New Year's call," Mother said firmly. "I don't want to hear another word. Put your clothes on."

We sighed loudly as we dressed ourselves. We would have to sit silently like little Buddhas and listen while our elders dredged up the past and gave it the annual overhaul. Even the prospect of Mrs. Matsui's magnificent holiday feast was dampened by the fact that we knew we would have to eat quietly like meek little ghosts and politely refuse all second helpings.

"Mama . . ." Henry shouted from his room. "What was that now, that New Year's greeting we have to say to the Matsuis? I've forgotten how it goes. '*Ake-mashite omede toh gozai masu. Konen mo, ahhh, konen mo . . .*' What comes after that? I can't remember."

Mother said, "*Soh, soh . . .* I want you all to say it properly when we arrive at the Matsui-san's home. It goes like this . . . *ake-mashite toh gozai masu*, which means 'This New Year is indeed a happy occasion.' Then you say *konen mo yoroshiku onegai itashi-masu*. 'I hope that the coming year will find us close friends as ever.' "

As we climbed up Yesler Hill to the Matsuis, we repeated the greeting over and over again. We raised our voices so we could hear ourselves better whenever a chunky bright orange cable car lurched up the hill like a lassoed bronco, inching its way furiously to the top.

The Matsui residence was a large yellow frame house which squatted grandly on an elevated corner lot. At the front door, Father and Mother and Mr. and Mrs. Matsui bowed and murmured, bowed and murmured. Standing behind our parents, we bowed vigorously, too. Then Mrs. Matsui looked at us expectantly and Mother pushed us forward. We bowed again, then started out in unison. "*Ake-mashite omede toh gozai masu.*" A long pause followed. We forgot the rest. Then Henry recalled a fragment, "*Konen mo . . . konen mo . . . ahhh*, something about *onegai shimasu.*"

The adults burst into laughter, bringing the affair to a merciful end.

In the living room, we waited patiently while Mrs. Matsui offered the best chairs to Father and Mother who politely refused them. Mrs. Matsui insisted and they declined. When at last we were all seated as Mrs. Matsui wanted — Father and Mother on the overstuffed brown

mohair chairs and the four of us primly lined up on the huge dav-
enport, our polished shoes placed neatly together and hands in our
laps — she brought in tea and thin, crisp, rice cookies. As she poured
the tea, she said, "Perhaps the little folks would rather have 'sodawata'
instead?"

Henry and Kenji smirked at each other while Sumiko and I hung
our heads, trying not to look eager, but Mother said quickly, "Oh, no,
please, Mrs. Matsui, don't trouble yourself. My children love tea." So
we sipped scalding tea out of tiny, burning teacups without handles
and nibbled at brittle rice wafers.

While the Matsuis and our parents reminisced about the good old
days, we thumbed through the worn photograph albums and old
Japanese tourist magazines. Finally Mrs. Matsui excused herself and
bustled feverishly around the dining room. Then she invited us in.
"*Sah,* I have nothing much to offer you, but please eat your fill."

"*Mah, mah,* such a wonderful assortment of *ogochi-soh,*" Mother bubbled.

Balding Mr. Matsui snorted deprecatingly. Mrs. Matsui walked
around the table with an enormous platter of *osushi,* rice cakes rolled
in seaweed. We each took one and nibbled at it daintily, sipping tea.
Presently she sailed out of the kitchen bearing a magnificent black and
silver lacquered tray loaded with carmine lacquer bowls filled with
fragrant *nishime.* In pearly iridescent china bowls, Mrs. Matsui served
us hot chocolatey *oshiruko,* a sweetened bean soup dotted with tender
white *mochi,* puffed up like oversized marshmallows.

Father and Mother murmured over the superb flavoring of each
dish, while Mr. Matsui guffawed politely, "*Nani,* this woman isn't
much of a cook at all."

I was fascinated with the *yaki-zakana,* barbecued perch, which, its
head and tail raised saucily, looked as if it were about to flip out of the
oval platter. Surrounding this centerpiece were lacquer boxes of des-
serts, neatly lined rows of red and green oblong slices of sweet bean
cakes, a mound of crushed lima beans, tinted red and green, called
kinton. There was a vegetable dish called *kimpira* which looked like a
mass of brown twigs. It turned out to be burdock, hotly seasoned with
red pepper.

Every now and then Mrs. Matsui urged us from the side line, "Please
help yourself to more food."

And each time, we were careful to say, "*Arigato,* I have plenty, thank
you," although I could have counted the grains of rice I had so far

consumed. I felt that a person could starve amidst this feast if he carried politeness too far. Fortunately, Mrs. Matsui ignored our refusals. She replenished our half-empty dishes and kept our teacups filled so that without breaking the illusion that we were all dainty eaters, we finally reached a semiconscious state of satiation.

We moved heavily to the parlor to relax. Mrs. Matsui pursued us there with more green, pickled radishes and *kazunoko,* fish eggs, and a bowl of fresh fruit. She brought out fresh tea and *yokan.* To turn down Mrs. Matsui's offer so often was very rude, so we accepted with a wan smile and firmly closed our mouths over the cake and chewed.

When Father and Mother finally came to their senses and decided it was time to go home, we nearly tore the door off its hinges in our rush to get out into the hallway for our wraps.

I staggered out at last into the frosty night, feeling tight as a drum and emotionally shaken from being too polite for too long. I hoped on our next call our hostess would worry less about being hospitable and more about her guests' comfort, but that was an impudent thought for a Japanese girl.

Jeanne Wakatsuki Houston

Manzanar is a Spanish word that means "apple orchard." Manzanar was also the name of a hastily built internment camp for Japanese and Japanese-Americans that was erected in the high desert country of the Owens Valley, just northeast of Los Angeles, in the early days of World War II. In 1942, when Jeanne Wakatsuki was seven years old, she, her mother, and her older brothers and sisters were ordered out of their house in Long Beach, California, and sent to Manzanar. Her father, a commercial fisherman who on the night after the attack on Pearl Harbor burned the Japanese flag he had brought with him to California from Hiroshima thirty-five years before, was already under arrest. Although his family did not know it, he had been sent off to an all-male camp in North Dakota.

The internees had been rounded up by federal order solely because of their race. Their mood was, Jeanne Wakatsuki Houston remembers, one of resignation best summed up by the Japanese phrase Shikata ga nai — "It cannot be helped; it must be done." *Three decades later, working with her husband, the novelist James D. Houston, she wrote* Farewell to Manzanar, *from which these excerpts are taken.*

From "Shikata Ga Nai," "A Common Master Plan," "Almost a Family," and "Manzanar, U.S.A.," *Farewell to Manzanar*

THE NAME MANZANAR meant nothing to us when we left Boyle Heights. We didn't know where it was or what it was. We went because the government ordered us to. And, in the case of my older brothers and sisters, we went with a certain amount of relief. They had all heard stories of Japanese homes being attacked, of beatings in the streets of California towns. They were as frightened of the Caucasians as Caucasians were of us. Moving, under what appeared to be government protection, to an area less directly threatened by the war seemed not such a bad idea at all. For some it actually sounded like a fine adventure.

Our pickup point was a Buddhist church in Los Angeles. It was very early, and misty, when we got there with our luggage. Mama had bought heavy coats for all of us. She grew up in eastern Washington and knew that anywhere inland in early April would be cold. I was proud of my new coat, and I remember sitting on a duffel bag trying to be friendly with the Greyhound driver. I smiled at him. He didn't smile back. He was befriending no one. Someone tied a numbered tag to my collar and to the duffel bag (each family was given a number, and that became our official designation until the camps were closed), someone else passed out box lunches for the trip, and we climbed aboard.

I had never been outside Los Angeles County, never traveled more than ten miles from the coast, had never even ridden on a bus. I was full of excitement, the way any kid would be, and wanted to look out the window. But for the first few hours the shades were drawn. Around me other people played cards, read magazines, dozed, waiting. I settled back, waiting too, and finally fell asleep. The bus felt very secure to me. Almost half its passengers were immediate relatives. Mama and my older brothers had succeeded in keeping most of us together, on the same bus, headed for the same camp. I didn't realize until much later what a job that was. The strategy had been, first, to have everyone living in the same district when the evacuation began, and then to get all of us included under the same family number, even though names had been changed by marriage. Many families weren't as lucky as ours and suffered months of anguish while trying to arrange transfers from one camp to another.

We rode all day. By the time we reached our destination, the shades were up. It was late afternoon. The first thing I saw was a yellow swirl across a blurred, reddish setting sun. The bus was being pelted by what sounded like splattering rain. It wasn't rain. This was my first look at something I would soon know very well, a billowing flurry of dust and sand churned up by the wind through Owens Valley.

We drove past a barbed-wire fence, through a gate, and into an open space where trunks and sacks and packages had been dumped from the baggage trucks that drove out ahead of us. I could see a few tents set up, the first rows of black barracks, and beyond them, blurred by sand, rows of barracks that seemed to spread for miles across this plain. People were sitting on cartons or milling around, with their backs to the wind, waiting to see which friends or relatives might be on this bus. As we approached, they turned or stood up, and some moved toward us expectantly. But inside the bus no one stirred. No one waved or spoke. They just stared out the windows, ominously silent. I didn't understand this. Hadn't we finally arrived, our whole family intact? I opened a window, leaned out, and yelled happily. "Hey! This whole bus is full of Wakatsukis!"

Outside, the greeters smiled. Inside there was an explosion of laughter, hysterical, tension-breaking laughter that left my brothers choking and whacking each other across the shoulders.

We had pulled up just in time for dinner. The mess halls weren't completed yet. An outdoor chow line snaked around a half-finished building that broke a good part of the wind. They issued us army mess kits, the round metal kind that fold over, and plopped in scoops of canned Vienna sausage, canned string beans, steamed rice that had been cooked too long, and on top of the rice a serving of canned apricots. The Caucasian servers were thinking that the fruit poured over rice would make a good dessert. Among the Japanese, of course, rice is never eaten with sweet foods, only with salty or savory foods. Few of us could eat such a mixture. But at this point no one dared protest. It would have been impolite. I was horrified when I saw the apricot syrup seeping through my little mound of rice. I opened my mouth to complain. My mother jabbed me in the back to keep quiet. We moved on through the line and joined the others squatting in the lee of half-raised walls, dabbing courteously at what was, for almost everyone there, an inedible concoction.

After dinner we were taken to Block 16, a cluster of fifteen barracks that had just been finished a day or so earlier — although finished was hardly the word for it. The shacks were built of one thickness of pine planking covered with tarpaper. They sat on concrete footings, with about two feet of open space between the floorboards and the ground. Gaps showed between the planks, and as the weeks passed and the green wood dried out, the gaps widened. Knotholes gaped in the uncovered floor.

Each barracks was divided into six units, sixteen by twenty feet, about the size of a living room, with one bare bulb hanging from the ceiling and an oil stove for heat. We were assigned two of these for the twelve people in our family group; and our official family "number" was enlarged by three digits — 16 plus the number of this barracks.

We were issued steel army cots, two brown army blankets each, and some mattress covers, which my brothers stuffed with straw.

The first task was to divide up what space we had for sleeping. Bill and Woody contributed a blanket each and partitioned off the first room: one side for Bill and Tomi, one side for Woody and Chizu and their baby girl. Woody also got the stove, for heating formulas.

The people who had it hardest during the first few months were young couples like these, many of whom had married just before the evacuation began, in order not to be separated and sent to different camps. Our two rooms were crowded, but at least it was all in the family. My oldest sister and her husband were shoved into one of those sixteen-by-twenty-foot compartments with six people they had never seen before — two other couples, one recently married like themselves, the other with two teenage boys. Partitioning off a room like that wasn't easy. It was bitter cold when we arrived, and the wind did not abate. All they had to use for room dividers were those army blankets, two of which were barely enough to keep one person warm. They argued over whose blanket should be sacrificed and later argued about noise at night — the parents wanted their boys asleep by 9:00 p.m. — and they continued arguing over matters like that for six months, until my sister and her husband left to harvest sugar beets in Idaho. It was grueling work up there, and wages were pitiful, but when the call came through camp for workers to alleviate the wartime labor shortage, it sounded better than their life at Manzanar. They knew they'd have, if nothing else, a room, perhaps a cabin of their own.

That first night in Block 16, the rest of us squeezed into the second room — Granny, Lillian, age fourteen, Ray, thirteen, May, eleven, Kiyo, ten, Mama, and me. I didn't mind this at all at the time. Being youngest meant I got to sleep with Mama. And before we went to bed I had a great time jumping up and down on the mattress. The boys had stuffed so much straw into hers, we had to flatten it some so we wouldn't slide off. I slept with her every night after that until Papa came back. . . .

The War Department was in charge of all the camps at this point. They began to issue military surplus from the First World War — olive-drab knit caps, earmuffs, peacoats, canvas leggings. Later on, sewing machines were shipped in, and one barracks was turned into a clothing factory. An old seamstress took a peacoat of mine, tore the lining out, opened and flattened the sleeves, added a collar, put arm holes in and handed me back a beautiful cape. By fall dozens of seamstresses were working full-time transforming thousands of these old army clothes into capes, slacks and stylish coats. But until that factory got going and packages from friends outside began to fill out our wardrobes, warmth was more important than style. I couldn't help laughing at Mama walking around in army earmuffs and a pair of wide-cuffed, khaki-colored wool trousers several sizes too big for her. Japanese are generally smaller than Caucasians, and almost all these clothes were oversize. They flopped, they dangled, they hung.

It seems comical, looking back; we were a band of Charlie Chaplins marooned in the California desert. But at the time, it was pure chaos. That's the only way to describe it. The evacuation had been so hurriedly planned, the camps so hastily thrown together, nothing was completed when we got there, and almost nothing worked. . . .

At seven I was too young to be insulted. The camp worked on me in a much different way. I wasn't aware of this at the time, of course. No one was, except maybe Mama, and there was little she could have done to change what happened.

It began in the mess hall. Before Manzanar, mealtime had always been the center of our family scene. In camp, and afterward, I would often recall with deep yearning the old round wooden table in our dining room in Ocean Park, the biggest piece of furniture we owned, large enough to seat twelve or thirteen of us at once. A tall row of elegant, lathe-turned spindles separated this table from the kitchen, allowing talk to pass from one room to the other. Dinners were always noisy, and they were always abundant with great pots of boiled rice, platters of home-grown vegetables, fish Papa caught.

He would sit at the head of this table, with Mama next to him serving and the rest of us arranged around the edges according to age, down to where Kiyo and I sat, so far away from our parents, it seemed at the time, we had our own enclosed nook inside this world. The grownups would be talking down at their end, while we two played our secret games, making eyes at each other when Papa gave the order to begin to eat, racing with chopsticks to scrape the last grain from our rice bowls, eyeing Papa to see if he had noticed who won.

Now, in the mess halls, after a few weeks had passed, we stopped eating as a family. Mama tried to hold us together for a while, but it was hopeless. Granny was too feeble to walk across the block three times a day, especially during heavy weather, so May brought food to her in the barracks. My older brothers and sisters, meanwhile, began eating with their friends, or eating somewhere blocks away, in the hope of finding better food. The word would get around that the cook over in Block 22, say, really knew his stuff, and they would eat a few meals over there, to test the rumor. Camp authorities frowned on mess hall hopping and tried to stop it, but the good cooks liked it. They liked to see long lines outside their kitchens and would work overtime to attract a crowd.

Younger boys, like Ray, would make a game of seeing how many mess halls they could hit in one meal period — be the first in line at Block 16, gobble down your food, run to 17 by the middle of the dinner hour, gulp another helping, and hurry to 18 to make the end of that chow line and stuff in the third meal of the evening. They didn't *need* to do that. No matter how bad the food might be, you could always eat till you were full.

Kiyo and I were too young to run around, but often we would eat in gangs with other kids, while the grownups sat at another table. I confess I enjoyed this part of it at the time. We all did. A couple of years after the camps opened, sociologists studying the life noticed what had happened to the families. They made some recommendations, and edicts went out that families *must* start eating together again. Most people resented this; they griped and grumbled. They were in the habit of eating with their friends. And until the mess hall system itself could be changed, not much could really be done. It was too late.

My own family, after three years of mess hall living, collapsed as an integrated unit. Whatever dignity or feeling of filial strength we may have known before December 1941 was lost, and we did not recover it until many years after the war, not until after Papa died and we began to come together, trying to fill the vacuum his passing left in all our lives.

The closing of the camps, in the fall of 1945, only aggravated what had begun inside. Papa had no money then and could not get work. Half of our family had already moved to the east coast, where jobs had opened up for them. The rest of us were relocated into a former defense workers' housing project in Long Beach. In that small apartment there never was enough room for all of us to sit down for a meal. We ate in shifts, and I yearned all the more for our huge round table in Ocean Park.

Soon after we were released I wrote a paper for a seventh-grade journalism class, describing how we used to hunt grunion before the war. The whole family would go down to Ocean Park Beach after dark, when the grunion were running, and build a big fire on the sand. I would watch Papa and my older brothers splash through the moonlit surf to scoop out the fish, then we'd rush back to the house where Mama would fry them up and set the sizzling pan on the table, with soy sauce and horseradish, for a midnight meal. I ended the paper with this sentence: "The reason I want to remember this is because I know we'll never be able to do it again." . . .

[Papa] arrived at Manzanar on a Greyhound bus. We all went down to the main gate to meet him, everyone but Woody's wife, Chizu, who was in the camp hospital. The previous day she'd given birth to Papa's first grandson. She named him George, in honor of Papa's return. Two of my sisters were pregnant at the time, and they were there at the gate in hot-weather smocks, along with Woody, who had left the hospital long enough to welcome Papa back, and Granny and Mama and the rest of the family, a dozen of us standing in the glare, excited, yet very reverent as the bus pulled in.

The door whished open, and the first thing we saw was a cane — I will never forget it — poking from the shaded interior into sunlight, a straight, polished maple limb spotted with dark lidded eyes where small knotholes had been stained and polished.

Then Papa stepped out, wearing a fedora hat and a wilted white shirt. This was September 1942. He had been gone nine months. He had aged ten years. He looked over sixty, gaunt, wilted as his shirt, underweight, leaning on that cane and favoring his right leg. He stood there surveying his clan, and nobody moved, not even Mama, waiting to see what he would do or say, waiting for some cue from him as to how we should deal with this.

I was the only one who approached him. I had not thought of him much at all after he was taken away. He was simply gone. Now I was so happy to see him that I ran up and threw my arms around his waist and buried my face in his belt. I thought I should be laughing and welcoming him home. But I started to cry. By this time everyone was crying. No one else had moved yet to touch him. It was as if the youngest, the least experienced, had been appointed to display what the others, held back by awe or fear, or some old-country notion of respect for the patriarch, could not. I hugged him tighter, wanting to be happy that my father had come back. Yet I hurt so inside I could only welcome him with convulsive tears. . . .

In Spanish, Manzanar means "apple orchard." Great stretches of Owens Valley were once green with orchards and alfalfa fields. It has been a desert ever since its water started flowing south into Los Angeles, sometime during the twenties. But a few rows of untended pear and apple trees were still growing there when the camp opened, where a shallow water table had kept them alive. In the spring of 1943 we moved to Block 28, right up next to one of the old pear orchards. That's where we stayed until the end of the war, and those trees stand in my memory for the turning of our life in camp, from the outrageous to the tolerable.

Papa pruned and cared for the nearest trees. Late that summer we picked the fruit green and stored it in a root cellar he had dug under our new barracks. At night the wind through the leaves would sound like the surf had sounded in Ocean Park, and while drifting off to sleep I could almost imagine we were still living by the beach.

Mama had set up this move. Block 28 was also close to the camp hospital. For the most part, people lived there who had to have easy access to it. Mama's connection was her job as dietician. A whole half of one barracks had fallen empty when another family relocated. Mama hustled us in there almost before they'd snapped their suitcases shut.

For all the pain it caused, the loyalty oath [a mandatory oath of "unqualified allegiance" to the United States] finally did speed up the relocation program. One result was a gradual easing of the congestion in the barracks. A shrewd house-hunter like Mama could set things up fairly comfortably — by Manzanar standards — if she kept her eyes open. But you had to move fast. As soon as the word got around that so-and-so had been cleared to leave, there would be a kind of tribal restlessness, a nervous rise in the level of neighborhood gossip as wives jockeyed for position to see who would get the empty cubicles.

In Block 28 we doubled our living space — four rooms for the twelve of us. Ray and Woody walled them with sheetrock. We had ceilings this time, and linoleum floors of solid maroon. You had three colors to choose from — maroon, black, and forest green — and there was plenty of it around by this time. Some families would vie with one another for the most elegant floor designs, obtaining a roll of each color from the supply shed, cutting it into diamonds, squares, or triangles, shining it with heating oil, then leaving their doors open so that passers-by could admire the handiwork.

Papa brought his still with him when we moved. He set it up behind the door, where he continued to brew his own sake and brandy. He wasn't drinking as much now, though. He spent a lot of time outdoors. Like many of the older Issei men, he didn't take a regular job in camp. He puttered. He had been working hard for thirty years and, bad as it was for him in some ways, camp did allow him time to dabble with hobbies he would never have found time for otherwise.

Once the first year's turmoil cooled down, the authorities started letting us outside the wire for recreation. Papa used to hike along the creeks that channeled down from the base of the Sierras. He brought back chunks of driftwood, and he would pass long hours sitting on the steps carving myrtle limbs into benches, table legs, and lamps, filling our rooms with bits of gnarled, polished furniture.

He hauled stones in off the desert and built a small rock garden outside our doorway, with succulents and a patch of moss. Near it he laid flat stepping stones leading to the stairs.

He also painted watercolors. Until this time I had not known he could paint. He loved to sketch the mountains. If anything made that country habitable it was the mountains themselves, purple when the sun dropped and so sharply etched in the morning light the granite dazzled almost more than the bright snow lacing it. The nearest peaks rose ten thousand feet higher than the valley floor, with Whitney, the highest, just off to the south. They were important for all of us, but especially for the Issei. Whitney reminded Papa of Fujiyama, that is, it gave him the same kind of spiritual sustenance. The tremendous beauty of those peaks was inspirational, as so many natural forms are to the Japanese (the rocks outside our doorway could be those mountains in miniature). They also represented those forces in nature, those powerful and inevitable forces that cannot be resisted, reminding a man that sometimes he must simply endure that which cannot be changed.

Subdued, resigned, Papa's life — all our lives — took on a pattern that would hold for the duration of the war. Public shows of resentment pretty much spent themselves over the loyalty oath crises. *Shikata ga nai* again became the motto, but under altered circumstances. What had to be endured was the climate, the confinement, the steady crumbling away of family life. But the camp itself had been made livable. The government provided for our physical needs. My parents and older brothers and sisters, like most of the internees, accepted their lot and did what they could to make the best of a bad situation. "We're here," Woody would say. "We're here, and there's no use moaning about it forever."

Gardens had sprung up everywhere, in the firebreaks, between the rows of barracks — rock gardens, vegetable gardens, cactus and flower gardens. People who lived in Owens Valley during the war still remember the flowers and lush greenery they could see from the highway as they drove past the main gate. The soil around Manzanar is alluvial and very rich. With water siphoned off from the Los Angeles–bound aqueduct, a large farm was under cultivation just outside the camp, providing the mess halls with lettuce, corn, tomatoes, eggplant, string beans, horseradish, and cucumbers. Near Block 28 some of the men who had been professional gardeners built a small park, with mossy nooks, ponds, waterfalls and curved wooden bridges. Sometimes in the evenings we could walk down the raked gravel paths. You could face away from the barracks, look past a tiny rapids toward the darkening mountains, and for a while not be a prisoner at all. You could hang suspended in some odd, almost lovely land you could not escape from yet almost didn't want to leave.

As the months at Manzanar turned to years, it became a world unto itself, with its own logic and familiar ways. In time, staying there seemed far simpler than moving once again to another, unknown place. It was as if the war were forgotten, our reason for being there forgotten. The present, the little bit of busywork you had right in front of you, became the most urgent thing. In such a narrowed world, in order to survive, you learn to contain your rage and your despair, and you try to re-create, as well as you can, your normality, some sense of things continuing. The fact that America had accused us, or excluded us, or imprisoned us, or whatever it might be called, did not change the kind of world we wanted. Most of us were born in this country; we had no other models. Those parks and gardens lent it an oriental character, but in most ways it was a totally equipped American small town, complete with schools, churches, Boy Scouts, beauty parlors, neighborhood gossip, fire and police departments, glee clubs, softball leagues, Abbott and Costello movies, tennis courts, and traveling shows. (I still remember an Indian who turned up one Saturday billing himself as a Sioux chief, wearing bear claws and head feathers. In the firebreak he sang songs and danced his tribal dances while hundreds of us watched.)

In our family, while Papa puttered, Mama made her daily rounds to the mess halls, helping young mothers with their feeding, planning diets for the various ailments people suffered from. She wore a bright yellow, long-billed sun hat she had made herself and always kept stiffly starched. Afternoons I would see her coming from blocks away, heading home, her tiny figure warped by heat waves and that bonnet a yellow flower wavering in the glare.

In their disagreement over serving the country, Woody and Papa had struck a kind of compromise. Papa talked him out of volunteering; Woody waited for the army to induct him. Meanwhile he clerked in the co-op general store. Kiyo, nearly thirteen by this time, looked forward to the heavy winds. They moved the sand around and uncovered obsidian arrowheads he could sell to old men in camp for fifty cents apiece. Ray, a few years older, played in the six-man touch football league, sometimes against Caucasian teams who would come in from Lone Pine or Independence. My sister Lillian was in high school and singing with a hillbilly band called The Sierra Stars — jeans, cowboy hats, two guitars, and a tub bass. And my oldest brother, Bill, led a dance band called The Jive Bombers — brass and rhythm, with cardboard fold-out music stands lettered J. B. Dances were held every weekend in one of the recreation halls. Bill played trumpet and took vocals on Glenn Miller arrangements of such tunes as *In the Mood, String of Pearls,* and *Don't Fence Me In.* He didn't sing *Don't Fence Me In* out of protest, as if trying quietly to mock the authorities. It just happened to be a hit song one year, and they all wanted to be an up-to-date American swing band. They would blast it out into recreation barracks full of bobby-soxed, jitterbugging couples:

> *Oh, give me land, lots of land*
> *Under starry skies above,*
> *Don't fence me in.*
> *Let me ride through the wide*
> *Open country that I love . . .*

Pictures of the band, in their bow ties and jackets, appeared in the high school yearbook for 1943–1944, along with pictures of just about everything else in camp that year. It was called *Our World.* In its pages you see school kids with armloads of books, wearing cardigan sweaters and walking past rows of tarpapered shacks. You see chubby girl yell leaders, pompons flying as they leap with glee. You read about the school play, called *Growing Pains* ". . . the story of a typical American home, in this case that of the McIntyres. They see their boy and girl tossed into the normal awkward growing up stage, but can offer little assistance or direction in their turbulent course . . ." with Shoji Katayama as George McIntyre, Takudo Ando as Terry McIntyre, and Mrs. McIntyre played by Kazuko Nagai.

All the class pictures are in there, from the seventh grade through twelfth, with individual head shots of seniors, their names followed by the names of the high schools they would have graduated from on the outside: Theodore Roosevelt, Thomas Jefferson, Herbert Hoover, Sacred Heart. You see pretty girls on bicycles, chicken yards full of fat pullets, patients back-tilted in dental chairs, lines of laundry, and finally, two large blowups, the first of a high tower with a searchlight, against a Sierra backdrop, the next a two-page endsheet showing a wide path that curves among rows of elm trees. White stones border the path. Two dogs are following an old woman in gardening clothes as she strolls along. She is in the middle distance, small beneath the trees, beneath the snowy peaks. It is winter. All the elms are bare. The scene is both stark and comforting. This path leads toward one edge of camp, but the wire is out of sight, or out of focus. The tiny woman seems very much at ease. She and her tiny dogs seem almost swallowed by the landscape, or floating in it.

Maya Angelou

Maya Angelou was born Marguerite Johnson in Saint Louis, Missouri, in 1928. When she was four her parents separated and she and her three-year-old brother, Bailey, went to live with their grandmother in rural Stamps, Arkansas. It was Bailey who renamed her Maya, his way of pronouncing "mine."

This excerpt from her autobiography, I Know Why the Caged Bird Sings, *begins when she is seven and has gone back to Saint Louis to live with her mother and her mother's new friend, Mr. Freeman — a visit that ends in tragedy. Before she was twenty Maya would find herself racing cars in Mexico, working as a streetcar conductor in San Francisco, acting as an amateur madam for two aging prostitutes. Later she would become an actress, a singer (touring Europe with a company performing* Porgy and Bess*), a poet, and a teacher at the University of Ghana. Her autobiography has now stretched to six volumes with no end in sight. "Each time I say I would like to cover ten years," she once observed. "But somehow I get into it, and I do maybe three years."*

Looking back to the violent end of her childhood that day in Mr. Freeman's apartment in Saint Louis, she has written, "I gave up some youth for knowledge, but my gain was more valuable than the loss."

From *I Know Why the Caged Bird Sings*

I HAD DECIDED that St. Louis was a foreign country. I would never get used to the scurrying sounds of flushing toilets, or the packaged foods, or doorbells or the noise of cars and trains and buses that crashed through the walls or slipped under the doors. In my mind I only stayed in St. Louis for a few weeks. As quickly as I understood that I had not reached my home, I sneaked away to Robin Hood's forest and the caves of Alley Oop where all reality was unreal and even that changed every day. I carried the same shield that I had used in Stamps: "I didn't come to stay."

Mother was competent in providing for us. Even if that meant getting someone else to furnish the provisions. Although she was a nurse, she never worked at her profession while we were with her. Mr. Freeman brought in the necessities and she earned extra money cutting poker games in gambling parlors. The straight eight-to-five world simply didn't have enough glamor for her, and it was twenty years later that I first saw her in a nurse's uniform.

Mr. Freeman was a foreman in the Southern Pacific yards and came home late sometimes, after Mother had gone out. He took his dinner off the stove where she had carefully covered it and which she had admonished us not to bother. He ate quietly in the kitchen while Bailey and I read separately and greedily our own Street and Smith pulp magazine. Now that we had spending money, we bought the illustrated paperbacks with their gaudy pictures. When Mother was away, we were put on an honor system. We had to finish our homework, eat dinner and wash the dishes before we could read or listen to *The Lone Ranger, Crime Busters* or *The Shadow.*

Mr. Freeman moved gracefully, like a big brown bear, and seldom spoke to us. He simply waited for Mother and put his whole self into the waiting. He never read the paper or patted his foot to radio. He waited. That was all.

If she came home before we went to bed, we saw the man come alive. He would start out of the big chair, like a man coming out of sleep, smiling. I would remember then that a few seconds before, I had heard a car door slam; then Mother's footsteps would signal from the concrete walk. When her key rattled the door, Mr. Freeman would have already asked his habitual question, "Hey, Bibbi, have a good time?"

His query woud hang in the air while she sprang over to peck him on the lips. Then she turned to Bailey and me with the lipstick kisses. "Haven't you finished your homework?" If we had and were just reading — "O.K., say your prayers and go to bed." If we hadn't — "Then go to your room and finish . . . then say your prayers and go to bed."

Mr. Freeman's smile never grew, it stayed at the same intensity. Sometimes Mother would go over and sit on his lap and the grin on his face looked as if it would stay there forever.

From our rooms we could hear the glasses clink and the radio turned up. I think she must have danced for him on the good nights, because he couldn't dance, but before I fell asleep I often heard feet shuffling to dance rhythms.

I felt very sorry for Mr. Freeman. I felt as sorry for him as I had felt for a litter of helpless pigs born in our backyard sty in Arkansas. We fattened the pigs all year long for slaughter on the first good frost, and even as I suffered for the cute little wiggly things; I knew how much I was going to enjoy the fresh sausage and hog's headcheese they could give me only with their deaths.

Because of the lurid tales we read and our vivid imaginations and, probably, memories of our brief but hectic lives, Bailey and I were afflicted — he physically and I mentally. He stuttered, and I sweated through horrifying nightmares. He was constantly told to slow down and start again, and on my particularly bad nights my mother would take me in to sleep with her, in the large bed with Mr. Freeman.

Because of a need for stability, children easily become creatures of habit. After the third time in Mother's bed, I thought there was nothing strange about sleeping there.

One morning she got out of bed for an early errand, and I fell asleep again. But I awoke to a pressure, a strange feeling on my left leg. It was too soft to be a hand, and it wasn't the touch of clothes. Whatever it was, I hadn't encountered the sensation in all the years of sleeping with Momma. It didn't move, and I was too startled to. I turned my head a little to the left to see if Mr. Freeman was awake and gone, but his eyes were open and both hands were above the cover. I knew, as if I had always known, it was his "thing" on my leg.

He said, "Just stay right here, Ritie, I ain't gonna hurt you." I wasn't afraid, a little apprehensive, maybe, but not afraid. Of course I knew that lots of people did "it" and that they used their "things" to accomplish the deed, but no one I knew had ever done it to anybody. Mr. Freeman pulled me to him, and put his hand between my legs. He didn't hurt, but Momma had drilled into my head: "Keep your legs closed, and don't leg nobody see your pocketbook."

"Now, I didn't hurt you. Don't get scared." He threw back the blankets and his "thing" stood up like a brown ear of corn. He took my hand and said, "Feel it." It was mushy and squirmy like the inside of a freshly killed chicken. Then he dragged me on top of his chest with his left arm, and his right hand was moving so fast and his heart was beating so hard that I was afraid that he would die. Ghost stories revealed how people who die wouldn't let go of whatever they were holding. I wondered if Mr. Freeman died holding me how I would ever get free. Would they have to break his arms to get me loose?

Finally he was quiet, and then came the nice part. He held me so softly that I wished he wouldn't ever let me go. I felt at home. From the way he was holding me I knew he'd never let me go or let anything bad ever happen to me. This was probably my real father and we had found each other at last. But then he rolled over, leaving me in a wet place and stood up.

"I gotta talk to you, Ritie." He pulled off his shorts that had fallen to his ankles, and went into the bathroom.

It was true the bed was wet, but I knew I hadn't had an accident. Maybe Mr. Freeman had one while he was holding me. He came back with a glass of water and told me in a sour voice, "Get up. You peed in the bed." He poured water on the wet spot, and it did look like my mattress on many mornings.

Having lived in Southern strictness, I knew when to keep quiet around adults, but I did want to ask him why he said I peed when I was sure he didn't believe that. If he thought I was naughty, would that mean that he would never hold me again? Or admit that he was my father? I had made him ashamed of me.

"Ritie, you love Bailey?" He sat down on the bed and I came close, hoping. "Yes." He was bending down, pulling on his socks, and his back was so large and friendly I wanted to rest my head on it.

"If you ever tell anybody what we did, I'll have to kill Bailey."

What had we done? We? Obviously he didn't mean my peeing in the bed. I didn't understand and didn't dare ask him. It had something to do with his holding me. But there was no chance to ask Bailey either, because that would be telling what we had done. The thought that he might kill Bailey stunned me. After he left the room I thought about telling Mother that I hadn't peed in the bed, but then if she asked me what happened I'd have to tell her about Mr. Freeman holding me, and that wouldn't do.

It was the same old quandary. I had always lived it. There was an army of adults, whose motives and movements I just couldn't undertand and who made no effort to understand mine. There was never any question of my disliking Mr. Freeman, I simply didn't understand him either.

For weeks after, he said nothing to me, except the gruff hellos which were given without ever looking in my direction.

This was the first secret I had ever kept from Bailey and sometimes I thought he should be able to read it on my face, but he noticed nothing.

I began to feel lonely for Mr. Freeman and the encasement in his big arms. Before, my world had been Bailey, food, Momma, the Store, reading books and Uncle Willie. Now, for the first time, it included physical contact.

I began to wait for Mr. Freeman to come in from the yards, but when he did, he never noticed me, although I put a lot of feeling into "Good evening, Mr. Freeman."

One evening, when I couldn't concentrate on anything, I went over to him and sat quickly on his lap. He had been waiting for Mother again. Bailey was listening to *The Shadow* and didn't miss me. At first Mr. Freeman sat still, not holding me or anything, then I felt a soft lump under my thigh begin to move. It twitched against me and started to harden. Then he pulled me to his chest. He smelled of coal dust and grease and he was so close I buried my face in his shirt and listened to his heart, it was beating just for me. Only I could hear the thud, only I could feel the jumping on my face. He said, "Sit still, stop squirming." But all the time, he pushed me around on his lap, then suddenly he stood up and I slipped down to the floor. He ran to the bathroom.

For months he stopped speaking to me again. I was hurt and for a time felt lonelier than ever. But then I forgot about him, and even the memory of his holding me precious melted into the general darkness just beyond the great blinkers of childhood.

I read more than ever, and wished my soul that I had been born a boy. Horatio Alger was the greatest writer in the world. His heroes were always good, always won, and were always boys. I could have developed the first two virtues, but becoming a boy was sure to be difficult, if not impossible.

The Sunday funnies influenced me, and although I admired the strong heroes who always conquered in the end, I identified with Tiny Tim. In the toilet, where I used to take the papers, it was tortuous to look for and exclude the unnecessary pages so that I could learn how he would finally outwit his latest adversary. I wept with relief every Sunday as he eluded the evil men and bounded back from each seeming defeat as sweet and gentle as ever. The Katzenjammer kids were fun because they made the adults look stupid. But they were a little too smart-alecky for my taste.

When spring came to St. Louis, I took out my first library card, and since Bailey and I seemed to be growing apart, I spent most of my Saturdays at the library (no interruptions) breathing in the world of penniless shoeshine boys who, with goodness and perseverance, became rich, rich men, and gave baskets of goodies to the poor on holidays. The little princesses who were mistaken for maids, and the long-lost children mistaken for waifs, became more real to me than our house, our mother, our school or Mr. Freeman.

During those months we saw our grandparents and the uncles (our only aunt had gone to California to build her fortune), but they usually asked the same question, "Have you been good children?" for which there was only one answer. Even Bailey wouldn't have dared to answer No.

On a late spring Saturday, after our chores (nothing like those in Stamps) were done, Bailey and I were going out, he to play baseball and I to the library. Mr. Freeman said to me, after Bailey had gone downstairs, "Ritie, go get some milk for the house."

Mother usually brought milk when she came in, but that morning as Bailey and I straightened the living room her bedroom door had been open, and we knew that she hadn't come home the night before.

He gave me money and I rushed to the store and back to the house. After putting the milk in the icebox, I turned and had just reached the front door when I heard, "Ritie." He was sitting in the big chair by the radio. "Ritie, come here." I didn't think about the holding time until I got close to him. His pants were open and his "thing" was standing out of his britches by itself.

"No, sir, Mr. Freeman." I started to back away. I didn't want to touch that mushy-hard thing again, and I didn't need him to hold me any more. He grabbed my arm and pulled me between his legs. His face was still and looked kind, but he didn't smile or blink his eyes. Nothing. He did nothing, except reach his left hand around to turn on the radio without even looking at it. Over the noise of music and static, he said, "Now, this ain't gonna hurt you much. You liked it before, didn't you?"

I didn't want to admit that I had in fact liked his holding me or that I had liked his smell or the hard heart-beating, so I said nothing. And his face became like the face of one of those mean natives the Phantom was always having to beat up.

His legs were squeezing my waist. "Pull down your drawers." I hesitated for two reasons: he was holding me too tight to move, and I was sure that any minute my mother or Bailey or the Green Hornet would bust in the door and save me.

"We was just playing before." He released me enough to snatch down my bloomers, and then he dragged me closer to him. Turning the radio up loud, too loud, he said, "If you scream, I'm gonna kill you. And if you tell, I'm gonna kill Bailey." I could tell he meant what he said. I couldn't understand why he wanted to kill my brother. Neither of us had done anything to him. And then.

Then there was the pain. A breaking and entering when even the senses are torn apart. The act of rape on an eight-year-old body is a matter of the needle giving because the camel can't. The child gives, because the body can, and the mind of the violator cannot.

I thought I had died — I woke up in a white-walled world, and it had to be heaven. But Mr. Freeman was there and he was washing me. His hands shook, but he held me upright in the tub and washed my legs. "I didn't mean to hurt you, Ritie. I didn't mean it. But don't you tell . . . Remember, don't you tell a soul."

I felt cool and very clean and just a little tired. "No, sir, Mr. Freeman, I won't tell." I was somewhere above everything. "It's just that I'm so tired I'll just go and lay down a while, please," I whispered to him. I thought if I spoke out loud, he might become frightened and hurt me again. He dried me and handed me my bloomers. "Put these on and go to the library. Your momma ought to be coming home soon. You just act natural."

Walking down the street, I felt the wet on my pants, and my hips seemed to be coming out of their sockets. I couldn't sit long on the hard seats in the library (they had been constructed for children), so I walked by the empty lot where Bailey was playing ball, but he wasn't there. I stood for a while and watched the big boys tear around the dusty diamond and then headed home.

After two blocks, I knew I'd never make it. Not unless I counted every step and stepped on every crack. I had started to burn between my legs more than the time I'd wasted Sloan's Liniment on myself. My legs throbbed, or rather the insides of my thighs throbbed, with the same force that Mr. Freeman's heart had beaten. Thrum . . . step . . . thrum . . . step . . . STEP ON THE CRACK . . . thrum . . . step. I went up the stairs one at a, one at a, one at a time. No one was in the living room, so I went straight to bed, after hiding my red-and-yellow stained drawers under the mattress.

When Mother came in she said, "Well, young lady, I believe this is the first time I've seen you go to bed without being told. You must be sick."

I wasn't sick, but the pit of my stomach was on fire — how could I tell her that? Bailey came in later and asked me what the matter was. There was nothing to tell him. When Mother called us to eat and I said I wasn't hungry, she laid her cool hand on my forehead and cheeks. "Maybe it's the measles. They say they're going around the neighborhood." After she took my temperature she said, "You have a little fever. You've probably just caught them."

Mr. Freeman took up the whole doorway. "Then Bailey ought not to be in there with her. Unless you want a house full of sick children." She answered over her shoulder, "He may as well have them now as later. Get them over with." She brushed by Mr. Freeman as if he were made of cotton. "Come on, Junior. Get some cool towels and wipe your sister's face."

As Bailey left the room, Mr. Freeman advanced to the bed. He leaned over, his whole face a threat that could have smothered me. "If you tell . . ." And again so softly, I almost didn't hear it — "If you tell." I couldn't summon up the energy to answer him. He had to know that I wasn't going to tell anything. Bailey came in with the towels and Mr. Freeman walked out.

Later Mother made a broth and sat on the edge of the bed to feed me. The liquid went down my throat like bones. My belly and behind were as heavy as cold iron, but it seemed my head had gone away and pure air had replaced it on my shoulders. Bailey read to me from *The Rover Boys* until he got sleepy and went to bed.

That night I kept waking to hear Mother and Mr. Freeman arguing. I couldn't hear what they were saying, but I did hope that she wouldn't make him so mad that he'd hurt her too. I knew he could do it, with his cold face and empty eyes. Their voices came in faster and faster, the high sounds on the heels of the lows. I would have liked to have gone in. Just passed through as if I were going to the toilet. Just show my face and they might stop, but my legs refused to move. I could move the toes and ankles, but the knees had turned to wood.

Maybe I slept, but morning was there and Mother was pretty over my bed. "How're you feeling, baby?"

"Fine, Mother." An instinctive answer. "Where's Bailey?"

She said he was still asleep but that she hadn't slept all night. She had been in my room off and on to see about me. I asked her where Mr. Freeman was, and her face chilled with remembered anger. "He's gone. Moved this morning. I'm going to take your temperature after I put on your Cream of Wheat."

Could I tell her now? The terrible pain assured me that I couldn't. What he did to me, and what I allowed, must have been very bad if already God let me hurt so much. If Mr. Freeman was gone, did that mean Bailey was out of danger? And if so, if I told him, would he still love me?

After Mother took my temperature, she said she was going to bed for a while but to wake her if I felt sicker. She told Bailey to watch my face and arms for spots and when they came up he could paint them with calamine lotion.

That Sunday goes and comes in my memory like a bad connection on an overseas telephone call. Once, Bailey was reading *The Katzenjammer Kids* to me, and then without a pause for sleeping, Mother was looking closely at my face, and soup trickled down my chin and some got into my mouth and I choked. Then there was a doctor who took my temperature and held my wrist.

"Bailey!" I supposed I had screamed, for he materialized suddenly, and I asked him to help me and we'd run away to California or France or Chicago. I knew that I was dying and, in fact, I longed for death, but I didn't want to die anywhere near Mr. Freeman. I knew that even now he wouldn't have allowed death to have me unless he wished it to.

Mother said I should be bathed and the linens had to be changed since I had sweat so much. But when they tried to move me I fought, and even Bailey couldn't hold me. Then she picked me up in her arms and the terror abated for a while. Bailey began to change the bed. As he pulled off the soiled sheets he dislodged the panties I had put under the mattress. They fell at Mother's feet.

In the hospital, Bailey told me that I had to tell who did that to me, or the man would hurt another little girl. When I explained that I couldn't tell because the man would kill him, Bailey said knowingly, "He can't kill me. I won't let him." And of course I believed him. Bailey didn't lie to me. So I told him.

Bailey cried at the side of my bed until I started to cry too. Almost fifteen years passed before I saw my brother cry again.

Using the old brain he was born with (those were his words later on that day) he gave his information to Grandmother Baxter, and Mr. Freeman was arrested and was spared the awful wrath of my pistol-whipping uncles.

I would have liked to stay in the hospital the rest of my life. Mother brought flowers and candy. Grandmother came with fruit and my uncles clumped around and around my bed, snorting like wild horses. When they were able to sneak Bailey in, he read to me for hours.

The saying that people who have nothing to do become busybodies is not the only truth. Excitement is a drug, and people whose lives are filled with violence are always wondering where the next "fix" is coming from.

The court was filled. Some people even stood behind the church-like benches in the rear. Overhead fans moved with the detachment of old men. Grandmother Baxter's clients were there in gay and flippant array. The gamblers in pin-striped suits and their makeup-deep women whispered to me out of blood-red mouths that now I knew as much as they did. I was eight, and grown. Even the nurses in the hospital had told me that now I had nothing to fear. "The worst is over for you," they had said. So I put the words in all the smirking mouths.

I sat with my family (Bailey couldn't come) and they rested still on the seats like solid, cold gray tombstones. Thick and forevermore unmoving.

Poor Mr. Freeman twisted in his chair to look empty threats over to me. He didn't know that he couldn't kill Bailey . . . and Bailey didn't lie . . . to me.

"What was the defendant wearing?" That was Mr. Freeman's lawyer.

"I don't know."

"You mean to say this man raped you and you don't know what he was wearing?" He snickered as if I had raped Mr. Freeman. "Do you know if you were raped?"

A sound pushed in the air of the court (I was sure it was laughter). I was glad that Mother had let me wear the navy-blue winter coat with brass buttons. Although it was too short and the weather was typical St. Louis hot, the coat was a friend that I hugged to me in the strange and unfriendly place.

"Was that the first time the accused touched you?" The question stopped me. Mr. Freeman had surely done something very wrong, but I was convinced that I had helped him to do it. I didn't want to lie, but the lawyer wouldn't let me think, so I used silence as a retreat.

"Did the accused try to touch you before the time he or rather you say he raped you?"

I couldn't say yes and tell them how he had loved me once for a few minutes and how he had held me close before he thought I had peed in the bed. My uncles would kill me and Grandmother Baxter would stop speaking, as she often did when she was angry. And all those people in the court would stone me as they had stoned the harlot in the Bible. And Mother, who thought I was such a good girl, would be so disappointed. But most important, there was Bailey. I had kept a big secret from him.

"Marguerite, answer the question. Did the accused touch you before the occasion on which you claim he raped you?"

Everyone in the court knew the answer had to be No. Everyone except Mr. Freeman and me. I looked at his heavy face trying to look as if he would have liked me to say No. I said No.

The lie lumped in my throat and I couldn't get air. How I despised the man for making me lie. Old, mean, nasty thing. Old, black, nasty thing. The tears didn't soothe my heart as they usually did. I screamed, "Ole, mean, dirty thing, you. Dirty old thing." Our lawyer brought me off the stand and to my mother's arms. The fact that I had arrived at my desired destination by lies made it less appealing to me.

Mr. Freeman was given one year and one day, but he never got a chance to do his time. His lawyer (or someone) got him released that very afternoon.

In the living room, where the shades were drawn for coolness, Bailey and I played Monopoly on the floor. I played a bad game because I was thinking how I would be able to tell Bailey how I had lied and, even worse for our relationship, kept a secret from him. Bailey answered the doorbell, because Grandmother was in the kitchen. A tall white policeman asked for Mrs. Baxter. Had they found out about the lie? Maybe the policeman was coming to put me in jail because I had sworn on the Bible that everything I said would be the truth, the whole truth, so help me, God. The man in our living room was taller than the sky and whiter than my image of God. He just didn't have the beard.

"Mrs. Baxter, I thought you ought to know. Freeman's been found dead on the lot behind the slaughterhouse."

Softly, as if she were discussing a church program, she said, "Poor man." She wiped her hands on the dishtowel and just as softly asked, "Do they know who did it?"

The policman said, "Seems like he was dropped there. Some say he was kicked to death."

Grandmother's color only rose a little. "Tom, thanks for telling me. Poor man. Well, maybe it's better this way. He *was* a mad dog. Would you like a glass of lemonade? Or some beer?"

Although he looked harmless, I knew he was a dreadful angel counting out my many sins.

"No, thanks, Mrs. Baxter. I'm on duty. Gotta be getting back."

"Well, tell your ma that I'll be over when I take up my beer and remind her to save some kraut for me."

And the recording angel was gone. He was gone, and a man was dead because I lied. Where was the balance in that? One lie surely wouldn't be worth a man's life. Bailey could have explained it all to me, but I didn't dare ask him. Obviously I had forfeited my place in heaven forever, and I was as gutless as the doll I had ripped to pieces ages ago. Even Christ Himself turned His back on Satan. Wouldn't He turn His back on me? I could feel the evilness flowing through my body and waiting, pent up, to rush off my tongue if I tried to open my mouth. I clamped my teeth shut, I'd hold it in. If it escaped, wouldn't it flood the world and all the innocent people?

Grandmother Baxter said, "Ritie and Junior, you didn't hear a thing. I never want to hear this situation nor that evil man's name mentioned in my house again. I mean that." She went back into the kitchen to make apple strudel for my celebration.

Even Bailey was frightened. He sat all to himself, looking at a man's death — a kitten looking at a wolf. Not quite understanding it but frightened all the same.

In those moments I decided that although Bailey loved me he couldn't help. I had sold myself to the Devil and there could be no escape. The only thing I could do was to stop talking to people other than Bailey. Instinctively, or somehow, I knew that because I loved him so much I'd never hurt him, but if I talked to anyone else that person might die too. Just my breath, carrying my words out, might poison people and they'd curl up and die like the black fat slugs that only pretended.

I had to stop talking.

I discovered that to achieve perfect personal silence all I had to do was to attach myself leechlike to sound. I began to listen to everything. I probably hoped that after I had heard all the sounds, really heard them and packed them down, deep in my ears, the world would be quiet around me. I walked into rooms where people were laughing, their voices hitting the walls like stones, and I simply stood still — in the midst of the riot of sound. After a minute or two, silence would rush into the room from its hiding place because I had eaten up all the sounds.

N. Scott Momaday

N. Scott Momaday's father was a Kiowa Indian, an artist, a trader in Indian art, and a sometime employee of the Indian Service. His mother was part white, from a Tennessee family, and part Cherokee. Scott was born in Oklahoma in 1934 and given the Kiowa name Tsoai-talee.

He once described the land where he was born and where his grandparents lived:

> *The hardest weather in the world is there. Winter brings blizzards, hot tornadic winds arise in the spring, and in the summer the prairie is an anvil's edge. The grass turns brittle and brown, and it cracks beneath your feet. There are green belts along the rivers and creeks, linear groves of hickory and pecan, willow and witch hazel. At a distance in July and August the steaming foliage seems almost to writhe in fire. Great green and yellow grasshoppers are everywhere in the tall grass, popping up like corn to sting the flesh, and tortoises crawl about on the red earth, going nowhere in the plenty of time.*

Momaday grew up on various Kiowa and Navajo reservations, went to Stanford University, became an expert on an obscure New England poet named Frederick Goddard Tuckerman, and then rediscovered his Kiowa roots with The Way to Rainy Mountain, *a memory book of Kiowa tales and legends. His novel* House Made of Dawn *won the Pulitzer Prize in 1969. He has also published several volumes of poetry. The following excerpt is from his memoir of his family.*

From *The Names: A Memoir*

IN MY EARLIEST YEARS I traveled a number of times from Oklahoma to the Navajo reservation in New Mexico and Arizona and back again. The two landscapes are fixed in my mind. They are separate realities, but they are sometimes confused in my memory. I place my feet in the plain, but my prints are made on the mountain.

I was much alone. I had no brothers or sisters, and as it happened in my childhood, much of it, my peers were at removes from me, across cultures and languages. I had to create my society in my mind. And for a child this kind of creation is accomplished easily enough. I imagined much.

When I was three years old my head must have been full of Indian as well as English words. The sounds of both Kiowa and Navajo are quite natural and familiar to me, and even now I can make these sounds easily and accurately with my voice, so well established are they in my ear. I lived very close to these "foreign" languages, poised at a crucial time in the learning process to enter into either or both of them wholly. But my mother was concerned that I should learn English as my "native" language, and so English is first and foremost in my possession. My mother's love of books, and of English literature in particular, is intense, and naturally she wanted me to share in it. I have seen Grendel's shadow on the walls of Canyon de Chelly, and once, having led the sun around Hoskinini Mesa, I saw Copperfield at Oljeto Trading Post.

In 1936 Haske Noswood, a Navajo friend, invited my parents and me to come to Gallup, New Mexico, where my mother and father hoped to find work in the Indian Service. We arrived at the time of Naa'ahoohai, the old celebration of the Navajos which had by that time become the Intertribal Indian Ceremonial. The Navajos came from far and wide to Gallup, which is called in Navajo Na'nizhoozhi, the "place of the bridge" on the Rio Puerco. We lived in the Del Mar Hotel, across from the old Harvey House on the Santa Fe Railroad, and I slept in a bureau drawer. My father found a temporary job: he painted signs for the traders in the Ceremonial exhibit hall at fifty cents a sign. And later he got on as a truck dispatcher with the Roads

Department, Indian Service, at Shiprock, which is called in Navajo Naat'aaniineez (literally "tall chief"; the town takes its name from the great monolith that stands nearby in an arid reach of the San Juan Basin). The name Shiprock, like other Anglicizations in this region, seems incongruous enough, but from certain points of view — and from the air, especially — the massive rock Naat'aaniineez resembles very closely a ship at sea. Soon thereafter my mother was offered the job of switchboard operator at Shiprock Agency, which she accepted, and we were a solvent and independent entity. My parents have told me time and again what an intoxication were those days, and I think back to them on that basis; they involve me in a tide of confidence and well-being. What on earth was not possible? I must have been carried along in the waves of hope and happiness that were gathered in the hearts of my young and free and beautiful parents.

In the years between 1936 and 1943 we lived on the Navajo reservation at Shiprock, New Mexico, and at Tuba City, then Chinle, Arizona. There were in that span of time a number of sojourns away from home — to Oklahoma, to Kentucky, even to Louisiana (where my aunt Ethel lived at the time), and for several months my mother and I, while my father waited in Oklahoma to be drafted into the army (it turned out that he wasn't drafted, though the war was raging then), lived on the San Carlos Apache reservation in the southeastern quandrant of Arizona — but "home" was particularly the Navajo country, Dine bikeyah. My earliest playmates and schoolmates were Navajo children and the children of Indian Service employees. Just at the time I was learning to talk, I heard the Navajo language spoken all around me. And just as I was coming alive to the wide world, the vast and beautiful landscape of Dine bikeyah *was* my world, all of it that I could perceive.

Memory begins to qualify the imagination, to give it another formation, one that is peculiar to the self. I remember isolated, yet fragmented and confused, images — and images, shifting, enlarging, is the word, rather than moments or events — which are mine alone and which are especially vivid to me. They involve me wholly and immediately, even though they are the disintegrated impressions of a young child. They call for a certain attitude of belief on my part now; that is, they must mean something, but their best reality does not consist in meaning. They are not stories in that sense, but they are storylike, mythic, never evolved but evolving ever. There are such things in the world: it is in their nature to be believed; it is not necessarily in them to be understood. Of all that must have happened to and about me in those my earliest days, why should these odd particulars alone be fixed in my mind? If I were to remember other things, I should be someone else.

There is a room full of light and space. The walls are bare; there are no windows or doors of which I am aware. I am inside and alone. Then gradually I become aware of another presence in the room. There is an object, something not extraordinary at first, something of the room itself — but what I cannot tell. The object does not matter at first, but at some point — after a moment? an hour? — it moves, and I am unsettled. I am not yet frightened; rather I am somewhat surprised, vaguely anxious, fascinated, perhaps. The object grows; it expands farther and farther beyond definition. It is no longer an object but a mass. It is so large now that I am dwarfed by it, reduced almost to nothing. And *now* I am afraid, nearly terrified, and yet I have no will to resist; I remain attentive, strangely curious in proportion as I am afraid. The huge, shapeless mass is displacing all of the air, all of the space in the room. It swells against me. It is soft and supple and resilient, like a great bag of water. At last I am desperate, desperately afraid of being suffocated, lost in some dimple or fold of this vague, enormous thing. I try to cry out, but I have no voice.

Restore my voice for me.

How many times has this memory been nearly recovered, the definition almost realized! Again and again I have come to that awful edge, that one word, perhaps, that I cannot bring from my mouth. I sometimes think that it is surely a name, the name of someone or something, that if only I could utter it, the terrific mass would snap away into focus, and I should see and recognize what it is at once; I should have it then, once and for all, in my possession.

It is a bright, hot day, but the arbor is cool. The smooth gray wood of the benches is cool to the touch. The worn patchwork covers are cool and soft. The red, hard-packed earth of the floor is dark and cool. It is quiet and sleepy inside. I love this place. I love the cool well water that I bring in a dipper to my mouth.

> One time the creek was backed up, and my dad . . .
> Was it that time he saw the animal, the . . .
> Yes, that was it; that was the time.

We set out, my father and I, in the afternoon. We walk down the long grade to the ravine that runs diagonally below, up again and through the brambles. The sun burns my skin. I feel the stiff spines and furry burrs at my legs and hear the insects humming there all around. We walk down into the shadows of Rainy Mountain Creek. The banks are broad and the mud is dry and cracked, broken into innumerable large facets like shards of pottery, smooth, delicately curved, where the water has risen and then withdrawn and the sun has baked the bank. The water is brown and runs very slowly at the surface; here and there are glints of light and beams that strike through the trees and splash on the rocks and roots and underbrush. We cross the creek on a log and climb up the west bank where the woods are thicker. There is a small clearing, and inside the clearing is a single tree that was bent down to the ground and tied as a sapling; and so it remains curved, grown over in a long, graceful arc, its nimble new branches brushing whorls on the ground. It is one of my delights, for it is a wonderful, lively swing. My father lifts me up and I take hold of the slender, tapered trunk, and then he pulls me down and lets me go. I spring up, laughing, laughing, and bob up and down.

We continue on, through fields now, to "across the creek," as the house there was always called when I was a child. It is Keahdinekeah's house, built for her by my grandfather; but when you are a child you don't think of houses as possessions; it does not occur to you that anyone has ownership in them. "Across the creek" is where Justin Lee lives, a cousin not much older than I, with his sister, Lela, and his parents, Jim and Dorothy Ware, and his grandmother Keahdinekeah.

It seems reasonable to suppose that I visited my great-grandmother on other occasions, but I remember only this once, and I remember it very well. My father leads me into her room. It is dark and close inside, and I cannot see until my eyes become accustomed to the dim light. There is a certain odor in the room and not elsewhere in the house, the odor of my great-grandmother's old age. It is not unpleasant, but it is most particular and exclusive, as much hers as is her voice or her hair or the nails of her hands. Such a thing has not only the character of great age but something also of the deep self, of one's own dignity and well-being. Because of this, I believe, this old blind woman is like no one I have ever seen or shall ever see. To a child her presence is formidable. My father is talking to her in Kiowa, and I do not understand what is being said, only that the talk is of me. She is seated on the side of her bed, and my father brings me to stand directly in front of her. She reaches out for me and I place my hands in hers. *Eh neh neh neh neh.* She begins to weep very softly in a high, thin, hollow voice. Her hands are little and soft, so soft that they seem not to consist in flesh and bone, but in the softest fiber, cotton or fine wool. Her voice is so delicate, so surely expressive of her deep feelings. Long afterwards I think: That was a wonderful and beautiful thing that happened in my life. There, on that warm, distant afternoon: an old woman and a child, holding hands across the generations. There is great good in such a remembrance; I cannot imagine that it might have been lost upon me.

Lester and I, when we were little, used to go to my aunt's house in a wagon.
Where?
She lived over by the Wichitas; I thought of it as being far away.
Was it far away?
I thought so. At night we heard wolves in the mountains.

I am lying in bed beside an open window in the house. The room is dark, and the moonlight is brilliant on the yard outside. Everything is recessed in those marvelous blue depths of the summer night; the grass and the leaves glisten. The arbor is white and gleaming across the way, the screens black and opaque until someone inside strikes a match, and the little flame, set away in that darkness, is intensely bright for a moment, then gone out; and then a cigarette glows there, now and then visible. On such evenings the family sits there in the arbor without lamps, letting the night take hold of them, savoring the cool air. But in the house it is warm. It would be uncomfortably warm were it not for that same most delicate breeze that steals in at the window. It is impossible to say how clean and delicious it is. I hear voices from the arbor, low, monotonous, indistinct — and now and again laughter; there are crickets and frogs across the range of the night, everywhere, nowhere. And at long intervals I hear trucks passing along the highway on the south side of the house, in the red cut of the knoll, the high-pitched singing of the tires. There is something unspeakably lonely in that sound, and in that respect it is like the faraway whistle of a train, or the wind at Keet Seel. It is so familiar to me, a sound which seems to pervade my memory of those Indian evenings in Oklahoma; and yet I think it has nothing to do with me, after all; it might as well be the whir of a star moving across infinity. The door opens and the room flares up in yellow light; around the walls slivers of shadows leap to the lamp in my grandmother's hand. She places the lamp on a bureau, looses her long braids, dresses for bed. And then she prays aloud in Kiowa, standing, her eyes closed tight in concentration and earnestness. Her voice goes on and on; it is strange-sounding, rich, rhythmical, hypnotic. I try to hold on to it, to stay awake inside it, but I slip away at last into sleep. I awaken, and the voice, my father's voice, laps softly against my mind:

and the man went on in the same way, pointing the arrow all around

and it is warm in the bed, under heavy blankets, and there is a taut wind at the windows, and the winter is coming on. Deer are huddled in the Carizos; horses are braced against the cold at Lukachukai.

Dawn is on the desert for a long time, and the air is clean and cold; it feels like frost, and it draws the skin tight about the hands and face. Look across the dunes wrinkled with light and shadow; the colors, before they deepen, are the colors of shells or of birds' eggs.

My father is at the wheel of a new green pickup, and I am sitting beside him, hugely pleased to be along. The dashboard is gray-brown and to me very beautiful; there are bright knobs in it. My father is wearing gloves, soft leather gloves, and that is unimaginably fine. My dog Blackie is at the rear window, riding high to the wind, looking, laughing in at me. I look out in every direction to see who will notice us, for we are wonderful to behold, speeding along in the new truck, handsome, handsome, our eyes glittering; and otherwise, too, there is so much to see; the wide world is enchanted. The little truck bounces over the dirt roads of the Navajo reservation, raises a great rooster tail of red dust. It is summer and there is a sharp glare on the sand, on the cottonwood leaves. There is a jolt which rattles my bones, and the buckboard bucks; snowflakes are whirling on the sharp wind. My mother and I hold on, on the way to Oraibi. The old man sitting above us is wearing gloves; he talks to the team and crouches in his striped blanket. I am freezing. Then there is a mug of coffee, steaming, in my mother's hands. She holds it out to me and I take it in both my hands and bring it to my lips. It is black and bitter and good, better to hold than to taste. Perhaps it is my first taste of coffee. The sky is bleak and immense, streaked with smoke. I not only hear the beat of the drums; I feel it, too, and I feel the voices of the singers. It is a particular music which touches me, moves inside me like my blood. I listen. The whistle moans and the engine swerves ahead and the cars lurch and whine on the rails, rolling on the long, horizontal axis, shifting under me. I go here and there, back and forth, on trains. I am known by sight to the crews of the Santa Fe; the nurse on the *Scout* looks out for me. One man, a wily black, crooked as a hairpin, comes to stop my crying. He tells me that children who cry on the train are put in a sack and dropped off at Winslow. His uniform glitters with bits of brass.

A wiry old man comes out of the trading post at Tuba City. Squatting, he opens a can of whole tomatoes with a knife; he pours sugar from a sack, a lot of it, on the tomatoes and eats them from the can, with his knife. He has a good belt, old plaques. Nizhoni yei!

Monument Valley: red to blue; great violent shadows, planes and prisms of light. Once, from a window in the wall of a canyon, I saw men on horseback, far below, two of them, moving slowly into gloaming, and they were singing. They were so far away that I could only barely see them, and their small, clear voices lay very lightly and for a long time on the distance between us.

The valley is vast. When you look out over it, it does not occur to you that there is an end to it. You see the monoliths that stand away in space, and you imagine that you have come upon eternity. They do not appear to exist in time. You think: I see that time comes to an end on this side of the rock, and on the other side there is nothing forever. I believe that only in *dine bizaad*, the Navajo language, which is endless, can this place be described, or even indicated in its true character. Just there is the center of an intricate geology, a whole and unique landscape which includes Utah, Colorado, Arizona, and New Mexico. The most brilliant colors in the earth are there, I believe, and the most beautiful and extraordinary land forms — and surely the coldest, clearest air, which is run through with pure light.

The long wall of red rocks which extends eastward and for miles from Gallup, New Mexico, describes something of the hard, bright beauty of the continent at its summit. The Continental Divide runs down and intersects this wall at Coolidge. In the long reach of country which lies between Coolidge and the red rock wall there are cattle and sheep, rabbits and roadrunners, all delightful to a child. And there are trains. In the middle distance is the Santa Fe Railroad. Trains, most often long, slow-going freight trains, move there, one after another without end — and so they moved there when I was a child. They were small and nearly silent in the distance, and they bore upon the land in an easy, nearly discreet way. They seemed not to intrude, that is, as machines do in so many of the landscapes of our time; or perhaps this is merely *my* sense of things, having long ago taken that countryside as I found it, cut through with glinting rails and puffing trains. Like the red wall above them, they made an ordinary stratum on the scene. I try to imagine that large expanse without them, but then there is a flaw in the design. For in my mind's eye, too, a train stitches black across the plain.

Gallup is a rough-edged town of dubious character and many surfaces of rich color. It is a place of high tensions and hard distinctions. I once heard someone say that Gallup is the last frontier town in America; there is a certain truth to that, I believe. On a given day you can see in the streets of Gallup cowboys and Indians, missionaries and miscreants, tradesmen and tourists. Or you can see Billy the Kid or Huckleberry Finn or Ganado Mucho — or someone who is not impossibly all these worthies in one, Everyman realized in some desperate notion of himself.

To the child I was in the thirties Gallup was a wonderful, enchanted city, wonderful in its high tones and wide motions, wonderful in its din and audacity. It was almost too much for a child to take in, a child who had come fresh from the deep interior of the reservation. Gleaming automobiles passed endlessly along Route 66; mammoth, steaming locomotives drew up at the Harvey House; covered wagons rolled along the Rio Puerco. And there was a fabulous booty in the store windows! I can still feel the child's excitement of that place. Years afterwards, in the ancient city of Samarkand, in the old bazaar there, I had precisely the same *gladness* in me that I had when I was a child come on a Saturday morning from Naat'aaniineez to Na'nizhoozhi.

Harry Crews

The title that novelist Harry Crews (b. 1935) gives the autobiography of his first ten years is simple enough: A Childhood. *Its subtitle is more provocative —* The Biography of a Place. *"The biography of a childhood," he writes, is necessarily "the biography of a place, a way of life gone forever out of the world." The place is Bacon County, Georgia. "The rest of the country was just beginning to feel the real hurt of the Great Depression" Crews recalls, "but it had been living in Bacon County for years."*

Harry's father was a sharecropper. "I've always thought that because my daddy died before I could ever know him, he became a more palpable presence than he would ever have been had he lived." This excerpt from A Childhood *consists of Harry's earliest memories.*

When he became sixteen he left home to join the Marine Corps. Later would come the University of Florida and nearly a dozen novels, including Naked in Garden Hills *and* Karate Is a Thing of the Spirit.

From *A Childhood: The Biography of a Place*

IT HAS ALWAYS SEEMED TO ME that I was not so much born into this life as I awakened to it. I remember very distinctly the awakening and the morning it happened. It was my first glimpse of myself, and all that I know now — the stories, and everything conjured up by them, that I have been writing about thus far — I obviously knew none of then, particularly anything about my real daddy, whom I was not to hear of until I was nearly six years old, not his name, not even that he was my daddy. Or if I did hear of him, I have no memory of it.

I awoke in the middle of the morning in early summer from the place I'd been sleeping in the curving roots of a giant oak tree in front of a large white house. Off to the right, beyond the dirt road, my goats were trailing along in the ditch, grazing in the tough wire grass that grew there. Their constant bleating shook the warm summer air. I always thought of them as my goats although my brother usually took care of them. Before he went to the field that morning to work, he had let them out of the old tobacco barn where they slept at night. At my feet was a white dog whose name was Sam. I looked at the dog and at the house and at the red gown with little pearl-colored buttons I was wearing, and I knew that the gown had been made for me by my Grandma Hazelton and that the dog belonged to me. He went everywhere I went, and he always took precious care of me.

Precious. That was my mama's word for how it was between Sam and me, even though Sam caused her some inconvenience from time to time. If she wanted to whip me, she had to take me in the house, where Sam was never allowed to go. She could never touch me when I was crying if Sam could help it. He would move quietly — he was a dog not given to barking very much — between the two of us and show her his teeth. Unless she took me somewhere Sam couldn't go, there'd be no punishment for me.

The house there just behind me, partially under the arching limbs of the oak tree, was called the Williams place. It was where I lived with my mama and my brother, Hoyet, and my daddy, whose name was Pascal. I knew when I opened my eyes that morning that the house was empty because everybody had gone to the field to work. I also knew, even though I couldn't remember doing it, that I had awakened sometime in midmorning and come out onto the porch and down the steps and across the clean-swept dirt yard through the gate weighted with broken plow points so it would swing shut behind me, that I had come out under the oak tree and lain down against the curving roots with my dog, Sam, and gone to sleep. It was a thing I had done before. If I ever woke up and the house was empty and the weather was warm — which was the only time I would ever awaken to an empty house — I always went out under the oak tree to finish my nap. It wasn't fear or loneliness that drove me outside; it was just something I did for reasons I would never be able to discover.

I stood up and stretched and looked down at my bare feet at the hem of the gown and said: "I'm almost five and already a great big boy." It was my way of reassuring myself, but it was also something my daddy said about me and it made me feel good because in his mouth it seemed to mean I was almost a man.

Sam immediately stood up too, stretched, reproducing, as he always did, every move I made, watching me carefully to see which way I might go. I knew I ought not to be outside lying in the rough curve of root in my cotton gown. Mama didn't mind me being out there under the tree, but I was supposed to get dressed first. Sometimes I did; often I forgot.

So I turned and went back through the gate, Sam at my heels, and across the yard and up the steps onto the porch to the front door. When I opened the door, Sam stopped and lay down to wait. He would be there when I came out, no matter which door I used. If I went out the back door, he would somehow magically know it and he would be there. If I came out the side door by the little pantry, he would know that, too, and he would be there. Sam always knew where I was, and he made it his business to be there, waiting.

I went into the long, dim, cool hallway that ran down the center of the house. Briefly I stopped at the bedroom where my parents slept and looked in at the neatly made bed and all the parts of the room, clean, with everything where it was supposed to be, just the way mama always kept it. And I thought of daddy, as I so often did because I loved him so much. If he was sitting down, I was usually in his lap. If he was standing up, I was usually holding his hand. He always said soft funny things to me and told me stories that never had an end but always continued when we met again.

He was tall and lean with flat high cheekbones and deep eyes and black thick hair which he combed straight back on his head. And under the eye on his left cheek was the scarred print of a perfect set of teeth. I knew he had taken the scar in a fight, but I never asked him about it and the teeth marks in his cheek only made him seem more powerful and stronger and special to me.

He shaved every morning at the water shelf on the back porch with a straight razor and always smelled of soap and whiskey. I knew mama did not like the whiskey, but to me it smelled sweet, better even than the soap. And I could never understand why she resisted it so, complained of it so, and kept telling him over and over again that he would kill himself and ruin everything if he continued with the whiskey. I did not understand about killing himself and I did not understand about ruining everything, but I knew the whiskey somehow caused the shouting and screaming and the ugly sound of breaking things in the night. The stronger the smell of whiskey on him, though, the kinder and gentler he was with me and my brother.

I went on down the hallway and out onto the back porch and finally into the kitchen that was built at the very rear of the house. The entire room was dominated by a huge black cast-iron stove with six eyes on its cooking surface. Directly across the room from the stove was the safe, a tall square cabinet with wide doors covered with screen wire that was used to keep biscuits and fried meat and rice or almost any other kind of food that had been recently cooked. Between the stove and the safe sat the table we ate off of, a table almost ten feet long, with benches on each side instead of chairs, so that when we put in tobacco, there would be enough room for the hired hands to eat.

I opened the safe, took a biscuit off a plate, and punched a hole in it with my finger. Then with a jar of cane syrup, I poured the hole full, waited for it to soak in good, and then poured again. When the biscuit had all the syrup it would take, I got two pieces of fried pork off another plate and went out and sat on the back steps, where Sam was already lying in the warm sun, his ears struck forward on his head. I ate the bread and pork slowly, chewing for a long time and sharing it all with Sam.

When we had finished, I went back into the house, took off my gown, and put on a cotton undershirt, my overalls with twin galluses that buckled on my chest, and my straw hat, which was rimmed on the edges with a border of green cloth and had a piece of green cello-phane sewn into the brim to act as an eyeshade. I was barefoot, but I wished very much I had a pair of brogans because brogans were what men wore and I very much wanted to be a man. In fact, I was pretty sure I already was a man, but the only one who seemed to know it was my daddy. Everybody else treated me like I was still a baby.

I went out of the side door, and Sam fell into step behind me as we walked out beyond the mule barn where four mules stood in the lot and on past the cotton house and then down the dim road past a little leaning shack where our tenant farmers lived, a black family in which there was a boy just a year older than I was. His name was Willalee Bookatee. I went on past their house because I knew they would be in the field, too, so there was no use to stop.

I went through a sapling thicket and over a shallow ditch and finally climbed a wire fence into the field, being very careful of my overalls on the barbed wire. I could see them all, my family and the black tenant family, far off there in the shimmering heat of the tobacco field. They were pulling cutworms off the tobacco. I wished I could have been out there with them pulling worms because when you found one, you had to break it in half, which seemed great good fun to me. But you could also carry an empty Prince Albert tobacco can in your back pocket and fill it up with worms to play with later.

Mama wouldn't let me pull worms because she said I was too little and might damage the plants. If I was alone in the field with daddy, though, he would let me hunt all the worms I wanted to. He let me do pretty much anything I wanted to, which included sitting in his lap to guide his old pickup truck down dirt roads all over the county.

I went down to the end of the row and sat under a persimmon tree in the shade with Sam and watched as daddy and mama and brother and Willalee Bookatee, who was — I could see even from this distance — putting worms in Prince Albert cans, and his mama, whose name was Katie, and his daddy, whose name was Will, I watched them all as they came toward me, turning the leaves and searching for worms as they came.

The moment I sat down in the shade, I was already wondering how long it would be before they quit to go to the house for dinner because I was already beginning to wish I'd taken two biscuits instead of one and maybe another piece of meat, or else that I hadn't shared with Sam.

Bored, I looked down at Sam and said: "Sam, if you don't quit eatin my biscuit and meat, I'm gone have to cut you like a shoat hog."

A black cloud of gnats swarmed around his heavy muzzle, but I clearly heard him say that he didn't think I was man enough to do it. Sam and I talked a lot together, had long involved conversations, mostly about which one of us had done the other one wrong and, if not about that, about which one of us was the better man. It would be a good long time before I started thinking of Sam as a dog instead of a person. But I always came out on top when we talked because Sam could only say what I said he said, think what I thought he thought.

"If you was any kind of man atall, you wouldn't snap at them gnats and eat them flies the way you do," I said.

"It ain't a thing in the world the matter with eatin gnats and flies," he said.

"It's how come people treat you like a dog," I said. "You could probably come on in the house like other folks if it weren't for eatin flies and gnats like you do."

That's the way the talk went until daddy and the rest of them finally came down to where Sam and I were sitting in the shade. They stopped beside us to wipe their faces and necks with sweat rags. Mama asked if I had got something to eat when I woke up. I told her I had.

"You all gone stop for dinner now?"

"I reckon we'll work awhile longer," daddy said.

I said: "Well then, can Willalee and me go up to his house and play till dinnertime?"

Daddy looked at the sun to see what time it was. He could come within five or ten minutes by the position of the sun. Most of the farmers I knew could.

Daddy was standing almost dead center in his own shadow. "I reckon so," he said.

Then the whole thing had to be done over again. Willalee asked his daddy the same question. Because my daddy had said it was all right didn't mean Willalee's daddy would agree. He usually did, but not always. So it was necessary to ask.

We climbed the fence and went across the ditch and back through the sapling thicket to the three-track road that led up to the shack, and while we walked, Willalee showed me the two Prince Albert tobacco cans he had in his back pockets. They were both filled with cutworms. The worms had lots of legs and two little things on their heads that looked like horns. They were about an inch long, sometimes as long as two inches, and round and fat and made wonderful things to play with. There was no fence around the yard where Willalee lived and the whole house leaned toward the north at about a ten-degree tilt. Before we even got up the steps, we could smell the food already cooking on the wood stove at the back of the house where his grandma was banging metal pots around over the cast-iron stove. Her name was Annie, but everybody called her Auntie. She was too old to work in the field anymore, but she was handy about the house with ironing and cooking and scrubbing floors and canning vegetables out of the field and berries out of the woods.

She also was full of stories, which, when she had the time — and she usually did — she told to me and Willalee and his little sister, whose name was Lottie Mae. Willalee and my brother and I called her Snottie Mae, but she didn't seem to mind. She came out of the front door when she heard us coming up on the porch and right away wanted to know if she could play in the book with us. She was the same age as I and sometimes we let her play with us, but most of the time we did not.

"Naw," Willalee said, "git on back in there and help Auntie. We ain't studying you."

"Bring us the book," I said.

"I git it for you," she said, "if you give me five of them worms."

"I ain't studying you," said Willalee.

She had already seen the two Prince Albert cans full of green worms because Willalee was sitting on the floor now, the lids of the cans open and the worms crawling out. He was lining two of them up for a race from one crack in the floor to the next crack, and he was arranging the rest of the worms in little designs of diamonds and triangles in some game he had not yet discovered the rules for.

"You bring the book," I said, "and you can have two of them worms."

Willalee almost never argued with what I decided to do, up to and including giving away the worms he had spent all morning collecting in the fierce summer heat, which is probably why I liked him so much. Lottie Mae went back into the house, and got the Sears, Roebuck catalogue and brought it out onto the porch. He handed her the two worms and told her to go on back in the house, told her it weren't fitting for her to be out here playing with worms while Auntie was back in the kitchen working.

"Ain't nothing left for me to do but put them plates on the table," she said.

"See to them plates then," Willalee said. As young as she was, Lottie Mae had things to do about the place. Whatever she could manage. We all did.

Willalee and I stayed there on the floor with the Sears, Roebuck catalogue and the open Prince Albert cans, out of which deliciously fat worms crawled. Then we opened the catalogue at random as we always did, to see what magic was waiting for us there.

In the minds of most people, the Sears, Roebuck catalog is a kind of low joke associated with outhouses. God knows the catalogue sometimes ended up in the outhouse, but more often it did not. All the farmers, black and white, kept dried corncobs beside their double-seated thrones, and the cobs served the purpose for which they were put there with all possible efficiency and comfort.

The Sears, Roebuck catalogue was much better used as a Wish Book, which it was called by the people out in the country, who would never be able to order anything out of it, but could at their leisure spend hours dreaming over.

Willalee Bookatee and I used it for another reason. We made up stories out of it, used it to spin a web of fantasy about us. Without the catalogue our childhood would have been radically different. The federal government ought to strike a medal for the Sears, Roebuck company for sending all those catalogues to farming families, for bringing all that color and all that mystery and all that beauty into the lives of country people.

I first became fascinated with the Sears catalogue because all the people in its pages were perfect. Nearly everybody I knew had something missing, a finger cut off, a toe split, an ear half-chewed away, an eye clouded with blindness from a glancing fence staple. And if they didn't have something missing, they were carrying scars from barbed wire, or knives, or fishhooks. But the people in the catalogue had no such hurts. They were not only whole, had all their arms and legs and toes and eyes on their unscarred bodies, but they were also beautiful. Their legs were straight and their heads were never bald and on their faces were looks of happiness, even joy, looks that I never saw much of in the faces of the people around me.

Young as I was, though, I had known for a long time that it was all a lie. I knew that under those fancy clothes there had to be scars, there had to be swellings and boils of one kind or another because there was no other way to live in the world. And more than that, at some previous, unremembered moment, I had decided that all the people in the catalogue were related, not necessarily blood kin, but knew one another, and because they knew one another there had to be hard feelings, trouble between them off and on, violence, and hate between them as well as love. And it was out of this knowledge that I first began to make up stories about the people I found in the book.

Once I began to make up stories about them, Willalee and Lottie Mae began to make up stories, too. The stories they made up were every bit as good as mine. Sometimes better. More than once we had spent whole rainy afternoons when it was too wet to go to the field turning the pages of the catalogue, forcing the beautiful people to give up the secrets of their lives: how they felt about one another, what kind of sicknesses they may have had, what kind of scars they carried in their flesh under all those bright and fancy clothes.

Willalee had his pocketknife out and was about to operate on one of the green cutworms because he liked to pretend he was a doctor. It was I who first put the notion in his head that he might in fact be a doctor, and since we almost never saw a doctor and because they were mysterious and always drove cars or else fine buggies behind high-stepping mares, quickly healing people with their secret medicines, the notion stuck in Willalee's head, and he became very good at taking cutworms and other things apart with his pocketknife.

The Sears catalogue that we had opened at random found a man in his middle years but still strong and healthy with a head full of hair and clear, direct eyes looking out at us, dressed in a red hunting jacket and wading boots, with a rack of shotguns behind him. We used our fingers to mark the spot and turned the Wish Book again, and this time it opened to ladies standing in their underwear, lovely as none we had ever seen, all perfect in their unstained clothes. Every last one of them had the same direct and steady eyes of the man in the red hunting jacket.

I said: "What do you think, Willalee?"

Without hesitation, Willalee said: "This lady here in her step-ins is his chile."

We kept the spot marked with the lady in the step-ins and the man in the hunting jacket and turned the book again, and there was a young man in a suit, the creases sharp enough to shave with, posed with his foot casually propped on a box, every strand of his beautiful hair in place.

"See, what it is," I said. "This boy right here is seeing that girl back there, the one in her step-ins, and she is the youngun of him back there, and them shotguns behind'm belong to him, and he ain't happy."

"Why he ain't happy?"

"Cause this feller standing here in this suit looking so nice, he ain't nice at all. He's mean, but he don't look mean. That gal is the only youngun the feller in the jacket's got, and he loves her cause she is a sweet child. He don't want her fooling with that sorry man in that suit. He's so sorry he done got hisself in trouble with the law. The high sheriff is looking for him right now. Him in the suit will fool around on you."

"How it is he fool around?"

"He'll steal anything he can put his hand to," I said. "He'll steal your hog, or he'll steal your cow out of your field. He's so sorry he'll take that cow if it's the only cow you got. It's just the kind of feller he is."

Willalee said: "Then how come it is she mess around with him?"

"That suit," I said, "done turned that young girl's head. Daddy always says if you give a man a white shirt and a tie and a suit of clothes, you can find out real quick how sorry he is. Daddy says it's the quickest way to find out."

"Do her daddy know she's messing round with him?"

"Shore he knows. A man allus knows what his youngun is doing. Special if she's a girl." I flipped back to the man in the red hunting jacket and the wading boots. "You see them shotguns behind him there on the wall? Them his guns. That second one right there, see that one, the double barrel? That gun is loaded with double-ought buckshot. You know how come it loaded?"

"He gone stop that fooling around," said Willalee.

And so we sat there on the porch with the pots and pans banging back in the house over the iron stove and Lottie Mae there in the door where she had come to stand and listen to us as we talked even though we would not let her help with the story. And before it was over, we had discovered all the connections possible between the girl in the step-ins and the young man in the knife-creased suit and the older man in the red hunting jacket with the shotguns on the wall behind him. And more than that we also discovered that the man's kin people, when they had found out about the trouble he was having with his daughter and the young man, had plans of their own to fix it so the high sheriff wouldn't even have to know about it. They were going to set up and wait on him to take a shoat hog out of another field, and when he did, they'd be waiting with their own guns and knives (which we stumbled upon in another part of the catalogue) and they was gonna throw down on him and see if they couldn't make two pieces out of him instead of one. We had in the story what they thought and what they said and what they felt and why they didn't think that the young man, as good as he looked and as well as he stood in his fancy clothes, would ever straighten out and become the man the daddy wanted for his only daughter.

Before it was over, we even had the girl in the step-ins fixing it so that the boy in the suit could be shot. And by the time my family and Willalee's family came walking down the road from the tobacco field toward the house, the entire Wish Book was filled with feuds of every kind and violence, maimings, and all the other vicious happenings of the world.

Since where we lived and how we lived was almost hermetically sealed from everything and everybody else, fabrication became a way of life. Making up stories, it seems to me now, was not only a way for us to understand the way we lived but also a defense against it. It was no doubt the first step in a life devoted primarily to men and women and children who never lived anywhere but in my imagination. I have found in them infinitely more order and beauty and satisfaction than I ever have in the people who move about me in the real world. And Willalee Bookatee and his family were always there with me in those first tentative steps. God knows what it would have been like if it had not been for Willalee and his people, with whom I spent nearly as much time as I did with my own family.

There was a part of me in which it did not matter at all that they were black, but there was another part of me in which it had to matter because it mattered to the world I lived in. It mattered to my blood. It is easy to remember the morning I found out Willalee was a nigger.

It was not very important at the time. I do not know why I have remembered it so vividly and so long. It was the tiniest of moments that slipped by without anybody marking it or thinking about it.

It was later in the same summer I awoke to a knowledge of myself in the enormous, curving oak roots. It was Sunday, bright and hot, and we were on the way to church. Everybody except daddy, who was sick from whiskey. But he would not have gone even if he were well. The few times he ever did go he could never stand more than five or ten minutes of the sermon before he quietly went out a side door to stand beside the pickup truck smoking hand-rolled Prince Albert cigarettes until it was all over.

An aunt, her husband, and their children had come by to take us to the meeting in their car. My aunt was a lovely, gentle lady whom I loved nearly as much as mama. I was out on the porch waiting for my brother to get ready. My aunt stood beside me, pulling on the thin black gloves she wore to church winter and summer. I was talking nonstop, which I did even as a child, telling her a story — largely made up — about what happened to me and my brother the last time we went to town.

Robert Jones figured in the story. Robert Jones was a black man who lived in Bacon County. Unlike any other black man I knew of, though, he owned a big farm with a great shining house on it. He had two sons who were nearly seven feet tall. They were all known as very hard workers. I had never heard anybody speak of Robert Jones and his family with anything but admiration.

". . . so me and Hoyet was passing the cotton gin and Mr. Jones was standing there with his wife and. . . ."

My aunt leaned down and put her arm around my shoulders. Her great soft breast pressed warmly at my ear. She said: "No, son. Robert Jones is a nigger. You don't say 'mister' when you speak of a nigger. You don't say 'Mr. Jones,' you say 'nigger Jones.'"

I never missed a stroke in my story. ". . . so me and him was passing the cotton gin and nigger Jones was standing there with his wife. . . ."

We were all dutiful children in Bacon County, Georgia.

William Humphrey

From the memoirs of John Adams on, hunting has been a recurring theme in these childhood recollections, a ritual as much as a sport or a way of providing food for the table. It is often the only ritual that links father and son. William Humphrey (b. 1924), whose Texas novels have included Home from the Hill *and* The Ordways, *remembers his first shotgun and his first hunting trips with his father in this excerpt from* Farther Off from Heaven, *his account of the Fourth of July weekend when his father died. The year is 1937; the place, Clarksville and nearby Paris, Texas.*

Humphrey writes:

> *On the day he lay fighting for his life in the Paris hospital, my father was just thirty-eight. And I, though just thirteen, had done more hunting than most men of thirty-eight. My father had bought me my first gun, a .22 rifle, and taught me to shoot it when I was still too little to hold it up without a prop. He was my prop, squatting and resting the barrel on his shoulder while I fired.*

From *Farther Off from Heaven*

MY FIRST SHOTGUN cost a nickel. One chance on the punchboard in a diner on the Paris road where my father stopped one day just when it was getting time his boy, about to turn twelve — which was to say, going on thirteen — had a shotgun and learned how to use it. It was a four-shot bolt-action .410 — the smallest of all the gauges. Being the lightest to carry, the cheapest to shoot, and the one with the least kick, it was the gauge boys were apprenticed on. From that beginning the grades up were 20, 16 and 12. It ought to have been just the other way 'round. Throwing the smallest charge and carrying the least far, the .410 ought to have been the gun for the most refined wingshot — the one in a thousand who is born, not made.

Now instead of stationary targets I began shooting at moving ones, or rather, I followed with the gun waiting for them to stop moving and become stationary. Finally, before the bird flew out of range or the rabbit hopped out of sight, I fired, and watched it fly on, hop faster. "You're trying to aim. Don't. You've got to shoot at where it's going to be," my father told me. "If you shoot at it, then you've shot at where it just was." For my age I was a pretty good rifleman — and for a wingshot I was a pretty good rifleman. To my father it was being a wingshot that separated the men from the boys. He was the best of them all, and I, his only son, his sole hope for a successor, could not get the hang of it. My father was patient with me but I was impatient with myself.

During my twelfth summer I would meet my father at the garage at quitting time and we would drive out of town to the nearby farms where mourning doves flocked to feed on the sorghum and the durum and to the stock-ponds to drink. That was the summer I shared with my chum Pete Hinkle a passion for casting, painting and warring with lead soldiers, and after a day of this, Pete sometimes went with my father and me dove shooting. I was not embarrassed to have Pete see me miss time after time, for Pete was no better shot than I was, though with his gun, a 20-gauge double barrel, he ought to have been.

We crouched in the tall grass at the edge of the pond, the telltale white of our faces shaded by long cap-bills. A whistle from my father signalled the approach of a bird: one if from the left, two from the right. He gave first chance at every bird that winged in to us, and Pete and I took turns missing them, sometimes missing the same one in turn, before my father brought it down. It ran head-on into the charge of shot waiting for it in the air, crumpled and fell. It was left to lie where it fell. When the day was over, Pete and I gathered them up like nuts from a thrashed tree, wading for those fallen into the pond, searching for the others among the grass, my father directing us to them, he having marked them down, and kept tally of the bag.

In the course of the summer both Pete and I unavoidably got a little better at it. I began to think that the knack was not hopelessly beyond me after Pete lent me his gun a few times. My improvement with the 20 gauge raised my self-confidence and I shot better with my own gun. I had learned what deceptive birds doves are. They looked slow and as if they ought to be easy to hit but they were fast and their flight erratic and unpredictable, capable of sudden acceleration, full of dips and flares, tricky as a pilot dodging flak. You swung from behind, passed it firing and followed through, stringing out the charge in a path on the air ahead of the bird. And you still missed a great many more than you hit.

My performance on doves qualified me to be taken quail shooting in the fall. For, although quail are actually easier to hit than doves, they occupy a higher niche in the hierarchy of game birds, possibly because of their comparative scarcity, possibly because they are more prized on the plate. Whatever the reason, the rule is immemorial and inviolable: doves are boys' game, quail men's.

But I could not hit them. On this superior bird, this man's game, and being privileged for the first time to shoot over dogs, I did less well than I had done on doves. The joy of shooting over field dogs had been impressed upon me but it was something that until now I had had to take on faith from my father, just as I took on faith (although about this I had reservations) that the time would come when I would enjoy doing what he had recently told me men did with women.

His bird dogs at that time — "ours," he now began calling them — were Mack and Kate, brother and sister English setters, he white speckled with black, she black spotted with white. Though still young, they were, in my father's opinion, already the best dogs he had ever owned. They were completing their training as I was commencing mine. We could look forward to years of pleasure out of them.

He was right about the joy of watching good bird dogs at work — maybe about that other business too, then. To see Mack and Kate divide a field between them in quarters and cover its every yard, their tails like flags for us to follow, watch one of them suddenly brake, stiffen, straighten its tail, and the other one then come to honor its set, to watch them inch up on the covey just enough to hold it, not enough to flush it, was as thrilling as my father had told me it was.

That was my job: to flush the covey, and it was one reason I could not hit the birds. They could never be seen until they broke, for they were the color of autumn, of nature: of dead leaves, dry grass, twigs, mottled rocks, sunshine and shadow, and, up to the last moment, they could hug the earth as though made of it. When I kicked and they burst at my feet it was as though I had stepped on a landmine. Like shell fragments they went whirring off in all directions. Their flight was low to the ground and short. You had to be steady, cool and quick, and I could never recover from my shock in time to get off a sensible shot before they had all pitched to the ground. To think of ever being able to drop one, then swing on a second, even a third, on a single rise, as my father did consistently, seemed as unlikely for me as did that other business. The long fall season reached closing day without my having cleanly killed a single bird. Some at which we had both fired my father credited to me, but he was just being fond.

By then — closing day — no longer was the burst at my feet when I kicked quite so explosive. The big coveys, disbanded by gunning, thinned by predators, were broken up into singles, doubles, triples now. Still, I was sluggish in my responses, and instead of pointing my gun, I pottered.

We had had the morning to hunt. Now it was almost noon and we were working our way back to the car, my father's game pockets, as always, bulging, mine, as always, empty, when, emerging from a woods into a clearing, the two dogs simultaneously set. Tails stiff and straight out behind them, heads high, they seemed to be holding the birds transfixed by their steady stare.

When I kicked, three birds flushed, two one way, one another. So rapid were my father's two shots that they seemed one, and to each a bird, in a burst of feathers, fell. I in my pottering way was following the lone bird, when my father swivelled, found it and fired. He scored a clean miss. I fired, and in a third burst of feathers on the air, that bird fell.

I acted as though I was used to doing it daily. So did my father, and he was offhand in his congratulations to me. But he was almost visibly puffed with pride. That he himself had missed the bird doubled his pleasure.

Forgotten were the uncountable number of quail he had brought down in his time whenever he told the story of that one of mine. Before long he was omitting to mention the two he had gotten on that rise before I killed the one he had shot at and missed.

Counting my one, we took home fifty-three quail that day. Game was not a treat for us, it was the staple of our diet; butcher's meat was the rarity in our house. My girl-mother, until late in the night, plucking birds into a washtub and sneezing as the feathers or the down tickled her nose, is one of my most vivid images of her, as is the one of my father stepping on the tail of a squirrel and peeling it out of its skin. Despite my mother's thoroughness as a housekeeper, pinfeathers and wisps of fur floated around doorjambs and lingered in corners of our house. The habit of watching for birdshot in my meat was so ingrained in me that I sometimes forgot and did it while eating fried chicken.

Yet it would have surprised my father to be called a gamehog. He was simply providing for his family. To the question, "What if everybody killed as many as you do?" he would have answered. "But not everybody does" (refraining out of modesty from saying, "*Nobody* does"), and would have expected that answer to quiet the fears of anybody concerned (in those days few were) over the future of wildlife. He heard men complain about the scarcity of game, but he had been hearing that all his life, and always from the same ones: those who were not very good hunters. There were good years and bad years, as there had always been, as there were for any of nature's crops. The long recent drought had had an effect, but that was coming to an end now, and once the birds and the animals rebuilt their numbers, we would see good times again.

That one closing-day quail of mine earned me the right to be taken a time or two that winter to shoot over the water, at the game bird supreme: wild ducks. Only a time or two, for duck shooting is where not merely the boys but the lesser men are separated from the men. Not just because ducks are the hardest to hit of all moving targets, but also because duck shooting is done under conditions demanding uncommon patience, stamina and strength.

The use of live decoys in shooting ducks had been outlawed the previous year, or maybe the one before that; but my father was never a strict observer of any of the game laws. In this he was not alone among hunters in our parts — just the most flagrant violator. Game laws were unenforceable there in those times. No effort was even made to enforce them. The post of warden, if not vacant, was held by somebody I had never heard of. Somebody who wisely worked not very hard at the job. To have done so would have made a man highly unpopular there where men had always hunted for meat, and took it as their fundamental and inalienable right to go hunting whenever they felt like it and to be limited in their kill by nothing but their own prowess — and where judges and juries agreed with them wholeheartedly. Gentlemen-sportsmen are not found on the frontier; and although the frontier was gone, and my father was one of those responsible, men like him had yet to learn this. Federal game laws like those protecting migratory birds they thought were something applicable to the other states of the Union, perhaps, but not to Texas.

My father kept his flock of live decoys in our back yard — whenever we moved, they moved with us — and he still drove through the square with them quacking loudly in their cage affixed to the rear of the model T touring car he used for hunting, and which could get with equal ease through the mud of Sulphur Bottom or the sand spread thickly for miles by the Red River in its periodical risings. Mallards, his were: three dozen of them, the imbalance between the sexes favoring hens over drakes. Siren-songs they quacked to their former fellows.

The wildfowler loves foul weather. Then the birds are on the wing. When days are short they must be active during the few daylight feeding hours. Rain and fog hamper their vision. Fearing freezing of their feeding grounds, they are on the move. The gunner endures these conditions in order to take advantage of the pressures they put upon the birds. Always on my initiatory expeditions to the Red River, it had been raining, was raining, and was going to rain — cold, cutting rain, often mixed with sleet, with a steady north wind driving it.

Even the model T could get us only so near the water. From our stopping place we proceeded on foot — all thirty-eight of us.

My father had rigged a stout cord, like a trotline, to which, every few feet, instead of a fishhook, was attached a snap swivel. Each duck was banded on one leg, and like convicts in a chain gang marshalled out of their van and manacled and marched to their work on the road, they were snapped to this cord — we two their shotgunned guards. Leading the column was always the same bird, an old drake that had established himself as gang-boss.

When the decoys were on the water we took our places in the blind, my father wiping out behind us with a bough the footprints we left in the wet sand. The blind was a pit dug into the sandbar and slant-roofed with reeds. To see out, I stood on a crate.

Our watch of the gray skies would go long unrewarded. Then out of the mist they would suddenly appear like a squadron of fighter planes in formation streaking to intercept the enemy. Immune to the seductive quacking of our decoys, some, high out of range, swept on. But another flock would bank and turn, circle, circle again more narrowly, dip, dive, and then you could hear the whistle of their wings as they swooped low overhead. "Pintails," my father would whisper, or "Mallards." What he said that gave him the most satisfaction was "Canvasbacks!"

He considered that the new law limiting duck shooters to three shots, one in the firing chamber and two in the magazine, was also for those who chose to obey it. As he always had, he carried five in his hammerless pump 12 gauge with the long, full-choked barrel, and I was to see him drop five birds on one pass, beginning with the hindmost and working forward so the flock could not count its losses.

When hit, ducks did not fold up and tumble down. Their speed seemed hardly to slow. They sailed on in a steadily falling trajectory and crashed into the water like a plane with its pilot dead at the controls.

The newly established daily limit on ducks was twenty-five. Since I was not able to fill mine myself, my father did it for me. That was only fair, as I was a beginner, and handicapped, undergunned. I tried my father's big gun and did no better with it than with the .410, getting nothing but a bruised shoulder in reward. I never minded. I was started now, in me my father was rediscovering the joys of just starting, and under his eager tutelage I was sure to show steady improvement.

On mornings when my father took me hunting with him we would get to the woods at about the hour my mother and I had gotten to the Paris hospital in the ambulance with him that morning. But in the woods it would seem like the hour just before Creation. It was as if God said again each day, "Let there be light." Looking just as they must have on the first day, the woods took shape out of the void. The change seemed chemical, like a photographic print in the developer in the dimness of the darkroom, the image appearing out of nothingness, then rapidly becoming distinct, recognizable, familiar. The transformation in my father seemed chemical, too. Perhaps even more in recent years, when illness and disappointment and worry had borne him down, that old boyish wonder of his whenever he went to the woods made a boy of him again. In me he saw the boy he once had been and then for a time he was one again himself. My oneness with him gave me some of his sense of oneness with that world.

He and I had long ago dispensed with talk while hunting. I knew what was expected of me. If, for instance, we were there now, as soon as the woods were light I would have crept around to the other side of that oak, and that first squirrel that came out to feed and chatter would now be lying on the ground, brought down by that keen right eye that would never look down a gun barrel again.

Gloria Steinem

Childhood is a luxury not everyone has been able to afford. Gloria Steinem (b. 1934) — journalist, political activist, founding editor of Ms. *magazine — spent much of her childhood taking the role of the adult in a relationship with her mother, Ruth, who was often too confused to care for herself.*

This excerpt is taken from the essay "Ruth's Song (Because She Could Not Sing It)." What happened to Ruth later? "I'd like to tell you that this story has a happy ending," Gloria Steinem writes. "The best I can do is one that is happier than its beginning." Ruth spent Gloria's college years living near a hospital, returning to it at her own request when "she felt the old terrors coming back." Approaching sixty, she stayed briefly at a Quaker farm that served as a halfway house and then for the next twenty years was able to live free of hospital care, at times supporting herself as a salesclerk. She died just before her eighty-second birthday.

From "Ruth's Song
(Because She Could Not Sing It)"

HAPPY OR UNHAPPY, families are all mysterious. We have only to imagine how differently we would be described — and will be, after our deaths — by each of the family members who believe they know us. The only question is, Why are some mysteries more important than others?

The fate of my Uncle Ed was a mystery of importance in our family. We lavished years of speculation on his transformation from a brilliant young electrical engineer to the town handyman. What could have changed this elegant, Lincolnesque student voted "Best Dressed" by his classmates to the gaunt, unshaven man I remember? Why did he leave a young son and a first wife of the "proper" class and religion, marry a much less educated woman of the "wrong" religion, and raise a second family in a house near an abandoned airstrip; a house whose walls were patched with metal signs to stop the wind? Why did he never talk about his transformation?

For years, I assumed that some secret and dramatic events of a year he spent in Alaska had made the difference. Then I discovered that the trip had come after his change and probably been made because of it. Strangers he worked for as a much-loved handyman talked about him as one more tragedy of the Depression, and it was true that Uncle Ed's father, my paternal grandfather, had lost his money in the stockmarket Crash and died of (depending on who was telling the story) pneumonia or a broken heart. But the Crash of 1929 also had come long after Uncle Ed's transformation. Another theory was that he was afflicted with a mental problem that lasted most of his life, yet he was supremely competent at his work, led an independent life, and asked for help from no one.

Perhaps he had fallen under the spell of a radical professor in the early days of the century, the height of this country's romance with socialism and anarchism. That was the theory of another uncle on my mother's side. I do remember that no matter how much Uncle Ed needed money, he would charge no more for his work than materials plus 10 percent, and I never saw him in anything other than ancient boots and overalls held up with strategic safety pins. Was he really trying to replace socialism-in-one-country with socialism-in-one-man? If so, why did my grandmother, a woman who herself had run for the school board in coalition with anarchists and socialists, mistrust his judgment so much that she left his share of her estate in trust, even though he was over fifty when she died? And why did Uncle Ed seem uninterested in all other political words and acts? Was it true instead that, as another relative insisted, Uncle Ed had chosen poverty to disprove the myths of Jews and money?

Years after my uncle's death, I asked a son in his second family if he had the key to this family mystery. No, he said. He had never known his father any other way. For that cousin, there had been no question. For the rest of us, there was to be no answer.

For many years I also never imagined my mother any way other than the person she had become before I was born. She was just a fact of life when I was growing up; someone to be worried about and cared for; an invalid who lay in bed with eyes closed and lips moving in occasional response to voices only she could hear; a woman to whom I brought an endless stream of toast and coffee, bologna sandwiches and dime pies, in a child's version of what meals should be. She was a loving, intelligent, terrorized woman who tried hard to clean our littered house whenever she emerged from her private world, but who could rarely be counted on to finish one task. In many ways, our roles were reversed: I was the mother and she was the child. Yet that didn't help her, for she still worried about me with all the intensity of a frightened mother, plus the special fears of her own world full of threats and hostile voices.

Even then I suppose I must have known that, years before she was thirty-five and I was born, she had been a spirited, adventurous young woman who struggled out of a working-class family and into college, who found work she loved and continued to do, even after she was married and my older sister was there to be cared for. Certainly, our immediate family and nearby relatives, of whom I was by far the youngest, must have remembered her life as a whole and functioning person. She was thirty before she gave up her own career to help my father run the Michigan summer resort that was the most practical of his many dreams, and she worked hard there as everything from bookkeeper to bar manager. The family must have watched this energetic, fun-loving, book-loving woman turn into someone who was afraid to be alone, who could not hang on to reality long enough to hold a job, and who could rarely concentrate enough to read a book.

Yet I don't remember any family speculation about the mystery of my mother's transformation. To the kind ones and those who liked her, this new Ruth was simply a sad event, perhaps a mental case, a family problem to be accepted and cared for until some natural process made her better. To the less kind or those who had resented her earlier independence, she was a willful failure, someone who lived in a filthy house, a woman who simply would not pull herself together.

Unlike the case of my Uncle Ed, exterior events were never suggested as reason enough for her problems. Giving up her own career was never cited as her personal parallel of the Depression. (Nor was there discussion of the Depression itself, though my mother, like millions of others, had made potato soup and cut up blankets to make my sister's winter clothes.) Her fears of dependence and poverty were no match for my uncle's possible political beliefs. The real influence of newspaper editors who had praised her reporting was not taken as seriously as the possible influence of one radical professor.

Even the explanation of mental illness seemed to contain more personal fault when applied to my mother. She had suffered her first "nervous breakdown," as she and everyone else called it, before I was born and when my sister was about five. It followed years of trying to take care of a baby, be the wife of a kind but financially irresponsible man with show-business dreams, and still keep her much-loved job as reporter and newspaper editor. After many months in a sanatorium, she was pronounced recovered. That is, she was able to take care of my sister again, to move away from the city and the job she loved, and to work with my father at the isolated rural lake in Michigan he was trying to transform into a resort worthy of the big dance bands of the 1930s.

But she was never again completely without the spells of depression, anxiety, and visions into some other world that eventually were to turn her into the nonperson I remember. And she was never again without a bottle of dark, acrid-smelling liquid she called "Doc Howard's medicine": a solution of chloral hydrate that I later learned was the main ingredient of "Mickey Finns" or "knockout drops," and that probably made my mother and her doctor the pioneers of modern tranquilizers. Though friends and relatives saw this medicine as one more evidence of weakness and indulgence, to me it always seemed an embarrassing but necessary evil. It slurred her speech and slowed her coordination, making our neighbors and my school friends believe she was a drunk. But without it, she would not sleep for days, even a week at a time, and her feverish eyes began to see only that private world in which wars and hostile voices threatened the people she loved.

Because my parents had divorced and my sister was working in a faraway city, my mother and I were alone together then, living off the meager fixed income that my mother got from leasing her share of the remaining land in Michigan. I remember a long Thanksgiving weekend spent hanging on to her with one hand and holding my eighth-grade assignment of *Tale of Two Cities* in the other, because the war outside our house was so real to my mother that she had plunged her hand through a window, badly cutting her arm in an effort to help us escape. Only when she finally agreed to swallow the medicine could she sleep, and only then could I end the terrible calm that comes with crisis and admit to myself how afraid I had been.

No wonder that no relative in my memory challenged the doctor who prescribed this medicine, asked if some of her suffering and hallucinating might be due to overdose or withdrawal, or even consulted another doctor about its use. It was our relief as well as hers.

But why was she never returned even to that first sanatorium? Or to help that might come from other doctors? It's hard to say. Partly, it was her own fear of returning. Partly, it was too little money, and a family's not-unusual assumption that mental illness is an inevitable part of someone's personality. Or perhaps other family members had feared something like my experience when, one hot and desperate summer between the sixth and seventh grade, I finally persuaded her to let me take her to the only doctor from those sanatorium days whom she remembered without fear.

Yes, this brusque old man told me after talking to my abstracted, timid mother for twenty minutes: She definitely belongs in a state hospital. I should put her there right away. But even at that age, *Life* magazine and newspaper exposés had told me what horrors went on inside those hospitals. Assuming there to be no other alternative, I took her home and never tried again.

In retrospect, perhaps the biggest reason my mother was cared for but not helped for twenty years was the simplest: her functioning was not that necessary to the world. Like women alcoholics who drink in their kitchens while costly programs are constructed for executives who drink, or like the homemakers subdued with tranquilizers while male patients get therapy and personal attention instead, my mother was not an important worker. She was not even the caretaker of a very young child, as she had been when she was hospitalized the first time. My father had patiently brought home the groceries and kept our odd household going until I was eight or so and my sister went away to college. Two years later when wartime gas rationing closed his summer resort and he had to travel to buy and sell in summer as well as winter, he said: How can I travel and take care of your mother? How can I make a living? He was right. It was impossible to do both. I did not blame him for leaving once I was old enough to be the bringer of meals and answerer of my mother's questions. ("Has your sister been killed in a car crash?" "Are there German soldiers outside?") I replaced my father, my mother was left with one more way of maintaining a sad status quo, and the world went on undisturbed.

That's why our lives, my mother's from forty-six to fifty-three, and my own from ten to seventeen, were spent alone together. There was one sane winter in a house we rented to be near my sister's college in Massachusetts, then one bad summer spent house-sitting in suburbia while my mother hallucinated and my sister struggled to hold down a summer job in New York. But the rest of those years were lived in

Toledo where both my mother and father had been born, and on whose city newspapers an earlier Ruth had worked.

First we moved into a basement apartment in a good neighborhood. In those rooms behind a furnace, I made one last stab at being a child. By pretending to be much sicker with a cold than I really was, I hoped my mother would suddenly turn into a sane and cheerful woman bringing me chicken soup à la Hollywood. Of course, she could not. It only made her feel worse that she could not. I stopped pretending.

But for most of those years, we lived in the upstairs of the house my mother had grown up in and that her parents left her — a deteriorating farm house engulfed by the city, with poor but newer houses stacked against it and a major highway a few feet from its sagging front porch. For a while, we could rent the two downstairs apartments to a newlywed factory worker and a local butcher's family. Then the health department condemned our ancient furnace for the final time, sealing it so tight that even my resourceful Uncle Ed couldn't produce illegal heat.

In that house, I remember:

. . . lying in the bed my mother and I shared for warmth, listening on the early morning radio to the royal wedding of Princess Elizabeth and Prince Philip being broadcast live, while we tried to ignore and thus protect each other from the unmistakable sounds of the factory worker downstairs beating up and locking out his pregnant wife.

. . . hanging paper drapes I had bought in the dime store; stacking books and papers in the shape of two armchairs and covering them with blankets; evolving my own dishwashing system (I waited until all the dishes were dirty, then put them in the bathtub); and listening to my mother's high praise for these housekeeping efforts to bring order from chaos, though in retrospect I think they probably depressed her further.

. . . coming back from one of the Eagles' Club shows where I and other veterans of a local tap-dancing school made ten dollars a night for two shows, and finding my mother waiting with a flashlight and no coat in the dark cold of the bus stop, worried about my safety walking home.

. . . in a good period, when my mother's native adventurousness came through, answering a classified ad together for an amateur acting troupe that performed Biblical dramas in churches, and doing several very corny performances of *Noah's Ark* while my proud mother shook metal sheets backstage to make thunder.

. . . on a hot summer night, being bitten by one of the rats that shared our house and its back alley. It was a terrifying night that turned into a touching one when my mother, summoning courage from some unknown reservoir of love, became a calm, comforting parent who took me to a hospital emergency room despite her terror at leaving home.

. . . coming home from a local library with the three books a week into which I regularly escaped, and discovering that for once there was no need to escape. My mother was calmly planting hollyhocks in the vacant lot next door.

But there were also times when she woke in the early winter dark, too frightened and disoriented to remember that I was at my usual after-school job, and so called the police to find me. Humiliated in front of my friends by sirens and policemen, I would yell at her — and she would bow her head in fear and say "I'm sorry, I'm sorry, I'm sorry," just as she had done so often when my otherwise-kindhearted father had yelled at her in frustration. Perhaps the worst thing about suffering is that it finally hardens the hearts of those around it.

And there were many, many times when I badgered her until her shaking hands had written a small check to cash at the corner grocery and I could leave her alone while I escaped to the comfort of well-heated dime stores that smelled of fresh doughnuts, or to air-conditioned Saturday-afternoon movies that were windows on a very different world.

But my ultimate protection was this: I was just passing through, a guest in the house; perhaps this wasn't my mother at all. Though I knew very well that I was her daughter, I sometimes imagined that I had been adopted and that my real parents would find me, a fantasy I've since discovered is common. (If children wrote more and grownups less, being adopted might be seen not only as a fear but also as a hope.) Certainly, I didn't mourn the wasted life of this woman who was scarcely older than I am now. I worried only about the times when she got worse.

Pity takes distance and a certainty of surviving. It was only after our house was bought for demolition by the church next door, and after my sister had performed the miracle of persuading my father to give me a carefree time before college by taking my mother with him to California for a year, that I could afford to think about the sadness of her life. Suddenly, I was far away in Washington, living with my sister and sharing a house with several of her friends. While I finished high school and discovered to my surprise that my classmates felt sorry for me because my mother *wasn't* there, I also realized that my sister, at least in her early childhood, had known a very different person who lived inside our mother, an earlier Ruth.

She was a woman I met for the first time in a mental hospital near Baltimore, a humane place with gardens and trees where I visited her each weekend of the summer after my first year away in college. Fortunately, my sister hadn't been able to work and be our mother's caretaker, too. After my father's year was up, my sister had carefully researched hospitals and found the courage to break the family chain.

At first, this Ruth was the same abstracted, frightened woman I had lived with all those years; though now all the sadder for being approached through long hospital corridors and many locked doors. But gradually she began to talk about her past life, memories that doctors there must have been awakening. I began to meet a Ruth I had never known.

. . . A tall, spirited, auburn-haired high-school girl who loved basketball and reading; who tried to drive her uncle's Stanley Steamer when it was the first car in the neighborhood; who had a gift for gardening and who sometimes, in defiance of convention, wore her father's overalls; a girl with the courage to go to dances even though her church told her that music itself was sinful, and whose sense of adventure almost made up for feeling gawky and unpretty next to her daintier, dark-haired sister.

. . . A very little girl, just learning to walk, discovering the body places where touching was pleasurable, and being punished by her mother who slapped her hard across the kitchen floor.

. . . A daughter of a handsome railroad-engineer and a schoolteacher who felt she had married "beneath her"; the mother who took her two daughters on Christmas trips to faraway New York on an engineer's free railroad pass and showed them the restaurants and theaters they should aspire to — even though they could only stand outside them in the snow.

. . . A good student at Oberlin College, whose freethinking traditions she loved, where friends nicknamed her "Billy"; a student with a talent for both mathematics and poetry, who was not above putting an invisible film of Karo syrup on all the john seats in her dormitory the night of a big prom; a daughter who had to return to Toledo, live with her family, and go to a local university when her ambitious mother — who had scrimped and saved, ghostwritten a minister's sermons, and made her daughters' clothes in order to get them to college at all — ran out of money. At home, this Ruth became a part-time bookkeeper in a lingerie shop for the very rich, commuting to classes and listening to her mother's harsh lectures on the security of becoming a teacher; but also a young woman who was still rebellious enough to fall in love with my father, the editor of her university newspaper, a funny and charming young man who was a terrible student, had no intention of graduating, put on all the campus dances, and was unacceptably Jewish.

I knew from family lore that my mother had married my father twice: once secretly, after he invited her to become the literary editor of his campus newspaper, and once a year later in a public ceremony, which some members of both families refused to attend as the "mixed marriage" of its day.

And I knew that my mother had gone on to earn a teaching certificate. She had used it to scare away truant officers during the winters when, after my father closed the summer resort for the season, we lived in a house trailer and worked our way to Florida or California and back by buying and selling antiques.

But only during those increasingly adventurous weekend outings from the hospital — going shopping, to lunch, to the movies — did I realize that she had taught college calculus for a year in deference to her mother's insistence that she have teaching "to fall back on." And only then did I realize she had fallen in love with newspapers along with my father. After graduating from the university paper, she wrote a gossip column for a local tabloid, under the name "Duncan MacKenzie," since women weren't supposed to do such things, and soon had earned a job as society reporter on one of Toledo's two big dailies. By the time my sister was four or so, she had worked her way up to the coveted position of Sunday editor.

It was a strange experience to look into those brown eyes I had seen so often and realize suddenly how much they were like my own. For the first time, I realized that she might really be my mother.

I began to think about the many pressures that might have led up to that first nervous breakdown: leaving my sister whom she loved very much with a grandmother whose values my mother didn't share; trying to hold on to a job she loved but was being asked to leave by her husband; wanting very much to go with a woman friend to pursue their own dreams in New York; falling in love with a co-worker at the newspaper who frightened her by being more sexually attractive, more supportive of her work than my father, and perhaps the man she should have married; and finally, nearly bleeding to death with a miscarriage because her own mother had little faith in doctors and refused to get help.

Did those months in the sanatorium brainwash her in some Freudian or very traditional way into making what were, for her, probably the wrong choices? I don't know. It almost doesn't matter. Without extraordinary support to the contrary, she was already convinced that divorce was unthinkable. A husband could not be left for another man, and certainly not for a reason as selfish as a career. A daughter could not be deprived of her father and certainly not be uprooted and taken off to an uncertain future in New York. A bride was supposed to be virginal (not "shopworn," as my euphemistic mother would have said), and if your husband turned out to be kind, but innocent of the possibility of a woman's pleasure, then just be thankful for kindness.

Of course, other women have torn themselves away from work and love and still survived. But a story my mother told me years later has always symbolized for me the formidable forces arrayed against her.

"It was early spring, nothing was open yet. There was nobody for miles around. We had stayed at the lake that winter, so I was alone a lot while your father took the car and traveled around on business. You were a baby. Your sister was in school, and there was no phone. The last straw was that the radio broke. Suddenly it seemed like forever since I'd been able to talk with anyone — or even hear the sound of another voice.

"I bundled you up, took the dog, and walked out to the Brooklyn road. I thought I'd walk the four or five miles to the grocery store, talk to some people, and find somebody to drive me back. I was walking along with Fritzie running up ahead in the empty road — when suddenly a car came out of nowhere and down the hill. It hit Fritzie head on and threw him over to the side of the road. I yelled and screamed at the driver, but he never slowed down. He never looked at us. He never even turned his head.

"Poor Fritzie was all broken and bleeding, but he was still alive. I carried him and sat down in the middle of the road, with his head cradled in my arms. I was going to *make* the next car stop and help.

"But no car ever came. I sat there for hours, I don't know how long, with you in my lap and holding Fritzie, who was whimpering and looking up at me for help. It was dark by the time he finally died. I pulled him over to the side of the road and walked back home with you and washed the blood out of my clothes.

"I don't know what it was about that one day — it was like a breaking point. When your father came home, I said: 'From now on, I'm going with you. I won't bother you. I'll just sit in the car. But I can't bear to be alone again.'"

I think she told me that story to show she had tried to save herself, or perhaps she wanted to exorcise a painful memory by saying it out loud. But hearing it made me understand what could have turned her into the woman I remember: a solitary figure sitting in the car, perspiring through the summer, bundled up in winter, waiting for my father to come out of this or that antique shop, grateful just not to be alone. I was there, too, because I was too young to be left at home, and I loved helping my father wrap and unwrap the newspaper around the china and small objects he had bought at auctions and was selling to dealers. It made me feel necessary and grown-up. But sometimes it was hours before we came back to the car again and to my mother who was always patiently, silently waiting.

At the hospital and later when Ruth told me stories of her past, I used to say, "But why didn't you leave? Why didn't you take the job? Why didn't you marry the other man?" She would always insist it didn't matter, she was lucky to have my sister and me. If I pressed hard enough, she would add, "If I'd left you never would have been born."

I always thought but never had the courage to say: *But you might have been born instead.*

Richard Rodriguez

*Richard Rodriguez (b. 1944) grew up in Sacramento, California, the same
city Lincoln Steffens had explored as a boy on horseback three-quarters of a
century before. "I was a bilingual child," he recalls,*

> *a certain kind — socially disadvantaged — the son of working-class par-
> ents, both Mexican immigrants. In the early years of my boyhood, my
> parents coped very well with America. My father had steady work. My
> mother managed at home. They were nobody's victims. Optimism and
> ambition led them to a house (our home) many blocks from the Mexican
> south side of town. We lived among the gringos and only a block from
> the biggest, whitest houses. It never occurred to my parents that they
> couldn't live wherever they chose. Nor was the Sacramento of the fifties
> bent on teaching them a contrary lesson.*

> *Relatives were the only guests at their house.*

> *For one day, enormous families of relatives would visit and there would
> be so many people that the noise and the bodies would spill out to the
> backyard and front porch. Then, for weeks, no one came by. (It was
> usually a salesman who rang the doorbell.) Our house stood apart. A
> gaudy yellow in a row of white bungalows. We were the people with the
> noisy dog. The people who raised pigeons and chickens.*

*Richard Rodriguez later studied at Stanford and Columbia universities and
did graduate work in English literature in London and Berkeley.*

From "Complexion," *Hunger of Memory*

WHEN I WAS A BOY the white summer sun of Sacramento would
darken me so, my T-shirt would seem bleached against my slender
dark arms. My mother would see me come up the front steps. She'd

wait for the screen door to slam at my back. "You look like a *negrito*," she'd say, angry, sorry to be angry, frustrated almost to laughing, scorn. "You know how important looks are in this country. With *los gringos* looks are all that they judge on. But you! Look at you! You're so careless!" Then she'd start in all over again. "You won't be satisfied till you end up looking like *los pobres* who work in the fields, *los braceros*." (*Los braceros*: Those men who work with their *brazos*, their arms; Mexican nationals who were licensed to work for American farmers in the 1950s. They worked very hard for very little money, my father would tell me. And what money they earned they sent back to Mexico to support their families, my mother would add. *Los pobres* — the poor, the pitiful, the powerless ones. But paradoxically also powerful men. They were the men with brown-muscled arms I stared at in awe on Saturday mornings when they showed up downtown like gypsies to shop at Woolworth's or Penney's. On Monday nights they would gather hours early on the steps of the Memorial Auditorium for the wrestling matches. Passing by on my bicycle in summer, I would spy them there, clustered in small groups, talking — frightening and fascinating men — some wearing Texas *sombreros* and T-shirts which shone fluorescent in the twilight. I would sit forward in the back seat of our family's '48 Chevy to see them, working alongside Valley highways: dark men on an even horizon, loading a truck amid rows of straight green. Powerful, powerless men. Their fascinating darkness — like mine — to be feared.)
"You'll end up looking just like them."

Regarding my family, I see faces that do not closely resemble my own. Like some other Mexican families, my family suggests Mexico's confused colonial past. Gathered around a table, we appear to be from separate continents. My father's face recalls faces I have seen in France. His complexion is white — he does not tan; he does not burn. Over the years, his dark wavy hair has grayed handsomely. But with time his face has sagged to a perpetual sigh. My mother, whose surname is inexplicably Irish — Moran — has an olive complexion. People have frequently wondered if, perhaps, she is Italian or Portuguese. And, in fact, she looks as though she could be from southern Europe. My mother's face has not aged as quickly as the rest of her body; it remains smooth and glowing — a cool tan — which her gray hair cleanly accentuates. My older brother has inherited her good looks. When he was a boy people would tell him that he looked like Mario

Lanza, and hearing it he would smile with dimpled assurance. He would come home from high school with girl friends who seemed to me glamorous (because they were) blonds. And during those years I envied him his skin that burned red and peeled like the skin of the *gringos*. His complexion never darkened like mine. My youngest sister is exotically pale, almost ashen. She is delicately featured, Near Eastern, people have said. Only my older sister has a complexion as dark as mine, though her facial features are much less harshly defined than my own. To many people meeting her, she seems (they say) Polynesian. I am the only one in the family whose face is severely cut to the line of ancient Indian ancestors. My face is mournfully long, in the classical Indian manner; my profile suggests one of those beak-nosed Mayan sculptures — the eaglelike face upturned, open-mouthed, against the deserted, primitive sky.

"We are Mexicans," my mother and father would say, and taught their four children to say whenever we (often) were asked about our ancestry. My mother and father scorned those "white" Mexican-Americans who tried to pass themselves off as Spanish. My parents would never have thought of denying their ancestry. I never denied it: My ancestry is Mexican, I told strangers mechanically. But I never forgot that only my older sister's complexion was as dark as mine.

My older sister never spoke to me about her complexion when she was a girl. But I guessed that she found her dark skin a burden. I knew that she suffered for being a "nigger." As she came home from grammar school, little boys came up behind her and pushed her down to the sidewalk. In high school, she struggled in the adolescent competition for boyfriends in a world of football games and proms, a world where her looks were plainly uncommon. In college, she was afraid and scornful when dark-skinned foreign students from countries like Turkey and India found her attractive. She revealed her fear of dark skin to me only in adulthood when, regarding her own three children, she quietly admitted relief that they were all light.

That is the kind of remark women in my family have often made before. As a boy, I'd stay in the kitchen (never seeming to attract any notice), listening while my aunts spoke of their pleasure at having light children. (The men, some of whom were dark-skinned from years of working out of doors, would be in another part of the house.) It was the woman's spoken concern: the fear of having a dark-skinned son or daughter. Remedies were exchanged. One aunt prescribed to her sisters the elixir of large doses of castor oil during the last weeks of pregnancy. (The remedy risked an abortion.) Children born dark grew up to have their faces treated regularly with a mixture of egg white and lemon juice concentrate. (In my case, the solution never would take.) One Mexican-American friend of my mother's, who regarded it as a special blessing that she had a measure of English blood, spoke disparagingly of her husband, a construction worker, for being so dark. "He doesn't take care of himself," she complained. But the remark, I noticed, annoyed my mother, who sat tracing an invisible design with her finger on the tablecloth.

There was affection too and a kind of humor about these matters. With daring tenderness, one of my uncles would refer to his wife as *mi negra*. An aunt regularly called her dark child *mi feito* (my little ugly one), her smile only partially hidden as she bent down to dig her mouth under his ticklish chin. And at times relatives spoke scornfully of pale, white skin. A *gringo*'s skin resembled *masa* — baker's dough — someone remarked. Everyone laughed. Voices chuckled over the fact that the *gringos* spent so many hours in summer sunning themselves. ("They need to get sun because they look like *los muertos*.")

I heard the laughing but remembered what the women had said, with unsmiling voices, concerning dark skin. Nothing I heard outside the house, regarding my skin, was so impressive to me.

In public I occasionally heard racial slurs. Complete strangers would yell out at me. A teenager drove past, shouting, "Hey, Greaser! Hey, Pancho!" Over his shoulder I saw the giggling face of his girl friend. A boy pedaled by and announced matter-of-factly, "I pee on dirty Mexicans." Such remarks would be said so casually that I wouldn't quickly realize that they were being addressed to me. When I did, I would be paralyzed with embarrassment, unable to return the insult. (Those times I happened to be with white grammar school friends, *they* shouted back. Imbued with the mysterious kindness of children, my friends would never ask later why I hadn't yelled out in my own defense.)

In all, there could not have been more than a dozen incidents of name-calling. That there were so few suggests that I was not a primary victim of racial abuse. But that, even today, I can clearly remember particular incidents is proof of their impact. Because of such incidents, I listened when my parents remarked that Mexicans were often mistreated in California border towns. And in Texas. I listened carefully when I heard that two of my cousins had been refused admittance to an "all-white" swimming pool. And that an uncle had been told by some man to go back to Africa. I followed the progress of the southern black civil rights movement, which was gaining prominent notice in Sacramento's afternoon newspaper. But what most intrigued me was the connection between dark skin and poverty. Because I heard my mother speak so often about the relegation of dark people to menial labor, I considered the great victims of racism to be those who were poor and forced to do menial work. People like the farmworkers whose skin was dark from the sun.

After meeting a black grammar school friend of my sister's, I remember thinking that she wasn't really "black." What interested me was the fact that she wasn't poor. (Her well-dressed parents would come by after work to pick her up in a shiny green Oldsmobile.) By contrast, the garbage men who appeared every Friday morning seemed to me unmistakably black. (I didn't bother to ask my parents why Sacramento garbage men always were black. I thought I knew.) One morning I was in the backyard when a man opened the gate. He was an ugly, square-faced black man with popping red eyes, a pail slung over his shoulder. As he approached, I stood up. And in a voice that seemed to me very weak, I piped, "Hi." But the man paid me no heed. He strode past to the can by the garage. In a single broad movement, he overturned its contents into his larger pail. Our can came crashing down as he turned and left me watching, in awe.

"*Pobres negros,*" my mother remarked when she'd notice a headline in the paper about a civil rights demonstration in the South. "How the *gringos* mistreat them." In the same tone of voice she'd tell me about the mistreatment her brother endured years before. (After my grandfather's death, my grandmother had come to America with her son and five daughters.) "My sisters, we were still all just teenagers. And since *mi pápa* was dead, my brother had to be the head of the family. He had to support us, to find work. But what skills did he have! Twenty years old. *Pobre.* He was tall, like your grandfather. And strong. He did construction work. 'Construction!' The *gringos* kept him digging all day, doing the dirtiest jobs. And they would pay him next to nothing. Sometimes they promised him one salary and paid him less when he finished. But what could he do? Report them? We weren't citizens then. He didn't even know English. And he was dark. What chances could he have? As soon as we sisters got older, he went right back to Mexico. He hated this country. He looked so tired when he left. Already with a hunchback. Still in his twenties. But old-looking. No life for him here. *Pobre.*" . . .

Complexion. My first conscious experience of sexual excitement concerns my complexion. One summer weekend, when I was around seven years old, I was at a public swimming pool with the whole family. I remember sitting on the damp pavement next to the pool and seeing my mother, in the spectators' bleachers, holding my younger sister on her lap. My mother, I noticed, was watching my father as he stood on a diving board, waving to her. I watched her wave back. Then I saw her radiant, bashful, astonishing smile. In that second I sensed that my mother and father had a relationship I knew nothing about. A nervous excitement encircled my stomach as I saw my mother's eyes follow my father's figure curving into the water. A second or two later, he emerged. I heard him call out. Smiling, his voice sounded, buoyant, calling me to swim to him. But turning to see him, I caught my mother's eye. I heard her shout over to me. In Spanish she called through the crowd: "Put a towel on over your shoulders." In public, she didn't want to say why. I knew.

That incident anticipates the shame and sexual inferiority I was to feel in later years because of my dark complexion. I was to grow up an ugly child. Or one who thought himself ugly. (*Feo.*) One night when I was eleven or twelve years old, I locked myself in the bathroom and carefully regarded my reflection in the mirror over the sink. Without any pleasure I studied my skin. I turned on the faucet. (In my mind I heard the swirling voices of aunts, and even my mother's voice, whispering incessantly about lemon juice solutions and dark, *feo* children.) With a bar of soap, I fashioned a thick ball of lather. I began soaping my arms. I took my father's straight razor out of the medicine cabinet. Slowly, with steady deliberateness, I put the blade against my flesh, pressed it as close as I could without cutting, and moved it up and down across my skin to see if I could get out, somehow lessen, the dark. All I succeeded in doing, however, was in shaving my arms bare of their hair. For as I noted with disappointment, the dark would not come out. It remained. Trapped. Deep in the cells of my skin.

Throughout adolescence, I felt myself mysteriously marked. Nothing else about my appearance would concern me so much as the fact that my complexion was dark. My mother would say how sorry she was that there was not money enough to get braces to straighten my teeth. But I never bothered about my teeth. In three-way mirrors at department stores, I'd see my profile dramatically defined by a long nose, but it was really only the color of my skin that caught my attention.

I wasn't afraid that I would become a menial laborer because of my skin. Nor did my complexion make me feel especially vulnerable to racial abuse. (I didn't really consider my dark skin to be a racial characteristic. I would have been only too happy to look as Mexican as my light-skinned older brother.) Simply, I judged myself ugly. And, since the women in my family had been the ones who discussed it in such worried tones, I felt my dark skin made me unattractive to women.

Thirteen years old. Fourteen. In a grammar school art class, when the assignment was to draw a self-portrait, I tried and I tried but could not bring myself to shade in the face on the paper to anything like my actual tone. With disgust then I would come face to face with myself in mirrors. With disappointment I located myself in class photographs — my dark face undefined by the camera which had clearly described the white faces of classmates. Or I'd see my dark wrist against my long-sleeved white shirt.

I grew divorced from my body. Insecure, overweight, listless. On hot summer days when my rubber-soled shoes soaked up the heat from the sidewalk, I kept my head down. Or walked in the shade. My mother didn't need anymore to tell me to watch out for the sun. I denied myself a sensational life. The normal, extraordinary, animal excitement of feeling my body alive — riding shirtless on a bicycle in the warm wind created by furious self-propelled motion — the sensations that first had excited in me a sense of my maleness, I denied. I was too ashamed of my body. I wanted to forget that I had a body because I had a brown body. I was grateful that none of my classmates ever mentioned the fact.

I continued to see the *braceros*, those men I resembled in one way and, in another way, didn't resemble at all. On the watery horizon of a Valley afternoon, I'd see them. And though I feared looking like them, it was with silent envy that I regarded them still. I envied them their physical lives, their freedom to violate the taboo of the sun. Closer to home I would notice the shirtless construction workers, the roofers, the sweating men tarring the street in front of the house. And I'd see the Mexican gardeners. I was unwilling to admit the attraction of their lives. I tried to deny it by looking away. But what was denied became strongly desired.

In high school physical education classes, I withdrew, in the regular company of five or six classmates, to a distant corner of a football field where we smoked and talked. Our company was composed of bodies too short or too tall, all graceless and all — except mine — pale. Our conversation was usually witty. (In fact we were intelligent.) If we referred to the athletic contests around us, it was with sarcasm. With savage scorn I'd refer to "animals" playing football or baseball. It would have been important for me to have joined them. Or for me to have taken off my shirt, to have let the sun burn dark on my skin, and to have run barefoot on the warm wet grass. It would have been very important. Too important. It would have been too telling a gesture — to admit the desire for sensation, the body, my body.

Fifteen, sixteen. I was a teenager shy in the presence of girls. Never dated. Barely could talk to a girl without stammering. In high school I went to several dances, but I never managed to ask a girl to dance. So I stopped going. I cannot remember high school years now with the parade of typical images: bright drive-ins or gliding blue shadows of a Junior Prom. At home most weekend nights, I would pass evenings reading. Like those hidden, precocious adolescents who have no real-life sexual experiences, I read a great deal of romantic fiction. "You won't find it in your books," my brother would playfully taunt me as he prepared to go to a party by freezing the crest of the wave in his hair with sticky pomade. Through my reading, however, I developed a fabulous and sophisticated sexual imagination. At seventeen, I may not have known how to engage a girl in small talk, but I had read *Lady Chatterley's Lover.*

It annoyed me to hear my father's teasing: that I would never know what "real work" is; that my hands were so soft. I think I knew it was his way of admitting pleasure and pride in my academic success. But I didn't smile. My mother said she was glad her children were getting their educations and would not be pushed around like *los pobres.* I heard the remark ironically as a reminder of my separation from *los braceros.* At such times I suspected that education was making me effeminate. The odd thing, however, was that I did not judge my classmates so harshly. Nor did I consider my male teachers in high school effeminate. It was only myself I judged against some shadowy, mythical Mexican laborer — dark like me, yet very different.

Language was crucial. I knew that I had violated the ideal of the *macho* by becoming such a dedicated student of language and literature. *Machismo* was a word never exactly defined by the persons who used it. (It was best described in the "proper" behavior of men.) Women at home, nevertheless, would repeat the old Mexican dictum that a man should be *feo, fuerte, y formal.* "The three *F*'s," my mother called them, smiling slyly. *Feo* I took to mean not literally ugly so much as ruggedly handsome. (When my mother and her sisters spent a loud, laughing afternoon determining ideal male good looks, they finally settled on the actor Gilbert Roland, who was neither too pretty nor ugly but had looks "like a man.") *Fuerte*, "strong," seemed to mean not physical strength as much as inner strength, character. A dependable man is *fuerte. Fuerte* for that reason was a characteristic subsumed by the last of the three qualities, and the one I most often considered — *formal.* To be *formal* is to be steady. A man of responsibility, a good provider. Someone *formal* is also constant. A person to be relied upon in adversity. A sober man, a man of high seriousness.

I learned a great deal about being *formal* just by listening to the way my father and other male relatives of his generation spoke. A man was not silent necessarily. Nor was he limited in the tones he could sound. For example, he could tell a long, involved, humorous story and laugh at his own humor with high-pitched giggling. But a man was not talkative the way a woman could be. It was permitted a woman to be gossipy and chatty. (When one heard many voices in a room, it was usually women who were talking.) Men spoke much less rapidly. And often men spoke in monologues. (When one voice sounded in a crowded room, it was most often a man's voice one heard.) More important than any of this was the fact that a man never verbally revealed his emotions. Men did not speak about their unease in moments of crisis or danger. It was the woman who worried aloud when her husband got laid off from work. At times of illness or death in the family, a man was usually quiet, even silent. Women spoke up to voice prayers. In distress, women always sounded quick ejaculations to God or the Virgin; women prayed in clearly audible voices at a wake held in a funeral parlor. And on the subject of love, a woman was verbally expansive. She spoke of her yearning and delight. A married man, if he spoke publicly about love, usually did so with playful, mischievous irony. Younger, unmarried men more often were quiet. (The *macho* is a silent suitor. *Formal.*)

At home I was quiet, so perhaps I seemed *formal* to my relations and other Spanish-speaking visitors to the house. But outside the house — my God! — I talked. Particularly in class or alone with my teachers, I chattered. (Talking seemed to make teachers think I was bright.) I often was proud of my way with words. Though, on other occasions, for example, when I would hear my mother busily speaking to women, it would occur to me that my attachment to words made me like her. Her son. Not *formal* like my father. At such times I even suspected that my nostalgia for sounds — the noisy, intimate Spanish sounds of my past — was nothing more than effeminate yearning.

High school English teachers encouraged me to describe very personal feelings in words. Poems and short stories I wrote, expressing sorrow and loneliness, were awarded high grades. In my bedroom were books by poets and novelists — books that I loved — in which male writers published feelings the men in my family never revealed or acknowledged in words. And it seemed to me that there was something unmanly about my attachment to literature. Even today, when so much about the myth of the *macho* no longer concerns me, I cannot altogether evade such notions. Writing these pages, admitting my embarrassment or my guilt, admitting my sexual anxieties and my physical insecurity, I have not been able to forget that I am not being *formal.*

So be it.

Joe Brainard

Joe Brainard (b. 1942) is a painter who grew up in Tulsa, Oklahoma, moved to New York City in the early 1960s, and has made something of a career out of remembering. He has published at least four "I Remember" books, all of which follow the same format: a litany of paragraph after paragraph of short memoirs, each beginning with the phrase "I remember . . ." and covering subjects that range from Christmas pageants in Tulsa to gay bars in New York. But Brainard is at his best when he focuses, as he does in this selection, on those compulsively important but trivial details of high-school life in the late 1950s.

Another of his books includes an essay entitled "People," which reads, in its entirety: "If I'm as normal as I think I am, we're all a bunch of weirdos."

From *I Remember*

I REMEMBER "Spam."

I remember when I was very young thinking that shaving looked pretty dangerous.

I remember rubber thongs and how they started out being 99¢ a pair and how they ended up being incredibly cheap (like 19¢ a pair) and the sound they made flopping against bare soles.

I remember chicken fried steak.

I remember "Kraft's" sandwich spread.

I remember not trusting pressure cookers.

I remember a blue glass mirror store front in Tulsa with one piece missing.

I remember "Sloppy Joes."

I remember shoulder pads. Cinnamon toothpicks. And "John Doe."

I remember little electric fans that could "cut your fingers right off" if you got too close.

I remember little boxes of cereal that opened up in back so you could eat it right out of the box. I remember that sometimes they leaked.

I remember cedar chests. (And the smell of)

I remember "blond oak."

I remember when the bigger the cuffs on blue jeans were the better.

I remember "5-Day Deodorant Pads."

I remember "The Arthur Murray Party."

I remember pony tail clips.

I remember "Chef Boy-ar-dee Spaghetti."

I remember baby shoes hanging from car rear-view mirrors.

I remember bronzed baby shoes. Shriner hats. And the Campbell Soup kids.

I remember cold cream on my mother's face.

I remember two-piece bathing suits. Alphabet soup. Ozzie and Harriet. And pictures of kidney-shaped swimming pools.

I remember a photograph in "Life" magazine of a woman jumping off a building.

I remember not understanding how the photographer could have just stood there and taken that picture.

I remember not understanding how very ugly or deformed people could stand it.

I remember a girl in junior high school who had a very thin black mustache.

I remember not understanding why women in dresses didn't freeze their legs off in the winter time.

I remember a girl who had dead corsages all around her circular dressing table mirror.

I remember a brief period in high school when it was popular to spray a silver streak in your hair.

I remember that I was a year ahead of everyone in high school by wearing sneakers but I missed the point a bit because I always kept mine spotlessly clean.

I remember seeing a 3-D movie once and wearing red and green cellophane glasses. And 3-D comic books too.

I remember a series of Cadillac ads with beautiful diamond and ruby and emerald necklaces, according to the color of the car in the ad.

I remember the little monkey so small he would fit in the palm of your hand that you had to sell so much of something for in order to get free. (Seeds or magazines or something like that)

I remember in many comic books a full page ad packed solid with rings. I remember especially one skull ring I always wanted.

I remember a red liquid medicine for cuts in a little brown bottle that "won't sting" but it always did.

I remember stories about babies being born in taxi cabs.

I remember when Arthur Godfrey caused a big scandal by driving his airplane drunk and having a crash and killing someone, or something like that.

I remember the little appliqued diver on all Jantzen swim suits.

I remember filling the ice trays too full and trying to get them back to the refrigerator without spilling any.

I remember not finding "The Little King" very funny.

I remember a piece of old wood with termites running around all over it the termite men found under our front porch.

I remember when one year in Tulsa by some freak of nature we were invaded by millions of grasshoppers for about three or four days. I remember, downtown, whole sidewalk areas of solid grasshoppers.

I remember a shoe store with a big brown x-ray machine that showed up the bones in your feet bright green.

I remember the "Goodyear" tire foot with wings. And the flying red horse.

I remember that watermelon is 99% water.

I remember posture pictures being taken at school and being told that I had *really* bad posture. And that was that.

I remember fire insurance ads of homeless families all wrapped up in blankets.

I remember little black and white Scottie dogs (plastic) each with a magnet on the bottom. I can't remember exactly what they "did" tho.

I remember prophylactic machines in gas station bathrooms.

I remember that a used prophylactic was found one morning by the principal laying in the outstretched hand of "The Great Spirit": a big bronze sculpture of an Indian on a horse looking up at the sky. That was in high school. Or maybe it was a used kotex.

I remember talk about one drug store that was easy to get them at.

I remember a short dumpy girl with long hair and pierced ears and giant tits that was supposed to be an easy lay.

I remember every other Saturday having to get a haircut. And how the barber was always clicking his scissors even when he wasn't cutting anything.

I remember a long brown leather strap. Beat-up magazines. And kids who cried. (And then got suckers)

I remember the bright red hair tonic that looked more like something to drink, and a white strip of tissue paper being wrapped tightly around my neck.

I remember watching my hair fall and accumulate.

I remember being afraid that the barber might slip and cut my ear.

I remember that once he did.

I remember at the end of a haircut getting my neck dusted off with a soft brush full of nice smelling powder. And getting swirled around to look in the mirror and how big, afterwards, my ears were.

I remember the *very* ornate chrome foot rest. And the old Negro shoeshine man.

I remember having an itchy back all the way home.

I remember a tower on top of a building in Tulsa that changed colors every five minutes. But only green and yellow and white.

I remember miniature hats in miniature hat boxes in a men's hat store window. You got one free when you bought someone a gift certificate for a hat.

I remember balloon sleeves. And no sleeves.

I remember "bouffants" and "beehives." (Hairdos)

I remember when "beehives" really got out of hand.

I remember school desk carvings and running my ball point pen back and forth in them.

I remember noisy candy wrappers when you don't want to make any noise.

I remember when those short sleeved knitted shirts with long tails (to wear "out") with little embroidered alligators on the pockets were popular.

I remember plain camel hair coats that rich girls in high school wore.

I remember "socialite corner" (2nd floor) where only kids who belonged to social clubs met and chatted before school and in between classes.

I remember that to be in a social club you either had to live on the South side of town (I lived on the North) or else you had to be good looking (I wasn't) and usually both.

I remember that popular boys always had their blue jeans worn down just the right amount.

I remember madras plaid shirts and sports coats and how they had to be washed a few times before they had the right look.

I remember "French kissing" and figuring out that it must have something to do with the tongue since there isn't anything else in the mouth except teeth.

I remember that shaking or holding hands with a girl while you scratched her palm with your middle finger was somehow "dirty." (Often done as a joke and the girl would turn red and scream)

Frank Chin

Frank Chin, a playwright, calls himself a Chinaman — not a Chinese-American, a term he considers assimilationist and effete. A Chinese-American, Chin believes, is what other Americans want him to be. A Chinaman is his own man.

He also claims that he does not write "autobiography or autobiographically." The autobiography, he says, "is a literary form peculiar to civilizations founded on religion, developed from religious confession. Confusian civilization is founded on history, not religion. My 'Confessions of the Chinatown Cowboy' is an allusion to the fact that autobiography was introduced into Asia by Christian missionaries as a tool of conversion, behavior modification and the extinguishing of history."

The grandson of a steward on the Southern Pacific Railroad, Chin was born in Berkeley, California, in 1940 and was raised during the World War II years in the Mother Lode country of the Sierra Nevada. After the war he lived in Chinatowns in Oakland, where his parents worked, and San Francisco, and started affecting a black cowboy outfit that made him look, he recalls, like "a Chinaman dressed for a barn dance." Later came some time at the University of Iowa and the University of California, and a job on the Southern Pacific, where he became the first brakeman of Chinese extraction, wearing the old gold watch the railroad had given his grandfather for good and faithful service.

His plays include The Year of the Dragon *and* The Chickencoop Chinaman.

The following excerpts are from an essay on Chinese stereotypes.

From "Confessions of the Chinatown Cowboy"

IN THE CODE OF CHINATOWN, only fools and finks took English language, or Chinese language or words, written words, spoken words seriously as language. Language as it was known in the world was emasculating, sissy stuff . . . that's how we compensated for the humiliation of all the time being heard talking in language lessons by Chinese folks and American people who never heard any sense from us when we opened up. Instead of real talk, we memorized phrases that worked, kept a stock of cliches we could string up in combos for any occasion and say nothing at all, no more. Polite, short, and out. Out without being corrected, a "I'm fine thank you," and swoop free . . . we'd pulled one on the *fan gwai* whiteman. There were two kinds of talkers among us, two kinds of clowns, for only clowns talked. Talking made you a clown. On the street, if you kept your hands loose, not so down at tight as to look a chicken, but loose enough not to be mistaken for action, and kept everybody laughing, you wouldn't get beat up. "I'm going to beat the shit out of you," a big guy with a gang says, "Well, you better hurry up, man, cuz I gotta get to Chinese school," you say, making it a joke, making them busy with some fun. That was practical language skills of the here and now school. There was something of a man in that clown act, but not the one where you talk college white. That college white in your mouth was the sound of shame on us, the sound of teachers calling us stupid, and you talking like a teacher grading papers meant you were too good for Chinatown and Chinamen. It meant if you were thinking of graduating the town for whiteness, you'd better. Hungry, all the time hungry, every sense was out whiffing for something rightly ours, chameleons looking for color, trying on tongues and clothes and hairdos, taking everyone else's, with none of our own, and no habitat, our manhood just never came home. Everything was copycat. Hunger and copycat. We had a lot of stutterers, thumbsuckers. The sound of whiteness inevitably crept into our tongue, became the sound of good grades and making good, and Chinatown didn't want us anymore. The language I wrote, that Thom Gunn, the first real poet I ever met, and writer Philip Roth told me wasn't English, making me go "huh?" the sounds out of my mouth a black migrant worker giving me a lift in Florida told me was "pretty good language for a Chinese person," is just good enough to turn off many in Chinatown. What they hear in the way I talk is a message white schools put in the sound, a message I don't mean . . .

that I've turned my back on Chinatown and become white, worse than white. To become white, you shit in your blood, hate yourself and all your kind. For *juk sing* to become "Chinese" (Pass for *juk hok*) means the same thing, a treatment, a session between electrodes, called an education. . . .

Every stereotype is based on a grain of truth I'm told by friends not really telling me that sissiness is a Chinese cultural trait that has somehow survived six generations of Chinese-America, but honestly suggesting that my "heritage" is responsible for the notable lack of Chinese-American presence in American culture. We have a fine popular reputation, but no popularly known works or political, literary, or artistic spokesmen. What we are really as Chinese-Americans is explained in terms of what was done to us here, what we were made to be, in the same way that the passive, subtly anti-American character of American prisoners of war home from the Korean conflict is explained in terms of what was done to them, what three years of controlled environment made them be. We haven't been here undergoing brainwashing for a mere three years but six generations.

In the late 19th Century, after the railroads had made San Francisco an elephants' graveyard for Chinaman, Christian missionaries and a California State law outlawing Chinese from all schools but "Chinese schools" confirmed our worst fears and contrived to help us out of America by creating the "Chinese schools" of Chinatown . . . the same schools Chinatown parents against busing look to for the preservation of what they've come to believe to be "Chinese culture." White missionaries and the Chinese Benevolent Association still run most of these schools in San Francisco and Chinatowns all over the country and Canada. Some of us are convinced the schools and the concept of being Chinese-American taught in these schools are ours. And the whites love us for it. Luckily . . . I think, luckily . . . for me different lessons were taught at my Chinese school.

From five to seven at night, after "American" school, I went to Wah Kue Chinese School, under Chinese Nationalist Party headquarters in Oakland. My mother had gone to this Chinese school, and my aunts and uncles. The wood of this old building smelled of them. The building smelled old of a lot of people . . . and we smelled too, of hot feet in hightopped rubber soled black and white basketball shoes and the sweat of the quick two hours on the court, between schools. One day the teacher who lived upstairs behind Party headquarters was late. We didn't hear his step working down the old stairs. But people were walking up there. Then they came down. Two men. One, a real smiler, standing on the teacher's platform told us Mr. Wong was dead. The girls sighed and the boys . . . for us it was good news. The old man used to beat us. He had a ruler with the measures marked off with brass tacks. One end of the ruler had the Chinese word for "big" carved in it. I used to think he hit us with that thing because we were born here. I still have a scar. The other man was our new teacher, Mr. Mah, a skinny. He wore his blue suit the way lunch wears a papersack.

Mr. Mah taught math and engineering at a university, the name of which he wouldn't mention, during the day, then he would drive his white Chevy down to the town to teach us Chinese. One day he stomped in with a newspaper and shouted at us, in real Chinatown buck buck bagaw, an angry quick-tripping tongue promiscuously roaming all the languages we knew, raping them of sense. He said he'd been on the way to school when he saw a headline "JOE" and he said to himself, "Joe Stalin alive?" and stopped the car and bought the paper. "And you know what it said?" He opened up the paper and showed us, "Joe DiMaggio Marries Marilyn Monroe!" And he was off into how crappy American journalism was, who the Tribune's publisher, Senator William Knowland, was, the China lobby, Mme. Claire Chenault, pounding his way to sense the way we told big movies up in front of class, on rainy days when we couldn't go to the yard at recess or P.E. period. There we are, kids. I was ten, eleven, maybe twelve. And he's talking about Chinatown and Chou En-Lai, the Long March, and how the Chinese in America have done nothing but keep their place, preserving a Chinese culture white men invented for them to preserve. He named names, raged against the Chinese-Americans who were horrified at the sound of the words "Chinatown" and "Chinaman." "Who made Chinaman ashamed to be called Chinaman?" he asked. "Not the Chinamen who came over as Chinamen, who were called Chinamen all the time, answered to Chinamen, worked hard and died as Chinamen . . . not the Chinamen, but the whites, the 'Americans' the 'Chinese-Americans' work so hard to please." The Chinamen were our ancestors he said. The price we were paying for getting along here, for being accepted was our pride. "Give up your fathers, forget the Chinamen and talk about Chinese art!"

I used to keep him talking and screaming a show for us the whole two hours, to get out of doing my Chinese lessons. I'd go to the library and read books on China, go through the papers for stuff on Korea, the French in Indo-China, Joe McCarthy, what was being said about Chinatown, and next day, when we're opening up our books, casually ask, something like "Who was Joe Stilwell?"

Then I began to hear around the town that people thought he talked like a Commie. The kids told their parents and they talked, and I felt it was my fault. McCarthy was going then. Mr. Mah was dumping on McCarthy too and the whole Red Scare, while the Chinese Nationalists through the Chinese Benevolent Association were forming a new Chinatown organization, the Anti-Communist League, a group that, not surprisingly, loved Chiang and hated Mao. I'm ten. Commies are bad. And to get out of my lessons, and for fun, I've been making this man talk like a Commie.

He used to drive me home to the restaurant, and we'd talk in the car. I'd invite him to dinner in the kitchen, but he never came, even when I said he could eat in front, he never came. I told him I was sorry, that I didn't want to get him in trouble but there was talk about him being a Commie, and that's why kids were dropping out of the school. There was a new school down the street, a free one, but that wasn't why the kids were being pulled out in the middle of the semester. I told him I'd been making him jump and scream to get out of doing my Chinese lessons. He hissed, turned his head around this way and that, pounded the steering wheel. "I hate the Communists!" he said. He'd welcomed them at first, thought there would be more freedom under them, enough for him to start a school. He started a school and was kicked out of the country. But he was glad to see China in the hands of the Chinese for a change. Did I know they were producing steel? Yes, he'd told us. There was *that* pride, for he was still Chinese, and would always be, in the same way he hoped we would be "Chinamen."

He told me he'd started a school on Taiwan and the Nationalists kicked him out. "I'm not a Nationalist. I am not a Communist! I am a Chinese. I am a teacher," he said. He said he wanted us to know there was no shame in being born here, that it was all right not to be a Chinese from China, that it was all right not to be a white American. That "Chinamen," those yellow men that worked on the railroad, the people whites collapsed mines on, paved over and built towns on, called names on, made laws against, and made their children want to forget . . . they, the Chinamen, were good men. They'd fought. There'd been brave men who stood out among them. Their fights and their brave men had been forgotten in favor of remembering white champions standing up for Chinese (these champs had been bought, and trained by the Chinese Benevolent Association, hip to the fact whites didn't like Chinese to be so aggressive and obnoxious as to speak for themselves, but would listen to another white man) and perpetuating the myth of timid, meek, passive Chinamen. He said their children's children, if not their children, should be proud of them Chinamen. And I was one of the children's children. I didn't know what he was talking about. All I knew was that I'd done it again. I'd triggered nerves in this man and made him cry and angry.

The Joe McCarthy thing caught Mr. Mah when the university came out with loyalty oaths. I learned this later. Much later, looking for the man, years later. He wasn't an American citizen. He couldn't in good conscience sign an oath of loyalty to America . . .

The school closed with a party. There were now five students left. A slow change had been working in Mr. Mah the past few weeks. One day he asked us all what we wanted to be. I said "artist or writer." Bill wanted to write sports. Calvin, some kind of science. He told us all to go into engineering, and we knew something was wrong, for before he was saying we should grow up and make Chinese-America AP-PEAR! And becoming an engineer was to disappear. We all brought goodies to the party. Calvin's sister made a cake. She's married, a mother and a schoolteacher now. Calvin became an engineer, gave it up and is now an orthopedic surgeon. Bill Wong is a staff writer for the *Wall Street Journal*. We had a party eating off the ping pong tables, the five of us . . . the fifth changes sheets and sweeps rooms in a large motel near where the school used to be . . . and Mr. Mah. He gave things from the school. The school bell, ping pong sets, swords, Mr. Wong's studded ruler went and nobody seemed to want anything else. He asked me what I did when I was on my own, what I did for fun. I told him I went to the library, read books on China, newspapers, Edgar Allan Poe, Sherlock Holmes. He asked Calvin, my best friend, what he did for fun. Calvin said he listened to baseball on the radio. And the skinny Mr. Mah, rattling around in his blue suit, pointed at me, and told me to stop. "Stop!" he shouted, and hit the top of the table with his hand, "Stop reading! Go home and listen to baseball on the radio!"

McCarthy only helped. It was the five of us, like the characters in those old Chinese swordslingers we watched and mixed up with Westerns to make a Chinatown soul, we the master's loyal proteges of I SHOT JESSE JAMES, who brought down his school and him toppling.

We'd done what the Communists, the Nationalists, the Sino-Japanese War, WW2, The Revolution, Korea, the whole world and Joe McCarthy alone couldn't do. He, Mr. Mah, was the Invincible Enemy on Golden Mountain, and now he was bowed. We made him stop being obnoxious, set him on the path to a healthy attitude toward prejudice, an acceptance of the "Aramco" psychology, assimilation into America without violence. He was the best teacher we'd ever had, and the bravest. Now he was the most broken man we'd ever seen in our lives. He looked like everything he hated, at last and finally a "Chinese-American." As with most of Chinese-America and dutiful housewives . . . the price of acceptance was his soul, but he didn't pay it up. We had to take it from him.

Jim Carroll

Jim Carroll (b. 1950) is a former high-school basketball star turned poet turned rock singer, who has recited his poems on MTV, had his adolescent diary published in the Paris Review, *and had a glossy fashion magazine call him "the new Rimbaud."*

Carroll, the son of a Lower East Side New York bartender, attended an expensive uptown private school on a scholarship and made no secret of his drug habit. His Basketball Diaries, *from which these excerpts are taken, is an artfully artless off-the-cuff reverie of the 1960s version of a Dead End Kid on the make. It would have been the perfect part for a spaced-out thirteen-year-old James Cagney.*

From "Fall 63" and "Fall 64," *The Basketball Diaries*

FALL 63

TODAY was my first Biddy League game and my first day in any organized basketball league. I'm enthused about life due to this exciting event. The Biddy League is a league for anyone 12 yrs. old or under. I'm actually 13 but my coach Lefty gave me a fake birth certificate. Lefty is a great guy; he picks us up for games in his station wagon and always buys us tons of food. I'm too young to understand about homosexuals but I think Lefty is one. Although he's a great ballplayer and a strong guy, he likes to do funny things to you like put his hand between your legs and pick you up. When he did this I got keenly suspicious. I guess I better not tell my mother about it. I don't want to describe the first game; I played bad and we lost anyway. I was nervous, I took my girlfriend Joan to the game which was at 153rd St., a Negro church called Minisink. Our team is from Madison Sq. Boys' Club on E. 29th St. The starting team consists of two Italians, two spades and me.

When the game was over and we were waiting on the subway platform at 155th, Tony Milliano started a fight with Kevin Dolon. Tony
is a huge monster who loves to fight; Kevin is a wise ass little prick.
Some guys tried to break it up but Tony wouldn't let them and kept
on yelling, "I want blood!" It was scary but interesting; I don't like to
fight but I love watching others fight. Kevin asked me to jump Milliano
from behind but he was too big for me to get involved. Who wanted
to help that little fucker anyway? He's forever getting me in trouble
down at St. Agnes grade school, where we go. Just today he snitched
to Sister Mary Grace about me spitting on the first graders from the
lunch room window.

It was the warmest October day that I ever saw today, so we skipped
practice (Tony and Yogi and I) and decided to take a little ride down
to the ferry and over to Staten Island. After polishing off a hero at
LUCY's we hopped on the back fender of the 2nd Ave. bus and rode
down to the ferry basin. Once I fell off a bus like that on a sharp turn
and almost got my balls crushed under the back wheel, but this ride
was smooth enough and we got off and deposited our nickels in the
turnstiles and were off. Just as the boat is pulling out of the dock,
Tony takes out a bottle of CARBONA cleaning fluid and a few rags and
suggests that we do a little sniffing to get high. I was up for this idea
because Carbona is one of the finest cheap highs you can get, even
stronger than model glue. We slipped up to the top deck of the ship
and wet our rags and raised them to our faces. After four deep whiffs
we were sailing someplace else, bells ringing through my ears and
little lights flashing through my eyes. I pictured myself paddling across
a river with black water, only the canoe was going backwards instead
of forwards, with clouds that were faces laughing spooky fun-house
laughs which wouldn't stop echoing. More sniffs and more freaky
visions, the ringing bell sound always getting louder the more I breathe
the stuff into my lungs. I kept it up for about ten minutes, but by then
I was getting too dizzy to handle it and I had to fling down the rag and
make it to the side rail, sick as possible. I began puking wildly. My eyes
felt like bowling balls and they were watering like mad. Tony and
Yogi had done themselves in too and they ran over to join in the
ceremony. Then we recovered enough to hear shouts from the bottom deck and wiping off our eyes we realized that we had zeroed in
over the head of some dude. More unfortunate was the fact that the

guy was fantastically huge and and looked horribly pissed. We wasted no time in making it to the nearest hiding spot, knowing the guy would be up after us any second. We got to the other side of the boat and did a quick Steve McQueen act, over the rail and down to the lowest deck. Then we ducked into the bathroom and into the last toilet stall, locking the door and sweating our balls off. We hung on in there, reading the little pencilled-in obscenities until the boat docked. After about ten minutes we sent Yogi out to see if the coast was clear. He came back and signalled us out and we ran our asses off the boat, through the terminal onto the nearest bus. We came to a nice park somewhere in the middle of the island and played ball with the local weaklings all day, taking on everyone, even guys as old as sixteen or so. It was almost dark when we caught our ferry back to the city again, keeping a sharp lookout for our friend and vowing we'd never sniff that stuff on any ferry again.

We played tonight in some big time 13-year-old and younger tournament way far up in the Bronx, a ritzy neighborhood called Riverdale . . . giant stone private houses . . . lots of ivy and swimming pools, that whole bit. It seemed like a trip to Utica from down here at the Boys' Club on E. 29th, but Lefty drives like a bitch so it wasn't too bad. Carson managed to get car sick again and he couldn't hold it back so he had to puke into one of Lefty's leather work gloves that we found under a spare tire in the back of the wagon. No one told Lefty about that though, so cheers to him next time some work pops up that needs gloves. We arrived at the gym of Riverdale High and the place was pretty fucking fancy, you bet your ass. Plenty of light from nice high ceilings and lots of lame basketball fans in the stands. We go to the locker rooms right away since we're half an hour late already. Our team is good at getting dressed quick because we're the type of team that wears their uniforms all day. Game or no game, we just don't dig carrying around those little fag bags with our stuff in them, we just whip off our shirt and pants and we're out on the court in a minute. After the game, it was the same thing, no showers, of course, just up with our pants and on with our shirts and out the door.

So we go onto the court and here are these guys we're playing all duded up in blue and gold uniforms with little stars all over them, and going through these perfect warm-up drills. We were pretty raggy next to those guys but we went over o.k. with the crowd because we're these tough ragamuffins from the lower east side, all poor and shaggy, and all these nice parents who have a few cars and smoke pipes and shit, well, they were gonna cheer the underdogs from the ghetto right along, whippie, that was so nice of them. So we took a few warm-up shots and went over and sat down and Lefty told us to use the press against them from the start. By the end of the first four minutes we were ahead by 23 points and the pretty boys from Lake Peekskill, or wherever the fuck they were from, didn't know what to do. They called a timeout. We stopped the press out of sheer pity and the rest of the half wasn't as exciting. They seemed to all have lead in their asses and never heard of the word "drive," so we constantly drove in for easy show-off layups or feeds to our big men. We fast broke so much Lefty told us to cool it before the guys that ran the thing started checking birth certificates and finding out that half our guys were ringers. One of our forwards, this tall spade with a baby face, must have been playing in these 13 and under farces for the past ten years, no shit. Score 53–20, at the half.

The locker room during the half was one of the most uncool scenes during the season. Three of our guys got caught by Lefty sniffing glue in the toilet stalls. I was lucky to flush down mine in time so old coachie thought I was in there legit. Lefty would take a lot of shit but he didn't dig any glue sniffing, so those suckers had to sit out the second half. Another thing that strangely enough really pisses off Lefty is anyone using that popular little expression "motherfucker," as if he, who has no hesitations about grabbing guys' balls and cocks in the middle of the team prayer in the huddle before the game, was some great moralist or something. Anyway, with the other starters out, I get to score all the points and wind up with forty-two, which felt good because I haven't really been scoring that many lately. I can also see little Most Valuable Player trophies in my head if this keeps up. We won by an awful lot. After the game they gave us free sodas and shit and all the local people stood in the lobby as we left and patted us on the back and said, "Nice game, son," and all, the whole scene strictly out of "Leave It To Beaver," all the old men Fred MacMurray types in tweed suits and the women, a pack of poodle walkers, standing around with a lot of make-up and sort of thinking how cute we were. They had these teased up bleached hair-dos that reminded me exactly of the higher priced 14th St. whores. I wanted to ask one if she wanted to suck it off but we just hopped into the car for that bitch trip downtown. It's a Friday night and we all wanted to go to the East

River Park and get drunk, do reefer and sniff glue. And that's exactly what we did.

Today we moved our last piece of furniture into our apartment in my new neighborhood at the upper tip of Manhattan. I've been up here before and got a pretty good image of the general bullshit of the local population. Fuck, they take the lamest cake in town. Hallways in my new building and each park bench filled with chattering old Irish ladies either gossiping or saying the rosary, or men long time here or younger ones right off the boat huddling in floppy overcoats in front of drug stores discussing their operations, ball scores, or the Commie threat. Guys my age strictly All-American, though most of the various crowds do the beer-drinking scene on weekends. My cousin Kevin did introduce me to a few weed-heads up here once, and today I ran into them and goofed with some ball playing. Most likely they'll be my scene. Nice basketball courts around here, at least.

Of course, the worst bullshit about this move is having to go back to a fucking Catholic school just in the middle of a goof year in a Public joint. That scene is simple, Catholic schools are sheer shit, madmen in fucking collars who in their pious minds can never be wrong, running around with their rubber straps beating asses red for the least little goofing, and pushing into a bunch of stiff noodle-sized brains that "Who made us? . . . ," "God made us . . . ," horse drip. The old biddy penguins they call nuns are even worse. I'm cracking back the first cat who tries that "bend over" shit, hoping they give me the boot quick. I've already got a scholarship set for that plush Private School next year, so I'm going to breeze easy for the rest of this grammar school bit. I'm meeting Kevin in the morning and we're supposed to get drunk, it'll be cool 'cause then I can pull the "sleeping over at his house" bit and not get snagged by Moms. I'll tell her the smell of paint gets me sick 'cause they're painting tomorrow; that ought to work.

FALL 64

It's my first day at the ultra-rich private school that I got a scholarship to come to. I had a hard time trying to figure out what I was doing there, and I got funny looks from everyone and thought how funny it was all those Jewish kids singing away those old Christian tunes like that at the chapel service in the morning. Some teacher in back of me kept poking on my shoulder to get me to sing but I just sat there with a bored look on my face. Before the first class I spoke with a nice enough little guy named Eggie Blaumgarden, whose old man owns a big diamond cutting firm, very impressive to me. It turns out that he's a great tennis star (sixth in the East for his age) and he's interested in art. "Got a few Renoirs over at my place," he lays on me, "come over for dinner some time and check 'em out." Sure thing Eggie. Then I got into hot water with Mr. Brothers, fancy Oxford graduate Latin teacher, who freaks out when I answer a question "Yah" instead of "Yes, sir." He keeps me after class and explains how he understands, with mounds of sympathy, how my family are lowly slobs and all but to discipline myself to proper replies and other classroom etiquette. Sure thing. Then at lunch the headmaster, Mr. Belt, comes over and sits at my table and tells me that my hand should be removed from sight while dining. I thought he meant the hand that I held the fork with, so I sat there for half a minute puzzled until I realized it was the other hand he was talking about. He's an overly sincere type guy, you know the kind, like a politician, they always wind up screwing you sooner or later. Frankly I don't dig the guy. I feel like farting and blowing up the 257 years of fine tradition of this place. After lunch I spent a little time in the school trophy room, which is actually a sort of lounge where there are fancy v-shaped sofas and all that and a walnut cabinet with all the school's trophies in it (not many, I might add, in fact, I've got more trophies at home than this place got in 257 years). So I'm minding my own business reading *Time* magazine when some guy from my own class, Larry Labratory, I think his name is, tries to insist that he was reading the magazine first. "Nice try there, champ," I say, "but I've been sitting here ten minutes now, you see?" So, can you picture this, he actually tries to take the thing from me, the prick, and for lack of a more peaceful solution, I get up and punch him out. His nose bleeding, he gets up and whimpers off, probably to squeak to some teacher. Sure enough, he's back in two minutes, with some old man from the History Dept., pointing dead at me, a handkerchief held up to his bleeding mug. It was only the testimony on my behalf by Eggie Blaumgarden that saved me from getting into a big hassle and being sent down to Mr. Bluster, our principal. Everyone seemed to hate that guy Larry Labratory anyway, so I drew a little applause from the lounge clique when the history guy shook off.

After boring afternoon History classes, I decided to hang around a while and watch the football team work out. Strictly lame, let me tell you, I could round up any ten friends of mine from downtown or uptown and whip their asses. Some senior asked me to hold the ball for him while he practiced field goals, thinking I was just another jerk-ass freshman. I did, and this guy kicked the thing like it was a bag of shit or something. I say, "Let me try one," and he says OK, thinking he's doing this little punk a big favor. I stepped back, took two strides forward, and breezed one over from 32 yards (this is in loafers, don't forget) and the guy just knelt there with his mouth hung open. I thought his jock would fall off and roll right down the leg of his clean little uniform. Then I tipped off to the subway, secretly loving everything about this crazy place.

I went back down the old neighborhood today, had to go to the wake of this old friend of mine, Bobby Sachs. I planned to make it downtown earlier to visit some people but got hung up at school cleaning desks and shit for cutting out once too often. This drag clean-up lasts until 4:30, though to tell the truth I didn't do a lick of work 'cause some dumbie was in charge and I hung out in the bathroom all the while and read about that wise-ass dwarf Alexander Pope. I wasn't missed and signed out with the rest of the crew on time. I made it down to the funeral place about five and there must have been every guy from 29th to 14st St. there. I talked to all these old friends for half an hour just as a cover 'cause I was trying to avoid having to look at Bob's dead body in the center of the room. I never saw a body in a casket in my life, even at my grandmom's wake my parents didn't make me go.

Bobby died of leukemia. He got it two years ago but had such a strong body (he was always the best at sports) that he kept fighting it off. They gave him six months at first, then he turned a trick and got better . . . even got out for awhile, though it was a different person when you saw him, then he went back in a year ago, like his brother was telling me, the line on his hospital chart just fell straight down in a perfect angle. I looked at his body and it was death for the first time in my life. His face was thin and wrinkled, almost ape-like, his hair just grey patches on his scalp. He looked sixty years old, and he was sixteen. I couldn't believe how skinny his arms were . . . it was like having the skeleton of someone you knew put in front of you.

I left dazed out in the streets like I had just come out of a four hour movie I didn't understand. I thought about that face all night, and death. I almost flipped and I took two reds even to knock me out but they don't feel like they're working.

The posh private school I go to is only a few blocks away from Central Park. Consequently, in the warmer part of the fall we have gym periods in the park consisting mainly of touch football. It's nice in a way to get to spend an hour in the park playing ball twice a week but the bullshit end of the stick is the walk over there in your corny ass little gym shorts and white tee shirts. It doesn't bother the rest of the lames in my freshman class but personally I don't dig the shit you take from the black cats and PRs that live in the neighborhood, their whistling and what not, calling us all rich little faggots . . . Dig it, I could bust the ass off any of those dudes woofing at us from the public basketball courts on Amsterdam if it was worth my time, but lately I've been wearing bluejeans over instead of that other shit and lagging behind all the other kids, so everything is cool, as long as the head-master don't catch an eye of me and give me another lecture on the "rules" of the school. Fuck dumb rules, let me wear what I want . . . No trouble from Mr. Doolittle, the cat that runs the phys. ed. here because he's the basketball coach too and he never gives me any hassles.

But today when we got in the park, I laid back from the rest and got high on a little reefer walking along the horse trail, I get to the field and start playing and I'm stoned and goofing on the whole scene but digging the game too, though my coordination was a little off level. So anyway I finished up and he toots his little whistle and time to get back for boring Latin class. Not too boring today though I figure because I still got a good half reefer left and I lag back again, squat in a patch of bushes and light up to make my man Virgil a little more interesting. All is cool, but all is not cool for long. I hear a sudden hoofing sound heading my way full blast and I know it ain't no Lone Ranger and Tonto. Fuck! It's two horse patrol cops giddy-apping right into the goddamn bushes. I toss the joint in back of me pronto just as one cop is off his horse and standing right in front of me in a fucking clump of bushes . . . "What the hell you in here for, you punkbastard, I think we got a good idea." I looked at the guy, wrecked out of my brain, and tell him I was sneaking a smoke before I went back to school after my gym class out here. The cop asks me where my teacher is but they're probably back at the school by now so that's what I tell the man. He tells me to get out of the bushes and I figure shit, lucky he ain't

looking for the joint, but then in that case what the fuck do they think
I was doing, beating off or something? We're in the open now and he
says to his partner something about me fitting the description. I look
up at the other cat on his horse still and, holy duck fuck, it's my little
league coach from the old neighborhood, Steve Malone. "JIM?" He
almost falls off the goddamn horse, "What the hell are you doing?" I
tell him in stoned dialogue, "School down block . . . go . . . play ball
class . . . gym, you know . . . smoke . . . sneak behind . . . high Steve,
good to see yer." I realize it was total gibberish and try to start again
but he breaks in and tells me not to sound so nervous, that they were
looking for some guy who molested some little girl the other day in
the bushes around there and he had red hair so they did a charge
when they saw me, then he nods to his partner and tells him who I am
. . . In fact, he goes on telling him about the no-hitter I pitched to win
our team the championship and all and starts bragging about the
smart move he made in that game having a guy steal third who later
got in on a sacrifice etc. I'm looking at the guy blasted out still thinking
about the grass and he's blabbing about weirdos raping kids, winding
up with a description of the speech he made at the League dinner for
winning coach of the year. I was also missing half my class in Latin. I
tell him finally I gotta go back to school and he just nods and waves a
tiny gesture and keeps on rambling about goddamn baseball to the
other guy who is all ears and starting to tell Steve about his own
coaching experiences out in Flatbush or some fucking place. I get into
Latin just before the bell rings and put on a fake limp coming in
telling him I got hurt in gym and had to see the nurse. He swallowed
it in a vague kind of way.

   Today at school we had our annual Thanksgiving fast for the benefit of the poor and hungry blacks we hear of scattered throughout
the South. Anyone who sympathizes with the injustice of poverty in
the South does not eat his meal as a symbol of this injustice. I'm sure
it interests a starving black in Mississippi that I am not eating my
lunch today. Frankly, I was too embarrassed to be the only cat in the
school to eat his meal so I snuck down to the corner and copped a
cheeseburger. Symbolic gestures are certainly self-satisfying but they
are not too nourishing for anyone anywhere. Somebody is conning
everyone else and themselves with plain dumb ideas as performed
here today. What happens to the food they prepared today? All that
turkey and mashed potatoes would probably seem pretty dried out if

we shipped it down South, even by air mail. It would have been interesting to point out that there are a lot of hungry dudes walking down Columbus Ave. that could have dug a free meal. But some of them might be drug addicts and shit and they'd no doubt make a big mess out of the lunch room that all the black cleaning women would have a hard time cleaning up. I suggest that tomorrow somebody symbolically stick a stale drum stick of today's lunch up the ass of whoever was humane enough to organize this farce.

Sheyann Webb and
Rachel West Nelson

*In 1965, when the Reverend Martin Luther King, Jr., came to Selma, Ala-
bama, to organize a voter registration drive, Sheyann Webb was eight and
Rachel West, her next-door neighbor in the segregated George Washington
Carver Homes housing project, was nine. More aware than many adults of the
importance of the events happening just down the block at the Brown Chapel
AME Church, these young spiritual descendants of Charlotte Forten became
involved in nonviolent demonstrations that climaxed in a dramatic confron-
tation with the Alabama National Guard on a bridge on the outskirts of town,
and in the historic march to Montgomery. In 1979 they told their stories to
Frank Sikora, who recorded them in the book* Selma, Lord, Selma.

From *Selma, Lord, Selma:*
Girlhood Memories of the Civil-Rights Days

SHEYANN

DURING THOSE EARLY DAYS of the church meetings, before the first
marches, I would be the only child there. I'd sit in back and listen. I
hadn't told my mother and father about missing school.

It was on the third or fourth day that Theo Bailey, who was about
sixteen at the time, came back to where I was sitting and asked me why
I wasn't in school.

I thought for a moment, then asked him: "Why ain't you?"
"I'm taking some time off," he said.
And I replied, "Me too."

Later, he had introduced me to Hosea Williams, and after we had
talked for awhile Williams had asked me if I could sing. I told him I
could. So we began practicing singing some of the freedom songs —
*Ain't Gonna Let Nobody Turn Me 'Round, O Freedom, This Little Light of
Mine,* and some of the others. I knew them all. So it was decided —

and I don't remember exactly how — that I would be singing at some of the mass rallies to be held.

So I was now a part of the movement; the worry I had had about missing school vanished.

That evening when Rachel got home, we walked around the block several times, talking about the meetings. I told her about the songs.

"You gonna sing up there in front of everybody?" she asked. "Ain't you gonna be scared?"

"I don't know," I said. "I never been up there before a bunch of people."

There were more than eight hundred people at that first rally held at Brown Chapel the night of Sunday, January seventeenth, and some of the teachers were in that crowd. I didn't look at them.

Rachel and I — dressed in our best dresses and wearing ribbons — sat in the front row; I think we must have arrived an hour early. The Reverend Reese started the meeting with a short talk about the first march to be held the following day. After several minutes, he said it was time for a song and called for me.

I sang and the people all joined in. After a few stanzas of *Ain't Nobody Gonna Turn Me 'Round*, I noticed that Rachel was up there with me, beaming and singing her heart out. We would do a lot of singing together in the coming weeks.

Now, the singing at those meetings had a purpose; it wasn't just for entertainment. Those songs carried a message. They were different from Negro spirituals, which — as beautiful as they are — told of some distant hope while carrying the burdens of this life. Freedom songs cried out for Justice right now, not later.

The words were simple and clear. They could be changed to meet the needs of the time:

> *Ain't gonna let George Wallace turn me 'round,*
> *turn me 'round, turn me 'round,*
> *Ain't gonna let George Wallace turn me 'round,*
> *I'll keep a-walkin', I'll keep a-talkin',*
> *Marchin' up to freedom lan'.*

They spoke of our determination, our dignity:

> *We shall not, we shall not be moved,*
> *We shall not, we shall not be moved,*

Just like a tree that's planted by the water,
We shall not be moved.

And some told of the ultimate sacrifice we were prepared to make
to achieve a dream:

O freedom, o freedom,
O freedom's over me, over me,
And before I'll be a slave,
I'll be buried in my grave,
And go home to my Lord
And be free.

Monday, January 18, was sunny and cool in Selma. There was a
whole crowd of people waiting outside the church when I left the
house. Dr. King was to arrive sometime that morning and the first
march was to be held. As I waited, squinting up the street for a
glimpse of him — for some reason I thought he'd come walking down
Sylvan Street — I listened as some men talked about Sheriff Clark
having a group of deputies waiting at the courthouse.

"Man, they got their clubs," one of them said. It made me more
than a little nervous. I couldn't know — and surely didn't know —
that the mayor of Selma, Joseph Smitherman, and the public safety
director, Wilson Baker, had reached an "agreement" with the sheriff
that there would be no undue force used. None of us could know that.
So we waited with an air of uncertainty, but also with resolve and
anticipation. Somebody started singing and the rest of us joined in;
the singing bolstered our spirits.

Suddenly a woman shouted, "There he comes," and a long black car
seemed to swish to the front of the church; there was a cheer as Dr.
King alighted, smiling and waving. Because of my size, I couldn't get
a good look at him. The crush of people straining forward wedged me
to the fringes.

It wasn't long then that we began lining up on the sidewalk.

It occurred to me then that on this day, at any moment after the
first step, somebody might die. We began moving forward, walking
two or three abreast. It was about two blocks to Alabama Avenue and
there Baker stopped us. I later learned that he told Dr. King that we
didn't have a parade permit. So we broke up into small groups and
walked piecemeal to the downtown.

Some of the people went into restaurants and stores with lunch counters and were served. I stayed with Mrs. Margaret Moore and we walked through the downtown for several minutes, then returned to the church. It wasn't until later that I learned that a white man attacked Dr. King as he registered at the Hotel Albert, located on Broad Street.

That night at the rally, me and Rachel sang again. There would be another march the next day, we were told. There was a tremendous cheer. Until then, I had been a little disappointed in the size of the crowd that had turned out for the march. But when I heard the shouting and the applause, I felt more confident.

I remember it was during one of those first rallies that I got up there by myself and sang a song that surely told what we had to face:

> *I went down to the County jail,*
> *Had no money to pay the bail,*
> *Keep your eyes on the prize,*
> *O Lord, O Lord.*

RACHEL

Coming home from the church that night of January 18, I more than anything, wanted to miss school and march that next day. I made up my mind that I would just stay out and go with Shey.

My mother was fixing cups of instant coffee in the kitchen, and soon the visitors to our home — James Bevel and the others — came in. I would talk to her later, I thought.

There weren't enough chairs in the kitchen or the living room and people were sitting on the floor, drinking coffee and talking. The next day would be rough, they said. The word had come to us that Sheriff Clark would no longer abide by any "agreements" made earlier that day.

"We'll have some folks arrested tomorrow," my father had said. "That sheriff'll be after us."

He had been with the marchers that day and, he said, he had sized up the situation. There had been looks of hostility from many white bystanders. And Sheriff Clark, he added, had looked like a caged tiger, stalking about, fuming.

I don't think I can ever describe the feeling I had on that night and the others that followed. There was a togetherness, a camaraderie that would never again be felt in the years to come. I lay on the living room floor, listening to the grown-ups talk about the pending troubles that could, and would, come.

Folks were going to have to lay their bodies on the line, James Bevel was saying. He was one of Dr. King's aides. Nella, seventeen, who was my oldest sister, sat cross-legged on the floor, listening. The others of us were sprawled around beside her, wondering about what was ahead as we listened.

There was Juliette, thirteen, Diane, ten, Charlene, sixteen, Alice, fourteen, Roderick, eight, Mark, six, and Carl, twelve. The littlest was Bonnie, age four. I'm not sure she knew what was going on for sure, but she sat up with us like she did. Lonzy, Jr., eighteen, was living in Cincinnati at the time.

The people were saying that Dr. King can't do this thing by himself; it's going to take people, people, people. These white folks aren't going to back down for nothing. It's going to take people out there every day. There's going to be people arrested, thrown in jail, maybe even some gettin' their heads busted. It may be even worse than that. We just didn't know.

The things that frightened me the most were the horsemen Sheriff Clark had — they were called "possemen" — and the thought of somebody planting a bomb at the church; or a sniper.

I could imagine Brown Chapel erupting in smoke and flame as had the Sixteenth Street Baptist Church in Birmingham [on September 15, 1963] when Addie Mae Collins, Cynthia Wesley, Denise McNair, and Carole Robertson had died. I never knew them personally, but there was a kinship between all us black folks, a bond that tied the Montgomery bus-boycott people to the Birmingham people and finally to us here in Selma.

Here, there was more at stake than just sitting at a counter or having a "white only" sign removed from a public restroom or riding in front of a bus. Gaining the right to vote would, in itself, Bevel was saying, open up all the other doors that had been closed.

We stayed up very late that night; the talk continued and later somebody started singing softly — some of the freedom songs — and the rest of us hummed along. Then we prayed. The message was clear: We could not be afraid — not of the bombs, nor the clubs, nor those horses Jim Clark had, nodding and tossing in the alley behind the courthouse. I had been told of them that day.

My brothers and sisters, one by one, fell asleep on the floor, and my father would pick them up and carry them to their bedroom. But I fought the sleep. Outside, the wind on this winter night made buzzing and whining sounds as it whipped through the apartments.

It had been such a special night. Here we were, Catholics, Baptists, whites, blacks, all in one place; we had all been to Brown Chapel and what denomination you were made no difference. That night convinced me that what was happening in Selma would not just be Dr. King's movement, or the people's movement, but something greater. Something, I thought, almost divine. I fell asleep in the confort that I was being watched over.

In our house wanting to march and marching were two different things. When I asked next morning if I could miss school, my mother was very short. "Miss school? And have the sisters coming here looking for you? No, ma'am!"

It would be later in the movement before she would change her mind.

SHEYANN

I was the youngest, certainly the smallest, of the "regulars" in the demonstrations. And I was the first of the children. The others would start in February. But when I went I was the only one missing school. This march was on another sunny, but cold, day. We gathered at Brown Chapel that morning and sang songs and listened to the leaders — among them Dr. King and Hosea Williams — telling us why we were there and how to march, like two abreast. I was with Mrs. Margaret Moore again.

We started up the sidewalk. I think there must have been two hundred and fifty of us, I'm not sure. It wasn't a great number, I know that.

Now, we knew that sooner or later we would have an encounter with Sheriff Jim Clark; it was going to happen on this day. I was about half-way or more back in the line of marchers, and as we went along we began singing some of the freedom songs. We went south to Alabama Avenue, then turned west; the courthouse was four blocks further. We passed the Selma City Hall, where a group of white people stood watching us. Some of them laughed, I remember, but I didn't hear any shouts or jeering. Then we got to the courthouse.

We had been there for twenty or thirty minutes, standing, talking, singing a few songs, when I heard this disturbance toward the front.

Then folks began shouting and crying out; I saw the sheriff with a hand behind the neck of Mrs. Amelia Boynton, running with her and hollering. Before this had happened, Clark and Dr. King had exchanged some words. I didn't hear them. Then the incident with Mrs. Boynton took place. Later I learned that she had asked him if she could go into the courthouse, and he said she could, but added, "You stay inside once you get there." Well, it was the lunch hour and all the courthouse workers left so Mrs. Boynton came out and when the sheriff saw her, he just got mad. He ran her down the street to a sheriff's car and had her arrested and taken away to the city jail. It had happened so quickly that I didn't get scared, but all the people around me began to get excited.

Then the sheriff began to shout at us. Suddenly people were moving, jamming together in a tight circle, edging together protectively, like a wagon train.

Deputies, with sticks and those long cattle prods moved toward us. I squeezed tight on Mrs. Moore's hand; there was a sudden urge to back away, even turn and run. Somebody shouted, "Y'all are under arrest!"

I looked up at Mrs. Moore. "Me, too? Are they arrestin' me?"

Her face was blank. "Don't be scared," she said. "Don't be. Just stay close. Don't let go of my hand."

I saw some of them deputies push our people, saw some of them use the cattle prods and saw men and women jump when the electric ends touched against their bodies. People were shouting. A man stumbled; a sign fell from my view as a marcher reacted to the shock. My toes were stepped on and I lost my balance several times as we were wedged together. Then they moved us away from the courthouse and began marching us down Alabama Avenue, back toward the city hall.

I was now holding onto Mrs. Moore with both of my hands, watching so I wouldn't get touched with one of the prods. We were being moved like cattle. But once we got away from the courthouse the shouting stopped and the deputies stayed about five yards away from the edges of the rank. A lot of people, black and white, were on the sidewalks, watching. We were taken to the city hall; the jail was located up on the second floor. We must have been there standing in line for about a half hour when an officer came to me and asked why I was there.

"Because they made us all come here," I said.

"I know that," he said. "But why are you here in the first place? Why aren't you in school, where you belong?"

I shrugged. I was a little afraid then.

"Who told you to go to the courthouse with these people?"

"Nobody. I just come."

"If nobody told you, then why did you come?"

"To be free," I said. Several of the people nearby muttered "Um-hmmms."

And he said, "If you want to be free, then go home. That's where you're free, not here. Go on home, now."

There were sixty people jailed that day, and while I wasn't one of them, I had come close. It taught me a lesson. I knew that being part of this movement would not be without its moments of fear. I had felt that fear that day; all the people had. But we had stayed together and by doing so had overcome it. At the time, I couldn't appreciate the historic significance of the day, that a pattern of passive resistance to the sheriff's anger and aggressive behavior was established. It would go on and reach a point where the sheriff would run out of jail space to put the people. The last thing I remembered that day as I left the city hall and walked home, was the sound of those people inside — some of them were singing.

Woke up this mornin'
With my mind stayed on freedom.

If they could sing, I thought, then I could go on marching.

It was later that day that my parents learned for certain — although I suspected my mother knew earlier — that I had been missing school. One of the teachers had called. My father, John Webb, was a stocky man of medium stature, and he had a temper. When he confronted me that evening with the truancy report, I looked for it to surface. At first, I didn't answer when he asked me why I had been missing.

"Now, John," said my momma, coming to my rescue, "Shey's goin' to the church and all because she believes it's right and because we can't vote."

"She's supposed to be in school." He was sitting on the couch in the living room. Then, to me, he said, "You wanna grow up to be dumb?"

I shook my head and told him, "But it don't do no good to be smart if you still be a slave."

"Who told you that?" he asked. "We're not slaves."

"But we ain't free, either. That's why we gotta march."

"Workin' folks don't have time to march," he said.

"Well, Daddy," I said, "don't you wanna be free?"

He had shaken his head, ending the discussion. Later, when I told told him I wanted to continue in the demonstrations, he hadn't committed himself, but his eyes had twinkled a trace of amusement. I read the looks as approval.

RACHEL

. . . One of the first ministers to come live with us was a Presbyterian priest named Samuel Morris. Now he had just planned to stay a few days but when he saw what was happening — this was in February, the early part — he decided he was going to stay; he sent for his wife and three children. One of them was a boy who was about seven and he was enrolled with us at St. Elizabeth Catholic School. So he would walk with us each day to and from classes. I think they put him there because it would have been too much trouble to enroll him in the public school; besides, he would be with us.

When we walked to school we'd often see some white kids who would be going to Parrish High School, which did not allow blacks to attend. They never bothered us. But this one day I saw some of them watching us as we walked with this little white boy. I remember there were some shouts at us, some hooting. But we kept walking. Next day, it was the same thing. Me and my sister Diane and this boy just kept walking; I was afraid to look at them or say anything. They were bigger kids, maybe fourteen or fifteen, maybe even older, some of them. Well, we got to school, but all that day I was worried about it, because it was the second day in a row they had been watching us. I guess it made them mad seeing us blacks walking to school with the white boy. I remember wishing it would rain hard so his father would come pick us up in his car. But it didn't happen. When we got out that afternoon me and Diane and the boy started home and we walked as fast as we could. The school was on Broad Street near Good Samaritan Hospital and we had to go across the railroad tracks, then to Jeff Davis, then turn left there and go another four blocks or so before we got to Sylvan Street. We'd be pretty safe there, because that's where the apartments started.

But before we got to the railroad tracks which crossed Broad Street, we saw this group of white boys again, maybe ten of them. They was

running around and wrestling with each other and showing out. I
remember we stopped and talked about going back to school, but then
decided to go ahead, because there were lots of cars around and we
didn't think they'd do anything. Well, about the time we got near the
tracks they saw us and they quit their jumping around and stood for
awhile. None of them said anything. We kept walking. Then one of
them yelled something about the "little white nigger." I was scared to
death then. Diane kept looking straight ahead and I did, too. But one
of them boys said, "Hey! Where y'all goin' with that white nigger?"
And the other ones started laughing and hollering at us.

So Diane looked at them and said, "You talkin' to us?" And one of
them, a bigger one, says, "Who you *think* we're talkin' to?"

So she doesn't say nothing more. But I says, "We just walkin' this
here boy home." I was hoping when they heard that they'd go and
leave us alone. But they hollered some more and it scared the boy and
he took my hand. There was nothing for me to do but hold it. So there
was quiet for awhile. Then a shout. And something hit on the ground
beside me.

"They throwin' rocks?" Diane said.

All of a sudden they all picked up rocks from the railroad bed and
started throwing. I remember closing my eyes and ducking, then
grabbing the boy's hand tighter and pulling him as I started running
as hard as I could go. And Diane was running and keeping her books
up over her head to keep from getting hit. We ran across the street
without even looking for cars and kept going down Jeff Davis. These
boys chased us part of the way. I don't know when they stopped
throwing and turned around, because I never looked back until we
were part way up Sylvan. Ahead of us at the church there were some
people and I knew we were safe. Diane stopped because some of them
asked why we were running — and I think the boy was crying — but
I kept going on to the house.

My mother was in the kitchen and she looked at me and says, "What
in the world? Why you breathin' so fast like that?"

And as I told her about what happened it made me scared and mad
at the same time, and I started crying and walking around the kitchen
and living room and saying that if I had been a boy I'd have picked up
some rocks myself and thrown them back.

Diane and the boy came in then and everyone was talking at once
and I remember my mother listening to me and then putting her
arms around me and patting me on the head. She tried to comfort me

but I knew it made her nervous, because later she and the minister's wife went off to themselves and were talking about it and I could see they were worried.

I was so upset I went up to the bedroom and sat staring out the window. It wasn't fair them chasing us and throwing rocks at us. I knew why they had done it. It was because the boy's parents were civil-rights workers. To those white boys they were outsiders who had come here to cause trouble. . . .

SHEYANN

My name was really Krisandra Sheyann, but everybody called me by the middle name, which I preferred. I don't know where Krisandra came from, other than the fact that my momma had liked it. Sheyann was a name that was handed down from her side of the family; my Great-Great Granmomma Wade had been named Sheyann. She had been a slave. Although we had never been able to find the exact site, the plantation where she had worked was located not far from Selma.

During those early days of the voting-rights drive in Selma, I found myself sometime thinking about Granmomma Wade. The stories she had told were limited because, Momma had told me, the people who had been slaves wanted to forget as much as they could.

One night, during that second week of the movement, I began to run a fever; I was coughing, my throat was getting raw.

"You been out in the cold and rain too much, young lady," Momma had said. Giving me orange-flavored baby aspirins and water, she insisted I stay in and go to bed. "Other folks can sing tonight."

I didn't argue with her, but lay listening to the wind blowing. It was good to be in a warm bed. I had been told that Granmomma Wade and the other slaves often lived in shanties with only one little stove for cooking and heat. Some of them had little clothing; I'd heard stories where they were even nearly naked when they worked in the field. I wondered if Sheyann Wade were living if she would be at the church. I bet she would. I bet she would have been in the marches.

Momma brought me some soup later, and we talked about Granmomma Wade.

"When they was freed," Momma said, "they all stayed right here in this county; I guess they didn't have no money to go up North. They just stayed right here and worked. And they didn't get paid much at all in them days."

I asked, "Did she say they ever tried to vote?"

Momma shrugged. "Well, in them days no women could vote, not even white ones. But she did say that some of the men did vote some but later they couldn't. The white folks had turned things around and cut them off. She said some tried later but the white men would tell 'em, 'Y'all niggers ain't ready to vote yet.' They put 'em off, and before long black folks just lose their rights."

I couldn't understand how that could happen.

" 'Cause they was scared," Momma said. "Granmomma Wade used to talk a little about it. She said she'd seen folks whipped. Even though they got free, some of 'em didn't forget. And they wasn't educated."

"Did they ever beat Granmomma Wade?'"

Momma shook her head. "She never did say. See, she was real old when I was a girl. She just never said a whole lot about it."

"You said them people who be slaves was scared," I had said. "So they never could vote. So today folks are still scared to go out there and they can't vote, either. See? We just like we was a whole hundred years ago."

She didn't answer me, just sat on the bed thinking, her eyes on the floor.

Later, almost asleep, I heard the sounds of the singing from the church; it seemed far away, almost a part of the wind. I lay there listening to the words:

> *O freedom, O freedom's over me,*
> *And before I'll be a slave,*
> *I'll be buried in my grave,*
> *And go home to my Lord*
> *And be free*

All of a sudden the thought struck me: *I might die.*

I might be in a march and someone would shoot and I'd be hit. Or I might be in the church when a bomb went off. Or I might be singing in front of the courthouse and a deputy might hit me with a club. *I might die.*

I had envisioned what it might be like: I saw my momma and daddy crying, following a little white casket across a brown field. Rachel would be there, holding a prayer book and flowers. And who else would be there? Would anyone in this whole world know? Or even care? I was very frightened. I jumped out of the bed, snapped on the lamp and sat there for more than an hour contemplating; I prayed for courage to face whatever was ahead. But it didn't halt the quivering of my hand, the shaking in my legs.

Maybe it was the fever that made me think those thoughts. But I took a piece of paper from the drawer, found a pencil, and began printing:

SHEYANN WEBB, 8 YEARS, WAS KILLED TODAY IN SELMA. SHE WAS ONE OF DR. KING FREEDOM FIGHTERS. SHE WAS A STUDENT AT CLARK SCHOOL SELMA. SHEYANN WANT ALL PEOPLE TO BE FREE AND HAPPY.

That done, I sat listening to the wind; it had such a menacing groan. I looked about the room, then ran to the door and hurried down the steps.

My momma and daddy slept in the bedroom downstairs; I ran in and began tugging at Momma's arm. She awoke, stared at me for a moment, then asked, "What's the matter?"

I told her, "I be scared."

Then I crawled in beside her. She raised up on one arm. "You been cryin'?" she asked.

"I scared I might die, Momma."

"What?" She was fully awake now. "Die! What you talkin' 'bout?"

I told her about the thoughts, and she cradled me close. "You not gonna die, doll," she crooned. "No, ma'am, you ain't. You quit that bein' scared now and go to sleep. You just lettin' all these things pile up and weigh that little heart down, that's what happen. My Lord, die! You ain't gonna die. I ain't lettin' nobody hurt my little girl."

She kept holding me close to her while I told her about the wind, how it had frightened me. Later, I fell asleep. But after that night my momma began taking part in the marches. She didn't join them, but every time we marched, she'd walk beside us, and when we'd be at the courthouse, I'd see her standing over on the sidewalk, keeping her eyes on me.

In later years, Momma would say that it was my courage and persistence that made her actively join the movement in Selma. I don't know about that. But my fears surely played a part.

That cold or touch of flu that I had kept me sidelined for several days.

Sooner or later it affected a lot of people, even Dr. King, I think. I remember one night I went to the church and found him sitting alone in the study. He must have been tired, or maybe not feeling well, or worried. Anyway, when I walked in, he didn't look at me, just kept sitting there. Then, he heard me and turned; he didn't smile.

"What do you want?" His voice was sharp, like he was busy and didn't want to be bothered. It surprised me, and I just stood there.

Turning back to the papers he had been reading, he repeated, "What do you want?"

"Freedom," I said.

He had turned quickly then, facing me. "What?" Then his face softened and he smiled. "I'm sorry," he said. "That's what we all want."

Acknowledgments

WHILE SEARCHING for suitable American autobiographies I received a lot of good advice, not all of which was followed. But I would especially like to thank Dr. Paul Clutz, Elizabeth Hogan, Charles Ruas, Shawn Wong, June Baensch, Al Silverman, Dana Gioia, Sandy Ogle, Arthur Ben Chidsey, Frances McCullough, Frank Scioscia, Ann Stanford, Lucy Rosenthal, Larry Shapiro, Gloria Norris, and Hilary Sterne.

I also wish to acknowledge the following for permission to use the selections listed:

Excerpts from *The Autobiography of John Adams* in *Diary and Autobiography of John Adams*, vol. 3, L. H. Butterfield et al., eds. © 1961 by the Massachusetts Historical Society. Reprinted by permission of Harvard University Press, Cambridge, Mass.

Excerpts from *Black Elk Speaks* by John G. Neihardt. Copyright John G. Neihardt 1932, 1959, 1961, etc. Published by Simon & Schuster Pocket Books and The University of Nebraska Press.

Excerpts from *My Father's House* by Pierrepont Noyes. Copyright 1937 by Pierrepont Noyes. Copyright © 1965 by Corinna Ackley Noyes. Reprinted by permission of Henry Holt and Company.

"A Boy on Horseback" from *The Autobiography of Lincoln Steffens*. Copyright 1931 by Harcourt Brace Jovanovich, Inc. Copyright renewed 1959 by Peter Steffens. Reprinted by permission of the publisher.

Excerpts from "A Little Girl's New York" by Edith Wharton. © February 18, 1938. Copyright renewed October 4, 1965, by William R. Tyler. First published in *Harper's*, March 1938. Reprinted by permission of the Watkins, Loomis Agency, Inc.

"Introduction to the Universe" from *Happy Days* by H. L. Mencken. Copyright 1939 by Alfred A. Knopf, Inc. Copyright renewed 1967 by August Mencken and Mercantile Safe Deposit and Trust Company. Reprinted by permission of the publisher.

"Mère and Père" from *Lanterns on the Levee: Recollections of a Planter's Son* by

William Alexander Percy. Copyright 1941 by Alfred A. Knopf, Inc. Copyright renewed 1969 by LeRoy Pratt Percy. Reprinted by permission of the publisher.

Excerpt and drawings from *Growing Pains* by Wanda Gág. Copyright 1940 by Wanda Gág. Copyright renewed © 1967 by Robert Janssen. Reprinted by permission of Coward, McCann & Geoghegan.

Excerpts from *Life Is for a Long Time* by Li Ling Ai. Reprinted by permission of Hastings House, Publishers.

Excerpt from *An Owl on Every Post* by Sanora Babb. Copyright © 1970 by Sanora Babb. Reprinted by permission of McIntosh and Otis, Inc.

Excerpts from *A Walker in the City*. Copyright 1951, 1979 by Alfred Kazin. Reprinted by permission of Harcourt Brace Jovanovich, Inc.

"The Little Store" by Eudora Welty. Copyright © 1975 by Eudora Welty. Reprinted by permission of Random House, Inc., from *The Eye of the Story: Selected Essays and Reviews* by Eudora Welty.

"The Bootleg Business" from *Army Brat* by William Jay Smith. Copyright © 1980 by William Jay Smith. Reprinted by permission of Persea Books, Inc.

Excerpt from *Homesick* by Jean Fritz. Text copyright © 1982 by Jean Fritz. Reprinted by permission of G. P. Putnam's Sons.

Excerpt from *Nisei Daughter* by Monica Sone. Copyright 1953, © renewed 1981 by Monica Sone. Reprinted by permission of Little, Brown and Company in association with The Atlantic Monthly Press.

Excerpts from *Farewell to Manzanar* by Jeanne Wakatsuki Houston and James D. Houston. Copyright © 1973 by James D. Houston. Reprinted by permission of Houghton Mifflin Company. Included in these excerpts is a quote from "Don't Fence Me In" by Cole Porter. © 1944 by Warner Bros. Inc. (renewed). All rights reserved. Used by permission.

Excerpt from *I Know Why the Caged Bird Sings* by Maya Angelou. Copyright © 1969 by Maya Angelou. Reprinted by permission of Random House, Inc.

Excerpt from *The Names: A Memoir* by N. Scott Momaday. Copyright © 1976 by N. Scott Momaday. Reprinted by permission of Harper & Row, Publishers, Inc.

Excerpt from *A Childhood: The Biography of a Place* by Harry Crews. Copyright © 1978 by Harry Crews. Reprinted by permission of Harper & Row, Publishers, Inc., and John Hawkins & Associates, Inc.

Excerpt from *Farther Off from Heaven* by William Humphrey. Copyright © 1976, 1977 by William Humphrey. Reprinted by permission of Delacorte Press/Seymour Lawrence. A Laurel/Seymour Lawrence Book.

Excerpt from "Ruth's Song (Because She Could Not Sing It)" by Gloria Steinem. Copyright © 1983 by Gloria Steinem. Reprinted by permission of

Henry Holt and Company from *Outrageous Acts and Everyday Rebellions* by Gloria Steinem.

Excerpts from *Hunger of Memory* by Richard Rodriguez. Copyright 1982 by Richard Rodriguez. Reprinted by permission of David R. Godine, Publisher, Inc.

Excerpt from *I Remember* by Joe Brainard. © copyright 1975 by Joe Brainard. Reprinted by permission of Full Court Press, Inc.

Excerpts from "Confessions of the Chinatown Cowboy" by Frank Chin. Copyright © Frank Chin 1972, 1987. First published in *Bulletin of Concerned Asian Scholars*, Fall 1972. Reprinted by permission of the author.

Excerpts from *The Basketball Diaries* by Jim Carroll. © Jim Carroll 1963–1978. To be published in 1987 by Viking Penguin Inc. Reprinted by permission of the author.

Excerpts from *Selma, Lord, Selma: Girlhood Memories of the Civil-Rights Days* by Sheyann Webb and Rachel West Nelson as told to Frank Sikora. © 1980 by The University of Alabama Press. Used by permission.